2.9-15

Fodor's

DOMINICAN REPUBLIC

1st Edition

Where to Stay and Eat
for All Budgets

Must-See Sights
and Local Secrets

Ratings You Can Trust

Fodor's Travel Publications New York, Toronto, London, Sydney, Auckland
www.fodors.com

FODOR'S DOMINICAN REPUBLIC

Editor: Douglas Stallings

Editorial Contributors: Eileen Robinson Smith, Elise Rosen, Michael de Zayas

Editorial Production: Evangelos Vasilakis, Jennifer DePrima
Maps & Illustrations: David Lindroth, Ed Jacobus, *cartographers*; Bob Blake, Rebecca Baer, *map editors;* William Wu, *information graphics*
Design: Fabrizio La Rocca, *creative director*; Guido Caroti, Siobhan O'Hare, *art directors*; Tina Malaney, Chie Ushio, Ann McBride, Jessica Walsh, *designers*; Melanie Marin, *senior picture editor;*
Cover Photo: David Deas/DK Stock/Getty Images
Production/Manufacturing: Matt Struble

1st Edition

ISBN 978-1-4000-0756-1

ISSN 1942-8723

SPECIAL SALES

This book is available at special discounts for bulk purchases for sales promotions or premiums. Special editions, including personalized covers, excerpts of existing books, and corporate imprints, can be created in large quantities for special needs. For more information, write to Special Markets/Premium Sales, 1745 Broadway, MD 6-2, New York, New York 10019, or e-mail specialmarkets@randomhouse.com.

AN IMPORTANT TIP & AN INVITATION

Although all prices, opening times, and other details in this book are based on information supplied to us at press time, changes occur all the time in the travel world, and Fodor's cannot accept responsibility for facts that become outdated or for inadvertent errors or omissions. So **always confirm information when it matters,** especially if you're making a detour to visit a specific place. Your experiences—positive and negative—matter to us. If we have missed or misstated something, **please write to us.** We follow up on all suggestions. Contact the Dominican Republic editor at editors@fodors.com or c/o Fodor's at 1745 Broadway, New York, NY 10019.

PRINTED IN THE UNITED STATES OF AMERICA

10 9 8 7 6 5 4 3 2 1

Be a Fodor's Correspondent

Your opinion matters. It matters to us. It matters to your fellow Fodor's travelers, too. And we'd like to hear it. In fact, we need to hear it.

When you share your experiences and opinions, you become an active member of the Fodor's community. That means we'll not only use your feedback to make our books better, but we'll publish your names and comments whenever possible. Throughout our guides, look for "Word of Mouth," excerpts of your unvarnished feedback.

Here's how you can help improve Fodor's for all of us.

Tell us when we're right. We rely on local writers to give you an insider's perspective. But our writers and staff editors—who are the best in the business—depend on you. Your positive feedback is a vote to renew our recommendations for the next edition.

Tell us when we're wrong. We're proud that we update most of our guides every year. But we're not perfect. Things change. Hotels cut services. Museums change hours. Charming cafés lose charm. If our writer didn't quite capture the essence of a place, tell us how you'd do it differently. If any of our descriptions are inaccurate or inadequate, we'll incorporate your changes in the next edition and will correct factual errors at fodors.com immediately.

Tell us what to include. You probably have had fantastic travel experiences that aren't yet in Fodor's. Why not share them with a community of like-minded travelers? Maybe you chanced upon a beach or bistro or B&B that you don't want to keep to yourself. Tell us why we should include it. And share your discoveries and experiences with everyone directly at fodors.com. Your input may lead us to add a new listing or highlight a place we cover with a "Highly Recommended" star or with our highest rating, "Fodor's Choice."

Give us your opinion instantly at our feedback center at www.fodors.com/feedback. You may also e-mail editors@fodors.com with the subject line "Dominican Republic Editor." Or send your nominations, comments, and complaints by mail to Dominican Republic Editor, Fodor's, 1745 Broadway, New York, NY 10019.

You and travelers like you are the heart of the Fodor's community. Make our community richer by sharing your experiences. Be a Fodor's correspondent.

Happy traveling!

Tim Jarrell, Publisher

CONTENTS

MAPS

ABOUT THIS BOOK

Our Ratings

Sometimes you find terrific travel experiences and sometimes they just find you. But usually the burden is on you to select the right combination of experiences. That's where our ratings come in.

As travelers we've all discovered a place so wonderful that its worthiness is obvious. And sometimes that place is so unique that superlatives don't do it justice: you just have to be there to know. These sights, properties, and experiences get our highest rating, **Fodor's Choice**, indicated by orange stars throughout this book.

Black stars highlight sights and properties we deem **Highly Recommended**, places that our writers, editors, and readers praise again and again for consistency and excellence.

By default, there's another category: any place we include in this book is by definition worth your time, unless we say otherwise. And we will.

Disagree with any of our choices? Care to nominate a place or suggest that we rate one more highly? Visit our feedback center at www. fodors.com/feedback.

Budget Well

Hotel and restaurant price categories from ¢ to $$$$ are defined in the opening pages of each chapter. For attractions, we always give standard adult admission fees; reductions are usually available for children, students, and senior citizens. Want to pay with plastic? **AE, D, DC, MC, V** following restaurant and hotel listings indicate whether American Express, Discover, Diner's Club, MasterCard, and Visa are accepted.

Restaurants

Unless we state otherwise, restaurants are open for lunch and dinner daily. We mention dress only when there's a specific requirement and reservations only when they're essential or not accepted—it's always best to book ahead.

Hotels

Hotels have private bath, phone, TV, and air-conditioning and operate on the European Plan (aka EP, meaning without meals), unless we specify that they use the Continental Plan (CP, with a continental breakfast), Breakfast Plan (BP, with a full breakfast), or Modified American Plan (MAP, with breakfast and dinner) or are all-inclusive (AI, including all meals and most activi-

ties). We always list facilities but not whether you'll be charged an extra fee to use them, so when pricing accommodations, find out what's included.

Many Listings

★	Fodor's Choice
★	Highly recommended
✉	Physical address
✛	Directions
⌂	Mailing address
☎	Telephone
🖷	Fax
⊕	On the Web
✆	E-mail
✎	Admission fee
☉	Open/closed times
Ⓜ	Metro stations
⊟	Credit cards

Hotels & Restaurants

🏨	Hotel
📶	Number of rooms
⚴	Facilities
¶◎|	Meal plans
✕	Restaurant
⚘	Reservations
⃠	Smoking
₿?	BYOB
✕🏨	Hotel with restaurant that warrants a visit

Outdoors

🏌	Golf
⛺	Camping

Other

☺	Family-friendly
⇨	See also
✉	Branch address
☞	Take note

Experience the Dominican Republic

1

WORD OF MOUTH

"Santo Domingo['s Zona Colonial] is a UNESCO World Heritage Site. There is a tropical wonderland at Saona Island. . . . Great golf in the Dominican Republic is that interests you."

—jmelzie

WHAT'S NEW

Boutique B&Bs in Santo Domingo's Zona Colonial

For decades there were few hotels (desirable or undesirable) in this most appealing quarter of the city, but that has turned around. More than a half-dozen petite hotels are now pleasing travelers. The Zona Colonial can be compared to New York's Greenwich Village in the 1960s, a magnet for artsy, intellectual, fun types. In fact, in most instances these urban sanctuaries are owned by expats who fit that description. The properties often reflect the personality of their charismatic owners. All are restorations, be they of ancient convents or 1920s mansions.

Regenerated Beaches & New Condos

Two modern engineering feats, the regeneration of Cabarete (broadened by some 114 feet) and Juan Dolio (lengthened by nearly 11,500 feet) beaches have proven to be key elements in regenerated tourism in the two cities. In Cabarete, the Ocean Point development on Kite Beach and Punta Goleta are adding top-notch housing stock for expats and vacationers in this former backpacker's haven. Juan Dolio has seen an even more miraculous rebirth. With their Costa del Sol condominiums, the Metro Group has led the new wave of conversions of old hotels and apartments into luxurious, beachfront condos. With these new housing developments, Juan Dolio is poised to become the equivalent of Miami's South Beach in the Caribbean.

Eco-Tourism in the Southwest

The natural beauty of this unspoiled province, where the mountains and rivers meet a pristine coastline, is an enticement for all tourists who think green. The region is a crossroads for bird-watchers, nature photographers, bush pilots, UNESCO workers stationed in Haiti, and other globetrotters who ply the roads less traveled. Three national parks preserve the landscape, while small eco-oriented lodges and villas are sprouting up. Peace Corps volunteers are organizing the local guides and artisans to teach them how tourism can make their lives better.

Cap Cana Keeps Growing

Years in the making, Altabella Sanctuary, the flagship hotel for the Cap Cana development south of the main body of Punta Cana hotels, opened its posh doors with 177 ocean-view suites. The next grand opening is expected to be the Golden Bear, a luxurious condo-style hotel. Coming in 2009 is the Fishing Lodge Cap Cana, another mid-size luxury hotel on the marina. The Ritz-Carlton Cap Cana, a billion-dollar mixed-use complex, should open with a big bang in 2010.

The Cruise-Ship Biz Is a Big Deal for the D.R.

Pirates once sailed these waters, but the blaggards have been replaced by cruisers, some half a million forecasted for 2008. This 60% increase over 2007 means that the island's cruise traffic now rivals Puerto Rico's. One major catalyst is that Santo Domingo has become a port of embarkation for Royal Caribbean's *Vision of the Seas*. The revitalization of the Don Diego Cruise Terminal, which lies just riverfront steps from the Zona Colonial, was a key element in the growth of the capital's cruise business. Nearby, the brand-new Sans Souci Port, with its tourist shops, will become the capital's new mother port in 2009.

DID YOU KNOW?

The D.R. Is a Growing Multiracial Mix

Multiculturalism characterizes the Dominican Republic, where the official language is Spanish and where 73% of the Dominicans are classified as mixed-race. Add to that a small 11% who are of African origin and 16% who are of European descent, and the cultural variety continues to grow. The next census will have to catch up with the number of *Norte Americanos* and other expats who have chosen to reside or retire here.

What Is Island Time?

You've heard tell of the phenomenon called island time, and in the D.R. this generally refers to the mindset that there is no point in hurrying. Here it is almost socially unacceptable. But the D.R. is really on a different island time than the United States. The local time zone is Eastern Caribbean Time. In winter the D.R. is one hour ahead of Eastern Standard Time in the United States. Since the D.R. does not observe daylight savings time, you might say it is the endless summer. But what this means in reality is that at sunset in winter, darkness really does fall . . . and suddenly.

The Peso Is a Good Deal for Americans

The official currency in the D.R. is the peso, with one Dominican peso equal to 100 *centavos*. Since the D.R. has such strong economic ties to the United States, U.S. greenbacks are not only widely accepted but also desired. Better, although the island's currency has increased in value, the D.R. is one place where the dollar is still quite strong. Although visitors are advised (officially) to exchange their dollars only at a bank, the truth is that independent *cambios* (currency-exchange offices) often give a slightly better rate and have longer hours. Ask any expat for the best exchange place.

The DR Has a Prosperous Japanese Community

Thanks to Generalissimo Rafael L. Trujillo, who implemented an immigration program in the 1950s, descendants of the 200 Japanese families that he "imported" to the fertile mountain region of Constanza, have prospered. Trujillo's original intention was to establish a strong agricultural community and bolster the area's economy. These industrious immigrants did just that, and today amid strawberry fields and flower farms, the prominent—though small—community of Japanese-Dominican families have prospered and built substantial homes in the Dominican "Alps."

Juan Luis Guerra Is Merengue's Superstar

Guerra is one Latin vocalist, musician, and composer who has broken through to the mainstream, both in the United States and abroad. In 2007 he won four Grammys at the 2007 Latin Grammy Awards. Atypically this folk hero was classically trained. He blends jazz-influenced merengue and sentimental *bachatas* (traditional country ballads) with his own hip lyrics. Merengue is the D.R.'s national form of music (and dance); traditionally, it combines the sounds of the aboriginal *guiro* (a metal "grater" that is scratched), the *tambora* (an African lap drum), and the accordion. Indeed, Guerra's renditions are refinements.

WHAT'S WHERE

1 **Santo Domingo.** Santo Domingo is a sprawling metropolis of some 3 million, but its soul is found within the historic blocks of its famous Zona Colonial. Southwest is the undeveloped eco-paradise around Barahona and its three national parks.

2 **The Southeast Coast.** East of Santo Domingo, the Boca Chica gives way to the luxury condos of Juan Dolio. Beyond La Romana and the famous Casa de Campo is beautiful Bayahibe Bay and Dominicus Beach.

3 **Punta Cana.** First-timers usually head to the all-inclusives in this east-coast enclave, which stretches from densely developed Baváro all the way north to Uvero Alto.

4 **Samaná.** The haunt of independent travelers has now been discovered and is no longer so remote. The region is traditionally known for its idyllic beaches, small inns, beachside restaurants, waterfalls, and excellent whale-watching.

5 **The North Coast.** This coast still has something for everyone, from the all-inclusive enclave of Playa Dorada, to the authentic city of Puerto Plata, to German-influenced Sosúa, to Cabarete, known for its windsurfing and kiteboarding.

6 **Santiago & the Cibao Valley.** Santiago's charm is its historic, Victorian-style downtown square. Nearby, the mountainous Cordillera Central offers white-water rafting, while the fireplaces at several small eco-lodges help thwart the nightly chill.

THE DOMINICAN REPUBLIC TODAY

Leonel Is President Once Again

Locals call him, simply, Leonel (lee-o-*nel*), but the full name of the D.R.'s president is Dr. Leonel Fernández Reyna. In 2008 the head of the Dominican Liberation Party (PLD) was reelected in 2008 for his third term (he first won his first four-year term in 1996, at the age of 42, but was not reelected until 2004). This handsome and intellectual *politico*, a former New Yorker, put the country on a sound economic path in the 1990s, curbing corruption and waste, fostering privatization, lowering unemployment and illiteracy, and awakening tourism. Leonel was defeated in 2000 by Hipólito Mejí, a so-called "man of the street," whose reign proved disastrous. It is said that when Leonel took over again in 2004, the treasury was nearly empty and that Hipólito's people took the chairs and air-conditioners with them. Hipólito left the country. The sales tax was raised to an unpopular 16% and to reduce crime in the capital, a midnight curfew on weeknights (2 AM on weekends) was established. Although the curfew has put some nightclubs out of business, the city is a safer place, and the extra money in government coffers is devoted to tourism infrastructure developments.

Tourism Is Expanding the Middle Class

What a difference 15 years has made as far as income and standard of living for Dominicans. Since 1992 tourism has grown to encompass 24% of the country's GDP, and car dealerships are opening up all over the island, this in a place where an automobile—never mind a luxury import—was inconceivable for most families. The government has announced plans to invest some $1 billion in tourism infrastructure developments by 2012. For many, education and social mobility have come through tourism. Although they may have grown up in a palm-thatched hut with a dirt floor, many tourism workers now own a home in a middle-class, suburban neighborhood. Poverty, however, is still omnipresent, from city slums to the most remote areas, especially near the Haitian border.

Dominican Yorkers Return Home

Many Dominicans who have been living in New York—sometimes for decades—are now starting to come home to retire and/or invest their hard-earned money. A new oceanfront condo development under construction in Guayacanes is an example of a Dominican York project. For decades, those sons and daughters who chose to try and get ahead in the States have sent their dollars home to their families. Remittances from Dominicans who live outside the country, particularly those one million brothers and sisters in New York, are now calculated to be $1 billion annually and is a top source of revenue for the country.

Baseball Heroes Help Out

Superstar athletes can be credited with bringing both their fame and hard-earned cash to their homeland. Their substantial salaries contribute to the country's economy, too, from the luxury penthouses they buy to the philanthropic donations that can turn around a whole hometown. Sammy Sosa, who started life as a shoeshine boy in San Pedro Macoris, has donated a sizeable fortune to that town. He owns an apartment in the capital's classy Malecón Center and a villa at Casa de Campo, as does Juan Marichal. Known for his flamboyant style, Marichal was one of the early Dominican record-

breaking pitchers and the first Dominican Hall of Famer (1983). His Juan Marichal Golf Tournament at Los Marlins Golf Course, held annually in Juan Dolio, has raised millions for the island's needy families. Another baseball legend has quietly begun building an upscale hotel and spa project in the mountains of Constanza.

Real Estate Values Rise

Property values are still rising quickly here, as much as 20% to 35% annually, and the Dominican real estate market has become an outlet for those who no longer feel secure investing at home in the United States. Most investment opportunities are within planned oceanfront developments, where absentee owners can rent their villas and condos through an on-site managerial office. The Samaná Peninsula, formerly considered remote, is booming thanks to its new international airport and improved highway access. As retirees and second-home owners in Florida and the southeast coast bail out, they have begun to seek out new condos in the D.R., where insurance on oceanfront property is just 0.075% of the purchase price, one of the factors being solid concrete construction.

Larimar & Amber Gain International Recognition

These indigenous semiprecious stones are starting to bring in big bucks to the island. For years amber was more the popular product, but as the novelty of wearing fossilized resin has held steady, interest in larimar is growng. Larimar, a pectoline that is the color of the Caribbean Sea, is being set in sterling silver with more upscale designs and is especially growing in popularity in Europe. Jewelers are having difficulty meeting demand since there is only one larimar mine in the world.

High Energy Prices Foster Innovation

Electricity in the Caribbean is higher than in the United States, but rates are among the highest in the Dominican Republic. And despite these exorbitant prices, regular power outages occur; in some neighborhoods they even occur daily. This has forced innovation. Wealthy homeowners have always had generators, but the growing cost of diesel fuel has created a surge in sales of efficient, compact fluorescent bulbs and solar hot water heaters to both homeowners and small inns and B&Bs. Apartment dwellers, particularly in Santo Domingo have small, battery-operated generators. People are also turning to wind power. As prices rise at the pump, more taxi drivers are turning their vehicles over to propane, which is a third of the cost; at approximately RD$10,000 (US$300, which is still real money in the D.R.), that is a modest investment to save for the long haul. Larger resorts that use a lot of power enter the sustainable realm by growing some of their own food and planting heat-absorbing trees to shade buildings.

TOP DOMINICAN REPUBLIC ATTRACTIONS

Strolling Through Santo Domingo's Zona Colonial

(D) If you believe in magic, you'll be enchanted with the Zona Colonial. Walk down Calle Las Damas, which may make you feel as if it were still 1590. The Zone is not just a medieval museum piece with cobblestone streets, but a hip, contemporary neighborhood. In-the-know travelers head to the bars and restaurants on Plaza España, where a convivial café scene can be experienced.

Whale-Watching in Samaná

(B) To cruise alongside a school of whales and photograph their playful antics is an experience you will not soon forget. The season lasts from January to March, when the humpbacks delight in the warm waters of the *Bahía de Samaná,* their breeding ground for centuries. By the end of January, as many as 4,000 whales are courting and cavorting in the Bay of Samaná.

Enjoying the Beach in Punta Cana

(A) Punta Cana is justifably famous for its beautiful beaches, which ring the easternmost cape over the course of 35 unbroken miles of sand, from Playa Uvero Alto in the north all the way to Playa Juanillo in the south, the latest are being turned into a tourist resort area with the luxurious Cap Cana development. From serene to savage, the beaches are sandy, white, and beautiful.

White-Water Rafting

(C) For travelers with a bigger taste for adventure, the D.R.'s adventure-sport center is Jarabacoa, in the so-called "Dominican Alps." From here, several companies offer white-water rafting trips on the Rio Yaque del Norte's Class III rapids, a trip that will take you through wild canyons, past soaring waterfalls, and into Class III rapids.

Playing Golf on a Great Course

(G) Golfers have long been drawn to the beautiful courses at Casa de Campo in La Romana, but there are many other beautiful courses, from the Playa Dorada course on the north coast, to Punta Cana's many great courses, to the Guavaberry and Los Marlins courses in Juan Dolio. And more new courses in development all over the D.R.

Snorkeling off Isla Saona

(H) This beautiful national park off the island's southeast coast has beautiful beaches and is surrounded by crystal-clear, aquamarine waters that are teeming with sea life, particularly starfish. A day here is an extremely popular excursion for travelers in La Romana or Bayahibe areas, as well as for visitors to Punta Cana.

Renting a Beachfront Villa

(E) A superb alternative for family reunions, destination weddings, golf forays, corporate retreats, and "Big Chill" reunions, the D.R.'s beautiful villas will get you out of the all-inclusive throngs. Some of these are fully staffed with chef, butler, maids, and more. And you can have a luxurious vacation on the D.R.'s north shore for less than a comparable villa on most other islands.

Kite- & Windsurfing

(F) Strong, steady winds and a clean shoreline have made Cabarete—especially Kite Beach—the North Coast's center for windsurfing, putting it on the map for sporty travelers with an adventurous spirit and excellent upper-body strength. But now the more exciting sport of kite surfing (and kiteboarding) is overshadowing the original, helping fliers go even higher.

QUINTESSENTIAL
DOMINICAN REPUBLIC

If you want to get a sense of Dominican culture and indulge in some of its pleasures, start by familiarizing yourself with the rituals of daily life.

Sample Some Sancocho

If there is a single Dominican specialty that could be called the national dish, it is this protein-rich stew that traditionally includes such key ingredients as chicken, pork, pumpkin, yucca, plantain, corn on the cob, and cilantro. The best version is served alongside hearty portions of rice and sliced avocado. After clubbing, *capitaleños* pile into late-night restaurants for their sancocho fix. Reputedly, the stew absorbs alcohol and lessens hangovers. Stop at any popular local restaurant at midday on Sunday, and it's almost a sure bet that you'll find sancocho on the menu. Of course, the best way to experience sancocho is when you can get yourself invited to someone's home and eat it like the Domincans do, family-style.

Ride the Gua-guas

If you want to feel what it's like to be a real Dominican, then you have to brave the local transportation. Gua-guas are local buses, which are often minivans, especially in the smaller towns. In Cabarete, for example, you just stand on the side of the road and wait for what looks like a speeding ambulance—a white van with a red light on top and a man hanging off the running board. Wave violently. The hanging man will bang his hand on the side, making the driver stop short. Watch what the other passengers give the hanger-on, and do likewise. It's usually *diez* (RD$10, about 30¢). In Santo Domingo, gua-guas are buses, often beaten-up school buses, though never yellow. As taxi rates increase, there's even more reason to take a gua-gua. And it's

a trip to see what locals bring aboard—kettle drums, a stack of Haitian artwork, full-size baby carriages.

Get Your Dance on at a Colmodon on Saturday Night

If you want to have a real peek through a window of Dominican culture, then you have to go dancing. A *colmodon* is larger than your average corner *colmado* (a small grocery store) and serves a larger purpose. It's part supermarket, part bar, and part social center. The colmodon will have tables and chairs, a TV always tuned to a baseball game or *telenovela,* and loud merengue and bachata music playing in the background. On weekends, the colmadons come alive, when many add a makeshift kitchen serving authentic Dominican fare including tostones, fried chicken, platanos, or arroz con pollo. Patrons dance in the street, and shots of local rum—chased by Presidente beer—help you feel the rhythms that you may never knew you had.

Take Yourself Out to a Ball Game

Dominicans are mad about baseball. Taking in a game is definitely doable and will definitely help you get down with the locals. For the full whammy, go to one of the top parks—in Santo Domingo, La Romana, or San Perdro de Macoris, the so-called "City of Shortstops." The betting is fast and furious, the bookies remarkably astute. Vendors have their individual style, whether they're peddling souvenirs, local snacks, Presidente beer, or mini-bottles of rum. Half-time is like no time you have ever seen. "Mascots" go through bizarre, often ribald antics. Merengue is played at ear-splitting levels, and fans dance hedonistically. This is a social event where you can make new friends as long as you pledge allegiance to their team.

IF YOU LIKE

The All-Inclusive Experience

The all-inclusive concept may be one of the most popular tourism promotions in recent history, even more beneficial than the swim-up bar. Although this crowd-pleaser began in Jamaica, the AI has reached its zenith in the Dominican Republic (particularly in Punta Cana), where your accommodations, meals, drinks, entertainment, tips, activities, and sometimes even spa treatments are included in one price tag.

Casa de Campo. Although hardly a traditional all-inclusive, the D.R.'s original luxury resort offers its best value to those guests who choose the AI plan; the side benefit is access to Casa's wonderful facilities and amenities, though golf is an additional cost.

Excellence Punta Cana. A sumptuous lovers' lair, this adults-only resort exudes romance and sensuality. The open-air, tropical lobby looks out on the heavenly beach. Swim-out suites open directly onto the lazy river pool that snakes around the grounds.

Iberostar Costa Dorada. It will dazzle you with its sprawling lobby, its hardwood benches and sculptures, and its curvaceous pool. As you swim, you can see the mountains and its expansive, rejuvenated beach. With good food, a great spa, and bright spirit, this is one of the North Coast's best resorts.

Paradisus Palma Real. Punta Cana's best all-inclusive is a show-stopper. The average suite, with flat-screen TV, CD player, balcony or terrace, and semi-open marble bathroom with jet showers and a Jacuzzi for two, is extraordinary. You won't need to upgrade.

Beautiful Beaches

Without exaggeration, the D.R.'s beaches are among the world's best. Beaches lined with coconut palms, with pearl-white to amber sands; beaches with looming, dramatic cliffs; pebbled beaches where mountain streams meet the sea, the country's coastline has them all.

Bahia de las Aquilas. This is the remote beach in the Southwest that everyone hears about and longs to go to. It takes some doing to get here, but it's oh so worth the effort.

The Coconut Coast. The beaches of Punta Cana—Juanillo, Punta Cana/Bávaro, El Cortecito, Arena Gorda, Macao, and Uvero Alto—are joined together in a 35-mi-long unbroken stretch of pearly sand with turquoise water.

Orchid Bay Beach. Near Cabrera on the North Coast, and named for the wild orchids that grow on its cliffs, it offers a large public beach seldom used by anyone but the residents in the luxury villas lining it. Swimmable in a couple of choice locations, this is an underutilized gem.

Playa Bahoruco. In front of the Southwest fishing village of the same name, this gorgeous stretch of virgin beach goes on for miles with unobstructed views. Taupe sand is under and around those white stones.

Playa Bayahibe. This glorious, half-moon cove is where you'll find the area's best all-inclusive resorts. At night, when no one is on it and the silver moon illuminates the phosphorescence, it is what Caribbean dreams are made of.

Nightlife

If you love the nightlife, then you're going to love the Dominican Republic. Dominicans are a fun-loving people, who like to drink, party, and dance. Dancing is a national passion—even more than baseball! Here, happy hour starts as early as 4 PM. Some then take a second siesta, so they can rest up before the usual late dinner and dancing after.

Casino Dominicus. This sparkling new, Las Vegas–style casino in Bayahibe has high, arched ceilings, the D.R.'s highest table limits, the only exclusive players' club, a 1,000-seat theater, a disco with local bands, restaurants, and shopping—all with a Caribbean flamboyance.

Hemingway's Café. Since the 1980s, this bar and restaurant has long been the spot in Playa Dorada to party if you're young or young at heart, offering a safe haven for both AI guests and expats. Merengue bands, a DJ, karaoke, and American-casual food keep the crowds coming.

Lax. The nightlife in Cabarete is known as a big beach party, with bar-hopping the name of the game. Open-air Lax spills onto the sand, attracting both the young and the ageless. The fun begins at happy hour, but the scene really comes alive after 10, when a DJ spins or a live band rocks.

Nowhere Bar. This bar in Santo Domingo's Zona Colonial is in a renovated 16th-century, two-story mansion. The place is hot, the crowd mostly young and affluent.

Great Food

The freshest seafood—eaten with views of the water from which it came—is one of the best aspects of dining in the D.R. Price is another plus. Although Dominican cuisine can be heavy, lighter, fresher cuisine can be found at upscale restaurants all over the island, particularly those owned by expats.

Jellyfish. Shaped like a double-decker yacht, this sophisticated open-air restaurant on the sands of Bávaro focuses on fresh seafood caught by local fishermen. Soothing music and soft lighting set the mood for romantic dining from fish right off the grill to the oven-baked lobster.

Lucia. At this Playa Dorada stunner, acclaimed chef Rafael Vasquez has created a menu that is both comprehensive and contemporary, with everything from tuna tartare with a smoking wasabi-lime sorbet, to rich foie gras with apples and spiced chocolate sauce.

Mesón D' Bari. For some 25 years, Señor Marisol has been feeding the locals in the capital's Zona Colonial from the recipes of his grandmother. Everyone is welcome at this late-night hangout.

Peperoni. Casa de Campo's Marina Chavón has a classy and contemporary Italian-accented restaurant that stretches its culinary muscles from osso buco and risotto to wood-oven pizzas to some Asian specialties.

La Terrasse. This casually charming Samaná restaurant offers one of the best beachfront dining experiences in the D.R. It's a standout primarily because of caring French–Spanish owners and their "sun-inspired" Mediterranean cuisine.

HISTORY YOU CAN SEE

Colonial Times

Christopher Columbus claimed the island for Spain on his first New World voyage in 1492, when he came looking for riches his Spanish patrons; Columbus's Bartholomeo founded Santo Domingo in 1496, and it became the cradle of Western civilization in the Americas. Columbus's son, Don Diego, resided here grandly before returning to Spain in 1532. Nicolas Ovando, the first governor, was an able ruler, but his mistreatment of the indigenous people was his black mark.

What to See: You can see some 300 surviving structures from the period in Santo Domingo's Zona Colonial (a UNESCO World Heritage Site). Although key buildings, such as the hospital and monastery, are now artistic ruins, some buildings have been beautifully restored. The **Plaza de España,** formerly the colony's warehouse row, now houses trendy restaurants with popular outdoor cafés. The urban mansion of the Governor of the Americas is now a luxury hotel, the **Sofitel Nicolas Ovando.** The focal point of Parque Colón, **Catedral Santa Maria de la Encarnation,** is reputedly the first cathedral in the Americas. **El Museo de las Casas Reales** is one of the Zone's most handsome colonial edifices; built in the Renaissance style, it was the seat of Spanish government and now functions as an art gallery and museum. The **Casa del Cordón** is believed to be the oldest surviving stone house from the early colonial period in the Western Hemisphere.

The Victorian Era

The 19th-century was a golden age for the island's tobacco-growing regions, when world prices reached their heights in the 1870s. While tobacco was grown in the fertile Cibao Valley around Santiago, it was shipped from such ports as Puerto Plata, bringing great wealth to that city, too. The trade made tobacco traders and merchants rich, and several Germans built impressive dwellings in the region. Although many such mansions are in disrepair, some have been restored; others are in the works.

What to See: The tobacco trade spawned opulent homes and handsome wooden buildings decorated with gingerbread fretwork, painted in eye-stopping Caribbean colors, which is notably present in all its faded glory in **Puerto Plata.** You can get a feeling for this bygone Golden Age in the magnificent Victorian-style gazebo in the central **Parque Independencia,** the **Museo del Ambar** (originally the urban residence of a German tobacco entrepreneur), and **Casa Cultura** (now a Dominican art gallery and performance space). The old Victorian neighborhoods continue northeast about eight blocks and also east toward the ocean. Many of the millionaire families in the charming, provincial city of Santiago still owe their fortunes to tobacco. Santiago's Old Town is also centered around its central park, **Parque Duarte.** Santiago's colorful past is seen in the facades of its 19th-century gingerbread houses that are scattered through the streets surrounding the park all the way to the **Fortaleza San Luis.**

The Trujillo Era

Generalissimo Rafael L. Trujillo ruled the Dominican Republic with an iron fist from 1930 until he was assassinated 1961. His reign was one of the bloodiest in the 20th century. After gaining power, he entered into several pushes to "whiten" the mixed-race nation. He was particularly against the immigration of Haitians to the D.R., and his policies caused the

deaths of thousands. At the same time, he had an open-door policy for Europeans, welcoming Jewish refugees during World War II and Japanese colonists afterward. He had a flamboyant style, drove yellow, big-finned Cadillacs, and was intent on leaving an architectural legacy behind. Indeed, he left a vast infrastructure in the country, including highways and other public works and monuments.

What to See: The most notable of Trujillo-commissioned structure is Santiago's massive **Monumento a los Héroes de la Restauración de la Republica,** a 230-foot monument topped by an allegorical figure of victory. The excellent, modern **Autopista del Este** (Highway 3) that connects Santo Domingo with Juan Dolio and La Romana was a "gift" to the nation in the late 1950s and also to Trujillo's son, Rafael, so that he would have a place to drive his race cars. The impressive **Palacio Nacional,** the white, neoclassical seat of government in Santo Domingo, which was completed in 1947, is emblematic of Trujillo's love of grandeur.

The New Millennium

It was as if the year 2000 signaled an awakening in the artistic sensibilities of Dominican architects, as their talent burst forth in compelling ways. The island nation was emerging as a tourist destination, and the revenue from tourism began to seep into the economy on every level. Neither architects nor developers were satisfied with the bland, concrete buildings and cookie-cutter mentality that predominated across the island. And upscale second-home buyers demanded something more interesting. The millennial revival has positively affected both the resort and residential categories and can be seen in important public works projects as well. In some cases, Dominican design has taken inspiration from its historic past, beginning with the 16th-century Spanish architecture.

What to See: The **Centro León** is the most impressive, new, architectural landmark in Santiago, a world-class museum and art gallery that was also designed to promote sensorial emotions. **Altabella Sanctuary Cap Cana Golf & Spa,** with its palatial main lobby and gorgeous stone facade, was inspired by 16th-century colonial styles. **Casa Colonial Beach & Spa Resort** in Playa Dorada may look like a restored colonial mansion, but as you can see on the inside, it's also got a contemporary feel. The classy **Hilton Santo Domingo** and the adjacent Malecón Center have attempted to blend modern with classical Spanish-colonial architecture to grand effect.

WHEN TO GO

The high season in the Dominican Republic is traditionally winter—from mid-December to the week after Easter—when northern weather is at its worst. This corresponds to the high season in the rest of the Caribbean. During the winter high season, you'll find a fairly even mix of Americans and Europeans at many resorts, though some resorts are favored more by Americans and some more than Europeans. There's a spike in travel by Europeans in the summer months, so even June through August can be busy in the D.R., unlike much of the rest of the Caribbean. This means that the island's resorts have no real "low" season, but you'll generally find the cheapest prices from September through November, during the height of hurricane season.

Carnival is an important event in the Dominican Republic, which is predominately a Catholic country; the most famous carnival celebration is in La Vega. The Dominican Republic Jazz Festival is an annual even in Cabarete each November. The same month sees the Dominican Republic International Film Festival at the Sun Village resort in Puerto Plata.

Climate

Weather in the Dominican Republic is warm year-round, but temperatures are generally cooler from November through April and warmer from May through October. The average daily temperature ranges from 78°F to 88°F. The coolest region is the Cordillera Central, around Jarabacoa and Constanza, where high temperatures can be in the 60s°F. The north coast is rainier during the winter months from November through April, the southern coast from May through October. Barahona, in the southwest, is the driest part of the country; Punta

Cana is about average, with peaks of precipitation in May, June, October, and November.

Toward the end of summer, of course, hurricane season begins in earnest, with the first tropical wave passing by in June; the season does not end until late November. In an odd paradox, tropical storms passing by leave behind the sunniest and clearest days you'll ever see.

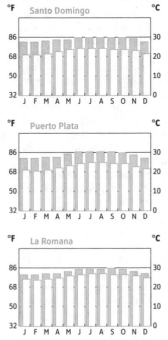

Santo Domingo

WITH AN EXCURSION TO BARAHONA

WORD OF MOUTH

"I can absolutely recommend the Sofitel Nicolas Ovando. This property is on the oldest street in the city, so [you] would be right in the heart of the Zona Colonial with all its history and sightseeing potential. The rooms/bathrooms are gorgeous, excellent breakfast buffet, charming pool. Santo Domingo is a beautiful, vibrant city filled with history and color."

—lifes2short

"My wife and I spent two months living in Santo Domingo this past summer (2007). The interior of the airport (Las Americas) went through a lot of upgrades/changes in just one year. The airport is very easy to navigate and fairly small."

—Lakeside 77

www.fodors.com/forums

By Eileen
Robinson
Smith

SANTO DOMINGO IS THE VIBRANT seaside capital of this emerging country. As the Dominican Republic grows up, this city, which for decades has had a cosmopolitan atmosphere and infrastructure that distinguished it from the rest of this island nation, only becomes more sophisticated. It's known throughout the Caribbean for its upscale hotels and restaurants, and certainly its nightlife.

There are many reasons why you might choose to fly into Santo Domingo instead of directly to Punta Cana or La Romana, including that it's often less expensive and there are more convenient flights into Las Americas International Airport than into some of the beach destinations. If this is the case, you can easily take a few days for an urban vacation and then couple it with a beach stay elsewhere on the island.

You might also be sent down by your company or have your own business dealings in this growing metropolis. Or you may be scheduled to attend an international conference at one of the deluxe high-rise hotels on the Malecón, the seaside boulevard that's one of the city's main thoroughfares. Plan on having your spouse or a special friend join you for a romantic getaway, and add a couple of days to your itinerary.

Perhaps you've heard about the city's Zona Colonial and, being a history buff, want the ambience and romanticism of such an old-world setting. That one square mile, which was the location of the original Spanish settlement to the island, was ruled in the 16th century by the family of its founder, Christopher Columbus. Achitectural landmarks include a number of firsts for the New World: the first cathedral, monastery, seminary, military fort, and university.

If you're bound for faraway ports on a cruise ship and Santo Domingo is your port of embarkation, you may have to overnight here. Don't hesitate to extend your stay, and enjoy a pre- or post-trip sojourn. Though it can be overwhelming, Santo Domingo is a genuine place, not simply a tourist area. It's the largest city in the Caribbean (with 3 million residents, both poor and rich); it's where the D.R.'s movers and shakers can be found. And as the country's economy has grown ever stronger, the old smoky cars are giving way to decent automobiles, the litter has decreased, and the hotels just keep getting better.

If you like getting dressed up and doing the town, the nightlife here is comparable to the glory days of the late 1950s and early '60s in the United States. People go out—couples, singles, and in groups—to have dinner and then go dancing at one of the clubs. Going a couple of rounds at one of the glitzy casinos is another choice, as are theaters and live music venues. Instead of hitting the diner for breakfast, Dominicans pile into late-night restaurants for *sancocho,* the protein-rich stew that is the national dish.

EXPLORING SANTO DOMINGO

The easiest away to start your trip to this fascinating city is to fly into Las Americas International Airport and proceed by taxi or prearranged transfer to downtown. Chances are you'll be staying in a hotel either in the Zona Colonial or on the Malecón (Av. George Washington), the seaside boulevard where most of the city's high-rise hotels are located. Much of your exploration can be done on foot—that's certainly true in the Zone—and it's easy to walk from one Malecón property to another. In other areas, including Piantini, you'll need to drive or be driven. At night it's not really safe to walk the Malecón alone, but if you're with a group it's usually fine. To be safe, take a hotel taxi. The most important thing is to have fun!

ABOUT THE RESTAURANTS

Santo Domingo's culinary repertoire includes Spanish, Italian, Middle Eastern, Indian, Japanese, and *nueva cocina Dominicana* (contemporary Dominican cuisine). If seafood is on the menu, it's bound to be fresh. The dining scene is the best in the country and probably as fine a selection of restaurants as you can find anywhere in the Caribbean. Keep in mind that the touristy places, such as those in the Zona Colonial—with mediocre fare and just-ok service—are becoming more and more costly, while the several fine-dining options, such as La Residence have lowered prices and are now offering daily specials for around $10. Supplement your entrée with a couple of appetizers, and you can have a nice dinner for less than $30 per person. Most notably, you'll have caring service and be sequestered in 'luxe surroundings away from the tourist hustle.

Some of the best restaurant choices are not in the tourist zones but in the business districts of the modern city and in the upscale residential neighborhoods where the wealthy *capitaleños* reside. Know that they typically dress for dinner and dine late. The locals usually start eating after 9:30 PM, when the Americans are just finishing their desserts.

Among the best Dominican specialties are *queso frito* (fried cheese), *sancocho* (a thick meat stew served with rice and avocado slices), *arroz con pollo* (rice with beans and fried chicken parts), *mofango* (mashed green plantains and shredded pork or chicken and chittlins), *pescado al coco* (fish in coconut sauce), *plátanos* (fried sweet plantains), and *tostones* (fried green plantains). Shacks and stands that serve cheap eats are an integral part of the culture and landscape, but eat street food at your own risk—more like your own peril. Presidente is the most popular local beer, but try a Bohemia, which has more flavor. Brugal rum is popular with the Dominicans, but Barceló *anejo* (aged) rum is as smooth as cognac, and Barceló Imperial is so special it's sold only at Christmas.

ABOUT THE HOTELS

Most of the better hotels are on or near the Malecón, with a growing collection of small, desirable properties in the trendy Zona Colonial, allowing you to feel part of that magical environment. Most of the hotels in the Zone are small boutique properties in colonial-era buildings.

The Malecón's high-rise hotels continue to offer a deluxe experience at prices that are exceptionally reasonable for a capital city. Seldom do you have to pay as much as $200, and that would be for the concierge level or a suite. Moderately priced American chains have made inroads into the country and offer stateside amenities, even luxury bedding programs and in-city pools, for less than the Malecón majors. Although these chain hotels do not have the same glamor or the primo locations, they're good choices, especially for the budget-conscious cruise-ship passengers who must spend a night before embarking. The pre- and post-cruise business has increased the weekend occupancy of some participating hotels by 20.

Always make your reservations at the smaller properties as far in advance as possible, as the posh surroundings, good service, and favorable pricing keep them full. Short-term apartment rentals are also available now if you want an extended vacation or are relocating or need time to do some house- or apartment-hunting. But these are typically not bargains.

WHAT IT COSTS IN DOLLARS					
	¢	$	$$	$$$	$$$$
Restaurants	under $8	$8–$12	$12–$20	$20–$30	Over $30
Hotels*	Under $80	$80–$150	$150–$250	$250–$350	Over $350
Hotels**	Under $125	$125–$250	$250–$350	$350–$450	Over $450

*EP, BP, CP **AI, FAP, MAP Restaurant prices are per person for a main course at dinner and do not include the 15% V.A.T. and 10% service charge. Hotel prices are per night for a double room in high season, excluding 15% V.A.T. and 10% service charge.

WHAT TO SEE

Parque Independencia separates the old city from modern Santo Domingo, a sprawling, noisy city with a population of close to 2 million. This park has rotating art (often replicas or poster art) and photography exhibits, too. These large "works of art" are night lighted and hung on the wall that encircles the park. Miraculously, people respect what the city is doing here and it never seems to disappear in the night.

A predominately Asian neighborhood just north of the Zona Colonial, on Mella and Duarte avenues, has been given a cosmetic face-lift to resemble San Francisco's Chinatown. This *barrio* now has an ornate archway as its entrance, with street signs and phone booths, etc., with Asian designs. Chinese businesses, particularly restaurants, already existed, and a museum and a plaza honoring Confucius are still in the works. However, local residents and expats are not frequenting it, saying that the restaurants aren't very good.

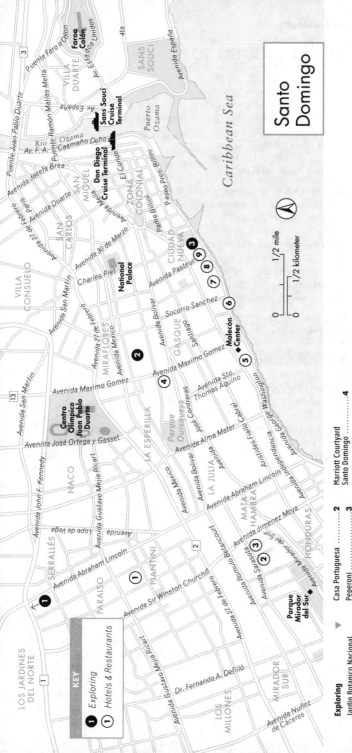

Santo Domingo

0   1/2 mile
0   1/2 kilometer

Caribbean Sea

KEY

● Exploring
① Hotels & Restaurants

Exploring

Jardin Botanico Nacional 1
El Malecón 3
Plaza de la Cultura 2

Restaurants

Adrian Tropical 6

Casa Portuguesa 2
Peperoni 3
Sophia's 1

Hotels

Hilton Santo Domingo 5
InterContinental
V Centerario 9

Marriott Courtyard
Santo Domingo 4
Meliá Santo Domingo
Hotel & Casino 8
Renaissance Jaragua
Hotel & Casino 7

2

SANTO DOMINGO TOP 5

Historical Sites. Santo Domingo's Zona Colonial is becoming known as one of the most appealing historic districts in the Caribbean. Check out the New World's oldest cathedral (which is still in service at Parque Colon), Casa Reales, or the Alcazar de Colón at Plaza de España.

Have a Beach Day. The capital is on the Caribbean but has no swimming beaches. Instead, go about an hour east and buy an inexpensive day-pass for the Barcelo Capella Resort in Juan Dolio. If you want a more in-depth look, head underwater with the professional German instructors at the dive center.

Wine & Dine. Partake in the city's sophisticated restaurant scene. There are restaurants galore in the Zona Colonial, in the top hotels along the Malecón, and in some upscale residential districts.

Shop 'til You Drop. Whether souvenir shopping on Calle El Conde, buying Dominican cigars and rum, or designer clothing in Piantini, you can find bargains here on quality goods.

Love the Nightlife. Head to one of the hotel lounges such as the one at the Hilton, which features live jazz, or else try one of the small, artsy bars in the Zone, then go dancing at one of the clubs. There are also more than a half-dozen casinos to choose from, each more attractive than the other.

THE ZONA COLONIAL

Fodor'sChoice ★ Spanish civilization in the New World began in Santo Domingo's 12-block Zona Colonial. As you stroll its narrow streets, it's easy to imagine this old city as it was when the likes of Columbus, Cortés, and Ponce de León walked the cobblestones, pirates sailed in and out, and colonists were settling the New World. Tourist brochures tout that "history comes alive here"—a surprisingly truthful statement. Every Thursday to Sunday night at 8:30, a typical folklorico show is staged at Parque Colón. At Plaza España, on Friday and Saturday nights, at 9 PM, there's typical costumed dancing. These meringue dancers, in turn, give onlookers a couple of lessons. During the Christmas holidays you'll be treated to an artisan's fair and live music concerts.

A fun horse and carriage ride throughout the Zone costs $20 an hour, or you can negotiate a carriage ride in lieu of a taxi. The steeds are no thoroughbreds, but they clip right along, though any commentary will be in Spanish. Drivers usually hang out in front of the Sofitel Nicolas de Ovando.

History buffs may want to spend a day exploring the Zone's many "firsts." You can get a free walking-tour map and brochures in English at the Secretaria de Estado de Turismo office at Parque Colón (Columbus Park), where you may be approached by freelance, English-speaking guides, who will want to make it all come alive for you. They'll work enthusiastically for $20 an hour for four persons. The licensed ones will have their ID tags on and will be wearing blue shirts. Those are the guides you want. Just make certain that you're clear on exactly how much they expect to be paid; if your guide is good (and many are), they will expect a tip at the end as well. Also, wear comfortable shoes; ladies don't even think about high-heels.

Numbers in the margin correspond to points of interest on the Zona Colonial Exploring map. Note: Hours and admission charges to sites are erratic.

4 **Alcazar de Colón.** The castle of Don Diego Colón, built in 1517, has 40-inch-thick coral-limestone walls. The Renaissance-style structure, with its balustrade and double row of arches, has strong Moorish, Gothic, and Isabelline influences. The 22 rooms are furnished in a style the viceroy of the island would have been accustomed to—right down to the dishes and the viceregal shaving mug. ✉ *Plaza de España, off Calle Emiliano Tejera at foot of Calle Las Damas, Zona Colonial* ☎ *809/687–5361* ✉ *RD$50* ☉ *Mon. and Wed.–Fri. 9–5, Sat. 9–4, Sun. 9–1.*

9 **Calle Las Damas.** The Street of the Ladies was named after the elegant
★ ladies of the court who, in the Spanish tradition, promenaded in the evening. Here you can see a sundial dating from 1753 and the Casa de los Jesuitas, which houses a fine research library for colonial history as well as the Institute for Hispanic Culture; admission is free, and it's open weekdays 8–4:30. If you follow the street going toward the Malecón, you will pass a picturesque alley fronted by a wrought-iron gate with perfectly maintained colonial structures that are owned by the Catholic Church. ✉ *Zona Colonial.*

10 **Casa Rodrigo de Bastidas.** There's a lovely inner courtyard here with
ᘓ tropical plants and galleries for temporary exhibitions. Within the Casa Rodrigo de Bastidas, the brilliant **Museo Infantils Trampolin** (☎ *809/685–5551* ⊕ *www.trampolin.org.do*) is a great destination for your kids even if they do not speak Spanish. This is the most kid-friendly venue in the city and the interactive experience (for parents, too) delves into paleontology, geology, ecology, biodiversity, water, and technology. It's a fun place and certainly stimulating, with earthquake and volcano simulations and a jungle gym made with giant, pretend body parts. Call in advance and you may be able to get a bilingual guide. ✉ *Calle Las Damas off Calle El Conde, Zona Colonial* ☎ *No phone* ✉ *Casa free, Museo Infantils Trampolin RD$100* ☉ *Tues.–Sun. 9–5.*

3 **Casa del Cordón.** This structure, built in 1503, is the western hemisphere's oldest surviving stone house. Columbus's son, Diego Colón, viceroy of the colony, and his wife lived here until the Alcazar was finished. It was in this house, too, that Sir Francis Drake was paid a ransom to prevent him from totally destroying the city. ✉ *Calle Emiliano Tejera and Calle Isabel la Católica, within Banco Popular, Zona Colonial* ☎ *No phone* ✉ *Free* ☉ *Weekdays 8:30–4:30.*

12 **Casa de Tostado.** The house was built in the early 16th century and was the residence of writer Don Francisco Tostado. Note its unique twin Gothic windows. It houses the Museo de la Familia Dominicana (Museum of the Dominican Family), which has exhibits on well-heeled 19th-century Dominican society. The house, garden, and antiquities have all been

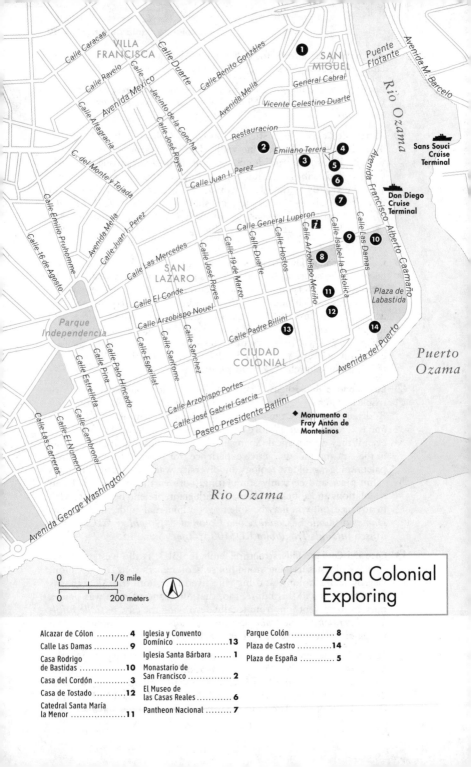

Zona Colonial
Exploring

restored. ✉*22 Calle Padre Bell-
ini, near Calle Arzobispo Meriño,
Zona Colonial* ☎*809/689–5000*
🎫*RD$50* 🕐*Thurs.–Tues. 9–2.*

⓫ Catedral Santa María la Menor. The
coral-limestone facade of the first
cathedral in the New World towers
over the south side of the Parque
Colón. Spanish workmen began
building the cathedral in 1514 but
left to search for gold in Mexico.
The church was finally finished in
1540. Its facade is composed of
architectural elements from the late

> **DID YOU KNOW?**
>
> You will see and hear the word
> *patrimonio* frequently in the Zona
> Colonial. Do you know what that
> is? As explained in the Casa de
> Reales, it's the legacy that we
> have received from the past. Our
> *patrimonio* is our cultural heritage,
> a strong institution of life and
> inspiration, our rock, our point of
> reference, our identity.

Gothic to the lavish Plateresque style. Inside, the high altar is made of
hammered silver. At this writing, a museum was being built for the cathedral's treasures. ✉*Calle Arzobispo Meriño, Zona Colonial* ☎*809/689–
1920* 🎫*Free* 🕐*Mon.–Sat. 9–4, Sun. masses begin at 6* AM.

⓭ Iglesia y Convento Domínico. This graceful building is still a Dominican
Church and Convent, having been founded in 1510. Note the prominent and beautiful rose window. In 1538, Pope Paul III visited here
and was so impressed with the lectures on theology that he granted the
church and convent the title of university, making it the oldest institution of higher learning in the New World. ✉*Calle Padre Bellini and Av.
Duarte, Zona Colonial* ☎*809/682–3780* 🎫*Free* 🕐*Tues.–Sun. 9–6.*

❶ Iglesia Santa Bárbara. This combination church and fortress, the only
one of its kind in Santo Domingo, was completed in 1562. ✉*Av. Mella,
between Calle Isabel la Católica and Calle Arzobispo Meriño, Zona
Colonial* ☎*809/682–3307* 🎫*Free* 🕐*Weekdays 8–noon, Sun. masses
begin at 6* AM.

❷ Monasterio de San Francisco. Constructed between 1512 and 1544, the
San Francisco Monastery contained the church, convent, and hospital
of the Franciscan order. Sir Francis Drake's demolition squad significantly damaged the building in 1586, and in 1673 an earthquake nearly
finished the job, but when it's floodlighted at night, the eerie ruins are
dramatic indeed. The Spanish government has donated money to turn
this into a beautiful cultural center, but we're still waiting. ✉*Calle
Hostos at Calle Emiliano, Zona Colonial* ☎*809/687–4722.*

❻ El Museo de las Casas Reales. This is a remarkable museum, which should
★ be seen. It helps to comprehend the discovery of the New World by
Christopher Columbus and the entire 16th-century epic. Housing
everything from Taíno archaeological finds to colonial artifacts, coins
salvaged from wrecks of Spanish galleons to authentic colonial furnishings, as well as a collection of weapons, the museum also has one of the
most handsome colonial edifices in the Zone. Built in the Renaissance
style, it was the seat of Spanish government housing the Governor's
office and the Royal Court. It has beautiful windows, for example,
done in the Plateresque style. Also, it functions as an art gallery, with

rotating art shows. When candle-lighted by night, it's truly magical and is often used as a wedding venue. ⊠ *Calle Las Damas, end of street, right before Plaza de España, Zona Colonial* ☎ 809/682–4202 ⊠ *RD$30* ☉ *Tues.–Sun. 9–5.*

7 Pantheon Nacional. The National Pantheon (circa 1714) was once a Jesuit monastery and later a theater. The real curiosity here is the military guard who stays as still as the statues, despite the schoolchildren who try to make him flinch. ⊠ *Calle Las Damas, near Calle de Las Mercedes, Zona Colonial* ☎ *No phone* ⊠ *Free* ☉ *Mon.–Sat. 10–5.*

8 Parque Colón. The huge statue of Christopher Columbus in the park named after him dates from 1897 and is the work of French sculptor Gilbert. Like all the parks in the Zona Colonial, this one has been restored. ⊠ *Calle El Conde at Arzobispo Meriño, Zona Colonial.*

14 Plaza de Castro. Calle Las Damas dead-ends as it goes in the direction of the Malecón. Few people ever make it past the junction of Calle Padre Bellini, thinking there's nothing to see. If you keep walking past the convent (you may hear the nuns singing in the chapel), just keep going until the street actually stops; simply make a right turn, and you'll find yourself in this delightful little park. Known almost solely to residents of the Zone, it's commonly called Plaza de Castro, though it was not named after the Cuban dictator but rather a Dominican poet, named Arturo Bautista Pellerano Castro. This is fitting, as it's an enchanting green space, peaceful, and free of litter. The new Coco Boutique Hotel fronts the park, and the co-owner, Eduardo, is probably the best bartender in the Zone. Have one of his fresh strawberry *mojitos* or a perfect martini. Sit at the table on the deck facing the plaza, or have it on the rooftop. Up there you can get comfy in a Balinese sunbed bed and count the ships that go sailing by. ⊠ *At end of Calle Las Damas.*

5 Plaza de España. This wide esplanade, which goes past the Casas de Reales in front of Don Diego Columbus' former palace, El Alcazar de Colón, is the area in the Zona Colonial where national holidays are celebrated. The annual Coca Cola–sponsored Christmas tree is here. It's bordered by what once were the ramparts of the original walled city. People enjoy the views of the Ozama River from here and watch the cruise-ship activity below at the terminal. Lovers stroll here by night, sharing a kiss under the gas lamps. When many people talk about the Plaza España, they are often referring to the half-dozen restaurants in a row, which are on the upper level of these 16th- and 17th-century warehouses. The popular seating for them is on their outdoor decks. ⊠ *Bordered by Calle Las Damas and Calle La Atarazana, Zona Colonial.*

NEED A BREAK?

Your explorations will surely take you to the Plaza España, and you'll want to take a breather in one of its restaurants. Angelo's (⊠ *Plaza de España, Zona Colonial* ☎ *809/686–3586*) has an eponymous, hands-on owner, and consequently service is better than good. From the old school, he is a suave and a gracious host. Although the restaurant is overly elegant and pricey, you can make a nice lunch from a cold beer and an appetizer. The third-floor terrace, with its lion's head fountain, is the where the "in" crowd sits.

ELSEWHERE IN SANTO DOMINGO

As for the other sights, if you only have two or three days, you should probably just take in those in the Colonial Zone. If you're looking to explore some of the city's major museums, most of them can be found in the Gazcue neighborhood, north of the Malecón.

Numbers in the margin correspond to points of interest on the Santo Domingo map. Note: Hours and admission charges to sites are erratic.

③ El Malecón. Avenida George Washington, better known as the Malecón, runs along the Caribbean and has tall palms, cafés, hotels, and sea breezes. ⊠ *Gazcue.*

① Jardin Botanico Nacional Dr. Rafael M. Moscoso. A tranquil, green oasis in a frenetic city, this is also one of the best botanical gardens in the Caribbean. A petite train will take you around for RD$20, or you can just stroll. If you have limited time, then just hit the high points that interest you. There's an arboretum, a small forest reserve, a Japanese garden, an orchid garden, and more. This is also the best place for bird-watchers in Santo Domingo, where you can see the common endemic birds and the special Palm Chat, a member of its unique family and the national bird of the Dominican Republic. The Hispaniolan Ornithological Society offers a free walk the first Sunday of very month at 7 AM. ⊠ *Av. República de Colombia, corner Los Proceres, Jardinas de Norte* ☎ *809/385–2611* ⊠ *RD$20* ☉ *Daily 9–5.*

② Plaza de la Cultura. Landscaped lawns, modern sculptures, and sleek buildings make up the Plaza de la Cultura, which is in the Gazcue, near the center of the city. There are several museums and a theater here. The works of 20th-century Dominican and foreign artists are displayed in the **Museo de Arte Moderno** (⊠ *Av. Maximo Gomez, between Avs. Mexico and Bolivár, Gazcue* ☎ *809/682–2154* ⊠ *RD$20* ☉ *Tues.–Sun. 10–5*). Native sons include Elvis Aviles, an abstract painter whose works have a lot of texture; his art

A BOOK OF BEAUTIFUL INTERIORS

While at the Museo de Arte Moderno look to buy the photographic book *Interiors* by Polibio Díaz, whose photography won him the Fifth Bi-annual Art Competition. The prize money enabled him to create this memorable photo essay that is far more than a coffee table book. He has a series of three photos each of interiors of humble, Dominican *casitas*. It's colorful, revealing, and often ribald, not to mention a real slice of Dominican life.

Cruising Into Santo Domingo

Santo Domingo has two cruise-ship terminals and has become a growing port for cruise passengers, including those of Royal Caribbean's *Vision of the Seas,* which is based in Santo Domingo at this writing. The Port of Don Diego is on the Ozuma River, facing the Avenida del Puerto, and across the street are steps that lead up to the main pedestrian shopping street of the Zona Colonial, Calle El Conde. A lovely yellow and white building, with stained-glass windows, and faux gas lights, it now has a small cafeteria, and potted palms soften the cordoned-off lines where passengers wait to have their tickets checked and to go through immigration. Just down the dock is an ATM machine; in front of that is a counter where you can get cold drinks and snacks. Across from it is a booth offering new self-guided audio tours.

The new Sans Souci Terminal complex is still a work in progress at this writing; it's slated for completion in summer 2008. It's diagonally across the river from Don Diego, on Avenida Francisco Alberto Caaman, and when it's fully operational, the new terminal will have stores and much more.

combines Spanish influences with Taíno and other Dominican symbols. Tony Capellan is one of the best-known artists, representing the D.R. in major international exhibitions. The temporary exhibits are often the most exciting and, well, contemporary. The **Museo del Hombre Dominicano** (✉ *Av. Maximo Gomez, between Avs. Mexico and Bolivár* ☎ *809/687–3623* ⊕ *www.museodelhombredominicano. org.do* ☎ *RD$20* ☉ *Tues.–Sun. 10–5*) traces the migrations of Indians from South America through the Caribbean islands. The **Teatro Nacional** (✉ *Av. Maximo Gomez, between Avs. Mexico and Bolivár* ☎ *809/687–3191*) stages fascinating performances in Spanish only, but don't let that stop you. When in Rome, you would go to an Italian opera, right? If you're in the neighborhood, it's worth stopping by to see if tours are being offered the day of your visit, even if you can't attend a performance; the space itself is beautiful.

WHERE TO EAT

Restaurants tend to be more formal in Santo Domingo than in the rest of the country. For lunch in a casual café in the Zone, for example, shorts (though never short-shorts) are acceptable, but not so at the better, fine-dining establishments, either for lunch or dinner. Similarly, at night in the better establishments, trousers and collared shirts are required for men and skirts, dresses, or resort-casual slacks appropriate for women. Ties aren't required anywhere, and few places still require jackets, even the finer establishments. Keep in mind that women tend to dress up here. If you're seated next to them in worn-out khakis and flip-flops, you will feel out of place.

ZONA COLONIAL

$$-$$$ ✕ **La Briciola.** This high-profile restaurant has attracted a clientele of well-heeled residents and international visitors, including politicos, Hollywood stars, and sports legends, including President Leonel, Andy Garcia, and Sammy Sosa since its opening in 1993. In the early 1990s, a group of friends from Milan made the momentous decision to restore a trio of 16th-century buildings in the Zone. This historical ambience, with seating in the brick-arched, Spanish courtyard, continues to be the magnet—much more than the food. Alas, the menu has not kept up with contemporary trends, nor are the plates garnished artistically. Yet, if you go with the house-made pastas and gnocchi; the oversize Briciola salad of arugula, shrimp, and shaved Parmesan cheese; and a grappa to cap your meal, you can have a lovely and romantic night out. The man playing the baby grand and the white twinkle lights add to all this. ⊠ *Arzobispo Meriño, corner Padre Bellini, Zona Colonial* ☎ *809/688–5055* ⌂ *Reservations essential* ☐ *AE, MC, V* ⊗ *No lunch Sun.*

$-$$$ ✕ **Café Bellini.** This café has always had a panache far and above its
★   counterparts, for the Italian owners also have the adjacent furniture design center. The moderne, wicker-weave barrel chairs, and the contemporary art and light fixtures, are all hip. The menu is the same at lunch and dinner. The democratic pricing usually offers a main course, such as the trio of raviolis (spinach, beet, and pumpkin), for about $10, which works for those on a slim budget. Also, know that an amuse bouche, perhaps a tomato brushetta, is usually satisfying. The addition of grilled portobellos to a classic arugula and shaved Parmesan salad is brilliant. Main courses are accompanied by pasta or grilled vegetables and potato. You can enjoy French and Italian liquors here (like pastis and grappa); dessert might be dark-chocolate mousse and fresh mango sorbet. Service is laudable, as is the music. ⊠ *Arzobispo Merino, corner of Padre Billini, Zona Colonial* ☎ *809/686–3387* ⌂ *Reservations essential* ☐ *AE, MC, V* ⊗ *Closed Sun. No lunch Mon.*

$-$$$ ✕ **El Grand Charolais.** This small, French-owned restaurant has, along with the crazy bovine motif, probably the best beef in the Zone. Calves' hides and steers' skulls are a wild contrast with the traditional, old-world tiles. In the back room art is on exhibit. As you listen to the subtle, international sounds, sup on French classics, including French chevre with mixed greens and a warm, *lardons* vinaigrette, not to mention an authentic Chateaubriand for two, with all of the accompanying vegetables. Top-shelf liquors and wines are a welcome sight, and—dazzle—there are big Bordeaux glasses! Try to reserve a front-room table, which is more atmospheric. Voila! ⊠ *Calle Hostos 151, Zona Colonial* ☎ *809/221–2052* ☐ *AE, MC, V* ⊗ *Closed Sun.*

$-$$ ✕ **Hard Rock Café Santo Domingo.** There are times that you may just want a perfect cheeseburger (here served with BBQ sauce on the bun) with onion rings, leaf lettuce, and a really strong American napkin. You can take that up a notch with a perfect Rockarita in a big goblet with a salted rim. Now that may cost a pretty peso once you add in tax, service, and a gratuity, which you will want to give since the service is efficient and in English. And, yes, the music videos are loud, but you can understand the words and sing right along. On the front terrace, which faces Parque de

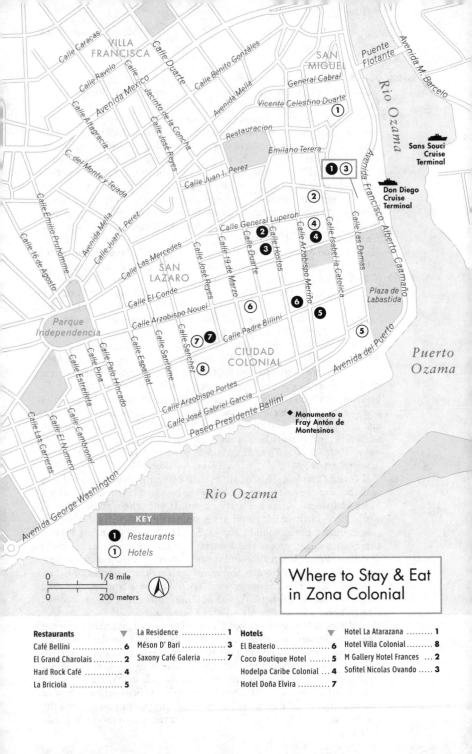

Where to Stay & Eat in Zona Colonial

KEY

● *Restaurants*

① *Hotels*

0	1/8 mile
0	200 meters

Restaurants ▼

Café Bellini	6
El Grand Charolais	2
Hard Rock Café	4
La Briciola	5
La Residence	1
Méson D' Bari	3
Saxony Café Galeria	7

Hotels ▼

El Beaterio	6
Coco Boutique Hotel	5
Hodelpa Caribe Colonial	4
Hotel Doña Elvira	7
Hotel La Atarazana	1
Hotel Villa Colonial	8
M Gallery Hotel Frances	2
Sofitel Nicolas Ovando	3

Colón and the cathedral, the music drops a decibel and you can people-watch. Servers even sweep up the litter. ⊠ *Calle El Conde 103, Zona Colonial* ☎809/686–7771 ⊟*AE, MC, V.*

$–$$ ✕**Mesón D' Bari.** Dominicans call this one a "long hitter"—as in base-ball, which will inevitably be on the TV at the bar. For more than 25 years, owner Sr. Marisol has been feeding the local Zoners the recipes of his grandmother. This simple, two-story Dominican restaurant has become a number-one hang-out for artists, baseball players, politicians, well-heeled capitale-ños, tourists, and even unaccompa-nied *gringas*, who feel comfortable here. The menu has really flavor-ful dishes, including creole-style eggplant, empanadas of crab and conch, grilled crabs, and stewed,

sweet orange peels. Sadly, the presentations are dated, so expect gar-nishes of shredded carrots and iceberg lettuce; a breakthrough is that there are now white geometric plates. Prices are up even though the culinary ambition is not. Live music usually happens on the weekends; otherwise, you'll hear some soothing music from decades past (think "Moon Glow"). Some of the owner's artworks are among the wall-to-wall local paintings. ⊠ *Calle Hostos 302, corner of Salomé Ureña, Zona Colonial* ☎809/687–4091 ⊟*AE, MC, V.*

$–$$$ ✕**La Residence.** This fine-dining enclave has always had the setting—
★   Spanish colonial architecture, with pillars and archways overlooking a courtyard—and an esoteric lunch-dinner menu with high prices that did not always deliver. Now it has a seasoned French chef serving clas-sic yet innovative cuisine with many moderately priced choices. The daily Menu del Chef has a main course for less than $10. It could be brochettes of spit-roasted duck, chicken *au poivre* , or vegetable risotto. You could start with a salad of panfried young squid for about $5 and go bonkers over the $3 dark- and white-chocolate terrine. Veer from the daily specials menu, and prices certainly higher but still fair; even the grilled fillet and braised oxtail with foie gras sauce and wild mush-rooms is reasonable. ⊠ *Sofitel Nicolas de Ovando, Calle Las Damas, Zona Colonial* ☎809/685–9955 ⊟*AE, MC, V.*

¢   ✕**Saxony Café Galeria.** This mom-and-pop operation serves only lunch, and offers a daily prix-fixe with several options—all vegetarian—for less than $4. Choices may include grilled eggplant Parmesan, empana-das, vegetarian meatballs, and tomato and avocado salad. Everything is freshly prepared and served with a familial smile; mom speaks English. The beverages of choice are fresh-squeezed juices, including *chinola* (passion fruit) and yogurt shakes. In time there may be a lunch buffet or even dinner service (don't be surprised if this little spot has grown up a bit by the time you arrive). Meanwhile, the restaurant also functions as a gallery of local art, much of which has been painted by the *dueno* (owner). ⊠ *Calle Padre Billini 205, next door to Hotel Doña Elvira- Zona Colonial* ☎ *809/221–6313* ⊟ *AE, MC, V* ⊘ *No dinner.*

BELLA VISTA

$$–$$$$ ✕ **Casa Portuguesa.** A newcomer near the Hotel Embajador, this is a darling of the privileged set. The decor is cutsey, with typical Portugal shawls, white lace, and shutters that give it a novel appeal. Portuguese tiles are even found in the restrooms. Authentic dishes include *bacalhua* (salt cod), *feijoada* (a hearty bean and pork stew from Brazil), and shellfish, notably clams and shrimp. All flavorful, the portions are usually large enough to share, which is good since this is not an inexpensive place. Service can be mediocre, and much of the wine list may have already said adios (the list is not kept up-to-date). Ask in advance to ensure that your favorite bottle or dish is available that evening to avoid disappointment. But if you sit back and enjoy the Portuguese ballads you can have a good time anyway. ⊠ *Av. Jardins del Embajador 10B, Bella Vista* ☎ *809/508–2063* ⌕ *Reservations essential* ⊟ *AE, MC, V* ⊘ *No lunch.*

PIANTINI

$–$$$$ ✕ **Peperoni.** One of Santo Domingo's long-standing, destination restaurants, Peperoni continues to evolve, which keeps it on the list of "in" places for well-heeled capitaleños of all ages. The menu is contemporary and multinational, and only the highest-quality ingredients are used. You many not make it past the appetizers, which include octopus with fava beans stewed in lemoncello vinaigrette, a warm goat cheese salad, and a sushi roll of sweet plantain, king crab, and avocado. But try to get to the main courses, giving the gnocchi, pastas, and risottos your first consideration. Service is laudable. Take the savvy wine steward's recommendations; an Italian or Chilean reserva works well with much of the menu. Sit out on the new deck under a market umbrella (though air-conditioned, the indoor dining room is smoky and too cold). ⊠ *Sarasota 23, at Plaza Universitaria, Piantini* ☎ *809/508–1330* ⊟ *AE, MC, V.*

$$–$$$$ ✕ **Sophia's.** Don't ask for Sophia; she doesn't exist. This high-profile, in-spot is owned by a prime Dominican family who appreciate fine food and wine, both of which are on exhibit there. With the outward formality of the old-guard institutions, including suited doormen and professional waiters, the setting is chi-chi, contemporary, with orchids galore and crisp white linens. When you see the first page of the menu you may be amazed that prices are so reasonable, including gourmet burgers, *nueva ensaladas,* and creative sandwiches for around $10. That is because both lunch and dinner share the same menu. Keep reading beyond the lunchier offerings, and the prices become more expensive. Starters begin at $10 and the mains range $10 to $34, the top spot being

held by a rack of lamb; sides are additional. To keep expenses down, order an innovative appetizer such as Japanese-style miso eggplant or a ceviche tasting, accompanied by a memorable bottle from the extensive wine list. Wrap it up with a warm guava cheesecake and an aged port. ⊠*Paseo de los Locutores 9, Piantini* ☎*809/620–1001* ⊟*AE, MC, V.*

GAZCUE

¢–$$ ✕**Adrian Tropical.** Hotel concierges still recommend this Malecón institution as having the best Dominican food (it's now a local chain of four). It's touristy, yes, but Dominicans still make up the majority of customers. You may want to try it for the three-tiered setting overlooking the ocean as well as the opportunity to see if the excellent sancocho (a rich, meaty stew), mofongo (stuffed mashed plantains), and other local favorites are as good as you hear. The *sopa de pescado* (fish soup) is the best this side of Mexico. You can also get wild and try the goat or pig's feet, or play it safe with grilled items and tropical sides like yucca. The restaurant serves both breakfast (from 7:30) and lunch (a buffet), but it's open 24 hours, and the clubbers come in for their late-night sancocho. ⊠*Av. George Washington 2, Gazcue* ☎*809/221–1764* ⊟*AE, MC, V.*

WHERE TO STAY

Santo Domingo's large, high-rise hotels are mostly along the Malecón, a short taxi ride from the Zona Colonial. But increasingly visitors want to stay in the Zone itself. The petite boutique hotels in the Zona Colonial are all reconstructions, some of architecturally significant colonial-era buildings. The French call these *hôtels de charme*. This atmospheric neighborhood has a large French contingent, perhaps fostered by the French Embassy, which is across the street from the Sofitel Nicolas Ovando, one of only two full-service hotels in the neighborhood. A member of the upscale French hotel group, this five-star property was a reconstruction of the residence of the city's first governor, Nicolas Ovando. So many visitors want to be based in the Zone that you'll now find several good B&Bs, the best of which are managed by their caring and sometimes resident owners.

ZONA COLONIAL

¢   🏨**El Beaterio.** As you sit in the coral stone lobby of coral stone with high ceilings, brick archways, and Spanish wrought-iron chandeliers, you're enmeshed in 500 years of history. The heavy Havanaesque lobby furniture and the orange, slippery bedspreads and curtains detract from the beauty. Still, this good small hotel has beautifully quiet (and dark) second-floor rooms with stone floors and small windows. Contemporary iron beds are attractive (room No. 7 is the best), although the bedframes can block your view of the wall-mounted TV. A French owner (absent) and French and Haitian staff make El Beaterio attractive to Francophiles. You'll pay an extra $10 per night for a/c, but prices

CLOSE UP

Sancocho Dominicano

The Dominican national dish is ideal for chilly nights. This recipe is courtesy of Villa Pajon, a rustic lodge nestled in the mountains of the Valle Nuevo. Ingredients (serves 8 people):

- 1 chicken (with bones), cut into pieces
- 8 pork chops
- 2 limes, juiced
- 4 cloves of garlic, mashed
- 1 large onion, chopped
- 1 Habañero pepper, chopped
- 1 bunch of cilantro, chopped
- 1 tablespoon salt
- 1 tablespoon bitter orange juice (fresh or Goya)
- 1 tablespoon apple cider vinegar
- 1 teaspoon oregano
- 2 tablespoons cooking oil
- 1 green plantain, peeled and cut into 1" pieces
- 1 lb. yucca, peeled and cut into 2" pieces
- 1 lb. pumpkin (auyama), peeled and cut into 2" pieces (butternut squash works, too)
- 1 corn on the cob, cut in half
- 8 to 12 cups water

Season the chicken pieces and pork chops with lime juice, garlic, onion, salt, cilantro, pepper, and oregano. Then sauté the meat and chicken in a large pot with the cooking oil for approximately 20 minutes. Add the water and cook until meat is almost done. Adjust the cooking time if necessary so you do not overcook the meat. Remove the meat from the cooking liquid, and strain the liquid, returning it to the pot. On high heat, bring the liquid to a boil, and add the plantain pieces, immediately reducing the heat to medium-high. Cook for five minutes, then add the yucca and pumpkin and cook for 10 minutes more. Finally, add the corn. When the vegetables are almost done, add the chicken and pork chops, vinegar, and bitter orange juice. Adjust the seasoning, if necessary, and cook for 20 more minutes on high.

Serve with white rice, concon*, avocado slices, and hot pepper sauce** if you like. *Concon: After the rice is done, remove most of it, leaving a little at the bottom of the pot. Turn the stove on medium-high and let the bottom of the rice turn golden and crispy, but be sure it does not burn. **Hot pepper sauce: Fill a small jar with one or more kinds of hot peppers. Add enough apple cider vinegar to cover all the peppers. Screw on the top and let it stand for a couple of days. The resulting vinegar will be hot, and you can use this to spice up the sancocho. The longer it stands, the hotter it gets! The jar can be refilled.

include tax. **Pros:** The included breakfast is quite good, convenient location with Duarte Park across the street, free Wi-Fi. **Cons:** Receptionists are too easily overwhelmed, the lobby and breakfast room are too dark, hotel accepts no credit cards or even travelers checks. ✉ *Calle Duarte 8, Zona Colonial* ☎ *809/687–8657* ⊕ *www.elbeaterio. com* 🛏 *11 rooms* ⚓ *In-room: no phone. In-hotel: no elevator, public Wi-Fi, no-smoking rooms* 🚫 *No credit cards* ⏹ *BP.*

2

¢–$ Coco Boutique Hotel. Behind the soft, Caribbean turquoise facade
★   you'll find a very un-typical B&B, not to mention white—almost everywhere: the reception and lounge, the stark wooden staircase, the grill-
work on the French doors; it's breathtaking, actually, with the dark
green plants offering the only contrast. New on the scene, Coco's,
which is a handsome renovation of a circa-1920s private home, has
developed a soul, and the silver-and-gold furnishings give it a hint
of Miami glitz as well. It's given personality by the young, charismatic owners, Elizabeth and her husband Eduardo, who is also the
Zone's most capable bartender. **Pros:** Amazingly quiet for the Zona
Colonial, opposite the picturesque Plaza Pellerano Castro, rooftop terrace with Balinese sunbeds where you can wave to the cruise ships.
Cons: Not steeped in creature comforts, bathrooms are small, as are
two front rooms. ⊠ *Arzobispo Porte 7, corner of Las Damas, Zona
Colonial, Santo Domingo* ☎ *809/685–8467* ⊕ *www.cocoboutique-
hotel.com* ➳ *5 rooms* ♿ *In-room: no phone, no TV. In-hotel: bar,
no elevator, laundry services, public Wi-Fi, parking (fee), no-smoking
rooms* ▤ *AE, MC, V* ⦾ *BP.*

$ Hodelpa Caribe Colonial. When you leave this little Hernando's Hide-
away, the caring staff will say, "Why so soon?" The art deco–style
lobby makes clever use of blue objets d'art, as does the high-tech Internet center. Rooms have white-gauze canopies on king-size beds; an all-
white honeymoon suite has a Jacuzzi. Splurge for a suite or a superior
room (though even those have tight bathrooms), rather than a subter-
ranean standard. Sit out on your balcony and wave to the neighbors.
On Friday nights a Mexican fiesta takes place on the side terrace, with
dancers, tequila action, and karaoke. **Pros:** Friendly staff, well-managed and efficient. **Cons:** Small bathrooms, standard rooms not on par
with others, subsequent renovated buildings have been done better.
⊠ *Isabel La Católica 59, Zona Colonial* ☎ *809/688–7799 or 888/403–
2603* ⊕ *www.hodelpa.com* ➳ *52 rooms, 2 suites* ♿ *In-room: safe. In-
hotel: restaurant, room service, bar, concierge, laundry service, public
Internet, parking (no fee)* ▤ *AE, MC, V* ⦾ *BP.*

¢–$ Hotel Doña Elvira. Housed in a colonial beauty some 500 years young,
this family-owned hotel is noteworthy for its exposed stone and brick
walls with high, mahogany-beamed ceilings. That look carries through
to the best room in the house, No. 11, with its open-air Moroccan tiled
bath and shower, which leads to a normal bathroom. A swimming pool
shaded by a mammoth mango tree is flanked by two stories of guest
rooms, the better ones being Nos. 2, 3, 6, and 7; the loft rooms you
don't want. The rooftop solarium and Jacuzzi can be a respite when
the orchids are in bloom and everything is in repair. In 2004, this was
the dream project of the owners Marc Bautil, of the Belgian consulate, and his wife, a Philippine-American business woman. Ask about
their two-bedroom apartment nearby, available for short-term rental.
Pros: As atmospheric as a Mexican hacienda, excellent location in the
Zone, cable TV. **Cons:** Employees are not properly in tune with good
service standards when the owners are away and working on other
projects, bedding, towels, and in-room artwork need to be upgraded,
open closets. ⊠ *Padre Bellini 209, Zona Colonial* ☎ *809/221–7415*

⊕*www.dona-elvira.com* ⇒*13 rooms* ⚷*In-room: safe, no phone. In-hotel: restaurant, bar, pool, no elevator, laundry facilities, public Wi-Fi, no-smoking rooms* ▤*MC, V* ▯◎▯*BP.*

¢–$ ▥**Hotel La Atarazana.** Ring the bell at this artistically renovated town house, and the white wrought-iron gate opens to a small foyer with a large mirror and long stems of tropical flowers. To the left is the kitchen and bar, to the rear a courtyard furnished with outdoor tables and market umbrellas. A waterfall flows down the coral stone wall; with bamboo and exotic greenery, it's an urban oasis. You may feel as if you're staying with friends—in this case Suzanne and Bernie. She's a Swiss-German economist, he's an architect who designed both the hotel and the contemporary lighting fixtures. Rooms, all upstairs, are minimalist and squeaky clean. The courtyard is the setting for the healthy, European-style breakfast and the rum-soaked cocktail hour. A small café offering meals is set to open at this writing. **Pros:** Superior service, excellent location near Plaza España but not on a touristy block, rooftop terrace offers views and shaded sitting areas. **Cons:** Front rooms (particularly the one closest to the police station) are noisy in the early morning, no luxurious creature comforts. ⊠*La Atarazana 19, next door to police station, Zona Colonial* ☎*809/706–5315* ⊕*www.hotel-atarazana.com* ⇒*7 rooms* ⚷*In-room: no a/c (some), no phone, Wi-Fi. In-hotel: bar, no elevator, laundry service, public Internet, public Wi-Fi, no-smoking rooms* ▤*AE, MC, V* ▯◎▯*BP.*

$ ▥**Hotel Villa Colonial.** A former home of the Leon banking family (circa 1920s), the French owner Lionel Bisteau has kept as much of the original as feasible, including the second-floor verandah, the columns and patterned tile floors so distinctive of the Zone. Room 8 has the most beautiful mustard-color replica tiles based on the damaged originals, which were fabricated by Dominican artist Candido Bido. In the reception area, contemporary art hangs and a Balinese sunbed provides a comfort zone. All of the furnishings in this three-year-old restoration are Indonesian, including beds' nouveau wooden canopies. Each room is unique, with colorful bedspreads matching the tile floors. Room rates include both breakfast and tax. **Pros:** Beautiful breakfast room and bar overlooking the petite pool, all rooms have Wi-Fi, low rates make this an exceptional value. **Cons:** Owner and staff have limited English, decor is somewhat spartan, hotel takes no credit cards. ⊠*Calle Sanchez 157, near Padre Bellini, Zona Colonial* ☎*809/221–1049* ⊕*www.villacolonial.net* ⇒*13 rooms* ⚷*In-room: no phone, Wi-Fi. In-hotel: no elevator, public Wi-Fi, no-smoking rooms* ▤*No credit cards* ▯◎▯*BP.*

$$ ▥**M Gallery Hotel Frances.** Discerning business travelers, American vacationers, celebs, and other luminaries (including Oscar de la Renta) opt for the intimate, refined luxury of this small, well-run hotel. A former Sofitel, it's still part of the Accor Group. French and Dominican flags fly over the arched, coral-stone entrance of the local landmark, a former French residence. Dark, hacienda-like rooms with tall, beamed ceilings (ask for second-floor corner room No. 205—it's soundproof) overlook the courtyard, an urban refuge with cast-iron balustrades and hanging ferns. Service throughout is exceptional, with English spoken. A romantic hideaway, it's probably not the best place for chil-

dren. **Pros:** Many fun, celebratory events, caring manager runs a tight ship. **Cons:** Rooms and furnishings are somewhat dated, evidence of neglect by Accor (promised renovations not done) since it's no longer a Sofitel. ⊠*Calles Las Mercedes and Arzobispo Meriño, Zona Colonial* ☎*809/685–9331 or 800/763–4835* ⊕*www.sofitel. com* ⏃*19 rooms* ⌂*In-room: safe, refrigerator. In-hotel: restaurant, room service, bar, no elevator, public Wi-Fi, parking (no fee)* ⊟*AE, MC, V* ⅠΟⅠ*BP.*

> **DID YOU KNOW?**
>
> An amazing litany of Hollywood stars have filmed on location in the D.R., primarily in the Zona Colonial, including Robert Redford, Andy Garcia, Matt Damon and Angelina Jolie, Vin Diesel, Dustin Hoffman, Bill Murray, Robert Duvall, Jaime Foxx, Colin Farrell, Amanda Bynes, and Chris Carmack. High-profile directors who have shot in the Zone include Robert De Niro and Andy Garcia.

$$$–$$$$ **Sofitel Nicolas Ovando.** This luxury
FodorśChoice hotel, sculpted from the residence of the first Governor of the Americas,
★ is the best thing to happen in the Zone since Diego Columbus's palace was finished in 1517. Colonial rooms have canopied king-size beds, tall ceilings, original stone window benches, and shutters. Some prefer the sunny (smaller) rooms in the contemporary annex; with the river views, these are smart examples of French minimalist style. The pool is shaded by trees and tropical plantings, and swimmers leave the sun for a fitness break in the gym. The bar is a social scene, particularly when the music man plays at cocktail hour, which includes complimentary hors d'oeuvres. **Pros:** Lavish breakfast buffet, beautifully restored historic section. **Cons:** Inconsistent service in the lovely restaurant, sometimes a bit too quiet. ⊠*Calle Las Damas, Zona Colonial* ☎*809/685–9955 or 800/763–4835* ⊕*www.sofitel.com* ⏃*100 rooms, 4 suites* ⌂*In-room: safe, refrigerator. In-hotel: restaurant, room service, bars, pool, gym, concierge, laundry service, public Internet, public Wi-Fi, parking (no fee), some pets allowed* ⊟*AE, MC, V* ⅠΟⅠ*BP.*

GAZCUE

$–$$ **Hilton Santo Domingo.** This has become *the* address on the Malecón
★ for businesspeople, convention attendees, and leisure travelers. The six luxurious executive floors are wired for business, each with three phones, Internet ports, actual corner offices with imposing desks and ergonomic leather chairs, and DSL lines. Suites are geared for longer stays and have kitchenettes. Creature comforts are satisfied with the plush duvets, rain showers, and surround sound in the bathrooms, oversize flat-screen TVs, and gorgeous sea views. Service might just be the best in the country, and rates are surprisingly moderate, particularly with online packages that include a lavish and healthy buffet breakfast. **Pros:** Sunday Brunch is one of the city's top tickets, great music in the lobby lounge, best service in Santo Domingo. **Cons:** Little about the hotel is authentically Dominican, hotel can be large and impersonal. ⊠*Av. George Washington 500, Gazcue* ☎*809/685–0000* ⊕*hilton-caribbean.com* ⏃*228 rooms, 32 suites* ⌂*In-room: safe, refrigerator,*

Ethernet. In-hotel: 2 restaurants, bars, pool, gym, spa, concierge, executive floor, public Internet, public Wi-Fi ⊟*AE, D, MC, V* |◎|*EP.*

$ 🖳 **InterContinental V Centenario.** This major Malecón property is still not one of InterContinental's glamour properties, but it does a lot right. All rooms—not just the luxe ones on the Club Level with sea-view balconies—have been redone in subtle earth tones, more masculine than tropical cheery. They don't have much local feel, but they are fine. The international cuisine at hotel restaurants is memorable, from the ample breakfast buffet to gastronomic dinners. Service is professional, and conferences run smoothly. Leisure time can be spent on the swanky pool deck, where discerning attendants dispense frosty drinks and plush, pastel towels, or at the classy casino. **Pros:** Good security, beautiful pool area, professional English-speaking staff. **Cons:** Rooms could be in a large chain hotel anywhere, service can be impersonal. ⊠*Av. George Washington 218, Gazcue* ☎*809/221–0000* ⊕*www. ichotelsgroup.com* ⇥*165 rooms, 31 suites* ᗜ*In-room: safe, refrigerator, dial-up (some). In-hotel: 2 restaurants, bars, tennis court, pool, gym, spa, concierge, executive floor, public Internet, parking (no fee), no-smoking rooms* ⊟*AE, MC, V* |◎|*EP.*

$ 🖳 **Marriott Courtyard Santo Domingo.** This American outpost near the U.S. Consulate is warm, friendly, and welcoming, suitable for a short layover. The architecture and its hot coral facade, which includes details such as wrought-iron lighting, are characteristic of a Mexican hacienda style, especially in the courtyard, where a fountain continually ejects water into the swimming pool. Dominicans take advantage of the special weekend and holiday packages, and if you do, opt for one that includes the *delicioso* breakfast buffet. Rooms are cookie-cutter but have laptop-size safes and coffeemakers; bedding is high-end, and you'll enjoy the fluffy pillows. The staff is warm, caring, and efficient—and most are bilingual. Many cruise passengers overnight here or add a weekend stay after their cruise because of the reasonable prices; however, you're still 3 mi from the Zona Colonial and the cruise-ship terminals. **Pros:** ATM machine in the lobby, near to Quisqueya Stadium for baseball games. **Cons:** Neighborhood is not exciting for tourists, not a luxury property. ⊠*Maximo Gomez Av. 50-A, La Esberilla* ☎*809/685–1010* 🖷*809/685–2003* ⊕*www.marriott. com* ⇥*243 rooms, 159 suites* ᗜ*In-room: safe, refrigerator, Ethernet. In-hotel: restaurant, bar, room service, pool, laundry facilities, laundry service, public Internet, public Wi-Fi, parking (no fee), no-smoking rooms* ⊟*AE, MC, V* |◎|*EP.*

$-$$ 🖳 **Meliá Santo Domingo Hotel & Casino.** Well-located on the Malecón, this deluxe high-rise is one of the closest to the Zona Colonial. The concierge-level rooms have always offered a pleasurable way to do business or have a pampered urban vacation. For about 15% more per person (above the cost of a regular room), you can get your clothes ironed, shoes shined, hook-up to a DSL line, have a free breakfast in the ocean-view lounge, and enjoy premium cocktails and hors d'ouvres during happy hour. Over the years, decor had become worn and, well, dated. But a major renovation, starting with the lobby and its domes, on to the meeting rooms, club level, then the remainder of the guest rooms, began in early 2008. **Pros:** Nightly lobby cocktail hour, free Wi-Fi in the lobby and concierge lounge, professional service staff and management. **Cons:** Unrenovated rooms are tired, the size of the hotel means less personal service, could use another restaurant. ⊠ *Av. George Washington 365, Gazcue* ☎ *809/221–6666* ⊕ *www. solmelia.com* ⇨ *241 rooms, 14 suites* ⭢ *In-room: safe, refrigerator, Ethernet (some). In-hotel: restaurant, room service, bars, pool, gym, laundry service, concierge, executive floors, public Internet, public Wi-Fi, parking (no fee), no-smoking rooms* ⊟ *AE, MC, V* ⧮ *EP.*

> ### COMPUTER HELP
>
> If you have a laptop problem or need parts or repair, go see Carlos Florian at **Host Computers** (⊠ *Calle El Conde, at Plaza Conde, basement level, across from Mercure Hotel, Zona Colonial* ☎ *809/685–2132, 809/867–8202 mobile*), who is the top hombre in Santo Domingo when it comes to computers. It's a Hewlett-Packard repair center, too. Carlos doesn't speak English (an assistant does), but he certainly knows computers.

$–$$ 🏨 **Renaissance Jaragua Hotel & Casino.** The sprawling, pink oasis is perennially popular, particularly with Americans, for its beautiful grounds and huge, free-form pool. Fountains splash and hot tubs gurgle. Saunas bake in what is the capital's largest fitness club—which was undergoing a needed renovation at this writing. Everything is bigger than life, from the rooms, where executive-size desks face the satellite TV, to the gigantic suites in the renovated main building to the generous lobby and huge, lively casino where bands heat up the action. It has the town's only cabaret theater. Comfy European linens and duvets make sleeping a dream vision. Management and staff are professional and caring. Check the Web for weekend packages, including even golf, and more. **Pros:** Hotel is busy and lively and will match any discount Internet rate, offers an optional all-inclusive plan (rare in Santo Domingo). **Cons:** Can be a bit too busy at times, nothing understated about the decor, some rooms outdated. ⊠ *Av. George Washington 367, Gazcue* ☎ *809/221–2222* ⊕ *www.marriott.com* ⇨ *292 rooms, 8 suites* ⭢ *In-room: safe, kitchen, refrigerator (some), dial-up (some). In-hotel: 3 restaurants, bars, tennis courts, pool, gym, spa, concierge, executive floor, public Internet* ⊟ *AE, D, MC, V* ⧮ *EP.*

APARTMENTS

It's difficult to find a short-term apartment rental in Santo Domingo, and the available apartments are not generally bargains. At this writing, there are no agencies who handle this type of rental in the capital, but you can find independently owned and rented apartments if you search sites like VRBO.com.

¢ 🏨 **Seaview Apartment Santo Domingo.** This spacious bi-level penthouse catches the Caribbean breezes and also offers views of the sea and passing ships, especially from the terrace, which has an outdoor Jacuzzi. Details, including the Italian marble floors, imported wood cabinetry, and a half-moon balcony, make this furnished apartment exceptional.

Its best feature is the oversize master bedroom with a decorator ceiling fan and marble bath. Fully equipped, the kitchen even has a microwave and battery-operated electricity inverter for back-up power. Two blocks from the seafront and some luxurious gated homes, it's on the third floor of a handsome apartment complex about 10 minutes from the central city and Zona Colonial ($4 in a cab). Maid service is three times per week for an additional fee; weekly rates are available. **Pros:** Safety features are good, bilingual owner/manager is hospitable and accommodating to guests, short-term or long-term, price includes electricity (a major plus here). **Cons:** Could use better bedding and pillows, decor not as upscale as the apartment itself, no Internet service at this writing. ⊠ *Residencia Patricia Calle 9 #19, at 9th St., Isabelita* ☎ *809/982–8300* ⊕ *www.kisskehyavacationrentals.com* ⌕ *3 bedrooms, 2 bathrooms* ᗢ *No phone, daily maid service, on-site security, hot tub, laundry facilities, no smoking* ⊟ *No credit cards.*

SPORTS & THE OUTDOORS

Don't come to Santo Domingo for an active vacation; you simply won't find the wide range of outdoor activities that are everywhere in the resort areas. All the large, modern hotels have fitness centers and swimming pools. It's not safe to swim off the Malecón. For tourists, the closest beaches to Santo Domingo are in Juan Dolio or, in a more limited way, Boca Chica. *For information on Boca Chica and Juan Dolio, see* ⇨ *Chapter 3, "The Southeast Coast."*

BASEBALL

Baseball is a national passion, and Sammy Sosa is still a legend in his own time. But he is just one of many celebrated Dominican baseball heroes, including pitcher Odalis Revela. Triple-A Dominican and Puerto Rican players and some American major leaguers hone their skills in the D.R.'s professional Winter League, which plays from October through January. Some games are held in the Tetelo Vargas Stadium in the town of San Pedro de Macorís, east of Boca Chica; others are held in Estadio Francisco A. Michelli in La Romana (about two hours east of Santo Domingo).

Ticket prices fluctuate and often change with the advent of the new season. If you go to the stadium, tickets range US$1–US$20. Always buy the most expensive seats, and try to go with a group, preferably with some new Dominican friends. When the Santo Domingo Liceys and Santiago Aquilas play, scalpers are in full force; it's akin to the Yankees playing the Mets in New York City.

Estadio Francisco A. Michelli (⊠ *Av. Padre Abreu, near monument, La Romana* ☎ *809/556–6188, 809/556–6188 to buy tickets by credit card*) is two hours east of Santo Domingo and not really suitable for a day trip, but if you decide to spend some time in Boca Chica or Juan Dolio it might be a possibility; and it's certainly doable if you're staying in one of the resorts in La Romana/Bayahibe area.

Estadio Quisqueya (⊠ *Av. Tieradentes at San Cristóbal, Naco, Santo Domingo* ☎ *809/540–5772, 809/616–1224 to purchase tickets by credit card*) is Santo Domingo's main baseball stadium. Because of the traffic and general chaos, it's usually easier if you hire a driver for the night if you're planning to attend a game independently since taxis can be difficult to hail after games when the demand is very high. The lines at the box office and time to get into the stadium vary depending on who is playing. You'll find few good dining options near the stadium.

Estadio Tetelo Vargas (⊠ *Av. Francisco Caamano Denó, San Pedro de Macoris* ☎ *809/529–3618, 829/529–3618 to purchase tickets by credit card*) is the main stadium in San Pedro de Macrois. From Santo Domingo, you might pay as much as $80 each way for the 90-minute trip, but the fares are more reasonable if you're staying 20 minutes away in Juan Dolio, from which the round-trip fare is about $30. From San Pedro de Macoris, it's $8 to the stadium by taxi.

Liga de Béisbol Stadiums (⊠ *San Domingo* ☎ *809/567–6371*) can be helpful with information if you're planning an independent trip to a baseball game.

GOLF

The D.R. has some of the best courses in the Caribbean, designed by some of the world's top course designers. Courses in Juan Dolio are the most easily accessible to clients of Santo Domingo hotels, which can arrange a golf outing for you. If you don't mind the distance (1½ hours one-way), the courses at Casa de Campo are stellar, but you must make advance reservations.

SHOPPING

Shopping in the capital is perhaps the best in the country. You can buy everything from inexpensive souvenirs to Italian designer shoes. *Mamajuana*—an herbal extract that is usually mixed with rum—is said to be the Dominican answer to Viagra. Brugal and Barcelo rums make good gifts or reminders of your island experience. Cigars, of course, are great guy gifts. Amber and larimar jewelry are lady pleasers and make reasonably priced jewelry gifts for young girls. Wood carvings of mahogany (although most are Haitian), as well as local and Haitian artwork and ceramics—notably the faceless dolls—are popular. High-end boutiques have fashions from Spain, France, Italy, and the United States, as well as from such noted Dominican designers as Oscar de la Renta and Jenny Polanco. If you go to a flea market or public market, yes, you can haggle, saying: *"Gracias no, es demasiado caro para mi!"* (No thanks, it's too expensive for me). But most prices in shops are set, except perhaps in some of the gift shops on Calle El Conde; if you must haggle, do it graciously.

CLOSE UP

Take Me Down to the Ballgame

Béisbol is the Domincans' passion and their pride for it has brought recognition, fame, and fortune to their shores. Sports fans should not miss the opportunity to take in a game—and that's true even if you might usually prefer shopping over a sporting event. This is a cross-cultural experience that can be unforgettable. Expect passionate and sometimes rowdy crowds but also great playing and a strong, competitive spirit.

David Keller, a coach for the Chicago Cubs, lives in Tampa and has been coming down to the D.R. during the winter season since the late 1990s. As he explains, "The first three weeks in December, the big kahunas come down like Tony Batista, Juan Acevedo, Migel Tejada, and Alberto Castillo. The Texas Rangers were down in December and rented a couple of penthouses on the new Juan Dolio Beach. I come down four to five times a year myself to coach and am now a hitting instructor. There is quite a competitive relationship between the Dominican and American players."

During one game that David attended, former Dominican President Hipolito threw the first ceremonial pitch for an Aquilas-Licey matchup. Dave saw the president making his way to the dugout and started to silently rehearse his Spanish, to be certain that his greeting would be *correcto*. Instead, when Hipolito saw him, he said: *"Hola, gringo! Deme cinco!"* ("Give me five!"). So much for protocol.

"One thing that differentiates a Dominican ball game is the fans," David emphasized. "To say they are enthusiastic doesn't cover it. They do love their teams! They don't get out of control so much now that the ruling was made that if a bottle or can is thrown from the home bleachers, the home team has to forfeit the game. Before, they had been known to throw things at the umpires when they made a bad call."

Going to your first game might be a little overwhelming with the noise, the craziness in the stands, and the high-decibel meringue. **Tropical Tours** (☎ *809/523–2028 at Casa de Campo, 809/556–5801 in La Romana*), a tour operator based at Casa de Campo, takes groups to the mid-size Francisco A. Michelli Stadium in La Romana from October through January, often coupling a game with a civilized dinner in town.

No peanuts and popcorn here, but *empanadas* with pepperoni and cheese and *pastellas* (seasoned ground beef with mashed plantains wrapped in a plantain leaf, to which you can add ketchup or mayo) are on the menu. The mascot for the home team, the Toros del Oeste (nicknamed Azucareros, as this is sugarcane country) rides around on a scooter. Between innings, fans dance wildly. The beer and rum flow. As passionate as Dominicans can be for the game, though, they are still on island time; even *aficionados* often come late, straggling in as late as the fourth inning.

AREAS & MALLS

Acropolis Mall, between Winston Churchill and Calle Rafael Augusto Sanchez, has become a favorite shopping arena for the young and/or hip capitaleñas. Stores like Zara and Mango, from Spain, have today's look without breaking budget. The **Malecón Center,** the latest complex, adjacent to the classy Hilton Santo Domingo, will house 170 shops, boutiques, and services plus several movie theaters, when it's completely occupied. In the tower above are luxury apartments, as well as Sammy Sosa, in one of the penthouses. **El Mercado Modelo,** a covered market, borders Calle Mella in the Zona Colonial; vendors here sell a dizzying selection of Dominican crafts.

One of the main shopping streets in the Zone is **Calle El Conde,** a pedestrian thoroughfare. With the advent of so many restorations, the dull and dusty stores with dated merchandise are giving way to some hip, new shops. However, many of the offerings, including local designer shops, are still of a caliber and cost that the Dominicans can afford. Some of the best shops are on **Calle Duarte,** north of the Zona Colonial, between Calle Mella and Avenida de Las Américas.

Piantini is a swanky residential neighborhood that has an increasing number of fashionable shops and boutiques. *(See Clothing, below)* Its borders run from Winston Churchill Avenida to Lope de Vega Avenida and from Calle Jose Amado Soler to 27 de Febrero Avenida. **Plaza Central,** between avenidas Winston Churchill and 27 de Febrero, is where you can find many top international boutiques. **Unicentro,** on Avenida Abraham Lincoln, is a major Santo Domingo mall.

SPECIALTY ITEMS

ART

Casa Jardin (⊠ *Balacer Gustavo Medjía Ricart 15, Naco* ☎ *809/565–7978*) is the garden studio of abstract painter Ada Balacer. Works by other women artists are also shown; look for pieces by Yolarda Naranjo, known for her modern work that integrates everything from fiberglass, hair, rocks, and wood to baby dresses.

Galería de Arte Mariano Eckert (⊠ *Av. Winston Churchill and Calle Luis F. Tomen, 3rd fl., Evaristo Morales* ☎ *809/541–7109*) focuses on the work of Eckert, an older Dominican artist who's known for his still lifes.

Galería de Arte Nader (⊠ *Rafael Augusto Sanchez 22, between Ensanche Piantini and Plaza Andalucia II, Piantini* ☎ *809/687–6674 or 809/544–0878*) showcases top Dominican artists in various media.

The gallery staff are well known in Miami and New York and work with Sotheby's.

Because their mix of Taíno, African, and European heritage, artisans creating modern Dominican art forms are using seeds, fiber, bones, coconut skin, cow horns, and African motifs. A good selection is found at **Jorge Caridad** (⊠*Arzobispo Merino, corner of General Cabral, Zona Colonial*).

> ## ART MIRRORS THE DOMINICAN HERITAGE
>
> Dominican arts and crafts reflect the country's diverse cultural heritage. The Spanish influence is evident in the painting and sculpture, while the Indian legacy is reflected in handmade craft items such as the concave trays, musical instruments, hammocks, and woven baskets.

Lyle O. Reitzel Art Contemporaneo (⊠*Plaza Andalucia II, Piantini* ☎*809/227–8361*) has, since 1995, specialized in contemporary art and showcases mainly Latin artists, from Mexico, South America, and Spain, and some of the most controversial Dominican visionaries.

Plaza Toledo Bettye's Galeria (⊠*Isabel la Católica 163, Zona Colonial* ☎*809/688–7649*) sells a fascinating array of artwork, including Haitian voodoo banners, metal sculptures, even souvenirs, chandeliers, and estate jewelry; the American expat owner, Bettye Marshall, has a great eye and can also rent you a room in one of her B&Bs.

CIGARS

★ **Cigar Club** (⊠*Av. 27 Febrero 211, Naco* ☎*809/683–2770*) is an upscale venue, selling a variety of fine cigars and one of the only places in the country where you can buy authentic Arturo Fuentes cigars. The club has a walk-in humidor as well as a lounge with a full bar, where you can enjoy fine wines, an aged rum, and Dominican coffee. It's open weekdays from 9 AM to midnight, until 3 on Saturday.

Cigar King (⊠*Calle El Conde 208, Baguero Bldg., Zona Colonial* ☎*809/686–4987*) keeps Dominican and Cuban cigars in a temperature-controlled cedar room.

Santo Domingo Cigar Club (⊠*Renaissance Jaragua Hotel & Casino, Av. George Washington 367, Gazcue* ☎*809/221–1483*) is a great place to find yourself a good smoke.

CLOTHING

Casa Virginia (⊠*C/Av. Roberto Pastoriza 255, Piantini* ☎*809/566–1535 or 809/566–4000*), one of the D.R.'s leading department stores, was founded in 1945 by the mother of the present Virginia, who took it to the next level, adding a great day spa. What a novel idea for ladies who love to shop *and* to spa. The store is stocked mostly with high-end designer clothing (including a Jenny Polanco department) and fashion finds, Italian jewelry, but also some moderately priced gift items.

★ **El Cofre del Pirata** (⊠*Calle Lic. Porfirio Herrera 23, 2nd Level, Piantini* ☎*809/540–2152*), a chic new boutique, carries dresses and tops from Betsy Johnson; the latest L.A. trends like Ed Hardy caps, jeans, and tees embellished with hand-embroidered Swarovski crystals; shoes from Dolce & Gabbana; Italian leather purses; perfume and cologne from Paris; and high-end costume jewelry. Owner Vianca Romero and her shop gals can give you a Dominican glamor makeover.

Plaza Central (⊠ *Avs. Winston Churchill and 27 de Febrero, Piantini* ☎ *809/541–5929*) is a major shopping center with high-end shops, including offers from upscale Dominican designer Jenny Polanco, who has incredible white linen outfits, artistic jewelry, purses, and more.

DUTY-FREE ITEMS

Centro de los Héroes (⊠ *Av. George Washington, Gazcue, Santo Domingo*) sells liquor, cameras, and the like.

HANDICRAFTS

Felipe & Co. (⊠ *Calle El Conde 105, Zona Colonial* ☎ *809/689–5810*) has a fascinating assortment of Dominican crafts and artwork, coffee, inexpensive "free spirit" jewelry, and some tropical clothing.

HOME FURNISHINGS

The exquisite **Nuovo Rinascimento** (⊠ *Plazoleta Padre Billini, Zona Colonial* ☎ *809/686–3387*), replete with contemporary furniture and antiques, has a treasure trove of Venetian linens and towels. Shipping can be arranged. The wooden hacienda doors open to a wonderful world of white sculptures and an inner courtyard with a lily-pad-dotted pool. Adjacent is Café Bellini offering authentic Italian cuisine in a striking contemporary setting.

JEWELRY

Ambar Tres (⊠ *La Atarazana 3, Zona Colonial* ☎ *809/688–0474*) carries a wide selection of items including high-end jewelry made with amber and larimar, the country's other indigenous, semiprecious stone. If you tour the in-house museum, you'll have a deeper appreciation of the gem.

L'Ile Au Tresor (⊠ *Calle El Conde, at Conde Plaza, lower floor, across from Mercure Hotel, Zona Colonial* ☎ *809/685–3983*) has a *Pirates of the Caribbean* theme, but that aside, it's fun and owned by a talented Frenchman named Patrick, who has some of the most attractive and creative designer pieces in native larimar, amber, and even pink conch. If you have never bought any of these lovely stones because the settings are usually cheesy, or if exquisite, too pricey, then this is your chance. His innovative custom work, with sterling or gold, can be done in 48 hours.

NIGHTLIFE

Santo Domingo's nightlife is vast and ever changing. Check with the concierges and hip *capitaleños*. Get a copy of the free newspaper *Touring, Aqui o Guía de Bares Restaurantes*—all available free at the tourist office and at hotels—to find out what's happening. At this writing there is still a curfew for clubs and bars; they must close at midnight during the week, and 2 AM on Friday and Saturday nights. There are some exceptions to the latter, primarily those clubs and casinos in hotels.

Amber & Larimar—The D.R.'s Indigenous "Gems"

As attractive as precious gems—and increasingly popular for jewelry—both here and even in France, larimar is actually a mineral and looks particularly attractive when paired with silver. This semiprecious stone is mined in the mountains of the southwest, in Bahoruco. It's the only place that this Caribbean blue pectolite has been found.

The national gem, amber, on the other hand, is actually a fossil—petrified tree resin that has been fossilized over a million or so years. Most amber is a golden color with brown tones, but it can be yellow and even black. It may have oddities like spiders and flies trapped inside.

Fakes are everywhere, plastic being pawned off as amber (it will float in water), blue beads as Larimar. Stick to the better jewelry shops, especially the Euro-owned ones, which have classy pieces with artistic design. So much of what is sold in the local shops has cheapie settings, which ruin the beauty of it.

Sadly, the curfew has put some clubs out of business, but it has cut down on the crime and late-night noise, particularly in the Zone.

BARS & CAFÉS

Doubles (⌧ *Calle Arzobispo Meriño 54, Zona Colonial* ☎809/688–3833) looks like a friend's place—that is, if you have a French friend who has a hip sense of interior design and would mix rattan furniture, antiques, subdued lighting, and candles in a space that's centuries old. Spanish tiles add interest to this atmospheric piano bar.

Marrakesh Café & Bar (⌧ *Hotel Santo Domingo, La Feria* ☎809/221–1511) is where a sophisticated after-work crowd gathers for American and international music and Casablanca style. Complimentary tapas come to the table, and you can get top-shelf liquors.

Don't think of the sandwich when you visit **Monté Cristo** (⌧ *Av. Jose Armado Soler at Av. Abraham Lincoln, Serralles* ☎809/542–5000), although the crowds can sandwich you in at this pub. The clientele spans the decades, music crosses the Americas, and there's a small dance floor. Both hot and cold tapas and sandwiches are served. It's open after work until late, and there's no cover. It's the only club where there's anything happening on a Tuesday night, which is a wine tasting.

Praia (⌧ *Calle Gustavo Mejia Ricart 74, Ensanche Naco* ☎809/540–8753) is a bar and wine lounge, popular with rich Dominicans and tourists. The contemporary design utilizes glass and steel for a cool, minimalist decor. Music is modern and electronic; drinks are expensive.

Punto Y Corcho (⌧ *Av. Abraham Lincoln at Gustavo Mejía Ricart, Piantini* ☎809/683–0533), on Plaza Andalucia, is where wine (by the glass and bottle) and local and international liquors are the order of the night. This is a great date- and late-night spot, and it tends to appeal to a more mature, sophisticated type.

El Sartan (⌧*Calle Hostos 153, Zona Colonial* ☎*809/686–9621*) might be considered a hole in the wall by some, but the crowd covers all classes of Dominicans, from the poorer Zone residents and the old men playing dominoes on the plastic tables on up to a wealthy and well-dressed group stopping by after an art opening. Funky, it's a real slice of life as it was before the neighborhood became so gentrified.

> **THE POLITUR IS YOUR FRIEND**
>
> You may see white SUVs with the word POLITUR cruising the streets; this is the tourist police, and their role is to protect and guide international tourists. Most have a working knowledge or English; some are trilingual. They play a leading role in making the tourist sector safer by eradicating unlicensed street vendors and controlling prostitution by both sexes.

Trio Cafe (⌧*Av. Abraham Lincoln N 12A, at Plaza Castilla Ensanche, Naco* ☎*809/412–0964*) is one of those places where the cool, older crowd comes to graze, drink, and dance, even though there's no real dance floor. They just stand around and groove, and chances are they will make new friends—as might you.

★ **Wine Tasting Room at El Catador** (⌧*Calle Jose Brea Péna 43, Piantini* ☎*809/540–1644*), an avant-garde wine bar, has been created by the major wine distributor El Catador, S.A. Cushy leather armchairs and hardwood floors help create a clubby atmosphere, where the focal point is an *enomalie,* where guests get to sample 16 different open bottles of fine wine. There's a contemporary selection of hors d'oeuvres, canapés and tapas, both hot and chilled. You will want to buy at least one of the 500 bottles of wine from around the wine-making world. It's open until 11 PM on weekdays, but only until 6 on Saturday.

CABARET

At **El Teatro La Fiesta** (⌧*Renaissance Jaragua Hotel & Casino, Av. George Washington 367, Gazcue* ☎*809/221–2222*) you can come to the cabaret, just like in the Broadway music and movie. This theater has revived the style of cabaret in Weimar Berlin of the 1930s. With the glitz and showmanship that characterize Broadway, there's nothing else like it in the D.R.

CASINOS

The action can heat up, but gambling here is more a sideline than a raison d'être. Most casinos are in the larger hotels of Santo Domingo. All offer slot machines, blackjack, craps, and roulette and, with a few exceptions, are generally open daily until midnight

> **DRESSING DOMINICANA**
>
> Dominican women tend to be flashy dressers. Expect to see a lot of glitter, with too-short skirts and too-tight slacks, not to mention a great deal of cleavage, wherever you go. And these are the good girls! Though outwardly flamboyant, they'll act in a ladylike manner. Treat them like ladies, or you may have to answer to their brothers.

(2 AM on Friday and Saturday). You must be 18 to enter, and jackets are required at the chic casinos in the capital. In Santo Domingo, several upscale hotels have casinos: Barceló Gran Hotel Lina; Meliá Santo Domingo; Hispaniola Hotel & Casino (attracts a younger crowd); Renaissance Jaragua; and the Hilton Santo Domingo.

Atlantis World Casino (⊠ *Av. George Washington 218, Gazcue* ☎ *809/688–8080*), adjacent to the InterContinental V Centenario, is one of the newest and most American-friendly casinos in the capital, with slots that accept dollars. Although there's no charge to enter the gaming room, the table minimums are higher than most, so the casino attracts a more upscale crowd through closing time—6 AM!

> **BAILE! BAILE!**
>
> Dance! Dance! The meringue is regarded as the Dominican national dance. Traditionally, it combines the sounds of the aboriginal *guiro* (a metal tube that is scratched to produce a continuous grating sound) and the *tambora* (a double-kinned African drum played on the lap) for rhythm, as well as the accordion. Over time, saxophones, trumpets, and trombones were added to produce the first meringue orchestras. The 1970s saw the introduction of electric pianos, and since then, synthesizers have given meringue a new sound, which increased its popularity even more abroad.

★ **Cirsa Majestic** (⊠ *Hilton Santo Domingo, 1st Level, Av. George Washington, Gazcue* ☎ *829/687–4853 or 809/685–0000*) is the newest of the Malecón casinos, and it's on par with its Las Vegas counterparts. From the time you walk through the grand entrance, majestic is the operative word here. There are 20 gaming tables (even baccarat); a VIP salon; 200 video slots; live music (national and international talent); a gastronomic restaurant; and more. It's the good life.

DANCE CLUBS

Dancing is as much a part of the culture here as eating and drinking. As in other Latin countries, after dinner it's not a question of *whether* people will go dancing but *where* they'll go. Move with the rhythm of the merengue and the pulsing beat of salsa (adopted from neighboring Puerto Rico). Among the young, the word is that there's no better place to party in the Caribbean than Santo Domingo's Zona Colonial. At this writing, in Santo Domingo almost all clubs have to close at midnight during the week, 2 AM on Friday and Saturday.

Aire (⊠ *Calle de Las Mercedes 313, Zona Colonial* ☎ *809/689–4163*), a long-standing, long-rocking gay and lesbian dance club has remained popular partly because of its appealing setting, a restored colonial home with a landscaped courtyard. There's always a crowd, but the dancing doesn't get going until after 11 PM. If you love classic rock and Top 40 but are not gay, go anyway; straights are welcome, but most of the couples on the dance floor will be male-male. Also, be aware that the drag shows can be raunchy.

Atarazana #9 (⊠ *Atarazana 9, Zona Colonial* ☎ *809/688–0969*) is just down the hill from Plaza España toward the river, an ideal location if you're staying in the Zone. The first level of this dance club has a bar and a stage, as well as large windows overlooking the historic streetscape. This place opens early, at 8 PM. It can be cheaper on Thursday nights due to special promotions.

Guácara Taina (✉ *Av. Mirador del Sur 655, Mirador Sur* ☎ *809/533–0671*) is a landmark, for it's the only *discoteca* in a cave, formerly inhabited by Taíno Indians as well as bats (Santo Domingo has a network of natural caves within its city limits). As you descend and see hundreds of heads bobbing and bodies gyrating among the stalactites, it's a unique sight. Banquettes and seating are in the limestone walls ornamented with Taíno pictographs. The fashionable crowd deserted it maybe 15 years ago, leaving it to the *turistas,* and now large groups of cruise-ship passengers. The cover charge is $10 and includes one drink and all the salsa you can dance to, but it's only open Thursday to Sunday.

LED (✉ *Hispaniola Hotel & Casino, Abraham Lincoln Ave. at Av. Independencia, La Feria* ☎ *809/476–7733 or 809/221–7111*) is in a hotel, so it's able to stay open later than the other clubs, and that is what has made this a favorite of the young and well-to-do party set. Many a graduation is celebrated here until the wee small hours of the *manana.*

Loft (✉ *Tiradentes 44, Naco* ☎ *809/732–4016*) is a modern and exclusive lounge with a grazing menu that includes sushi, bruschetta, hot wings, and nachos; later on, it segues into a large and popular disco with a great sound system and lighting.

Moon (✉ *Calle Hostos and Arzobispo Noel, Zona Colonial* ☎ *809/686–5176*) is a smaller club dedicated to electronic music and reggae. It generally appeals to the 18- to 24-year-olds.

★ **Nowhere Bar** (✉ *Calle Hostos 205, Zona Colonial* ☎ *809/877–6258*) is hot, and the crowd is mostly young and affluent, but all ages stop by; it seems to be especially popular with Americans in college here, who seem to have adopted the place. They hang on the first level, where the latest music from the States—plus hip-hop and house—is played. A DJ plays Dominican music on the second floor, packing in the locals. Thursday night is the infamous Ladies Night. On Friday and Saturday, local bands take the stage. An artistic renovation of a 16th-century, two-story mansion, this is the bar seen in the movie *Miami Vice.* It had another cosmetic redo in 2007 and is looking clean and refreshed. It's open Wednesday through Saturday.

BARAHONA & THE SOUTHWEST

Think of a trip to the Dominican Republic's southwestern provinces as an exotic safari. The variety of flamingos, crocodiles, iguanas, and many other kinds of animals is truly amazing. If you come to this wild part of the island, you can experience nature the way you were meant to, whether on solitary walks into the mountains or on day-long eco-tours. You have left the long lines and overpriced piña coladas. You will find friendly people who have not been jaded by tourism, not to mention food straight from the earth or the sea. Fishermen, farmers, and tradesmen still work and live here with their families, away from the established tourism zones. As we overheard one guest exclaim, "This has to be as beautiful as heaven . . . but I don't think heaven could be this beautiful!"

> ### CHICKENS DEAD OR ALIVE
>
> Stuck in traffic in Azua, you may be able to glimpse through the crowds a *pollera* (chicken shop) advertising *pollos vivo* (live chickens) for RD$20; *pollos matando* (dead chickens), on the other hand, are RD$26. If they ring its neck, apparently, it's six pesos extra. That's six pesos well spent!

This is the part of the D.R. where rivers still clear and cold from their mountain springs, meet the sea at pebbly beaches washed by gentle azure waves. And you can see for miles and miles down the undeveloped coastline. You'll enjoy trying the various beaches and investigating villages like La Bahoruco, San Rafael, Paraiso, and Los Patos. Eco-tourism is on the rise here, and the southwest continues to draw visitors looking to commune with nature, including ardent bird-watchers.

At this writing, this is a Dominican destination without the crowds, but which is so physically beautiful and unspoiled that each day will amaze you. You'll need three to five days to really appreciate what the region has to offer. If you put yourself in the hands of a guide or eco-tour company that knows its way around, you'll be able to make the most of your time. But you can also do it on your own, preferably in a 4x4 vehicle.

Barahona, your gateway to the southwest, is about 209 km (129 mi) southwest of Santo Domingo and about 120 km (80 mi) east of the Haitian border. The drive here from the capital (primarily on Highway 44 through the towns of Bani and Azua) takes between 3 and 3½ hours. If you take the Caribe Tours bus, it will make a pit stop in Azua, but there's no reason for independent travelers to stop. The populace here is unaccustomed to tourists, but they're accommodating and friendly.

ABOUT THE RESTAURANTS

In the Southwest, there are no fine-dining restaurants, with the exception of the restaurant at Casa Bonita and the *table d'hôte* at Casa Blanca (both hotel-based restaurants near Barahona). But you can find many good local and seafood restaurants with welcoming owners and staff. Expect simple local food for the most part, so expect to see a lot of sancocho, mofongo, and *chicharrones* (crispy pig skin fried with garlic), which come packaged here like potato chips. Restaurants are not too big on desserts; they keep it simple, with flan, white cheese and guava, *majarete* (corn pudding), and boiled orange peels, which can be quite tasty. Food tastes like it just came from the earth or the sea; when you see a 4-foot silver dorado paraded through a restaurant to

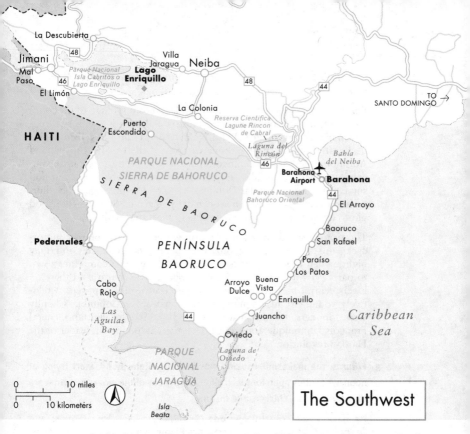

The Southwest

the kitchen, you know what you should be having for dinner. Credit cards are not accepted at many establishments.

ABOUT THE HOTELS

In addition to a noteworthy luxury property, most hotels in the southwest are simple; almost all the recommendable hotels in the region are small inns, and many offer meals (though breakfast is not always included in the base price). Hotels in the southwest normally quote rates in both pesos and dollars, though you'll be able to pay with either local or U.S. currency. Some hotels do not take credit cards.

WHAT IT COSTS IN DOLLARS					
	¢	$	$$	$$$	$$$$
Restaurants	under $8	$8–$12	$12–$20	$20–$30	Over $30
Hotels*	Under $80	$80–$150	$150–$250	$250–$350	Over $350
Hotels**	Under $125	$125–$250	$250–$350	$350–$450	Over $450

*EP, BP, CP **AI, FAP, MAP Restaurant prices are per person for a main course at dinner and do not include 16% tax and 10% service charge. Hotel prices are per night for a double room in high season, excluding 16% V.A.T. and 10% service charge.

BARAHONA

209 km (120 mi) southwest of Santo Domingo; approximately 3½ hours by car

Barahona is a noisy, smoky city; it's the least cosmopolitan of the country's mid-size metropolises, yet it's also a college town with two centers of higher learning, UCATEBA (Universidad Catolica y Tecnologica de Barahona) and the Barahona campus of the UASD (Universidad Autonoma de Santo Domingo). There's a Malecón (seafront promenade), which comes alive on the weekends and where you can find some of the more popular Dominican seafood restaurants. The colorful and lively market, which is open daily—even on Sunday—is a good photo opportunity and you'll be able to meet the locals.

The primary mode of transportation is the motor scooter or motorcycle, and there's an eternal buzz from them, which escalates on Friday nights when everyone in the entire region seems to come into town to party. Victorian houses give Barahona a little charm, and there's a lovely central park, but some of the streets are still unpaved. A relatively young city in a country where Christopher Columbus's family were founders, Barahona was founded in 1802 by Haitian General François-Dominique Toussaint Louverture, an important leader of the Haitian revolution.

NEED A BREAK? *Frituras,* **the makeshift cooking stands along Highway 44, start frying at noon, when they open for lunch almost every day of the week. Just what are they frying? Fish, chicken, and** *tostones.*

At Barahona's colorful **Mercado** (⊠ *Between J.-J. Pena Gomez and Jaime-Mota*) you can find good prices on locally made handicrafts, Haitian art, wooden *pilones* (mortars and pestles), and *giras* (a musical instrument that looks like a kitchen grater; a knife is stroked across it to make a metallic sound), which can be hung as wall decorations.

The city's characteristic **Parque Central,** in the center of town, is a downtown oasis, with some ancient shade trees, park benches, and a kiosk. Around it are some little, wooden creole houses painted Caribbean colors (some of these creole houses are little stores). Around the square are also the banks and a *gua-gua* stop.

Larimar is a semiprecious stone the color of the sea that is found only in the southwest region of the Dominican Republic. The **Larimar Mine** (⊠ *Carretera de la Costa Km 18, Bahoruco* ✉ *ialofaitulidrv@gmail. com* 🎫 *RD$1,500 for full-day tour* ☉ *Daily 8–6*) is one of the area's mines that can be visited. With the aid of a grant from U.S.A.I.D. and the assistance of Peace Corps volunteers, a new Bahoruco community collaboration will give visitors real-life tours of the mine, as well as a hands-on orientation of the history of larimar mining and processing, and visits to local workshops that make larimar jewelry. Eco-Tours (see ⇨ Tour Options *in* Southwest Essentials, *below*) offers organized group tours from Barahona and surrounding hotels. The cost of the full-day tour includes lunch, drinks, your guide, and the mine visit.

**EN
ROUTE**

Go southwest out of Barahona on Carretera de la Costa (also called Carretera Paraiso, Carretera Enriquillo, Highway 44, and Carretera Barahona–Pedernales) and watch the beauty unfold. Keeping the sea to your left and the mountains to your right, you'll pass through a series of seaside villages: Juan Esteban, Bahoruco, La Cienega (towns where four of the small hotels listed are found) and then onto San Rafael, then Paraiso and Los Patos, and Enriquillo, until you eventually go around the tip of the Pedernales Peninsula and on to the National Parks.

WHERE TO EAT

The region's best restaurants are all found in or around Barahona, but not all good food is cooked in real restaurants. In Bahía de las Aguilas, a pristine beach about two hours from Bahouruco by car (road to Pedernales), you can find rustic restaurants serving the freshest seafood you can find.

$–$$ ✕ **Las Brisas del Caribe.** This dining room, which was built by Catholic medics in 1947, has a certain charm, like an old black-and-white movie. It's an upscale restaurant and considered pricey by Barahona standards. Appetizers, such as the flavorful pumpkin soup, are well priced. Fresh fish is the obvious choice here, with shellfish a known specialty. A French expat always orders either the paella (for two) or the wonderful garlicky *parrilla mixta* for two, which has two grilled lobsters, squid, shrimp, and lambi (for about $20). That is living *la vida buena*! The restaurant is on a knoll with a loop of a driveway at the end of the seafront; the views of the water are best from the open-air terrace. ⊠ *Av. Enriquillo 1, next to Politur, Barahona* ☎ *809/524–2794* ▤ *MC, V.*

¢ ✕ **Melo Café.** You could easily pass by this nondescript, three-story building, which was once an office but now houses a café owned by Rafael of the Melo Coffee family and his wife Teresa. Teresa runs a clean-living (no alcohol) café, with good plates of eggs, omelets, and pancakes (a rarity here) for breakfast. Priced low enough for a Peace Corp volunteer's budget, the best beverages are the fresh fruit *batidos* (smoothies); try papaya, pineapple, or milk and bananas, all for less than 40 pesos. The *plat del dia* always offers rice and beans with perhaps a chicken fricassee or stewed pork, and a little salad, for just RD$125. You can get a club sandwich here, too (another rarity). Look for the blue awnings. ⊠*Anacaona 12, Barahona* ☎ *809/524–5437* ▤*No credit cards* ⊘ *Closed Sun. No dinner Fri. and Sat.*

$–$$ ✕ **Restaurant at Casa Bonita.** Whether it's lunch poolside at a teak table
★ shaded by a market umbrella or in the open-air dining room, it's a joy just to be in this glorious environment with its panoramic view of the sea. By night, tables are draped in white linen, and attentive waiters dressed in white guayabera shirts serve food as diverse as the international music playing in the background. Consulting chef Carlos Estevez has designed a Caribbean fusion menu that utilizes the fresh fish from the village and local produce. Shellfish—particularly shrimp—are well-utilized, either lime-marinated in cold salads or as coconut shrimp; there's also Asian-style tuna. Saturday is BBQ night with everything from hamburgers to octopus to lobster as well as a tempting lineup

Down Under in the Larimar Mines

A larimar mine is not like any mine you have ever seen, whether in West Virginia or Wales, but if you have never seen an active mining operation, this could be your chance. While the larimar that comes from the mine is beautiful, the mine is not. It is, as they say, earthy, even odiferous.

Try to ignore the heaps of litter, especially around the cooking shacks, and the disarmingly loud noise from the diesel generators that keep lights down under and also help bring in fresh air. Despite these drawbacks, the mine can be fascinating. There are some 25 holes in a given mine, many owned by small investors. Everyone knows whose hole is whose, despite the seeming disorganization. The individual miners are welcoming to visitors and will sometimes let them go down their shafts. The miners, who work 12 hours a day, range in age from 45 down to teenagers; all are Dominican or Haitian. The work itself can be hazardous, as two teenage miners discovered in 2007, when their oxygen supply failed and they died.

Each hole is perhaps the size of a typical table in a restaurant and about 20 to 30 feet deep, at which point the shaft narrows until it becomes horizontal, forcing you to crawl. Miners chip away at the larimar deposits, which are brought up in a bucket by a rope and pulley system. The miners ascend and descend foot by foot on wooden pegs. Armed security guards at the top ensure that no one takes a rock that doesn't belong to him.

The next time you see a display of larimar in a jewelry case, you will wonder why the prices aren't higher.

of vegetables and starches. It's divine, especially when accompanied by an appropriate match from the wine cooler. ⊠*Casa Bonita Tropical Lodge, Km 17, Carretera de la Costa, Bahoruco* ☎*809/476–5059* ⊟*AE, MC, V.*

$ ✕**Restaurant at Playa Azul.** Blue-and-white gingham tablecloths are the only decoration in the dining room, where you can see the Caribbean by day and hear its serenade you by night. If ocean breezes wane, particularly during breakfast, then flies can be a problem. There's an open kitchen, but you may wish it wasn't. Keep your order simple, such as lobster, fish, or fillet of beef on the grill, or a Dominican dish like fish soup, fillet of dorado in coconut sauce, or lambi vinaigarette, and you'll be fine. There's no wine by the glass—only bottles—but the bar does serve nice tropical cocktails. Local music is played, and when the teenage employees aren't at the controls, it's pleasant. ⊠*Playa Azul, Km 7, Carretera de la Costa, Juan Esteban* ☎*809/204–8010* ⊟*No credit cards.*

$ ✕**Restaurant Hotelito Oasi.** Sr. Giordano Mettifego is as good a chef as he is a photographer, which is how he made his living in his native Italy. After he "retired" to the D.R. with his young Dominican bride, Eva, this caballero became a restaurateur and hotelier. Pastas are his specialty; while other restaurants may do a carbonara, this is the real thing. Similarly, he makes his own gnocchi and authentic pizzas. A delicious sauce of fresh-peeled tomatoes with Italian olive oil arrives on fresh fish, and his octopus is marinated with the same fine oil and imported vinegar. Chicken Milanese is a delightful change, and there are great ice creams and lemon sorbet for dessert. His three young children make this a real family affair. The delicious bread? Giordano's 12-year-old daughter makes that. ⊠*Hotelito Oasi Italiano, Calle Jose Carrasco, Los Patos* ☎*809/918–6969* ▭*No credit cards.*

¢–$ ✕**Restaurant Los Robles.** On a Friday night, this Malecón eatery is abuzz, and not just from the drone of the *moto* scooters. Patrons watch sports on the TV out on the patio, and a pizza oven in the corner spits out orders to go while a grill turns out simple dishes like shrimp or chicken breast on a wooden board with fries or tostones. "Loaded" grilled sandwiches are man-size (and available 24 hours). This rough and rustic joint that's trying to please everyone, which it often does, is best known for *mofongo* (of many varieties like chicken, lobster, and lambi). Asopao has the addition of shellfish. The good news is that tax is included and a Presidente is only RD$54. The bad news is the cleanliness, which leaves something to be desired. ⊠*Av. Enriquillo, corner Av. Nuestra Santa del Rosario, Barahona* ☎*809/524–1629* ▭*MC, V.*

WHERE TO STAY

The best hotels in the southwest are around Barahona, the region's major city. Most of these are small and owner-managed, and some are quite good. Although we have recommended the best that the region has to offer, we've also stretched our standards to make some of these recommendations; please read both the pros and cons of each hotel here before making a reservation. The good news is that lodging in this part of the island is relatively cheap.

HOTELS ⊡**Casa Blanca.** Named after the Bogey and Bergman flick, this little
¢ hotel is just as much a crossroads for intriguing international visitor as
★ Rick's Bar Americain. Your fellow guests might be a New York basketball trainer or a globetrotter from Finland. Susanna Knapp, a charming Swiss woman, transformed this former doctor's home into a fine little inn. The main building houses the reception and dining area, while two guesthouses each have three Spartan but colorful, pristine rooms (four have three beds). All are set amid palm and almond tree orchards. Pathways lead to the cliffs and down steep steps to the virgin, private beach. You can expect a stimulating breakfast (RD$200 extra, and worth it); Susanna sets a lovely table strewn with bougainvillea and offers a most appealing *table d' hôte* for dinner that fosters camaraderie. Dinner possibilities may be fresh-caught fish and shellfish, a fish soup with coconut, or even Dominican Sancocho. Occasionally, Susanna takes nonguests for dinner (reservation only) for the steal of RD$400 to RD$800 (beg for a reservation!). **Pros:** This is an outpost of civility, excellent value and refinements for the price, food is among the area's finest. **Cons:** Lots of "nots" (no phones, TV, a/c, pool, or even credit cards), the only access is by an unpaved road, car a must to stay here. ⊠*10 Km, Carretera Paraiso, Juan Esteban* ☎*809/471–1230* ⊕*www. hotelcasablanca.com.do* ⇆*6 rooms* ♿*In-room: no a/c, no phone, no TV. In-hotel: restaurant, room service, bar, beachfront, laundry services, parking (no fee)* ▭*No credit cards* ⋈*EP.*

$–$$

Fodor'sChoice
★

🔲 **Casa Bonita Tropical Lodge.** This small gem was once the country home of the Schiffino family; well, it's still in the family but has been reborn as a small luxury hotel that still retains the warmth of a family-owned lodge. Acclaimed architect Rafael Selman has added new architectural elements, including some Indonesian design and thatched-roof cabanas have been brought to the next deluxe level, with contemporary lighting and natural materials like *tabla de palma* (wood slats of palm). Private balconies allow you to hear the river below and see the cloud forest above. The excellent breakfast is served in the palapa-topped restaurant that segues into the salon. Both overlook an infinity pool with its singular palm and the sea beyond. Unquestionably, this is the most stellar option in the entire southwest. **Pros:** Celestial, panoramic vistas allow you to chill and enjoy the area, manicures and massages can be had poolside, iPod-ready clock radios and Jacuzzi poolside. **Cons:** Hotel is somewhat remote, not all staffers are fluent in English. ⊠ *Km 17, Carretera de la Costa, Bahoruco* ☎ *809/476–5059, 809/540–5908 reservations* ⊕ *www.casabonitadr.com* ⇦ *12 rooms* ⏃ *In-room: refrigerator, Wi-Fi, no TV. In-hotel: restaurant, bar, pool, bicycles, parking (no fee)* ⊟ *AE, MC, V* ⦿ *BP.*

¢ 🔲 **Coral Sol Resort.** This is the only real eco-inn in the southwest. In fact, the construction may remind you of the rustic cabins found in U.S. national parks. But instead of evergreens, there are palm trees. The Dominican owners have creatively utilized the round white stones from their beach for the pathways and steps, sometimes painting them black to make a pattern. Resort may be a too-grand description for this place, but there's a pool with mismatched furniture and an inviting "clubhouse" where guests can mingle. Cabins are large and bisected with a slatted wood partition, each section with its own double bed and bathroom. In the rustic, open-air restaurant, the ladies do turn out some especially flavorful Dominican meals, such as fried fish with tomato sauce and both white beans and black beans. Management promises a soft-goods freshening. **Pros:** The caring resident owner is a true Barahona *caballero,* soothing and stress-free atmosphere, attractive to both families and eco-tourists. **Cons:** A little rough around the edges with few creature comforts, style and decor need help. ⊠ *Km 19, Carretera Paraiso, La Cienega* ☎ *809/233–4882* ⊕ *www.coralsolresort.com* ⇦ *9 rooms* ⏃ *In-room: no a/c, no phone, no TV. In-hotel: restaurant, room service, bar, pool, beachfront, parking (no fee)* ⊟ *No credit cards* ⦿ *MAP.*

¢ 🔲 **Hotel Costa Larimar.** The best option in downtown Barahona is not a destination hotel. Although the sign says this is WHERE YOUR DREAMS COME TRUE, it's doubtful that this will be your idea of a sweet dream. The facade and layout, including a pool within steps of the beach that fronts a small tree-covered isle, is quite inviting, but the beach furniture is falling apart and swimming in Barahona's own bay is not advisable. Guest rooms, although spacious and with "American" cable TV, have flat pillows on hard beds and less than upscale bedding. The elevator was broken during our last visit. However, you will be treated nicely, and the middling breakfast buffet is served by the pool. Nevertheless, don't add a full meal plan to your stay; the regular buffet grub just isn't worth it. Business travelers frequent here midweek, and Dominican families prevail on weekends. **Pros:** Bed with breakfast is a good value, nice children's playground, some rooms have private balconies and sea views (request one). **Cons:** Looks as if no money has been put into it this last decade, little English spoken, noisy families take over on weekends. ✉*Av. Enriquillo 6, Barahona* ☎*809/524–1111* ⊕*www. hotelcostalarimar.com* ☎*109 rooms* ⚘*In-room: safe. In-hotel: 2 restaurants, bars, pool, beachfront, laundry services, public Wi-Fi, parking (no fee)* ⊟*MC, V* ⊺⊘*BP.*

¢ ✗**Hotelito Oasi Italiana.** An oasis in this neighborhood of simple, one-room wooden casitas, this walled and gated complex is impressive from the street. Inside the compound are two buildings with a pool between. The first two-story building houses a restaurant and the owner's dwelling; the other building is the family's former home, now hotel rooms centered around a salon with Italian leather furniture and an attractive mural of exotic birds and banana trees. The bedrooms are not as attractive as the common areas, but three newer rooms have sea views and handsome desks and furnishings from the owner's native Italy, though at twice the price as the older rooms. What is certain is the sincere hospitality of Giordano and his family, not to mention their wonderful restaurant. **Pros:** The location is closer to the national parks than hotels near Bahoruco, great Italian restaurant, proximity to a fun beach. **Cons:** No phones though TVs promised, rooms and appliances were not particularly well-maintained, no English spoken. ✉*Calle Jose Carrasco, Los Patos* ☎*809/918–6969* ⊕*www.lospatos.it* ☎*7 rooms* ⚘*In-room: no phone, no TV. In-hotel: restaurant, bar, room service, pool* ⊟*No credit cards* ⊺⊘*BP.*

¢ ▦**Playa Azul.** New in 2006, this is one of the southwest's better lodging options overlooking a "private" beach snug in its tranquil shore. The rooms are quite comfortable, and there's cable TV, though no English-language channels. The hotel's architectural design is unattractive, just two stucco blocks of units, and the second tier rooms, which are right behind the first row (reserve these), have no sea views. Cheap is the operative word here: cheap furnishings, bathroom fixtures, construction, including the cracked plastic tables and sagging Presidente umbrellas around the pool. Although the co-owners are French (the couple's partner is Dominican), the decor is strictly local, and the only thing French here is the crepes. **Pros:** Good value for the money, nice rocking chairs on front porch and under thatch-capped gazebos. **Cons:** Lacks class or much spirit, young staff is green and poorly trained, though nice. ✉ *Km 7, Carretera Barahona–Enriquillo, Enriquillo* ☎*809/454–5375* ☎*16 rooms* ⚘*In-room: no phone. In-hotel: restaurant, bar, pool, beachfront, laundry service, parking (no fee)* ⊟*No credit cards* ⊺⊘*CP.*

¢ ▦**Ponte Vedra.** This stucco "apartotel" (all rooms are apartment-like, with kitchenettes) with stone details looks good from the outside, as does the bar–restaurant under a palapa next to the pool, which looks out to the sea. It even has a beach with sand versus pebbles. Some rooms, including No. 201, are ok; the two-room apartment can sleep six; however, others, such as No. 101, desperately need a fresh paint job. No rooms have true water views, nor does the hotel have a welcoming ambience. Although family-owned, the employees are not outstanding. And there is nothing eco about it. **Pros:** Location is convenient, nice pool and beach. **Cons:** Plastic flowers everywhere are indicative of decor, the little restaurant is not so good. ☒ *Km 12, Carretera Paraiso, El Arroyo* ☎ *809/341–8462 or 809/341–4698* ⊕ *www.pontevedracaribe.com* ⇋ *16 rooms* ☙ *In-room: kitchen. In-hotel: restaurant, bar, pool, beachfront, parking (no fee)* ▤ *MC, V* ⏍ *EP.*

A UNIQUE
HOUSE
$$

▦ **Casa de Tarzan.** Tarzan's House, an innovative, tri-level home, is deep in the tropical forest with decks overhanging a river. The ultimate escape for adventurous types is accessible only by a 4x4, horseback, or mountain bike, and all food and other necessities must be brought in. However, this eco-friendly house has its own spring water aqueduct, a generator, barbecue, and a lot of candle power. Cell phones can now get a signal, a plus that came with its total renovation. New bamboo furniture has been added, as well as *hamacas* (hammocks); one bedroom has three bunk beds. Reservations can be made directly through the English-speaking owner. To reach the house, you go up the drive to Casa Bonita but make a hard left before the hotel, onto a dirt road for some 30 minutes. Five rivers must be forded, but you will eventually reach the casa. **Pros:** You are at one with nature (the sound of the rushing river is omnipresent), can be a romantic getaway, especially with a full moon, a nearby local family acts as caretaker and can provide maid service or cook for you. **Cons:** This is a hard-core adventure only for the self-sufficient, the long trek here isn't feasible after dark. ☒ *Km 17, Carretera de la Costa, Bahoruco* ☎ *809/977–4280, 809/476–5059, or 809/540–5908* ✉ *polidiaz@codetel.net.do* ⇋ *4 bedrooms, 2½ bathrooms* ☙ *In-room: No a/c, no phone, no TV, kitchen* ▤ *No credit cards* ⟳ *2-day minimum.*

BEACHES

The reason the Dominican government has been slow to develop the southwest is that its *playas* are predominantly white stones and pebbles with some white-sand patches. Water shoes are necessary for safe walking and swimming on most beaches. That aside, the water, the sun, the unspoiled coastline, and the lack of hotels and development is inviting to the very types who are now discovering eco-tourism here. ⚠ **Caution: While this is still one of the safest areas in the country, drugs have come to the area by sea and by land over the Haitian border. They have made several fishermen wealthy and given others unwelcome habits, including fishing of a most unwelcome sort. They throw out a hook and line and snag the belongings of unsuspecting tourists frolicking in the sea. So keep an eye on your things. This is more likely to happen on a beautiful deserted beach.**

Playa El Quemaito. Although just down from Casa Blanca and Hotel Quemaito, this beach is seldom populated during the week, so never swim alone. It's usually dead calm because of a small reef; consequently, it's safe even for small children to swim here. White stones are interspersed with white patches of sand where you can put down your towel. There are no facilities. ☒ *Km 16, Carretera de la Costa, Bahoruco, 9 mi (16 km) southwest of Barahona.*

Playa Bahoruco. In front of the fishing village of the same name, this gorgeous stretch of virgin beach goes on for miles with unobstructed views. Taupe sand is underfoot surrounding all those white stones. Turn left at the sign for the former Barcelo Bahoruco Hotel. Surfers come for the small waves, and there is some undertow. You may see some small, blue larimar pebbles on the beach (otherwise you can buy them from local children). ⊠*Km 17, Carretera de la Costa, Bahoruco, 8 mi (17 km) southwest of Barahona.*

Playa St. Rafael. A few kilometers past Playa Bahoruco, the joy here is that a river comes right into the sea, and a rock dam makes a small waterfall, which, in turn, forms a pool. Little children scamper in and out of its frigid waters, and you certainly can join them. It's cold, yes, but safer than swimming in the sea, which has quite a strong undertow beneath the mild waves. Beach shacks here turn out tasty fried fish and *tostones.* You may even be able to get red snapper filets in coconut sauce. Parking is RD$40, which pays for the security guard. ⊠*Km 17, Carretera de la Costa, St. Rafael* ✛*25 km (12 mi) southwest of Barahona.*

NEED A BREAK?

Villa Mariam, formerly a private home up the steep hill from St. Rafael Beach, it has a wonderful icy waterfall, where you can bathe in its pools as you drink aged rum (though it's BYOB, and you may need it to brave the chilly waters). Lanai vines and tropical flowers, even orchids, grow wild and make it look like the mythical Eden. There's no restaurant or bar, but there are picnic tables, and you can bring your fried fish plates up from the beach. Admission RD$100, free to guests of Casa Bonita.

SPORTS & THE OUTDOORS

The Southwest is one very sporty place. Here the sportin' life ranges from bird-watching to spectator sports like cockfighting, and in between is horseback riding, trekking, mountain biking, snorkeling, surfing, and a host of other possibilities. *For information on the major tour companies that offer organized excursions in the region, see* ⇨ *Tour Options, in Southwest Essentials, below.*

BIRD-WATCHING

Hispaniola has 30 endemic bird species, not to mention many others that can be found throughout the Caribbean region. The three national parks in the Barahona region are great birding destinations. Kate Wallace, an American living in Santo Domingo, is an expert in this birding frontier and organizes birding tours through her company **Tody Tours** (⊠*Calle Jose Gabriel Garcia 105, Zona Colonial, Santo Domingo* ☎*809/686–0882* ⊕*www.todytours.com*). When her groups first arrive in Santo Domingo, she houses them at hotels in the Colonial Zone. A four-wheel-drive vehicle is hired, and they travel to the southwest, staying either at Casa Bonita or Hotel Quemaito, but cheaper camping options are also available at her own Villa Barrancoli. Bird-watching can be an expensive hobby, but tours are all individually designed and priced, depending on duration and choice of lodging.

COCKFIGHTING

Cockfighting is a tradition that persists in the Spanish islands of the Caribbean—in Puerto Rico, Cuba, and the Dominican Republic. The fact that these birds are put in a ring with spurs on their ankles and are expected to fight until death—and it is hoped that only one has to die—may seem like a horrid blood sport to the outsider, but it is a long-held tradition here, and it's an authentic experience (albeit one that is not for everyone). The high season for fights is June through November (roosters cannot fight during molting season from December to January). February through May are usually reserved for training. Given the tendency for blood splatters, the front rows may not be to everyone's taste. Bets are taken, but first-timers are urged to sit out their first time in the *gallera* until they get the system down.

The main cockfighting ring closest to Barahona is **La Gallera** (⊠ *Km 21, Carretera de la Costa, La Cienaga*). Fights (in season) are held on Saturday and Sunday nights, from 4 PM until the wee hours. If you want to take in a cockfight, you'll pay RD$500 for a front-row seat, RD$300 for a second-row seat; elsewhere, you'll pay RD$200 for a chair, or RD$75 for standing room.

HIKING & HORSEBACK RIDING

Horseback riding and hiking tours are popular with those who are fit and who want to have a real eco-experience. Since feet and hooves are the usual mode of locomotion in the mountains, certainly for those who live "in the bush," you'll have a chance to visit many small villages along the way and meet locals, who genuinely enjoy these visits. They may offer you coffee or fruit, a trademark is true Dominican hospitality since they have precious little for themselves. Guides can identify the different species of wild orchids and often do bird calls that attract beauties such as parrots, hummingbirds, papagayos, and even Hilgueros, which can make nine different sounds. You will also learn a little about how the residents live off the land and survive.

ECO-Tour Barahona (⊠ *Carretera Enriquillo, The Malecón, Edificio 8, Apt. 306, Paraiso* ☎ *809/243–1190, 809/395–1542 cell* ⊕ *www.eco-tour-repdom.com*) organizes such tours for all levels of trekkers, from greenhorn to advanced. Trips can be just a half-day (2 or 3 hours of walking or riding), a full day (5 to 8 hours), or several days, including camping at night. Hiking treks begin at $30 for a half-day tour without lunch to $50 for a full-day tour with lunch. Horseback riding begins at $40 for a half-day with no lunch, to $60 for a full day with lunch.

SHOPPING

The best products to buy in the southwest are indigenous and locally created. Different groups are spearheading artisan cooperatives and training programs to help the locals to help themselves.

In August 2007, a group of 12 females and one man formed La Asociación de Artesania de Paraìso, Arte Natural. Since May they had been meeting with Maya Matsuo, a volunteer of JICA (Japan's Agency of International Cooperation) that works with Fundeprocunipa. The group participated in the Festival of Organic Coffee in Polo during

Watch the Birdie

The national parks in the southwest part of the country provide the last remaining habitats for some 300 bird species in the Dominican Republic, including 30 that are endemic to Hispaniola. You have never seen anything like these Caribbean birds outside of an exotic pet store. Take the little tody, which has both a narrow- and broad-billed variety. These diminutive beauties are predominately green with red, pink, and yellow markings on white or gray breasts. They're very sweet.

Have you ever seen a parrot or parakeet out of captivity? Both the Hispaniolan parrot (*cotorra*) and its smaller cousin, the Hispaniolan parakeet (*perico*) can be sighted here. The Hispaniolan trogon (*papagayo*), which has a verdant green back and head, and gray chest that segues into ruby-red plumage, has a bright blue tail and is accented with black and white stripes on its wings. Should you see a low-flying vain hummingbird (*zumbador Cito*) suspended in motion over a fuchsia flower, you may need to catch your breath. Even more rare is his relative, the Antillean mango (*zumbador grande*); the male has a black mask, green face and throat, and purple tail. And then there are other birds normally associated with northern climes—owls, hawks, swallows, pigeons, quail-doves—though far more beautiful than their northern cousins, with vibrant colorings.

Birders come here in all sizes and shapes, from teenage students to fortysomethings and seniors. The ardent bird-watchers, including "twitchers," as some British aficionados are called, are in their own little feathered world here. They will arrive with tripods for their expensive cameras, not to mention equally expensive binoculars. Their floppy hats act as sunscreens. Of course, all true bird-watchers have their log books in which they record their sightings. They travel to exotic countries and spend thousands of dollars to be able to log views of nearly extinct species. The Dominican Republic—much of the Caribbean, actually—is a sleeper for bird-watching, often passed over for more well-known places like Costa Rica or Trinidad.

Expert guide, Kate Wallace is the Queen of the Bird-watchers. At an age when most well-brought up ladies are content to garden, she drives a four-wheel-drive vehicle like a professional truck driver at all hours of the morning and up steep mountain trails. Shepherding her people, she is deserving of respect as is the sport itself, which is certainly an activity with an eco-conscience.

the first weekend in June. Following that they exhibited and sold their products at the agency of ECO-Tours in Paraiso. In summer they sold their wares on certain days in various areas such as San Rafael Beach, and the River of Los Patos, where it meets the beach. They have now extended their market to Barahona, to the city's gift shops and restaurants.

One group of local artisans makes products under the label Arte Natural–Artisans of Paraiso, using only materials that are from the immediate area, including coconut, banana leaves, gourds, bamboo, coffee, rock, wood, feathers, palm leaves, and the like. Each member makes items in his or her own home, then the group meets periodically. Look for their label as you browse for gifts and souvenirs.

Melo Coffee (⊠*Anacaona 14, Barahona* ☎*809/524-2440*) is a family-owned company, and both the factory and offices of the company are here. Organic coffee is their business, and that is all they sell, beautifully packaged in dark green, one-pound bags for a mere RD$60. This beats taking home an ashtray with the name of the city. At **Taller Artesanal de Larimar Banesa** (⊠*Carretera Enriquillo 156, Bahoruco* ☎*829/401-8668 or 829/401-8591*) Mari and Cesar Feliz, who also only own and run the pharmacy in their little fishing village, sell their handmade larimar jewelry right in the little *farmacia*. Simple but attractive are the *bolitos* (necklaces of little larimar beads strung like pearls), which make perfect gifts for young girls. The larimar "eggs" make great paperweights. Many other designs are done with silver, and they also sell small wire sculptures.

NIGHTLIFE

In Barahona, nightlife consists mostly of local merengue clubs and discos in town and on the Malecón. Tourists should probably stick to the main restaurant and hotel bars unless accompanied by Dominican friends.

In *el campo* (the countryside), mostly on the weekends, evenings are spent at the *colmados* (little grocery stores, most with outdoor seating, on the coastal road). Locals can be seen drinking Presidente beer or *traigos* (shots of Dominican rum), eating plates of *pollo frito* (fried chicken) or *pescado frito* (fried fish) with tostones. Some of these turn into regional dance spots on weekends as well; during the week, you might see the same people watching a baseball game on TV. If you're looking for a good place to dance, ask any local or taxi driver, who can tell you about the best places and how to find them.

PEDERNALES

135 km (84 mi) southwest of Barahona; approximately 3 hours from Barahona by car

Pedernales is the name of the peninsula on the DR's southernmost shore where three national parks can be found. This is the biggest reason why eco-tourists are starting to gravitate here. The physical beauty and diversity of landscape is not inconsiderable. Pedernales is also the name of the town on the DR's border with Haiti, where the best of the natural sites are located, particularly in Parque Nacional Jaragua and the famous Bahía de Las Aguilas.

Much of the Pedernales region—namely Parque Nacional Jaragua and Parque Nacional Bahoruco—has been declared a Global Biosphere Reserve by UNESCO because of its vast and diverse habitats (a biosphere is an area of the planet where unique forms of earth, water, air, plants, and animals coexist). **Parque Nacional Jaragua** is one of three national parks in this region (the third is Lago Enriquillo). The park is named after a famous Taíno chief Jaragua, who defied the Spanish for more than a decade. (If you go on a guided trip, you can see some Taïno cave drawings.) Many scientists and hobbyists come here regularly for bird-watching, butterfly-watching, and even palm- (tree) watching. It's a place where you might spot flamingos, iguanas, and crocodiles, among other endemic, protected species in the surrounding lakes, mountains, rivers, and pristine beaches.

From Barahona to the park, you'll drive nearly 3 hours, from the small hotels in the Bahoruco/La Cienega area 2½ hours, from Los Patos 2 hours. There is now one decent hotel in Pedernales, where you can stay if traveling independently. It can beat getting up at dawn to make the drive. The park is a straight shot down Highway 44, the coastal road, from either Barahona or Pedernales. There's good signage for the entrance to the park as well as **Laguna de Oviedo**, about 1½ mi (3 km) from the little town of Oviedo.

The park occupies the southern part of the Pedernales Peninsula, with its stark and striking contrasts of seascapes and arid desertlike terrain, including a thorn forest, and there are marine turtles the greatest variety of bird species on the island of Hispaniola. The flocks of pink flamingoes that roam the shores of the Laguna de Oviedo on their spindly legs are the most photographed.

The park is a vast area of 1,500 square km (579 square mi), and to reach the interior you must have a strong, four-wheel-drive vehicle and a means of communication should you get stuck or break down. We strongly urge you not to attempt this trip on your own without the help of a seasoned guide or tour company.

When you arrive at the park's entrance, you'll be greeted by guides, who will direct you to parking and will line you up to get the boat tour to Laguna de Oveido, which takes about 3 hours. The cost of the boat trip is the same whether you have 2 people or 8, so it's cost-effective to buddy up with strangers. If you have time, climb the tower for a view of the shallow, brackish lagoon. It's best to arrive in the morning, between 8 and 9 AM before the wind gets up. The lagoon is so shallow that once you reach the mangroves, the boatman has to turn off the motor and push the boat. Yet, it's a wonderful way to quietly approach the flamingos and the roseate spoonbills, the pelicans, egrets, and frigate birds. Tours will take you to visit the flamingo colony, a couple of islets, and a cave with Taïno petroglyphs. The birds are more active at dawn, which means it's easier for you if you spend the night in Pedernales (see ⇨Where to Stay, *below*). The trip can include the south end of the lagoon, where the endemic iguana Ricordi, only found on Hispanola, can be seen. (Feed them only leaves, not any other snacks.) It's hot here, so bring plenty of water, sunscreen, and a hat.

The Alcoa Road, indicated by a park sign on the right, is one of the entrance points for the 800 square-km, mostly mountainous, **National Park Sierra de Bahoruco.** The intersection is actually about 10 km (6 mi) before the town of Pedernales. The road leads up to a pine forest and the site of the former bauxite mines. The view from the Hoyo de Pelempito of a wide rift valley is justly famous. The other entrance to the Sierra Park is on the north side, passing through Duverge on the south side of Lago Enriquillo, to Puerto Encondidio. This dusty road is also the entrance to Kate Wallace's camp. You must have a strong, four-wheel drive to get to see the wild orchids (some 166 species) and 49 species of birds (including the Hispaniolan parrots), in the pine forests of this interior park. It's definitely not advisable to do it on your own. Wallace's Tody Tours is one of the only recommendable alternatives.

At this writing, ECO-Tours of Barahona and Tody Tours offers excursions here, but two local guides' associations assisted by Peace Corps volunteers are also a possibility if you really want to go it alone (*see* ⇨ *Tour Options in Southwest Essentials, below*). ⊠ *Hwy. 44 W, 1½ mi (3 km) north of Oviedo* ⊠ *$3, $65 for tours of Laguna de Oviedo* ⊙ *Daily 8–5.*

WHERE TO STAY

If you don't want to get up at dawn to make the drive to Nacional Park Jaragua, there is now one recommendable, small hotel in Pedernales. It's simple, but owners Marino and Katya are welcoming and belong to the local eco-tourism organization. **Hostal Doña Chava** (⊠ *Calle 2da, Barrio Alcoa, Pedernales* ☎ *809/524–0332* ⊕ *www.donachava.com* ✆ *hostalchava@hotmail.com*) charges about RD$650 per night for a double. The Web site (in English) doesn't always work, but the e-mail usually does.

BEACHES

Bahía de Las Aguillas. This gorgeous white-sand beach may very well rank among the best you'll ever see, and it's reachable only by boat from the fishing village of Las Cuevas, south of Cabo Rojo, or by a difficult overland route that is not recommended for the inexperienced. Granted this is not for those who require fancy amenities. This is a pristine, isolated beach with absolutely no facilities, so bring a cooler of drinks, food, and whatever else you might need. But if you come prepared, you can spend a blissful couple of hours here.

The unmarked dirt road to Cabo Rojo is approximately 12 km (7.4 mi) east of Pedernales, off the highway to Oviedo. You'll first pass the limestone and cement plant; if you continue about 6 km (3.7 mi), you'll reach the town of Cabo Rojo; after another 10 minutes or so (approximately ½ mi), you'll reach the fishing village of Las Cuevas, and it's here that fishing boats can take you to the beach. Expect to pay $60 (but try bargaining); agree on a time the fisherman will return to pick you up. Offer to pay one-half on arrival and one-half when he picks you up. Las Cuevas also has a boat-rental operation and a decent seafood restaurant. The beach is also reachable by road if you have a 4x4 vehicle, but be sure to ask a local in Las Cuevas how to get there, and we highly recommend you do not take this route unless you're experienced driving in the area. If you don't want to make the trip unescorted, both AGUINAPE and ECO-Tours offer organized excursions (*see* ⇨ *Tour Options in Southwest Essentials, below*). At this writing, a new tourist center was expected to open in 2008 in Cabo Rojo, and you'll be able to arrange transportation there when it's open.

✉*Approx. 6.4 km (4 mi) south of Cabo Robo, 3 km (1.6 mi) south of Las Cuevas.*

Bahía El Cabo Rojo. This is the kind of unspoiled beach that Caribbean dreams are made of, with turquoise water and golden sand, where you can lay back and watch the pelicans dive for their dinner. You'll have to bring yours, for there are no facilities, just mangroves and dry thorn scrubs. If you're into beachcombing, you'll find more conch shells than you can carry. ✉*Hwy. 44, 12 km (7 km) east of, approximately 2 hrs, from Barahona.*

Playa Los Patos. This beautifully long beach is bisected by a river and well-populated with Dominican and international tourists every weekend. During the week, you may see the ladies of this poor *pueblito* bathing their children and doing their laundry in this, the shortest river in the Caribbean. Bordering the river is a row of colorful cooking shacks with names scrawled on the side. Consistently recommendable is Pulla, the fish-and-fried-potatoes queen. ✉*Hwy. 44, Los Patos ✛7 km (4 mi) south of Paraiso.*

Playa Paraiso. Bordering the main *calle* of this town, this is a good long beach, though it can be littered. Modern mid-rise apartment buildings face the beach, which attracts a fun, young crowd of expats, particularly Habitat for Humanities volunteers. ECO-Tours of Barahona has its main headquarters for the region in Paraiso. ✉*Hwy. 44, Paraiso ✛16 km (10 mi) south of San Rafael.*

SHOPPING

Marianne's Gift Shop (✉*Edificio 7, 2nd fl. left, Malecón de Paraiso, in office of ECO-Tour Barahona, Paraiso* ☎*809/243–1190, 809/395–1542 cell*) is run by Marianne Messmer, a French woman with a good sense of design, who sells handmade larimar jewelry as well as crafts made from such natural materials as coconut, banana leaves, and natural seeds from the region. She spearheads a cooperative group of local women, showing them how they can be productive artisans. Her shop is open from 10 to 6 daily.

LAGO ENRIQUILLO

Approx. 129 km (80 mi); approximately 2½ hours by car

La Descubierta is your gateway to Lago Enriquillo and a good shopping destination for local wares and, if you're lucky, Haiti's Barbancourt Rum. Organized tours to the lake do not stop in the town, but if you're driving, you may want to take a look, though it's hardly a life experience. Although the cold, natural pool of Las Barias Balneario, which is across the street from the town park, we recommend that you not swim in the water because of the possibility of disease, though Dominicans swim with few worries.

Lago Enriquillo. The largest lake in the Antilles is on an arid plain outlined by craggy mountains near the Haitian border. The saltwater lake is also the lowest point in the Antilles: 114 feet below sea level. It encircles wild, arid, and thorny islands that serve as sanctuaries for such exotic birds and reptiles as flamingos, iguanas, and—the indigenous American crocodile, which are said to number close to 500. It's an eerie place, where dead trees poke up from the salty water. Your best chance of seeing a croc is at dawn during the dry season between January and June. Flamingo sightings are more likely during their migration season, from April to July; after that, the lake level becomes higher, and the flamingoes decamp to the Bahamas (there are very few crocs visible as well).

Isla Cabritos Parque Nacional is a small island within Lago Enriquillo that is the habitat for hundreds of iguanas, as well as their larger cousins, American crocodiles. The word *cabritos* means little goats, and they roam the island, as do donkeys. You may see the droppings, but you will rarely see the goats or donkeys on a visit. Boats to the island leave from the national park dock in the town of Descubierta. The only facility on the island is a little green, wooden casita, where the island's history, the flora, and the wildlife are explained in detail in Spanish and in graphics. For independent travelers, a boat trip to the island is RD$3,500 (about $100), regardless of the size of the group. If you can wait for a sizable group, the price can be reduced to about $10 per person. The trip to the island takes an hour; the best time to pull together a group is in the morning—whatever size the group, be it 2 persons or 15. But you might have to wait some time for a group to come together. ECO-Tours runs organized trips to the island as well, which will allow you to book ahead (*see* ⇨ *Tour Options in Southwest Essentials, below*).■TIP➡ **There is shade and a couple of picnic tables on the island, but the island itself can be monstrously hot. Bring sunglasses, sunscreen, a long-sleeve shirt, insect repellent, and closed-toe shoes (there are a lot of burrs and cacti) for your trip. The national park (though not the island) has primitive restrooms, but bring your own toilet paper. The Association of Eco-Tourism Guides of Lago Enriquillo offers information on visiting the lake on its Web site.** ✉*Hwy. 48, 3 km (1.8 mi) east of Descubierta, on northwestern shore of Lago Enriquillo* ☎*809/816–7441 for Association of Eco-Tourism Guides of Lago Enriquillo* ⊕*www. lagoenriquilloguides.com* ✆*US$3* ☉*Daily 8–5.*

WHERE TO STAY

The drive from Barahona to La Descubierta is approximately 2½ hours. If you drive yourself and are too exhausted to make it back to your hotel, there are five very basic places to spend the night in La Descubierta; however, only two are recommendable. Both are simple, Dominican-owned hotels, so don't expect anything fancy. But you'll have a private room, possibly a private bath, a fan (perhaps a/c), and a friendly staff. Both hotels have emergency back-up generators to deal with power outages, which are not uncommon. Restaurants also keep it simple, serving rice and beans, empanadas, and fried chicken but little else. The Association of Eco-Tourism Guides of Lago Enriquillo can help you make reservations at one of the local hotels if you don't speak Spanish.

Hotel Iguana (⊠ *On main road west of park, LaDescubierta* ☏ *809/301–4815*) is the best of the local options and they can make you lunch or dinner if you notify them in advance. A room (no hot water) costs between RD$300 and RD$500; breakfast, lunch, or dinner is extra. **Mi Pequeño Hotel** (⊠ *Calle Padre Bellini, next to central park, La Descubierta* ☏ *809/762–6329 or 809/243–1080*) is an acceptable alternative to Hotel Iguana, although it's noisier because it's next to La Descubierta disco Saturday Night Fever. A double-room here costs about RD$400, but the hotel serves only breakfast.

SOUTHWEST ESSENTIALS

AIR TRANSPORT

Aeropuerto Internacional Maria Montez in Barahona is only open for charter flights. Unless you're paying the big bucks, you'll be flying into Santo Domingo first, and then making the three-plus-hour drive from there.

BUS TRANSPORT

Caribe Tours leaves from its terminal in Santo Domingo four times daily, with service to the town of Barahona; at this writing there were buses at 6:15, 9:45, 1:45, and 5:15; all stop in Azua; returns are at the same times from Barahona. The cost is a modest RD$220, but this is considered first-class transportation in these parts; it even has a bathroom (but bring your own paper, wipes, and hand sanitizer because the water in the sink never runs). The a/c on these buses is strong, so be prepared for the cold. The 3½-hour drive is reasonably efficient, not that much longer than driving yourself.

Information **Caribe Tours** (⊠ *Av. 27 de Febrero and Leopoldo Navarro, Santo Domingo* ☏ *809/521–5088 or 809/221–4422* ⊠ *Av. Uruguay and Calle Maria Montenez , Barahona* ☏ *809/524–4952* ⊕ *www.caribetours.com.do*).

CAR TRANSPORT

About half of the region's tourists rent a car and tour the area for three to five days, picking up their cars in Santo Domingo or at the airport. At this writing there are no rental-car agencies in the Barahona area, so you must pick up a car before coming into the Barahona area. For more information, *see* ⇨ Car Rentals *in* Santo Domingo Essentials, *below*. ⚠ **CAUTION Do not attempt to drive the nearly four hours from Santo Domingo to the Southwest after dark. If you arrive in Santo Domingo in the afternoon or evening, stay in a reasonably priced hotel and head out in the morning, whether by rental car or by bus. The truly scenic journey to Barahona by day is a treacherous run on unlighted, unfamiliar roads after dark. Livestock wander the roads as if they were pasture land.**

GUA-GUA TRANSPORT

Gua-guas are the local buses, which are actually white or beige mini-vans that can pack 'em in like chickens in a coop. They run hourly to Santo Domingo and have a/c but no bathrooms. Expect to pay about half the price of a Caribe Tours bus, but take one only in a desperate emergency.

They are a different story for shorter trips. The cost of one trip is about RD$5 to RD$10, and they offer a viable way to get between the little towns. In Barahona they leave from the east end of the central park, on Avenida 27 de Febrero. In the small towns, just stand on the side of the highway and wave them down.

INTERNET

Cybernet has the best Internet service in Barahona, with a bank of computers; it's conveniently open from 8 AM to 9 PM and charges about $1.25 per hour. Guanaba.net is an Internet center in La Cienega with nine computers, which have Skype to make Internet calls; it's open from 8:30 AM to 7:30 PM from Monday through Saturday, from 8:30 to 3 on Sunday. Expect to pay about $1 per hour.

Information **Cybernet** (✉ *Av. Uruguay, between Calles Cabral and Messon, Barahona*). **Guanaba.net** (✉ *Calle Duarte 35, across from Catholic Church, La Cienega).*

TAXI TRANSPORT

If you don't want to do the driving but still want a private transfer to the southwest, you can hire a taxi. Expect to pay at least $180 plus tip. If you take a tour with ECO-Tours or another company, transportation may be included. Don't expect to be able to arrange transportation if you arrive late in the day, or especially after dark.

Once you get to Barahona, taxis are not particularly organized. There are no metered cabs, and all of them seem to be on their last axle. If you arrive on the Caribe Tours bus with luggage, expect to pay RD$300 to RD$400 to get to the towns of Juan Esteban, Bahoruco, or La Cienaga, RD$600 to Los Patos. In town, you should have to pay only RD$100.

Once up in the countryside, the hotels have their trusted drivers who they will call on their cell phones for you. In La Cienega, there's a taxi stand where they all hang out right as you get into the town on the highway.

Moto conchos are motorcycle taxis—half the price and twice the risk. They are usually in bad condition, just like the car taxis. In Barahona they can be found at the central park, in front of Los Robles restaurant and along Avenida Luis E. Delmonte. In the country, you just flag them down, but if they stop and are going where you want to go, then they are for hire. Ask at your lodging what the fare should be.

TOUR OPTIONS

Aguinape is made up of experienced youths eager to provide services, who offer guide services for Bahía de las Aguillas; some are college students, athletes, and those active in their churches. They have taken classes with birding expert, Kate Wallace. The guides only speak Spanish, but a Peace Corps volunteer is usually available to go as a translator. Some of the young people are taking English classes.

Lago Enriquillo is once again a worthy destination, and a Peace Corps volunteer has worked to help set up the relatively new Association of

Eco-Tourism Guides of Lago Enriquillo, many of whom previously were with the Parks Department. Before the guide association was created there were only two boats on Lago Enriquillo, a small one (10 passengers), and a big one (25 passengers); now there's a third (15 passengers), and the guide association, which works in conjunction with ECO-Tour Barahona, does a creditable job of offering useful guided tours of the lake and Isla de Cabritos. Some tours visit a small Haitian village on the Dominican border called Mal Passe; it can be an upsetting experience to see the poverty on the other side of the border, but it's an experience nonetheless. The cost of these tours is RD$3,500 regardless of the size of the party, which is why it often pays to make advance arrangements through ECO-Tour Barahona to take a prearranged group tour; otherwise, show up in the morning and make your own arrangements once you can get a group together. The guide association can help you make local reservations if you're coming on your own from Barahona.

At this writing, there is only one full-service tour agency in the area, and it's a good one, owned by a French couple, Olivier and Marianne Messmer. For any of its full-day tours, ECO-Tour Barahona charges about $70 per person per day, including pick-up at your hotel, lunch (with nonalcoholic drinks), national park entrance fees, and boat tours (when applicable). Tours tend to be long (averaging 8 to 12 hours). The company employs English-, French-, and Spanish-speaking guides. This company organizes trips to all the national parks, Bahía de Las Aguillas, and Lago Enriquillo (also Isla de Cabritos).

Information AGUINAPE (☎ *809/214–1575* ⊕ *www.nuestrafrontera.org/aguinape/* ✍ *mrounsevilledrv@gmail.com*). **Association of Eco-Tourism Guides Lago Enriquillo Guides** (☎ *No phone* ⊕ *www.lagoenriquilloguides.com*). **ECO-Tour of Barahona** (✉ *Carretera Enriquillo, The Malecón, Edificio 8, Apt. 306, Paraiso* ☎ *809/243–1190 or 809/395–1542* ⊕ *www.ecotour-repdom.com*).

SANTO DOMINGO ESSENTIALS

To research prices, get advice from other travelers, and book travel arrangements, visit www.fodors.com.

TRANSPORTATION

BY AIR

Santo Domingo's Las Americas International Airport (SDQ), about 15 mi (34 km) east of Santo Domingo, has undergone many improvements since 2007, and giant color photos of smiling Dominicans now welcome visitors. It's still a major international destination, with many daily flights from the United States. Though much improved, it's still busy, and you really must allow a full two hours to check-in for an international flight.

La Isabela International Airport (JBQ), which opened in 2006 in Higuero, a northern Santo Domingo suburb, is the capital's domestic airport, servicing mostly intra-D.R. and charter flights.

For more information on flights to the Dominican Republic, see ⇨ By Air in the Transportation section in Dominican Republic Essentials.

AIRPORT TRANSFERS

If you book a package through a travel agent, your airport transfers will almost certainly be included in the price you pay. Look for your company's sign as you exit baggage claim. If you book independently, then you may have to take a taxi (approximately $40 for two persons whether you're going to Las Américas or La Isabela airport) or rent a car. Caribe Tours now has a bus that goes from the airport to downtown Santo Domingo for $10, if you're not burdened by much luggage. Prieto Tours also offers an airport shuttle service ($18 per person to Las Américas, $20 to La Isabela), with a minimum of two people; you must reserve this service in advance by phone or e-mail and pay in advance with a credit card. A private driver is also an option.

Airports **Las Américas International Airport** (*SDQ* ✉ *Santo Domingo* ☎ *809/412–5888*). **La Isabela International Airport** (*JBQ* ✉ *Higuero* ☎ *809/476–8152*).

Airport Transfers **Caribe Tours** (✉ *Av. 27 Febrero, esq. Leopoldo Navarro, Naco* ☎ *09/221–4422* ⊕ *www.caribetours.com.do*). **Prieto Tours** (✉ *Av. Francia 125, Gazcue* ☎ *809/685–0102* ✎ *resevas@prieto-tours.com*).

BY BUS

Privately owned, air-conditioned buses are the cheapest way to move around the country, and most of these originate in Santo Domingo. *For more information on bus travel in the Dominican Republic, see ⇨ By Bus in the Transportation section in Dominican Republic Essentials.*

BY CAR

You do not want a car in Santo Domingo, where both parking and traffic are very problematic, but you can rent a car in Santo Domingo to explore the country at your own pace. Most major car-rental companies have outlets at Las Américas Airport outside Santo Domingo since this is the airport of choice for most independent travelers who are likely to rent cars.

You can expect to pay as little as $55 for a manual compact car, $85 for an automatic with insurance, or $125 for an SUV from a major like Budget. You may also save money by renting from a local agency, but some travelers prefer the comfort of renting from a known quantity. It's usually cheaper to book your car in advance or book in conjunction with your hotel stay. If you want to rent a car for a day, you can often do so at a car-rental desk at your hotel and have it delivered.

Local Agencies **MC Auto Rental Car** (✉ *Las Américas Airport* ☎ *809/549–8911* ⊕ *www.mccarrental.com*). **Nelly Rent-a-Car** (✉ *Las Américas Airport* ☎ *809/530–0036, 800/526–6684 in U.S.*)

Major Agencies **Avis** (✉ *Las Américas Airport* ☎ *809/549–0468*). **Budget** (✉ *Las Américas Airport* ☎ *809/549–0351*). **Europcar** (✉ *Las Américas Airport*

☎ *809/549–0942*). **Hertz** (✉ *Las Américas Airport* ☎ *809/549–0454* ✉ *Santo Domingo*).

BY PUBLIC TRANSPORTATION

Public transit is not one of Santo Domingo's strong points. A system of local buses called *gua-guas* runs through the city. They're less than wonderful, walking being so much more enjoyable. Should you want to brave them—and, yes, they will get you out to Juan Dolio and Boca Chica beaches for a fraction of what a taxi costs—your hotel staffers will be able to tell you where the nearest stops are.

Similarly, there are *publicos,* beat-up old cars that drive the main drags picking up as many people as they can squeeze into a regular size car— seven, eight, or more. Even though it may not seem too bad, if you're one of the first ones in, as it goes along it will get progressively more crowded until you will want to jump out, no matter where you are.

A brand-new metro is scheduled to begin service at this writing in late 2008, though it will have only a handful of stops to begin with (and none in the Zona Colonial).

BY TAXI

Taxis, which are government regulated, line up outside hotels and restaurants. They're unmetered, and the minimum fare is about $4, but you can bargain for less if you order a taxi away from the major hotels. Though they're more expensive, hotel taxis are the nicest and the safest option. Freelance taxis aren't allowed to pick up from hotels, so they hang out on the street in front of them and can be half the cost per ride (over a hotel taxi) depending on the distance. Carry some small bills because drivers rarely seem to have change.

Recommendable radio-taxi companies in Santo Domingo are Tecni-Taxi (which also operates in Puerto Plata) and Apolo. Tecni is the cheapest, quoting RD$80 as a minimum per trip, Apolo RD$90. Hiring a taxi by the hour—with unlimited stops and a minimum of two hours—is often a better option if you're doing a substantial sightseeing trip. Tecni charges RD$240 per hour but will offer hourly rates only before 6 PM; Apolo charges RD$280 per hour, day or night. When booking an hourly rate, be sure to establish clearly the time that you start. There are also set rates to most out-of-town locations. Call Tecni-Taxi for a rate quote.

Information **Apolo Taxi** (☎ *809/537–0000, 809/537–1245 for a limo, must be booked far in advance*). **Tecni-Taxi** (☎ *809/567–2010, 809/566–7272 in Santo Domingo*).

CONTACTS & RESOURCES

BANKS & EXCHANGE SERVICES

You may need to change some money, particularly if you plan to spend any amount of time in Santo Domingo. The coin of the realm is the Dominican peso (written RD$). At this writing, the exchange rate was approximately RD$34 to US$1.

Independent merchants willingly accept U.S. dollars, because the peso can fluctuate wildly in value. However, change will be in pesos. You can find *cambios* (currency exchange offices) at the airport, as well as on the street, and in major shopping centers. A passport is usually required to cash traveler's checks, if they're taken. Save some of the official receipts with the exchange transaction, so if you end up with too many pesos when you're ready to leave the country, you can turn them in for dollars. Some hotels provide exchange services, but, as a rule, hotels and restaurants will not give you favorable rates—casino cages are better. Banco Popular has many locations throughout Santo Domingo, and its ATMs accept international cards, though you can get only pesos. Major credit cards (American Express not as often) are accepted at most hotels, large stores, and restaurants.

BUSINESS HOURS
Banks are open weekdays from 8:30 to 4:30. Post offices are open weekdays from 7:30 to 2:30. Offices and shops are open weekdays from 8 to noon and 2 to 6, Saturday from 8 to noon. About half the stores stay open all day, no longer closing for a midday siesta.

EMERGENCIES
Emergency Services **Ambulance & Fire & Police Emergencies** (☎ *911*). **Politur (Tourist Police Department)** (⊠ *Calle El Conde at Jose Reyes, Zona Colonial* ☎ *809/686–8639 or 809/221–4660*) officers speak English and are trained to deal with tourists.

Medical Clinics **Centro Médico Universidad Central del Este** (⊠ *Av. Máximo Gómez 68, La Esperilla* ☎ *809/221–0171*). **Clínica Abreu** (⊠ *Av Independencia, corner Calle Delegado, Gazcue* ☎ *809/688–4411 or 809/687–9654*). **Clínica Gómez Patino** (⊠ *Av. Independencia 701, Gazcue* ☎ *809/685–9131*).

24-hour Pharmacies **Farmacia San Judas Tadeo** (⊠ *Av. Independencia 57, Gazcue* ☎ *809/685–8165*). **Farmacia Vivian** (⊠ *Av. Independencia at Delgado, Gazcue* ☎ *809/221–2000*).

INTERNET, MAIL & SHIPPING
If you plan to send packages home, it's safer to use an international courier. FedEx has an office in Santo Domingo. EPS, a local courier service, helps to offset the limitations of the regular mail service in the D.R.; though not as quick as FedEx, it's certainly better and more reliable than the regular mail.

Paid Internet access of some kind is available in almost every hotel, though you may sometimes have access to only one slow and old terminal in the lobby, maybe with a Spanish keyboard. Wi-Fi is becoming more prevalent in the better hotels even the smaller boutique properties; it's usually free but generally exists only in the lobby and some public areas, rather than in your room, but that is slowly coming. There are dozens of Internet cafés in Santo Domingo, particularly on Calle El Conde. Look up; they're generally on the second stories.

Post Offices **Main Post Office** (⊠ *Isabel la Católica, across from Parque Colón, Zona Colonial*).

Shipping Companies EPS (⊠ *Calle Ortega Gaset, corner Calle Fantino Falco, Santo Domingo* ☎ *809/540–4005 or 800/200–5177*).

FedEx (⊠ *Av. de los Próceres, at Camino del Oeste* ☎ *809/565–3636 or 809/200–3138*).

Internet Cafés Centro de Internet (⊠ *Av Independencia 201, Gazcue* ☎ *809/238–5149*). **Connexion Internet** (⊠ *Calle El Conde, corner of Calle Espaillat, Zona Colonial* ☎ *809/689–6154*).

TOUR OPTIONS

When planning a city tour or investigating one farther afield, do make certain that you're aware of how much time is involved. For example, local tour companies sell city visitors excursions to La Catalina. They typically leave at 6:30 AM and return some 12 hours later! It can take you three hours just to get to where the boat disembarks, because you will usually have a long stop at least one area all-inclusive resort. You arrive back in the city, exhausted, at nearly 7 PM, and you will pay about $130. Forget about it!

New is the Audio Guide, a self-guided walking tour of the Zona Colonial. For US$30 you get information about 25 historical sights, admission to three museums and a nonalcoholic beverage at Hard Rock Cafe, and you get to walk at your own pace. The company targets cruise-ship passengers with its booth at the cruise pier, but anyone with a major credit card can rent the audio tour.

DomRep Tours, a European-owned travel agency, specializes in individual tours and eco-adventures—even to Jarabacoa and Barahona. With an office in the Zona Colonial, the company even offers city-breaks of two or three nights, including airport transfers, hotels, tours, and lunch. Guided private tours of the historical sights in the Zone are available as well as tours to the nearby beaches and sights, including some multiday trips.

EcodoTours, as the name implies, specializes in eco-adventures but also brings groups into the capital for city tours and will pick up individual travelers at their hotels. One excellent option this company offers is a "Santo Domingo Night Tour." Included is a drink, two disco admissions, and time at a casino for $49, a good deal since taxis to all these places can easily cost $40.

An agent for American Express, the well-established Prieto Tours gives tours of the city and surrounding area in English. For the latter, these large bus tours usually include guests from the all-inclusive resorts outside of the city. The company offers a good three-hour tour of the Zona Colonial for about US$25. If you have the stamina a six-hour tour takes in the Zone, El Faro, the Aquarium, and "modern" Santo Domingo, including lunch, museum entrances, and an hour of shopping time for your US$50.

A relatively new company, specializing in educational, adventure and incentive programs for groups, is Tours, Trips, Treks & Travel, founded by a veteran Iguana Mamas trip leader. Although based in Cabarete, the company will come into Santo Domingo and is especially good at helping to organize cultural excursions.

Private tour guides are another option, and you'll have to pay approximately $125 a day for a guide (more if the guide uses a private driver). Your hotel concierge will know the good English-speaking guides, though you may pay more than if you organized the tour yourself. Dré Broeders is a multilingual, licensed tour guide with 16 years of experience in the D.R. and can give a customized tour for two people or a group. His late-model car is clean and well-maintained, and he is very reliable. He will also pick up passengers from any of the area airports and bring them to any destination on the southeast coast. Although he lives in Juan Dolio, he's an expert on the Colonial Zone and runs a great tour.

Kate Wallace, a recognized birding authority who leads tours in various parts of the country, will lead private bird-watching tours in the Jardin Botanico Nacional Dr. Rafael M. Moscoso.

Information **Audio Guide** (✉ *Don Diego Cruise Terminal, Av. del Porto, Zona Colonial* ☎ *809/221–2221 for CTN television network*). **DomRep Tours** (✉ *Plaza Paseo del Conde, Calle El Conde 360 , Zona Colonial* ☎ *809/686–0278, 829/367–7421 cell* ⊕ *www.domreptours.com*). **Dré Broeders** (☎ *809/526–3533, 809/399–5766 cell* ✐ *drebroeders@hotmail.com or peralta162@gmail.com*).

EcodoTours (☎ *809/815–1074* ⊕ *www.ecodotours.com*). **Kate Wallace** (☎ *809/686–0882* ✐ *katetody@gmail.com*). **Prieto Tours** (✉ *Av. Francia 125, Gazcue* ☎ *809/685–0102* ⊕ *www.prietotours.com*). **Tours, Trips, Treks & Travel** (✉ *Cabarete* ☎ *809/867–8884 in Cabarete* ⊕ *www.4Tdomrep.com*).

VISITOR INFORMATION

Information **Dominican Tourism Office** (✉ *Palacio Bortello, Isabel la Catolica 103, across from Parque Colón, Zona Colonial* ☎ *809/686–3858* ⏱ *Mon.–Sat. 9–3*).

The Southeast Coast

BOCA CHICA, JUAN DOLIO, LA ROMANA, BAYAHIBE

WORD OF MOUTH

" We went to Casa de Campo because my [father-in-law] is an avid golfer and he has been there about two dozen times . . . Teeth of the Dog is a stunning course."

—Rabbit

By Eileen
Robinson
Smith

LAS AMÉRICAS HIGHWAY—BUILT BY THE dictator Trujillo so his son could race his sports cars—runs east along the coast from Santo Domingo to La Romana, nearly a two-hour drive. This highway changes names along the way and eventually becomes Highway 3 in La Romana. Midway are Santo Domingo's nearest long-established beach resorts, Boca Chica and Juan Dolio. The latter is undergoing an astounding renaissance at this writing, with major beach rejuvenation and new high-end condo developments; it may very well be poised to become the Caribbean's answer to Miami's South Beach.

Boca Chica, on the other hand, has been left to the low-budget travelers looking for cheap, all-inclusive resorts and sex tourists. Baseball fans may want to make a pilgrimage to Sammy Sosa's hometown, San Pedro de Macorís. Vestiges remain from its heyday in the early 20th century, when it was a thriving port and center of culture.

Sugar was king in the area surrounding the typical Dominican city of La Romana before it was made famous by the megagolf resort Casa de Campo.To its credit, Casa continues to reinvent itself. In the new millennium, Marina Chavón was born, and although skeptics thought it would be overkill—that there was not the demand in this area of the Caribbean from either sailboats or motor yachts to warrant such an extravagant facility—it has been so successful that an expansion was necessary.

Due east of La Romana is Bayahibe Bay, where you can find a handful of all-inclusive resorts, including several on Playa Dominicus, a glorious beach in an area originally settled by Italians, who introduced the locals to tourism. The beaches come as long, unbroken stretches and also as half-moons. This region is more and more becoming a less frenetic and more attractive alternative to the high-density tourist zone of the "far" east, that is, Punta Cana and Bávaro.

EXPLORING THE SOUTHEAST COAST

You can plot your course depending on which area of the southeast coast you choose to stay. One possibility is to break up your stay with half of your days spent in the Juan Dolio area, from where you can make easy forays into the capital and tour the Colonial Zone, take lunch at one of the great seafood restaurants in Boca Chica's beach, and dive the sites in the area. If you spend half of your time in La Romana or the Bayahibe/Dominicus area, you can take wonderful excursions, particularly to the islands that are in that region.

ABOUT THE RESTAURANTS

Dining options in the southeast are as varied as the quality of the accommodations. You can eat like the locals in little side-of-the-road Dominican cafés, where you will always find *moro* (the traditional mixture of rice and beans). There are a good number of international and seafood restaurants on the waterfront in the town of (old) Juan Dolio and nearby Guyacanes.

Some of the region's most sophisticated dining is found at the Casa de Campo resort and in its Altos de Chavón and Marina Chavón. The little town of Bayahibe has a handful of seafood restaurants, some with French and or Italian influences. Of course, much of the food consumption goes on at the all-inclusive resorts. Food quality will vary among the resorts and even within each individual hotel, from their buffeterias to their à la carte restaurants, where the abundance of food is legendary.

ABOUT THE HOTELS

Accommodation options are equally as varied. Juan Dolio is filled with new mid-rise condominiums for rent, smack on the newly rejuvenated beachfront; if you go across the street from the beach, you'll save money and find accommodations that are just as nice. A couple of all-inclusives still operate in Juan Dolio, and you can also find a few moderately priced apartments in town. The few inexpensive small hotels quickly fill up with backpackers, European retirees, and sex tourists. Boca Chica has lower-end all-inclusives that draw budget tourists. Casa de Campo dominates in La Romana (and has a new Four Seasons hotel on the way in 2009). There are nearly a half-dozen all-inclusive resorts in the Bayahibe/Dominicus area, as well as a few smaller inexpensive hotels.

WHAT IT COSTS IN DOLLARS					
	¢	$	$$	$$$	$$$$
Restaurants	under $8	$8–$12	$12–$20	$20–$30	Over $30
Hotels*	Under $80	$80–$150	$150–$250	$250–$350	Over $350
Hotels**	Under $125	$125–$250	$250–$350	$350–$450	Over $450

*EP, BP, CP **AI, FAP, MAP Restaurant prices are per person for a main course at dinner and do not include the 15% V.A.T. and 10% service charge. Hotel prices are per night for a double room in high season, excluding 15% V.A.T. and 10% service charge.

BOCA CHICA

34 km (21 mi) east of Santo Domingo, 13 km (8 mi) east of Las Américas International Airport.

The Boca Chica resort area is immediately east of Las Américas International Airport. A seasoned destination, Boca Chica is popular mainly with Dominicans and Europeans. Since it's the best beach area near Santo Domingo, it has long been popular with chic *capitaleños,* who considered this a chic place to sun and frolic on the light sand beach, their children splashing safely in the calmest of water. In the 1960s, when all beaches were declared public domain, the tide changed, and the scene went quickly downhill. The crowded, dusty town had become too boisterous and even raunchy, the nighttime scene dodgy and dangerous, with sex tourism being the primary reason. The good news is that now after 7 PM the city shuts down the main drag, Avenida Duarte, to vehicular traffic. So while there is still some daylight, it can be fun to

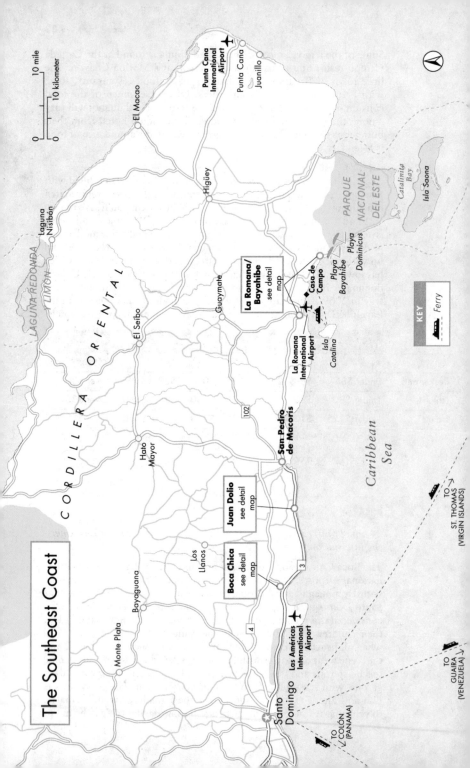

SOUTHEAST COAST TOP 5

Playing "The Teeth of the Dog."
The kings course of Casa de Campo continues to be ranked as one of the top golf courses in the Caribbean. Other great courses are at Guavaberry Resort and Metro Country Club.

An excursion to Altos de Chavón. This incredible re-creation of a 16th-century Italian hill town is filled with shops and restaurants.

Leisure time at Marina Chavón. Designed to look like the famed marina in Portofino, Casa de Campo's marina has been a yachting suc-cess and is a dining and shopping destination, too.

Diving La Caleta. Close to Juan Dolio, this underwater national park is considered one of the country's best sites.

Day trip to Isla Saona. Sail or speed out to this island to enjoy a day of sun and sea and snorkeling energized by a BBQ lunch buffet and rum libations. Playa Bayahibe is also a great beach if you want to stick closer to land.

have a cold beer at one of the makeshift bars, and rows of food stands sell cheap Dominican dishes, the best of which are fried fish (usually bones in) and *tostones*. Just be aware that hygiene is always a question mark at these stands.

WHERE TO EAT

Boca Chica is probably best enjoyed as a day trip from Santo Domingo, a chance to eat lunch, and swim in the sea. The trio of seafront restaurants that are the best of Boca Chica seem to be in a universal competition. Each is vying for a similar clientele of well-heeled *capitaleños* and repeat tourists, all of whom can be fickle in their tastes. If someone does it better—or splashier—they're on to the next place that is even more happening.

■TIP→ **An alternative to the restaurants recommended here is to buy a day-pass at the Oasis Hamaca Beach Resort for $55, which includes food, drinks, and access to the resort facilities and beach for the entire day. Although El Pelicano now belongs to the hotel, it's not a part of the resort's all-inclusive package. The resort does have several restaurants from which to choose, including a bountiful buffet, a seafront restaurant, and a beachside pizzeria.**

$$–$$$ ✕**Neptuno's Club.** Once a simple seafood spot, beautifully situated at the end of the pier—and owned by a grouchy German—Neptuno's is now trendy to the point of garishness. Not only is there draped white fabric everywhere, but also marine-blue sheer curtains. Cocktail seating is on white faux-leather couches. White is the color of the wood furnishings; the tables have blue cloths. The largest tables are around three huge Jacuzzis. A ladder goes down to the sea, but there are no chaises like you'll find nearby at Restaurant Boca Chica Marina. Most of the food is, of course, from the sea (and the prices are the highest of Boca Chica's trio of good restaurants). The menu includes sushi, a range of pastas,

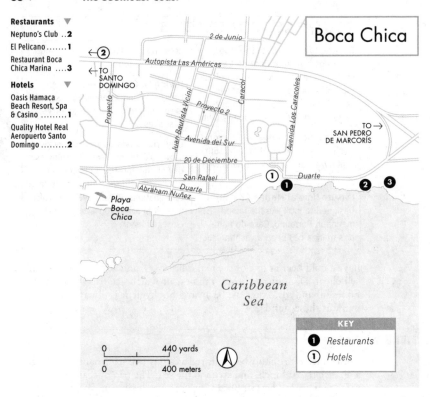

Boca Chica

grilled lobster, and even a few grilled meat offerings, as well as a host of sides, from risottos to grilled veggies. ✉ *Calle Duarte 12, Boca Chica* ☎ *809/ 523–4703* ▭ *AE, D, DC, MC, V.*

$–$$$ ✕**El Pelicano.** A fave over the years, this restaurant has evolved with the times. Now it has an expanded deck and a dozen or more chaises longues, and even Balinese sunbeds right in the gin-clear water. Here hip lounge music plays, but not so loud that it interferes with your fun. Begin with a mango daiquiri and establish your table under a market umbrella. While you wait for your order to arrive, float in a white hammock bed or jump in the shallow water. The best part is that this is the only one of the Boca Chica trio with a beach. Your food arrives on white geometric plates—and there are even linen napkins. Although the cuisine is not stellar, there are more hits than misses, including the mango and shrimp tempura with a wasabi vingairette. You might also want to consider the Bahamian conch or the squid with its own ink staining the rice. Any fresh fish on the *plancha* (grill) works—most certainly the garlicky lobster. Fifteen minutes from Las Americas Airport, this is an ideal place to endure a long layover. Enjoy your lunch, swim, sleep in the sun, and then shower in the clean locker rooms. Take a luscious hazelnut piña colada to go. ✉ *End of Calle Duarte, in front of*

Oasis Hamaca Beach Resort, Boca Chica ☎*809/523–4611 Ext. 830 or 747* ▭*AE, MC, V.*

$$–$$$ ✗**Restaurant Boca Chica Marina.** No, this is not a marina, but rather a ★ remarkable seafood restaurant that is presently the "in" spot for the young, fun, and moneyed locals and hip tourists. With a *nuevo* nautical theme, the whole restaurant is decorated with flowing white sails. Growing popularity has warranted an expansion, which means there are more chaise longues, Balinese sunbeds, and a second-floor dining room. If you want a primo table on the pier, try reserving one. Do bring your beach towel because you can jump in the sea (or descend by a ladder), but there is no beach here. Servers are semi-pros, and some are even semi-bilingual. Start with a baguette drizzled with olive oil and topped by quality Parmesan. The menu is vast with any manner and preparation of delectable *mariscos* (shellfish), from octopus to lobster, or you can have a perfectly grilled sea bass or red snapper fillet and a side of grilled veggies. The seafood is 100% fresh and local with the notable exception the excellent black tiger shrimp. And there's an admirable wine cave. ✉*Calle Duarte 12A* ☎*809/523–6702* ▭*AE, D, MC, V.*

WHERE TO STAY

Most of the properties in Boca Chica—virtually all one-star all-inclusive resorts—are not recommendable. The Hamaca (formerly the Coral Hamaca) is now owned by Spain's Globial Group, which has been working diligently to get the property back on track. The region has few, if any, hidden gems. Because the cheapest hotels and resorts are frequented by the *putas* and their johns, these are not where you want to be. The Quality Hotel is not strictly in Boca Chica, but rather adjacent to the airport free-trade zone, but its lack of a beachfront makes it less attractive to tourists and more to business travelers.

$$ 🏨**Oasis Hamaca Beach Resort, Spa & Casino.** When this resort opened ♺ back in the early 1990s, Boca Chica was brought to another level; then it plunged downward in quality. The Spanish group Globial bought the resort in 2006 and has begun to breathe life back into it. Among the highlights are a smashing new lobby bar with rustic wood slats, Mr. Roger's Bar overlooking the water, a beachside pizzeria, new deluxe spa, and a new casino, which has been relocated; pergolas with fabric have replaced beach umbrellas, and the Italian restaurant has an impressive new menu and beautiful decor. Breakfast is served at the beach. Beach rooms had been renovated, but garden rooms had not been finished at this writing. The crowd here is primarily European, especially Spanish (with a high volume of rowdy students), but Oasis wants and is courting the American market. If you're staying in the area a day or night pass is just $55. **Pros:** Roving trio serenades nightly in each restaurant, 24-hour service, some international liquors included. **Cons:** Low prices can draw a low-class clientele, high volume precludes real luxury or great service, beachside rooms with sea view are $30 to $40 extra. ✉*Calle Duarte, Box 2973, Boca Chica* ☎*809/523–6767 or 809/523–4611* ⊕*www.oasishotels.com* ⇥*588 rooms, 1 suite* ♿*In* *room: refrigerator. In-hotel: 6 restaurants, bars, tennis courts, pools, gym, spa, beachfront, diving, water sports, casino, children's programs (ages 4–12), public Internet, laundry services, parking (no fee)* ▭AE, MC, V ⏷AI.

$ ▦ **Quality Hotel Real Aeropuerto Santo Domingo.** This modern American chain is the closest hotel to Las Américas Airport and its adjacent Las Américas Free Zone industrial park, drawing both leisure and business travelers. The hotel is a welcoming sight to both expats and business people, sparkly clean and organized, with front desk staff in dark suit jackets over white shirts and ties. The only clue that you're in the Caribbean is the small outdoor pool and a thatch-roof gazebo. The modest lobby and public spaces are tastefully furnished with large mirrors and plantings. Guest rooms are not as appealing but are colorful, though unremarkable, and have much-appreciated irons and coffeemakers. The restaurant is not bad at all. Ask on arrival if a junior suite is available; you can sometimes get these for just $20 more per night. **Pros:** Freestanding spa with reasonable prices, free Internet and local calls, free American breakfast buffet. **Cons:** Not a true luxury property, though nice has a cookie-cutter feel, prices somewhat high compared to competition. ✉*Autopista Las Américas, Km 22.5, approximately 35 min east of Santo Domingo by car* ☎*809/549–2525* ⊕*www.gruporeal.com* ⇌*109 rooms, 15 suites* ♿*In-room: refrigerator, Ethernet; Wi-Fi (some). In-hotel: restaurant, room service, bar, pool, gym, spa, laundry facilities, laundry service, public Internet, public Wi-Fi, parking (no fee)* ▭AE, MC, V ⏷BP.

NIGHTLIFE

In Boca Chica you should stick to the nightlife in your hotel because this resort area is the nocturnal haunt of the *putas* and *putos*. It's pretty much ground zero for sex tourism in the D.R., a form of tourism we strongly discourage, not only because of its inherent illegality but also because of the dangers involved. Although the Politur (tourism police) are quite visible, crime—even the murders of European expats and tourists—have occurred in the Boca Chica area. If you're here at night, the newly renovated casino at the Hamaca is the closest thing to a safe haven.

BEACHES

Playa Boca Chica. You can walk far out into warm, calm, gin-clear waters protected by coral reefs. The strip with the rest of the mid-rise resorts is busy, particularly on weekends, drawing mainly Dominican families and some Europeans. But midweek is better, when the beaches are less crowded. One bad thing: if you choose to go to the public beach, you will be pestered and hounded by a parade of roving sellers of cheap jewelry and sunglasses, hair braiders, seafood cookers, ice-cream men, and masseuses (who are usually peddling more than a simple beach massage). Young male prostitutes also roam the beach and often hook up with older European and Cuban men. The best section of the public beach is in front of Don Emilio's (the blue hotel), which has a restaurant, bar, decent bathrooms, and parking. ⊠*Autopista Las Américas, 21 mi (34 km) east of Santo Domingo, Boca Chica.*

■TIP→ **Bring ear plugs. The Dominican Republic may be the noisiest country that you've ever visited. In addition to traffic noise, there's always high-volume Dominican music; by night, the music at the colmodons can be heard for a mile. And earplugs are almost impossible to buy in the D.R. Of course, an iPod can also help you drown out your surroundings.**

SPORTS & THE OUTDOORS

DIVING

Local dive aficionados will tell you that the south coast, including Boca Chica, Juan Dolio, Isla Catalina, and, most notably, the underwater national park La Caleta, offer the best diving in the country. La Caleta is a half-day trip from Boca Chica, and experienced divers can explore two sunken vessels—the *Limon,* a 115-foot tug boat, or the famous *Hickory,* a 130-foot freighter. Both lie in 60 feet of water. Isla Catalina requires a full day, but divers can discover black coral, huge sponges, and sea fans. (*For information on dive shops in the region, see* ⇨ *Diving under Sports & the Outdoors in Juan Dolio.*)

JUAN DOLIO

18 km (11 mi) east of Boca Chica, 52 km (32 mi) east of Santo Domingo, 78 km (48 mi) west of La Romana.

Like Boca Chica, Juan Dolio has a story of boom and bust. The resort area began life as a pristine beach and developed into *the* place to go on the southeast coast for sun and sea for residents of Santo Domingo, which is 40 minutes away. When the Europeans discovered it, the all-inclusive resorts started springing up. In the early 1990s, it was a pioneer in the all-inclusive concept, which caught on immediately, and no sooner was the blaze ignited than North Americans started to jump on it as well. But as soon as Punta Cana came online with its newer, more luxurious AIs and long expanses of palm-studded beach—with white sand at that—the *turistas* started to abandon Juan Dolio for the newer hot spot.

The resorts dropped their prices to try to stem the flood-tide of tourists heading farther east, but in doing so they had to cut food costs and service staff, the best of whom were already being recruited Punta Cana. As food went downhill and rooms became more shabby, Juan Dolio entered a years-long cycle of slow decline.

How things have changed. The year 2007 has brought the sounds of construction everywhere in Juan Dolio. And the beach here has been revitalized under a new program spearheaded by President Lionel Fernandez and the State Secretariat of Tourism. What a difference a "little" sand can make! It's now closer to Miami's South Beach than any other place in the D.R., which is finally striving to attract more chic tourists to its shores to supplement the bargain-basement, mass-market tourism of the past decade.

WHERE TO EAT

$–$$$ ✕ **Cala.** Like that gorgeous white lily, this restaurant has been called the
★   *flor de Juan Dolio*. And indeed it is a standout. A contemporary study
in white, the simple setting—from the outdoor terrace seating to the
pristine dining room to the impressive wine cave—invites you in, just
as the music draws you in. Gregarious owner, Michael Vega, who once
worked at Casa de Campo, runs a professional operation. Particularly
recommendable are the roasted red, yellow, and green peppers stuffed
with goat cheese blended with caramelized onions; filet mignon with
gorgonzola sauce and mashed potatoes green from puree of arugula;
and chocolate mousse with an unexpected yucca crust. ⊠ *Plaza Cas-
tilla, Blvd. Playa Juan Dolio, Villas del Mar, Juan Dolio* ☎ *809/526–
1108* ☴ *MC, V* ☉ *Closed Tues.*

$–$$ ✕ **DeliSwiss.** This small restaurant is owned by a veteran Swiss chef,
Walter Kleinerp, who is one of those interesting Caribbean characters
you usually only read about. Many diners come for the staggered terraces and the sounds, sight, and smells of the Caribbean just beyond.
The interior of the restaurant is dated and rather unimpressive—except
for the framed wine awards. The wine list itself is 22—yes, 22—pages,
but you'll get no written menu for the food. The cuisine is simple;
you can share a plate of European cheeses and meats from the deli
counter, including homemade bread and butter; or you can choose
the fishermen's daily catch in a perfect garlic sauce, an expensive lobster, or a meat such as pork tenderloin in a creamy peppercorn sauce.
If you make it to dessert—and you should—the German pastries are
a far-away dream: strawberry pie; stollen; pear cheesecake. ⊠ *Calle
Central 38, Guayacanes, Juan Dolio* ☎ *809/526–1226* ☴ *AE, MC, V*
☉ *Closed Mon. and Tues.*

$–$$ ✕ **Playa de la Pescador.** This restaurant's eastern European owner has
gained a loyal Euro clientele for eclectic cuisine washed down with
German and Belgian beers, grappa, cognacs, and good half-bottles on
the wine list. This rustic, two-story palapa offers romantic seating top-
side, on the sand, or in the open-air dining room. Pumpernickel bread
arrives with the well-priced, bilingual menu. Seafood comes off one
of the moored boats, so you can order the shellfish ceviche with con-
fidence. The mixed grilled shellfish is enough for two and can include
a lobster from the tank. Sunday is the big BBQ day, which is best
avoided. Lunch midweek is calm and you can find a chaise longue and
swim. Dinner waiters give the best service, but at breakfast the eggs
can come sunny-side up, just like the new day! You might walk in and
hear an Italian opera playing. Brava! ⊠ *Playa Guayacanes, Guyacanes*
☎ *809/526–2613, 809/862–8547 cell* ☴ *MC, V.*

$–$$$ ✕ **Restaurante Aura.** This hot, beach spot has been the buzz since it
opened in 2005, as it was the first to bring the South Beach experience
to Juan Dolio. The dining area is a large, thatched-roof structure, its
trendy white fabric tied back with a string of conch and sea shells. Try
relaxing on a partner chaise, a swinging beach bed, or a hedonistic
Balinese sunbed. On Sunday Aura is slammed, and sports cars and
luxury SUVs vie for parking spots in the lot. And, yes, the seafood is
good, from the *lambi* (conch) to the *langosta* (lobster), not to mention

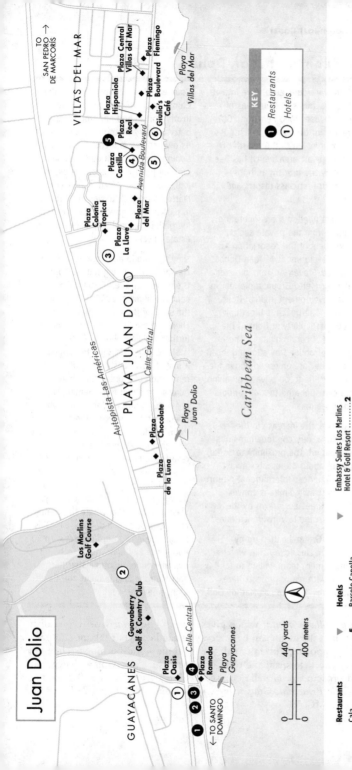

Juan Dolio

TO
SAN PEDRO →
DE MARCORÍS

VILLAS DEL MAR

Plaza
Hispaniola

Plaza Central
Villas del Mar

Plaza
Flemingo

Plaza
Castilla

Plaza
Real

Plaza
Boulevard

Giulia's
Café

Avenida Boulevard

Playa
Villas del Mar

Plaza
Colonia
Tropical

Plaza
La Llave

Plaza
del Mar

PLAYA JUAN DOLIO

Calle Central

Autopista Las Américas

Plaza
Chocolate

Plaza
de la Luna

Playa
Juan Dolio

Caribbean Sea

Los Marlins
Golf Course

Guavaberry
Golf & Country Club

Plaza
Oasis

Plaza
Ramada

Calle Central

GUAYACANES

← TO SANTO
DOMINGO

Playa
Guayacanes

KEY

1 Restaurants
① Hotels

0   440 yards
0   400 meters

Restaurants ▶
Cala 5
DeliSwiss 3
Playa de la Pescador 2
Restaurante Aura 1
Tommy's of Austria
at Cacique 4

Hotels ▶
Barcelo Capella
Beach Resort 3
Club Hemingway 5
Coral Park 4
Costa del Sol 6

Embassy Suites Los Marlins
Hotel & Golf Resort 2
Guesthouse Holland 1

3

The Rebirth of Juan Dolio

Children and adults alike were in awe as giant machines spit out tons of sand onto Juan Dolio beach in 2007. The rebirth of the beach, which goes for 2.5 mi, has led to the rebirth of the entire resort area, which has been targeted by the tourism authority as a site for first-class resorts and amenities.

The project needed the cooperation and funds from the private sector, and members of the Association for Tourism Development of Juan Dolio cooperated. Steven Ankrom, director of sales for Metro Group, a pioneer in upscale development in Juan Dolio, explained: "The beach is breathtaking now, particularly in front of the Costa del Sol condominiums. The government obliged by allowing local resorts to declare any sand above the high-water line to be private, meaning guests can sunbathe free of vendors and hair-braiders."

For families, the increase in the number of luxury condominums has been a big hit. The proximity to Santo Domingo (about 45 minutes away) and Las Américas International Airport (20 minutes away) means convenience. Retirees are drawn by the good prices and low insurance rates.

The Metro Group, headed up by visionary Dr. Luis Jose Asilis, was the first investment team willing to take a chance with major projects here, including the 18-hole Los Marlins Golf Course and adjacent Metro Country Club, which are now surrounded by luxury homes and apartments. Guavaberry Country Club has followed with its own course and country club, positioning the area as a golf destination, and not just for the *capitaleños*. The Embassy Suites, which is adjacent to Metro Country Club, was built in 2003 in part to offer good lodging for visiting golfers, as well as prospective real estate buyers.

Now the condo and condo-hotel construction is going full tilt. Metro Group opened their Costa del Sol condominiums in 2006, built from the shell of the former Metro Hotel. Their success has been a catalyst for further building. Next to Costa del Sol is Starfish Resorts' Club Hemingway, a mix of new construction and a total renovation of a preexisting hotel. Across the street from Hemingway's is a sister property, Coral Park, which offers tasteful two- and three-bedroom condos, nearly 50% of which are available for vacation rental. Other resorts are being built, including Maxim's Bungalows, which was slated at this writing to open in 2008. Another bourgeoning area is Guayacanes, just west of Juan Dolio, where the trendy restaurant Aura still dazzles. Las Olas, Metro's newest dream project with 16 floors and 227 apartments, is being built next door. Two miles farther east Metro is also building the Costa Blanca development.

the *parrillada mixta*, which gives you all your *mariscos* in one dish. Although the menu can be pricey, you can keep your tab more moderate by choosing a pizza or calzone from the wood-burning oven, a few of the excellent sushi and rolls, or a pasta (such as ravioli with eggplant and proscuitto). Nutella cheesecake is truly worth its $10 price tag. ✉ *Calle Principal, Guayacanes, Juan Dolio* ☎ *809/526–2319* 🖃 *AE, D, DC, MC, V.*

■TIP→ If you come to have lunch at Restaurante Aura, wear your bathing suit and pareo and bring a change of clothes and your shampoo. There are now showers in Aura's restrooms, which are a mix of contemporary fixtures and "rustic" materials. In the ladies' rooms, a 10-foot mirror artistically framed with conch and other shells will tell you if you're lookin' fine.

$-$$ ✗**Tommy's of Austria at Cacique.** This is one surprising find. Who would have guessed that behind an Austrian-owned bar of rather ill repute would be a beachfront restaurant run by another Austrian, Tommy Kreuzer, who serves up first-rate specialties from his homeland. Don't be intimidated by the blackboard specials in German; the menu itself is in five languages. One of the standouts is a humongous portion of baby pork roast with sauerkraut and caraway seeds and bread dumplings floating in jus. Any meat-and-potatoes lover will relish the pounded fillet of beef with peppers, dark brown gravy, and perfect fried potatoes. Other carnivores' dreams include the boiled beef and horseradish sauce and calves liver and onions. Tommy fixes pasta and the requisite seafood, but aren't you here for the Wiener schnitzel? ⊠ *Calle Principal, Playa Juan Dolio, Juan Dolio* ☎ *809/848–5306* ▭ *No credit cards* ⊙ *Closed Mon. and Tues. No lunch.*

WHERE TO STAY

VILLAS & CONDOS

When renting an apartment in the Juan Dolio area, be sure to ask about proximity to the beach (it's safer the closer you are), if an apartment building has an elevator (not all of them do), and if there are wrought-iron gates on doors and or windows (you want them for security reasons).

Ana-Christina Peralta (⊠ *Residencial Marie Michell 104, Juan Dolio* ☎ *809/526–3533, 809/399–5766 cell* ⊕ *www.guesthouse-holland.net. ms* ✐ *peralta162@gmail.com*), who owns Guesthouse Hollande along with her husband, manages a roster of 18 apartments and houses, which can be rented by the day, week, or month. Prices range from a low of $500 per month for a simple studio to $1,200 per month for an upscale home with private pool and sea views. Prices include water and electricity (normally a hefty expense here). Many clients book online where they can opt for transfers from the airport, as well as excursions and private tours. Ana-Christina does not ask for a security deposit to hold an apartment or even an advance payment, but no credit cards are accepted.

NEED A BREAK? If you're staying in an apartment in Playa Juan Dolio and don't want to do your own cooking, you can take a break at little Hotel Fior Loto (⊠ *Carretera Vieja, Playa Juan Dolio, 2 blocks past taxi stand on opposite side of street, Juan Dolio* ☎ *809/526–1146*) with a tasty breakfast for RD$80. Mara Sandri, the Italian owner of the *hotelito*, is in love with India, and the decor reflects her love. Later in the day, pull up a chair and have a beer with the backpackers and Italian retirees that make up the interesting mix of guests.

Know Your Juan Dolios

Do you know how to tell one Juan Dolio from the other? Since its resurgence, Juan Dolio is actually made up of two almost completely different places now. Approaching from Santo Domingo, you'll first come across Guyacanes, which is an adjacent small fishing village that has some development. It's at the westernmost end of Juan Dolio's main drag, called Calle Principal, about 3 km (2 mi) before the old town proper. If you're going to Guyacanes, it's faster to travel by the highway.

The original town of Juan Dolio is about 3 km (2 mi) east of here and is signposted PLAYA JUAN DOLIO/GUYACANES.

Some call this area Old Juan Dolio, Juan Dolio West, Oasis (pronounced with a long O, short a, see), or even Oasis Plaza. The beach rejuvenation includes the lovely horseshoe-shape stretch of sand in front of the main waterfront restaurants on the older part of the resort area.

The area characterized by the most condo development is still farther east and is called Villas del Mar, but you may also hear people call it New Juan Dolio. If you're traveling on the highway look for the sign that says CLUB HEMINGWAY or the billboard for BARCELO CAPELLA, and you'll know you've found it.

$$$–$$$$
★
Club Hemingway. One of the earliest and most impressive of the region's luxury condo developments includes both the renovation of an older hotel (towers 1, 2, 3) and new construction dating to 2005 (towers 4, 5). All face a century-old coconut grove and the beach, which is now wide and soft. Big pluses for famlies are the infinity pool that segues into a children's pool, a movie theater in the clubhouse, a pizzeria, and kids' playground. Many condos in the rental pool are beautifully decorated; two-bedroom units have two baths, three-bedroom units have three baths; daily maid service is available for an additional fee. Part of the allure is the boardwalks and piers with a restaurant designed by architect Carlos Reid and his sister Patricia Reid that is open only to owners and renters. It has exquisite seafood and new wave Dominican specialties. **Pros:** Beach has a lifeguard and safe swimming area, all units have full kitchens with microwaves, all interiors are consistently good, whether in the renovated or newly built towers. **Cons:** No credit cards accepted (even at these rates), the cheapest two-bedroom has only a lateral sea view, only 70% of units have full sea views. ✉ *Blvd. Playa de Juan Dolio, Villas del Mar, Juan Dolio* ☎ *809/526–2202* 🛏 *108 2-bedroom condos; 12 3-bedroom condos* Ꮜ *No phone, VCR (some), Ethernet (some), Wi-Fi (some), daily maid service, on-site security, pool, tennis, gym, beachfront, laundry facilities (some), no-smoking (some)* ▤ *No credit cards* ⚲ *4-day minimum during high season and holiday periods.*

$$–$$$
Coral Park. Ritzier Club Hemingway's sister property is directly across the street, which means it does not have sea views or its own beach, but you can use all of Club Hemingway's facilities at about half the price of that more elaborate resort. This condo–apartment complex, which was a total renovation of a former hotel, does have elevators and its own

3

quiet pool secluded in a Mexican hacienda-style courtyard. Apartments are truly stylish, with beautiful decor, and include an open kitchen with microwave, balconies, and two flat-screen TVs; daily maid service costs extra. The complex has a barbecue area and kids playground. It's an excellent value for the money, particularly for two couples or families. Winter and summer are both considered high season here. **Pros:** Good bedding, each apartment has an additional maid's room (big enough for kids), complex has an electrical generator. **Cons:** Cash only, no bathtubs, the higher the floor the more expensive but still no sea views. ⊠ *Blvd. Playa de Juan Dolio 1, Villas del Mar, Juan Dolio* ⇨ *12 1-bedroom condos, 16 2-bedroom condos* △*No phone, VCR (some), Ethernet (some), Wi-Fi (some), daily maid service, on-site security, pool, laundry facilities (some), no-smoking rooms* ⊟*No credit cards.*

$$-$$$
★
🏨**Costa Del Sol.** This condo complex is symbolic of the new Juan Dolio Beach. Architecturally speaking, it has a simplicity that flows, an undulation of off-white stucco that exactly mimics the 2.5 mi of new beachfront. When standing on a balcony, you feel as if you could reach the coco palms when they sway. The white-on-white lobby calms; the owners lounge (open to renters, too) is even more attractive with comfy salon furnishings, Wi-Fi, and a wide-screen TV. Some condos are long and narrow with a balcony as their focal point. Kitchens are adequate. The classy, Euro furnishings around the pool below complete the idyllic Caribbean picture. The Texas Rangers (as in baseball) recently rented a couple of penthouses and loved them. **Pros:** Incredible sea views, good value for the money (particularly for families), taxes are included in prices quoted. **Cons:** Rentals don't have standardized decor, so you get what you get, no real restaurant on-site, some staff need more training. ⊠ *Blvd. Juan Dolio, Villas del Mar, Juan Dolio* ☎*809/526–2236 or 809/526–2131* ⊕*www.rentalmetrocountry.com* ⇨*142 2-bedroom condos, 19 3-bedroom condos* △*Daily maid service, on-site security, beachfront, laundry facilities* ⊟*AE, MC, V* ❑*EP.*

NEED A BREAK?

Giulia's Café (⊠*Plaza Hispaniola, Blvd. Juan Dolio, Villas del Mar, Juan Dolio* ⊹*Across from Costa del Sol condos* ☎*809/526–1492*) **is a sports bar and café where you can grab a burger and beer while using the free Wi-Fi or watching baseball or boxing on satellite TV. You can also have a leisurely breakfast here. They have full meals but prices are nearly as high as the better restaurants, so why would you do that?**

¢ 🏨**Guesthouse Holland.** This little ground-floor studio apartment (with private entrance) is adjacent to that of the owner, Dré Broders. Attractive, with its handcrafted pine doors and kitchen cabinets, tile floors, and decorator window treatments, it has cable TV with some 60 channels (including some in English) and is within a Wi-Fi hot spot, though service costs $20 per week. The kitchen has a full refrigerator, stove, and oven. Basically, it has everything you need for a short or long stay, but the price and convenient location are the best selling points. The beach is across the street, and grocery stores, restaurants, bus stops, and the taxi stand are nearby. **Pros:** Safe with outside door locks and wrought-iron gates on door and windows, helpful and friendly multilingual landlords. **Cons:** Bedding and pillows could be better, no phone, decor a little drab. ✉*Residencial Marie Michell 104, Playa Juan Dolio, Juan Dolio* ☎*809/526–3533, 809/399–5766 cell* ⊕*www.guesthouse-holland.net.ms* ⇨*1-studio, 1 bathroom* ♨*In-room: no phone, safe. In-hotel: Wi-Fi, laundry facilities* ⊟*No credit cards.*

HOTELS & RESORTS

$$ 🏨 **Barcelo Capella Beach Resort.** This resort has always been the best of the all-inclusives in Juan Dolio and that much has not changed. After some years in decline, it's on the rise again and is now the only recommendable all-inclusive resort in Juan Dolio. The Capella's grounds are nearly palatial, and the mix of architecture, which ranges from Moorish to Spanish-Colonial, works beautifully. Guest rooms are all spacious, particularly in the quietest 1000 building; new decor throughout is colorful. In rooms are all the amenities, from coffeemakers to bathrobes. On the beach, which has been rejuvenated and extended, is the famous disco, a two-story palapa structure that doubles as an à la carte seafood restaurant for lunch and dinner. The principal buffet was relocated and now faces the sea. Food in all the restaurants, including the buffet, is a cut above once again. ■TIP➔ **You can purchase a day or night pass for a mere $45, which gets you either lunch or dinner and all your drinks; by day it's the beach and pools, by night the disco from 7 to 2 AM. Pros:** Dive shop under professional German ownership, nightly shows in amphitheater better than most, Aslan Spa quite nice. **Cons:** Runs at high occupancy, the crowd can be rowdy, 3000 and 4000 buildings have sea views but can be noisy. ✉*Blvd. Juan Dolio, Box 4750, Villas de Mar, Juan Dolio* ☎*809/526–1080, 809/221–0564, or 800/924–5044* ⊕*www.barcelohotels.com* ⇨*474 rooms, 23 suites* ♨*In-room: safe, refrigerator. In-hotel: 5 restaurants, room service, bars, tennis court, pools, spa, beachfront, diving, water sports, no elevator, children's programs (ages 4–12), laundry service, public Internet, parking (no fee)* ⊟*AE, D, MC, V* ♥○♥*AI.*

$ 🏨 **Embassy Suites Los Marlins Hotel & Golf Resort.** Dominicans are suitably impressed by the atrium lobby and subtropical plantings splashed by the waterfall in this all-suites hotel. Guests love the two rooms for the price of one (families especially love two TVs), and businesspeople can make an office in the living room, where there's a desk. In general, this place works—you'll see laptops open to Wi-Fi in all the public spaces—but that doesn't mean guests don't have fun. Guests make conversation at the complimentary hot breakfast in the morning and make new friends at the nightly, manager's cocktail hour, also complimentary. There's a free shuttle to the beach at Costa del Sol. **Pros:** Balconies overlook the pool and palapa bar, super management and staff, massages now available in-room. **Cons:** Not on the beach, living room ensemble very utilitarian with little style, complimentary snacks at happy hour not good for the waistline. ✉*Metro Country Club, Autovia del Este, Km 55, Juan Dolio* ☎*809/688–9999 or 800/362–2779* ⊕*www.los-marlins.embassysuites.com* ⇨*125 suites* ♨*In-room: safe, refrigerator. In-hotel: 3 restaurants, room service, bars, golf course, tennis courts, pool, gym, laundry service, public Internet, public WiFi, parking (no fee), no-smoking rooms* ⊟*AE, MC, V* ♥○♥*BP.*

NIGHTLIFE

There's not a great deal of nightlife in Juan Dolio. Often people simply continue their evening in the place where they had dinner, particularly if it's on the water. Some of these places have DJs on weekends. Those staying at resorts almost always dance the night away on-site. The American Casino is another popular option.

The American Casino (⊠ *Calle Principal, across from Coral Costa Caribe Hotel, Playa Juan Dolio, Juan Dolio* ☎ *809/526–3318*) is a particularly fun place that's innovative in its offerings, from Friday-night blackjack tournaments to inexpensive Wednesday slot tournaments. There are tables for roulette, craps, and Caribbean stud, and free drinks and sandwiches are handed out to players. Saturday night brings live, local bands. The casino is open from 8 PM to 4 AM and has free shuttles from area hotels and restaurants.

⚠ **An ATM outside the American Casino comes in handy but often runs out of cash. Remember that you get pesos, not dollars, and don't forget to retrieve your card as soon as the machine spits it out; otherwise, it may take it back.**

Casa Blanca Café & Piano Bar (⊠ *Calle Principal, Playa Juan Dolio, Juan Dolio* ☎ *No phone*) was inspired by the famous movie with Bogie and Bergman, so the walls are decorated with stills from the film. It's a fun hangout, either indoors or out on the terrace. On some Friday and Saturday nights a local music professor plays the piano, and everyone comes. This is also a great place for breakfast—a perfect cappuccino, a croissant, fresh-squeezed juice, and even eggs most of the time.

BEACHES

The coral reef off Juan Dolio Beach protects the natural marine habitat. The water here is relatively shallow, with gentle currents to keep things clean and clear. It's safe for kids and easy to snorkel.

Playa Juan Dolio (⊠ *Blvd. Playa Juan Dolio, Playa Juan Dolio, Juan Dolio*) is now glorious, especially in the Villas Del Mar area. Its regeneration, which goes for 2.5 mi, included the relocation of more than 14 million cubic feet of nearly white sand. It has led to the town's rebirth, and the tourism authority's goal is to turn Juan Dolio into the South Beach in the Caribbean, with condominium projects that demonstrate style and first-class amenities fit for the international jet set. The beach rejuvenation was continued to the horseshoe-shape public beach in Playa (Old) Juan Dolio, starting in front of Casa Blanca.

NEED A BREAK?

If you come off the beautiful new Playa Juan Dolio with a mighty thirst, plop yourself on a stool at Freedom Bar & Grill (⊠ *Blvd. Playa Juan Dolio, just before Barcelo Capella Beach Resort, Villas del Mar, Juan Dolio* ☎ *809/526–1958*), and ask for a cold Presidente, which is also known as *aqua verde* (green water) since it comes in a green bottle. Sue, the British owner who has lived in India, sells delicious rotisserie chickens and sides, and once you get a whiff of her aromatic chicken curry, you may simply have to have it.

SPORTS & THE OUTDOORS

DIVING

Local dive aficionados will tell you that the south coast, which includes Boca Chica, Juan Dolio, Isla Catalina, and, most notably, the underwater national park La Caleta, offer the best diving in the country. La Caleta is a half-day trip from Juan Dolio (about $70 for excursion plus $35 for a dive), and divers can explore two sunken vessels: the *Limon* is a 115-foot tug boat, and the famous *Hickory*, a 130-foot freighter that once functioned as a treasure-hunting vessel. Both lie in 60 feet of water. Isla Catalina is just another day in Paradise ($75 for transportation plus $35 a dive); divers can discover black coral, huge sponges, and beautiful sea fans. Cave diving in Cueva Taina is another possibility ($70 for the transportation plus $35 per dive). If you prefer snorkeling you can find the viewing good near the coral reef that rims the regenerated Playa Juan Dolio.

Neptuno Dive (⊠ *Barcelo Capella Beach Resort, Villas del Mar, Juan Dolio* ☎ *809/526–2005* ⊕ *www.neptunodive.com*), the PADI five-star dive shop at the Barcelo, has been taken over by a professional new German team. Dive instructors and dive masters are multilingual, speaking German, English, Spanish, French, and Italian. In addition to simple dives, you can also arrange certification or refresher courses. Among other options, Neptuno Dive does a half-day trip to La Caleta as well as an all-day excursion to Isla Catalina, which is great for the whole family, even if you aren't divers. That price includes food, drink, and the possibility of two tank dives. The Neptuno team has also explored Cueva Taina, a cave system near Santo Domingo, and offers dives here.

GOLF

The 7,156-yard, par 72, 21-hole course at **Guavaberry Golf & Country Club** (⊠ *Autovia del Este, Km 55, Juan Dolio* ☎ *809/333–4653* ⊕ *www.guavaberrygolf.com*), designed by Gary Player, has earned a reputation as one of the top courses in the country. Player designed it with an island hole and a wide putting area, beautifying it with bougainvillea and coral stone. Intimidating at first glance, it's a challenging but fair course with long fairways. Play costs $100, including a cart. The golf director is a PGA pro. A branch of the Montréal-based Golfologist Academy, which gives audiovisual analysis of your golf swing, opened in 2006. **Los Marlins Championshop Golf Course** (⊠ *Autovia del Este, Km 55, Juan Dolio* ☎ *809/526–1359*) is an 18-hole, 6,400-yard, par-72 course designed by Charles Ankrom. Guests of the adjacent Embassy Suites pay $45 for 18 holes including cart, $22 for 9 holes; nonguests pay $70 for 18 holes, $40 for 9. Golfers get 10% off at the Metro Country Club. A Fuentes Cigar Club, one of the few such clubs in the country, is on the second floor. Kids and moms can be seen on the 18-hole miniature golf range when the dads are playing the 18-

hole course. The tennis courts are night-lighted. A new deluxe spa is expected sometime in 2008. ■TIP➡ **If you're playing golf at Los Marlins, plan on taking your lunch at the adjacent Metro Country Club. You can sit in the air-conditioned dining room or outside on the terrace. Some of the menu items, particularly the starters, are especially good. Mains are reasonably priced. For example, it's hard to find a filet mignon anywhere for $10. Likewise, pasta dishes begin at $5.**

HORSEBACK RIDING

Guavaberry Equestrian Center (✉*Guavaberry Golf & Country Club, Autovia del Este, Km 55, Juan Dolio* ☎*809/333–4653*) has a clean stable, good stock, and English and Western saddles. Delightful hour-plus trail rides throughout the extensive grounds of the resort cost $25; complimentary transportation is provided from all Juan Dolio hotels.

SAN PEDRO DE MACORÍS

24 km (15 mi) east of Juan Dolio.

The national sport and the national drink are both well-represented in this city, an hour or so east of Santo Domingo. Some of the country's best baseball games are played in **Tetelo Vargas Stadium.** Many Dominican baseball stars have their roots here, including George Bell, Tony Fernandez, Jose Río, and Sammy Sosa. The **Macorís Rum** distillery is on the eastern edge of the city. From 1913 to the 1920s this was a very important town—a true cultural center—and mansions from that era are being restored by the Office of Cultural Patrimony, as are some remaining vestiges of 16th-century architecture and the town's cathedral, which has a pretense to the Gothic style, even gargoyles. There's a **Malecón,** a nice promenade along the port, and by night the beer and rum kiosks come alive. The Dominicans, Europeans, and now North Americans, who take self-catering apartments or condos in Juan Dolio, frequent San Pedro for it has the closest *supermercados,* which are Jumbo, Iberia (also has a big pharmacy), Zaglul—and other necessary businesses. *For information on baseball in San Pedro, see* ➪*Baseball in Sports & the Outdoors in Chapter 1, Santo Domingo.*

Some of the caves in the Dominican Republic are well worth exploring, even for nonaficionados. **Cueva Las Marvillas** is an incredible cave with the requisite stalactites and stalagmites, but its true highlight is a series of primitive Taíno cave paintings. Cement walkway steps and ramps make exploration easy; ramps are even sufficient to accommodate visitors in wheelchairs. The state-of-the-art lighting utilizes sensors, illuminating the artwork as you approach. Everything has been done so the cave can safely accommodate groups, which is the only way you can visit, as part of a guided tour. The grounds and semi-arid gardens are well-designed and maintained, as are the restrooms, museum, shop, and cafeteria. The tour takes about one hour. ✉*Off Las Américas Hwy., Cumayasa* ✛*16 km (10 mi) east of San Pedro de Macorís* ☎*809/696–1797* 🎫*$3* ⊙*Tues.–Sun. 10–6.*

SPORTS & THE OUTDOORS

BASEBALL

Baseball is more than just a game in the Dominican Republic; it's a passion. With so many famous Dominican baseball players coming from San Pedro, it's no wonder that the games here are particularly popular. Ticket prices fluctuate, but they range US$7–US$12. Always buy the most expensive seats. For more information on baseball in the Dominican Republic, see ⇨ Baseball *in* Sports & the Outdoors *in* Chapter 1, Santo Domingo. **Estadio Tetelo Vargas.** (⊠ *Av. Francisco Caamano Denó, San Pedro de Macorís* ☎ *809/529–3618*) is the local stadium.

LA ROMANA

48 mi (78 km) east of Juan Dolio.

La Romana is on the southeast coast, about a two-hour drive from Santo Domingo and the same distance southwest of Punta Cana. The international airport here has nonstop service to both the United States and Canada. The actual town of La Romana is not pretty or quaint, although it has a central park, an interesting market, a couple of good restaurants, banks and small businesses, a public beach, and Jumbo, a major supermarket. It is, at least, a real slice of Dominican life.

Casa de Campo is just outside La Romana. Although there are now more resorts in the area, this 7,000-acre luxury enclave put the town on the map. Marina Chavón, with its Mediterranean design and impressive yacht club and villa complex, is as fine a marina facility as can be found anywhere; the shops and restaurants at the marina are a big draw for all tourists to the area, as is Altos de Chavón, the re-created 16th-century Italian hill town on the grounds of Casa de Campo.

La Romana is about an hour east of Juan Dolio. If you go straight on Autovia del Este, the coastal highway changes into Highway 3. As you approach the town of La Romana, you'll pass the baseball stadium on your left. If you want to explore the downtown area, take Avenida General Luperón to the right, when the road splits, and you'll head straight to the central park, which is the main town square.

★ **Altos de Chavón,** a re-creation of a 16th-century Mediterranean village, sits on a bluff overlooking the Río Chavón, about 3 mi (5 km) east of the main facilities of Casa de Campo. There are cobblestone streets lined with lanterns, wrought-iron balconies, wooden shutters, courtyards swathed with bougainvillea, and **Iglesia St. Stanislaus,** the romantic setting for many a Casa de Campo wedding. More than a museum piece, this village is a place where artists live, work, and play. Dominican and international painters, sculptors, and artisans come here to teach sculpture, pottery, silk-screen printing, weaving, dance, and music at the school, which is affiliated with New York's Parsons School of Design. They work in their studios and crafts shops selling their finished wares. The village also has an archaeological museum and five restaurants.

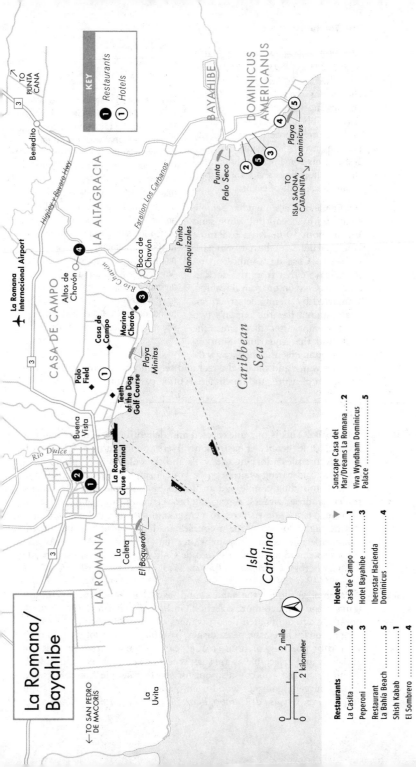

La Romana/Bayahibe

KEY

1 Restaurants
① Hotels

LA ALTAGRACIA

CASA DE CAMPO

La Romana Internacional Airport ✈

Benedito

TO
PUNTA
CANA

Higüey-Bavaro Hwy.

Altos de Chavón

Río Chavón

Farallón Los Carbanos

Boca de Chavón

BAYAHIBE

DOMINICUS
AMERICANUS

Punta
Palo Seco

Playa
Dominicus

② **5** **③** **④** **⑤**

TO
ISLA SAONA,
CATALINITA

Punta
Blanquizoles

Casa de
Campo

Polo
Field

①

Marina
Charón

③

Teeth
of the Dog
Golf Course

Playa
Minitas

Caribbean
Sea

Buena
Vista

Río Dulce

La
Caleta

El Boquerón

La Romana
Cruse Terminal

②
①

LA ROMANA

← TO SAN PEDRO
DE MACORÍS

La Uvita

Isla
Catalina

↑

0 ⊢——⊣ 2 mile
0 ⊢——⊣ 2 kilometer

Restaurants

La Casita **2**
Peperoni **3**
Restaurant
La Bahía Beach **5**
Shish Kabab **1**
El Sombrero **4**

▶ **Hotels**

Casa de Campo **1**
Hotel Bayahibe **3**
Iberostar Hacienda
Dominicus **4**
Sunscape Casa del
Mar/Dreams La Romana **2**
Viva Wyndham Dominicus
Palace **5**

3

A 5,000-seat **amphitheater** (☎809/523–2424 for Kandela tickets ⊕www.kandela.com.do) features *Kandela*, a spectacular musical extravaganza showcasing the island's sensuous Afro-Caribbean dance moves, music, and culture. Concerts and celebrity performances by such singers as Julio Iglesias, his son Enrique, Sting, and the Pet Shop Boys share the amphitheater's schedule of events.

Isla Catalina is a somewhat remote island with a beautiful white-sand beach about 10 mi from El Parque Nacional del Este) the national park (closer to Casa de Campo); many tours leave either from the dock at Altos de Chavón or from Bayahibe. Unmarred by manmade structures, Isla Catalina has the region's two most sought after dive sites, the Wall and the Aquarium. Snorkelers can sunbathe and then just walk into the water and out to the reef and see schools of tropical fish. The beach is a pleasure, and lunch here is often part of this tour.

> ## CAPTAIN KIDD'S SHIP DISCOVERED
>
> The big news in late 2007 was that the *Quedagh Merchant,* the ship belonging to the notorious Captain Kidd that was lost off the east coast of the D.R. in 1699, was discovered by a local resident 70 feet off Isla Catalina. The pristine shipwreck lies only 10 feet underwater. Experts (and locals) are amazed that no one ever looted the site, given its proximity to shore. It's among only a few pirate shipwrecks found in the Americas and will be turned into an underwater public preserve. As to whether a treasure has been found, no one's talking, and the site is under tight surveillance.

WHERE TO EAT

$$–$$$ ✕**La Casita.** This is one unexpected and delightful oasis in a town not revered for its beauty or gastronomy. Here you might be in Spain, with the ceramic tiles adorning the walls and the colorful wall plates. Professional and caring waiters guide you through the menu explaining that the founding couple had an Italian–Spanish marriage. The menu traverses those borders, zigzagging between clam soup and carpaccio, caprese, pastas, and risottos, to a casuela of shellfish and paella. Prices can be high, but many main courses are large enough to be shared. When offering a digestif, your waiter may suggest an Amaro-Averna (root-based and Sicilian) or Orujo de Galicia (a Spanish liqueur made from 29 herbs). ⊠*Francisco Richiez 57, La Romana* ☎*809/556–5932 or 809/349–5434* ▭*MC, V.*

$$–$$$$ ✕**Peperoni.** Although the name sounds as Italian as *amore,* this restaurant's menu is much more eclectic than Italian. It has a classy, contemporary, white-dominated decor; waiters are also dressed in white with long aprons. The classic pasta dishes, osso buco, and risottos with rock shrimp or porcinis, or house-made pear and goat cheese raviolis are authentic and delectable as are such specialties like curried shrimp with jasmine rice. But you can also opt for stylishly simple charcoal-grilled steaks, burgers, gourmet wood-oven pizzas, sandwiches, or even sushi and sashimi. ⊠*Casa de Campo, Plaza Portafino 16, Marina Chavón, La*

Romana ☎809/523–2228 ▤AE, MC, V.

¢–$$ ✕**Shish Kabab.** Fancy it is not, but this local institution has been family-owned for 37 years and gets a steady flow of guests from all walks of life. It has probably changed little over time, but now you're more likely to see the grown children taking care of business rather than papi, who emigrated from Palestine in his youth. Middle Eastern food is the main event here: deep-fried *kipes* (elliptical balls of seasoned raw wheat), hummus, and baba ganoush. Of course, there are shish kebabs and even breakfast after 10 AM. ⊠*Calle Castillo Marquez 32, La Romana* ☎809/556–2737 ▤MC, V ⊘*Closed Mon.*

GOING TO SANTO DOMINGO

Santo Domingo is reachable on a day trip from either La Romana or Bayahibe (easier still from Boca Chica or Juan Dolio), but if you're in La Romana or Bayahibe, you're better off going on an organized tour rather than renting a car. If in Juan Dolio or Boca Chica, you can hire a driver or even take a gua-gua; however, gua-guas drop off and pick up at Parque Enriquillo, which isn't the best place to be after dark, so be sure to head back before then.

$–$$$$ ✕**El Sombrero.** Tethered outside, a burro—appropriately named "Margarita"—draws visitors like a magnet to this casual restaurant, which is your best bet for lunch at Altos de Chavón. Inside, the open-air restaurant has all of your Mexican favorites. Some of the best are the Aztec soup (a fiery, chicken soup) and tequila-marinated shrimp. Since main courses are pricey—most are more than $20—many people just share a selection of appetizers (a sampling costs around $25) and save the pesos for Jimmy Buffet's favorite blender drink. The festive atmosphere is fired by the tequila bar, and strolling musicians add to the fiesta. ⊠*Casa de Campo, Altos de Chavón, La Romana* ☎809/523–3333 ▤AE, MC, V ⊘*No dinner Tues. and Wed.*

WHERE TO STAY

There's only one resort in La Romana, the fabled Casa de Campo, which has both a resort and villa component.

HOTELS

$$$$ ▦**Casa de Campo.** At the country's most illustrious resort, golfers vie for ⊘ tee times at the three famed Pete Dye–designed courses. Family reunions ★ in luxury villas are perennially popular. Regular rooms are called casitas and are in two-story, nondescript blocks (ask for one of the six newest), but inside they are soundproof and commodious, with down pillows, walk-in closets, and balconies overlooking the gardens. What's great is that each room (and villa) comes with a golf cart; there's an efficient shuttle, too. Minitas Beach, though not expansive, has had many new chic amenities added such as new Euro furnishings and Balinesse sunbeds. The restaurant at the beach looks amazing, with contemporary white sail installations and upgraded cuisine thanks to the new partnership with New York's Le Cirque; high up in Altos de Chavón a second Le Cirque restaurant was expected to open in 2008. Booking

just a room (EP) at Casa is possible, but few go this route because the all-inclusive plan is a better value, as are the golf packages. **Pros:** The luxurious new Cygalle Healing Spa opened in 2007, staff is excellent and most are long-term employees, organization and efficiency at this resort is stellar for the D.R. **Cons:** Not as beach-oriented as other D.R. resorts, so nongolfers may not feel quite as much at home, casitas do not have water views. ✉ *Box 140, La Romana* ☎ *809/523–3333 or 305/856–7083* ⊕ *www.casa-decampo.com.do* ⤳ *267 rooms, 150 villas* ⚷ *In-room: safe, refrigerator, kitchen (some), dial-up. In-hotel: 9 restaurants, bars, golf courses, tennis courts, pools, gym, spa, diving, water sports, bicycles, no elevator, children's programs (ages 1–18)* ▤ *AE, MC, V* ⭘*AI.*

> ### FOUR SEASONS CASA DE CAMPO
>
> The big news at Casa de Campo is that in 2009 a brand-new Four Seasons Hotel is expected to open on the expansive resort grounds, offering a new level of luxurious accommodations with access to all of Casa's great facilities, golf courses, and restaurants. The resort will be family-oriented and have its own large spa and beach.

VILLAS

Insiders will tell you that the best way to appreciate Casa de Campo is to rent an exclusive villa. Oceanfront mansions are ideal, but if you don't have that kind of money, you can still enjoy the good life in a modest two-bedroom home over looking a golf course. The houses in Las Cerezas and Las Piñas are moderately priced. Villa rentals at Casa de Campo fall into two basic categories: Classic and Exclusive, with similar pricing depending on the number of bedrooms and the season; you pay more for oceanfront or "special request" villas. All villas have telephones and safes; some have a dishwasher, DVD, VCR, or Jacuzzi. DSL and Wi-Fi connections may be requested.

A supplement allows you to dine and drink freely at all the resort's all-inclusive restaurants. Excel Concierge service offers maid and butler service, breakfast prepared in your villa, a welcome basket, and airport transfers (from La Romana only) for a cost of $35 per adult per night. Most rentals include at least one four-person golf cart so you can whip around the expansive resort grounds.

▮TIP➡ There's a Jumbo supermarket in La Romana, and this is the best place to stock up on supplies. The store also has a pharmacy, cafeteria, and Orange cell phone shop. You would best avoid Friday nights, when teens hang out there and there's a frenetic scene of just-paid shoppers mixing with the dating game.

Most of the villas at **Casa de Campo** (☎ *800/877–3643* ⊕ *www.casa-decampo.com.do*) can be rented through the resort's central reservations office. In general, this is one well-oiled, professional rental operation with a high-quality inventory and it boasts the largest number of rental villas in the Caribbean, with accommodations from 2 to 22 persons. A seven-night minimum stay applies during holiday periods. Some homeowners at Casa de Campo choose to rent their properties through smaller management companies.

Villas at Casa (☎*809/299–0722 cell* ⊕*www.VillasinDR.com*) is a small, personalized business that rents, manages, and sells Casa de Campo homes. The president, Gina Piantini, is a full-time Casa resident and is bilingual; she is also the on-site rental manager. Although the company manages 40 different villas, most are comfortable and stylish but moderately priced compared to some of the resort's luxury offerings. The company will also do your grocery shopping for $25 (maids will make breakfast and lunch, if requested). Since these are considered direct-from-owner rentals, not all units are always available. A $25 per villa per day resort fee allows private rental guests to tap into Casa's grand facilities. Check-in is at the villa owners' club at Casa reception; in addition to MC and V, cash, wire transfers, and checks are accepted for payment.

$$$ ⚏**Casa Bella.** Sophistication meets creativity here. Island-style furnishings are juxtaposed with traditional pieces. Inventive details like oversize candles imbedded in shells share the living room with contemporary touches, including a large, black LCD TV and excellent sound system dramatically placed on a white wall. This villa is special, ideal for savvy couples, business groups, or family reunions, preferably with adult children. A second-story sun deck is a welcome amenity. The kitchen has quality equipment, and the BBQ and picnic table are out on the stone patio that wraps around the pool. The palapa-topped gazebo with built-in benches is a good place to begin the night with a rum-something. **Pros:** Handsome cane furnishings, bedrooms are individually decorated, large back yard. **Cons:** Not directly on the beach (about 3–5 minutes away), fairly distant (8–10 minutes) to most resort facilities. ⊠*Casa de Campo, Las Piñas 3, La Romana* ⊕*www.casadecampo.com.do* ⤹*4 bedrooms, 4 bathrooms* ⚷*Safe, dishwasher, DVD, daily maid service, on-site security, pool, laundry facilities* ⊟*AE, MC, V* ⊚*EP.*

$$–$$$ ⚏**Casa Blanca.** Guests at this home feel like they're in an exclusive neighborhood, which they are—Bahía Minitas, and close to the beach at that. A brick circular drive sets the stage; a Japanese garden in the front makes yet another positive statement. All contribute to a great first impression that only gets better. If there are serious cooks in your group, they will love the chef's kitchen with its stainless steel appliances. This Exclusive Villa is super for business groups—particularly those with a strong female contingent, who will recognize a woman's touch in the decor—and will have a special appeal to post-boomers. The guys will enjoy hanging out in the den with its wide-screen TV and leather couches. A BBQ, wet bar, fridge, stove, and gazebo all help make this a great place for outdoor entertaining. **Pros:** This is a feel-good house, master bedroom with its whirlpool tub is especially spacious. **Cons:** Outdoor decor may be too bright for some, no water views, some 10 minutes by golf cart to resort facilities. ⊠*Casa de Campo, Bahía Minitas 1, La Romana* ⊕*www.casadecampo.com.do* ⤹*3 bedrooms, 3 bathrooms* ⚷*Safe, dishwasher, DVD, daily maid service, on-site security, pool, laundry facilities* ⊟*AE, MC, V* ⊚*EP.*

$$ 🏠**Golf Villa 183.** This tastefully decorated, classic Casa two-story home is in a long-established neighborhood, with a large pool as well as a high-tech, big-screen plasma TV and home theater system with professional stereo equipment. All of this could spell P-A-R-T-Y, but instead it mostly it provides good family entertainment, especially for teenagers. For large families or groups there's an ample dining room (with a/c) and a fully equipped kitchen with a wine cooler. The outdoor areas are equally geared to entertaining, and the large patio around the pool has stylish outdoor furnishings and a BBQ. Back indoors, the impressive master bedroom suite on the second floor has a spacious terrace with a dining table as well as its own cable TV and stereo sound system. Another bedroom is a queen-size suite, while the other two double rooms are perfect for sharing by noncouples. **Pros:** Plenty of space, homey ambience, master bath is stellar. **Cons:** Not on the beach, no sea views, some 10 minutes from the main resort facilities. ✉*Casa de Campo, Golf Villa 183, La Romana* 🌐*www.VillasinDR.com* 🛏*4 bedrooms, 4.5 bathrooms* ⚒*Dishwasher, DVD, daily maid service, cook (breakfast only), hot tub, pool, laundry facilities, no smoking* 🚭*MC, V* 🍴*BP.*

$$–$$$ 🏠**Lagos #10.** One of the first neighborhoods of Casa to be developed, Lagos is characterized by homes with back yards and solid construction. Those that have been substantially renovated, as #10 has been, have achieved that desirable marriage of character and up-to-date decor, in this case in a Mexican hacienda style. As a neighborhood, Lagos is relatively quiet, as its streets are not heavily trafficked arteries. Within this home's grounds you'll find a pool, a Jacuzzi, and a BBQ area. The master bedroom has a decidedly Mexican colonial ambience. Handsome, colorful area rugs on tile floors and textured walls give this villa charisma and, consequently, repeat clients. All four bedrooms have TVs; another is in the living room. That should keep kids or golf buddies content. There's a fully equipped kitchen, and a big plus is the free Wi-Fi. **Pros:** A cozy, homey atmosphere, nice oversize patio with handsome brown wicker furniture. **Cons:** No water view, maid doesn't speak English. ✉*Casa de Campo, Lagos 10, La Romana* 🌐*www.VillasinDR.com* 🛏*4 bedrooms, 4 bathrooms* ⚒*Dishwasher, DVD, Wi-Fi, daily maid service, cook (breakfast and lunch), on-site security, hot tub, pool, laundry facilities* 🚭*MC, V* 🍴*BP.*

SPORTS & THE OUTDOORS

Minetas Beach, the private beach for Casa de Campo guests on the resort's property, is about 15 minutes by golf cart (10 minutes by shuttle bus) from Casa de Campo's main campus. It's a surprisingly small strip of sand for the size of the resort (indeed, it has always been the resort's one true disappointment), but it has recently been rejuvenated with tons of white sand and is really much more attractive now. Stylish Euro-chaises and Balinese sunbeds, where one can have a massage, have been added. Sail installations at the upgraded beach restaurant all make for one chic Caribbean scene.

BASEBALL

Baseball is as much a passion in La Romana as it is in San Pedro de Macoris and Santo Domingo. Ticket prices fluctuate, but they will range US$7–US$12. Always buy the most expensive seats. For more information on baseball in the Dominican Republic, see ⇨Baseball *in* Sports & the Outdoors *in* Chapter 1, Santo Domingo. **Estadio Francisco A. Michelli** (⊠*Av. Padre Abreu, near monument, La Romana* ☎*809/556–6188*) is La Romana's baseball stadium. Tropical Tours does arrange baseball tours during the playing season.

BOATING

Sailing conditions are ideal, with constant trade winds. Favorite excursions include day trips to Isla Catalina and Isla Saona (see ⇨Bayahibe, *below*) and sunset cruises on the Caribbean. Prices for crewed sailboats of 26 feet and longer, with a capacity of 4 to 12 people, range from $120 to $700 a day. **La Marina Chavón** (⊠*Casa de Campo, Calle Barlovento 3, La Romana* ☎*809/523–8646*) has much going on, from sailing to motor yachting and socializing at the Casa de Campo Yacht Club.

FISHING

Marlin and wahoo are among the fish that folks angle for here (fishing is best between January and June). **La Marina Chavón** (⊠*Casa de Campo, Calle Barlovento 3, La Romana* ☎*809/523–8646*) is the best charter option in the area. Boats for deep-sea and river fishing are available as well. Costs to charter a boat with a crew, refreshments, bait, and tackle—generally range from $598 to $2,013 for a half day and from $796 to $3,334 for a full day.

GOLF

FodorśChoice
★

The Famed "Teeth of the Dog" at **Casa de Campo** (⊠*La Romana* ☎*809/523–3333* ⊕*www.casadecampo.com.do*), with seven holes on the sea, is ranked among the best golf courses in the Caribbean and the world. Green fees are $150 per round, per person. Pete Dye has designed this and two other globally acclaimed courses here: Dye Fore, close to Altos de Chavón, hugs a cliff that looks over the sea, a river, and the stunning marina (green fees $150); the Links is an 18-hole inland course (green fees $115). Avid golfers should inquire about the resort's three-day and one-week supplements, or the new Simply Golf Packages, which are a good value. Tee times for all courses must be reserved at least one day in advance by resort guests, sooner for nonguests.

HORSEBACK RIDING

The 250-acre **Equestrian Center at Casa de Campo** (⊠*Casa de Campo, La Romana* ☎*809/523–3333* ⊕*www.casadecampo.com.do*) has something for both Western and English riders—a dude ranch, a rodeo arena (where Casa's trademark "Donkey Polo" is played), guided trail rides, and jumping and riding lessons. Guided rides run about $35 an hour; lessons cost $56 an hour. There are early-morning and sunset trail rides, too. Handsome, old-fashioned carriages are available for hire, as well.

POLO

Casa de Campo is a key place to play or watch the fabled sport of kings, which is surprisingly lively and entertaining. The resort has always prided itself on the polo traditions it has kept alive since its opening in the 1970s. Matches are scheduled from October to June, with high-goal players flying in from France and Argentina. Private polo lessons ($60 an hour) and clinics are available for those who always wanted to give it a shot. Guavaberry Golf and Country Club in Juan Dolio is also constructing two polo fields at this writing.

TENNIS

La Terraza Tennis Club (⊠ *Casa de Campo, La Romana* ☎ *809/523–3333*) has been called the Wimbledon of the Caribbean. This 12-acre facility, perched on a hill with sea views, has 13 Har-Tru courts. Nonmembers are welcome (just call in advance); court time costs $28 an hour, and lessons are $55 an hour with an assistant pro, $69 with a pro.

SHOPPING

Altos de Chavón is a re-creation of a 16th-century Mediterranean village on the grounds of the Casa de Campo resort, where you can find art galleries, boutiques, and souvenir shops grouped around a cobbled square. Extra special is El Club de Cigaro.

La Marina Chavón, Casa de Campo's top-ranked marina, is home to more than 60 shops and international boutiques, galleries, and jewelers scattered amidst restaurants, an ice-cream parlor, Euro-style bars, and a yacht club. It's a great place to spend some leisure time shopping, sightseeing, and staring at the extravagant yachts. Ferretti Bertram Yachts sells the dream boats here if you are in the market. The chic shopping scene at the marina includes Burberry, Bleu Marine, Pucci, Benetti-Azimuth-Perini Nave, Gucci, Cartier-Montblanc, and Mondo Versace. Dominican designer Jenny Polanco's boutique now includes her line of jewelry and handbags. There's even a marvelous antique shop at the marina's end. Although upscale is the operative word here, this does not mean that you cannot buy a postcard, a pair of shorts, or a logo sweatshirt. Also, the supermercado Nacional at the marina has not only groceries but sundries, postcards, and snacks.

NIGHTLIFE

At Casa de Campo's main resort complex, in the Canoa Bar, there's often live music and danceable Latin music. Other than that, people usually hang out at the place where they went to dinner, like Peperoni's in the Marina, but the Victory Club is another option that is quite popular, even with nonresort guests.

Casino Santana Beach (⊠ *Santana Beach, between La Romana and San Pedro Macoris* ☎ *809/412–1104 or 809/412–5006*) is surprisingly sophisticated for a touristy beachside casino. It's right on the beach; there's a tropical terrace and an aquarium behind the roulette wheel. Drinks are on the house while you play, be it blackjack, Caribbean

Poker, Poker Hold-em, or the slots. The live music is nice, not crazy. Round-trip transport and drinks are free every night. The hours are from 8 PM to 4 AM nightly.

Victory Club (✉ *Casa de Campo, Paseo del Mar 10, Marina Chavón, La Romana* ☎ *809/523–2264*), a piano bar in a faux lighthouse at the very end of the marina's boardwalk, is like a vacation fantasy. Yes, drinks are expensive, but at least you don't have to pay just to sit down in the Italian designer chairs and black leather couches. In the salon–lounge is artwork, not to mention a muted plasma TV and fairy-tale vistas of the sea and moored yachts. The bar, which is shaped like a boat with a starry backdrop, has all of the fashionable drinks and wine choices— mostly Italian—and top-shelf champagnes. Food is served late—cheese, proscuitto, and the like as light bites, and also an assortment of ice creams and tropical sorbets.

BAYAHIBE

10.5 mi (17 km) east of La Romana via Hwy. 3.

Columbus dropped anchor here in 1494, Puerto Rican fishermen founded the town in the middle of the 19th century. Now many of the local fishermen either moonlight or have totally given up their poles and nets to skipper the speed boats that bring tourists back from Isla Saona. The small fishing village has flourished in modern times by embracing tourism, and in town Italian immigrants have opened gelato stands and seafood restaurants. Some vestiges remain from earlier times, including the 1925 green wooden church on the waterfront, from where a picture of the Virgin Divine Shepherdess is carried at the front of the annual marine procession.

Nearby is the Bamboo Beach Bar, this one owned by a French woman. Crêpes anyone? Tour buses roll in and park near the jam of souvenir shops and Haitian art vendors. On a side street, on the way to the new Bayahibe, a sprawl of attractive, low-rise apartments and duplexes rented by hotel executives and long-term snowbirds, is the Clinica Rural Bayahibe that Sunscape Casa del Mar "adopted" by cleaning, painting, and stocking it with medical supplies. And so Bayahibe village grows, an old-fashioned *colmado* next door to a dive shop, a small hotel here and there. As one dirt road after another is paved, the town grows less like a village. Around its periphery are nearly a half-dozen, densely populated all-inclusive resorts.

The small village of Bayahibe is about 2 km down a small road from Highway 3; signage is good; just watch for the water tower and then turn. A large parking lot on the waterfront is where buses park. Most of the resorts are on Playa Dominicus, just outside of town.

Dominicus Americus is a little treasure, having been developed mostly by Italians, who brought tourism to the local Dominicans. Very quaint, its original houses are painted mostly in Caribbean pastels—pinks, yellows, and blues. A more *moderne* wave of both apartments and single-family houses of all types is proliferating at this writing, and there's a little real estate boom going on. One main street holds most of the shops, from clothing stores to souvenir shops. (El Mundo is the largest and boasts that they have something for everyone.) And there are a few simple restaurants, bars, a supermarket, tour agencies where excursions are sold mostly to Isla Catalina and Isla Saona, and Stars disco. ✢ *About 5 min east of Bayahibe by car.*

Catalinita is an islet that is often a stopover on an Isla Saona trip, primarily for its popular dive site, Shark Point. The coral reef here offers excellent snorkeling as well. This is the tail end of Parque Nacional Del Este and is uninhabited, with none of the touristy infrastructure of Saona. This is more like a deserted island should be. Usually the stop includes traversing a mangrove forest. The water is transparent. ✢ *Approximately 25 min from Bayahibe by speedboat.*

Isla Saona, off the east coast of Hispaniola, is now a national park inhabited by sea turtles, pigeons, and other wildlife. Caves here were once used by Indians. The beaches are beautiful, and legend has it that Columbus once strayed here. Getting here, on catamarans and other excursion boats, is half the fun, but know that it can be a crowded scene. Vendors are allowed to bother visitors, and there are a number of beach shacks serving lunch and drinks. The largest island in the national park, it's no longer as pristine as a national park should be. ✢ *20 km (12.5 mi), approximately 35 min by Bayahibe by speedboat.*

WHERE TO EAT

$-$$ ✗ **Restaurant La Bahía Beach.** Small, homey, and smack on the beach, this restaurant allows you to eat in the open-air dining room shaded by a palm-thatched roof or take a beachside table. Kick your sandals off, and put your feet in the sand. Lemon-marinated fresh fish and shellfish are the obvious choices here; the mixed seafood grill is easily shared. Or you can try a Dominican rice dish, green rice with the garlic shrimp. The menu does span ethnic borders, so you can even have, say, shrimp in vodka sauce. The music is kept at an enjoyable decibel, and you can usually hang out for hours with no one trying to chase you out. ⊠ *Calle Principal/Playa Bahía, Bayahibe* ☎ *809/833–0055* ▭ *MC, V.*

WHERE TO STAY

Dominicus Americanus and Bayahibe Bay have always been popular with *capitaleños* and Europeans. North Americans are also checking in here and leaving satisfied, having missed nothing of high-density Punta Cana. The Sunscape Resort and Hotel Bayahibe are both in or near the little town; a bit farther away on Playa Dominicus—a truly gorgeous beach—the Iberostar, Viva Wyndham, and Coral Canoa share the sand. The two other resorts on Playa Dominicus (Oasis Canoa and Catalonia Grand Dominicus) are not recommended. The new Dreams resort was not open at this writing, so it is also not reviewed here.

¢ ⊞**Hotel Bayahibe.** This simple abode will appeal to budget travelers and long- term guests—even single females can feel safe, warm, and dry here. Rooms are at least one flight up and are a good size with sufficient windows. You will feel part of the village here, yet the hotel will give you wrist bands so that you can go to the same great beach as the AI guests at the nearby Suncape Casa del Mar (soon to become Dreams La Romana), though you will not be able to partake of the AI resort's included food or drinks. You can check your e-mail at the lobby computer, where there's nothing else but the reception desk. Breakfast is served in a small breakfast room adjacent to the lobby. ⊠*Calle Principal, Bayahibe, next to Casa Daniel* ☎*809/833–0159* ✎*hotelbayahibe@hotmail.com* ➫*20 rooms* ♿*In-room: refrigerator. In-hotel: public Internet* ➩*No credit cards* ⦿*BP.*

3

$$ ⊞**Iberostar Hacienda Dominicus.** Iberostar's reputation for excellent cui-
☾ sine has helped to cement its popularity with families and incentive
★ groups. The breakfast buffet is a "Yes!" El Colonial, the gourmet room, may be one of the best in the all-inclusive world. Its idyllic beach with its lighthouse bar doesn't hurt, either. The crowd here is an interesting mix with some very young adults, hip families with young kids, enough French to warrant the bars stocking Ricard, and senior citizens who are staying as long as three weeks. A manager's party honoring repeat guests can draw a crowd of more than 100 returnees, some who have decided this is the only place to be. Junior suites are worth the few dollars more. This resort has familial warmth as well as a definite fun quotient for singles. **Pros:** Fun resort, gorgeous beach, very family-friendly. **Cons:** Room decor is a bit outdated, always packed, reservations at à la carte restaurants not always available and must be made very early in the morning. ⊠*Playa Bayahibe, Bayahibe* ☎*809/688– 3600 or 888/923–2722* ⊕*www.iberostar.com* ➫*460 rooms, 38 junior suites* ♿*In-room: safe, refrigerator. In-hotel: 4 restaurants, bars, tennis courts, pools, gym, spa, beachfront, diving, water sports, no elevator, children's programs (ages 4–12), public Internet, public Wi-Fi* ➩*AE, MC, V* ⦿*AI.*

$$ ⊞**Sunscape Casa del Mar La Romana.** With its whimsical Victorian fret-
☾ work, the Sunscape Casa del Mar sits on an exceptional, palm-fringed
★ ribbon of white sand protected by a coral reef that offers great snor-keling from the beach. Overlooking the glorious sea-view pool and Oceana restaurant is the impressive Club wing. Rooms, particularly corner units with balconies, are exceptional with deluxe amenities for $50 per person more. The renovated Metamorphosis Spa definitely invites a visit; or have your massage in an open-air wooden hut. The proactive kids' Explorers Club (open until 10 PM) raises the resort's family profile substantially. ⚠ **CAUTION This resort is scheduled to become Dreams La Romana Resort & Spa in December 2008: by then, all rooms will be upgraded, although there will still be a separate Club level; two new discos will be added; a new casino; a convention center for 900 persons; and the lobby will become a grand "palapa" that will appear to be floating in a lagoon network with tropical plantings. Prices will go up. Much of this construction was in progress at this writing, and some may continue into 2009. Pros:** Caring and efficient staff, top-shelf liquors available at

the lobby bar for no extra charge. **Cons:** Large and busy property usually feels overly full, lines and seating in the buffet can be problematic. ⊠*Bayahibe Bay, Bayahibe* ☎*809/221–8880* ⊕*www.amresorts.com* ⤳*774 rooms, 37 suites* ⚘*In-room: safe, refrigerator, Wi-Fi (some). In-hotel: 8 restaurants, bars, tennis courts, pools, gym, beachfront, diving, water sports, bicycles, no elevator, children's programs (ages 3–12), public Internet, public Wi-Fi, parking (no fee)* ⊟*AE, MC, V* ⏨*AI.*

$$–$$$ ▣**Viva Wyndham Dominicus Palace.** Americans will prefer this classier
☾ sister to the nearby Viva Wyndham Dominicus Beach, which has a reputation for its excellent animation programs, for its sports, and for its fun atmosphere. An impressive white tent, big enough for a Greek (or Dominican) wedding, is a focal point of the long expanse of beach, which boasts a blue-flag designation for nonpolluted waters; by day it's a casual lunch spot, but night it becomes a romantic rendezvous. Guest rooms in the blocks, like the lobby, have a Spanish colonial style accented with Caribbean colors. The resort has a Green Globe designation for its eco-friendly policies. The Metamorphosis Spa, like all its counterparts, has earth tones, minimalist, contemporary decor and an extensive list of services. **Pros:** Absolutely fabulous blue-flag beach, professional dive center, great soothing Metamorphis Spa. **Cons:** Always busy, no interior transportation even though resort grounds are sprawling, reservations needed for à la carte restaurants. ⊠*Playa Bayahibe, Bayahibe* ☎*809/686–5658* ⊕*www.vivaresorts.com* ⤳*330 rooms* ⚘*In-room: safe, refrigerator, Wi-Fi (some). In-hotel: 7 restaurants, bars, tennis courts, pools, gym, spa, beachfront, diving, water sports, no elevator, children's programs (ages 4–16), public Internet, public Wi-Fi* ⊟*AE, MC, V* ⏨*AI.* ■TIP→ **A popular wedding destination, honeymoon packages with upgrades and additional amenities, are available for no extra charge. (Copy of marriage certificate must be shown at check-in.)**

BEACHES

Playa Bayahibe (⊠*Starts in the center of town, Bayahibe*), where several seafood restaurants are situated, is somewhat thin, with hard-packed taupe sand and no lounge chairs. However, as you move away from the village, a 10-minute walk along the shoreline, you'll reach the glorious, half-moon cove where you'll find the new Dreams resort (formerly Sunscape Casa del Mar). Although you'll be able to get to the cove and the soft sand, do bring a towel because the resort's security won't let you use the facilities. At night, when no one is on it and the silver moon illuminates the phosphorescence, it's the stuff that Caribbean dreams are made of.

Playa Dominicus (⊠*Dominicus Americanus*) has gin-clear water and just a very few waves at the entrance but absolutely no undertow. The Iberostar, Viva Wyndham, and Coral Canoa resorts all share this beach, and there's a small public section where the locals venture on weekends. The beach has some huts to purchase souvenirs and two restaurants on the sand as well.

SPORTS & THE OUTDOORS

DIVING

The beautiful beaches and excellent diving draw travelers above and below the waves here. If you're a diver, make sure you arrange your excursion with a dive operator rather than on a party boat. These waters and the treasures below are a joy.

Casa Daniel (✉ *Calle Principal, next to Hotel Bayahibe, Bayahibe* ☎ *809/833–0050* ⊕ *www.casa-daniel.com*) is a PADI dive center, so don't be confused by the name. It has an excellent, long-term reputation for professionalism, and the European dive instructors are multilingual and fun. They do it all: lessons from a resort course to advance open-water and rescue diving, certifications, wall diving, night diving, and all of the typical excursion areas. Among their dive sites are Dominicus Shallow, Tortuga, and St. George's Wreck, which is considered a major dive. Hotel pick-ups are free.

Parque Nacional Del Este is a virtual underwater museum, whose seabed is strewn with wrecked Spanish galleons. It's a joint project of the Ministry of Culture and La Romana/Bayahibe Hotel Association. As early as the 1970s a baseline coral reef monitoring program was established. Just 150 yards offshore you can see sunken anchors, cannons, and rifles at depths of 20 feet, which means snorkelers can view them just as easily as divers. For divers, this is a two-tank dive, and it's 30 minutes by boat from Bayahibe. Isla Saona and Isla Catalina are also technically a part of the national park.

Penon is another quick island stop before returning to Bayahibe from Saona, and it can also be a half-day trip for divers. It's considered a pretty dive site because it has an incredible diversity of marine life—rays, sharks, starfish, purple and yellow coral.

SHOPPING

Unlike Marina Chavón, Bayahibe is not really for serious shoppers. You'll encounter little souvenir shops all around the Bayahibe area, depending on where you're staying. Most carry the usual mamajuana, coffee, Brugal and Barcelo rum, Dominican cigars, Haitian art, and tschotkes from rope jewelry that the kids and teenagers favor to pareo fasteners made of coconut shells. Guests at Casa del Mar have a super JL Conchita Llach boutique in the lobby carrying Italian handbags and one-of-a kind jewelry pieces.

NIGHTLIFE

Nightlife in Bayahibe and Dominicus Americanus centers on the resort in which you're staying. If you're looking to travel beyond your resort, the ones with the most animated nightlife are the Wyndham "sisters," the Palace and the Beach. If not a guest there, you can buy a night pass for $85 that includes dinner and unlimited drinks as well as dancing in the disco. The new Casino Dominicus is the buzz in town.

Casino Dominicus (✉ *Calle Juan Ponce de Leon, Dominicus America-nus* ☎ *809/554–8917* ⊕ *www.casinodominicus.com*), across from the Iberostar, opened in late 2007. This sparkling new nightlight in Bayahibe has high, arched ceilings and offers Las Vegas–style gaming (boasting that it has the highest table limits in the country and the only exclusive players club). It showcases entertainment in Las Vegas–style shows in a 1,000-seat theater; there's also a disco with local bands, restaurants, and shopping—all with a Caribbean flamboyance. Gamblers can try their luck at one of 23 table games, 300 slots, or in the sports book. A nightly, continuous shuttle service runs from all major Bayahibe area resorts.

SOUTHEAST COAST ESSENTIALS

BY AIR

There are two convenient airports for travel to the Southeast Coast. There are more flights (and perhaps better fares) into Las Américas International Airport, which is about 15 mi (24 km) east of Santo Domingo and served by the widest variety of major airlines. This is the most convenient airport if you're staying in Boca Chica or Juan Dolio. If you're staying in La Romana or Bayahibe, then the best airport is La Romana/Casa de Campo International Airport. It's possible to fly into Punta Cana, but then you face a 2-hour drive to La Romana, or 3½-hour drive to Juan Dolio. *For information on specific airlines that fly into these airports, see* ⇨ *Air Travel in Domincan Republic Essentials.*

Upon arrival, if you have booked a package through a travel agent, your airport transfers will almost certainly be included in the price you pay. Look for your company's sign as you exit baggage claim. If you book independently, then you'll probably have to reserve a private driver, take a taxi, or rent a car.

AIRPORT TRANSFERS   There are no regular airport shuttle buses in the D.R., so plan on taking a taxi if you're traveling independently (or arrange airport transfers through your hotel or villa rental agent). Private drivers are also a possibility but will charge more.

Dré Broders is a licensed tour guide and private driver who speaks English, German, Dutch, Spanish, and French. He will pick up passengers from any of the area airports and bring them to any destination on the southeast coast. His late-model car is clean and well-maintained, his driving safe. His prices are often better than regular taxis, and he is 100% reliable.

Tropical Tours, the primary tour operator on the Southeast Coast, which has an office in Casa de Campo, also does airport transfers to the resort.

Information **Dré Broeders** (☎ *809/526–3533, 809/399–5766 cell* ✍ *peralta162@ gmail.com*). **Tropical Tours** (☎ *809/556–5801* ⊕ *http://tropicaltoursromana. com.do*).

Airports **Las Américas International Airport** (*SDQ* ✉ *Santo Domingo* ☎ *809/549-0450*). **Punta Cana International Airport** (*PUJ* ☎ *809/686-8790*). **La Romana/Casa de Campo International Airport** (*LRM* ☎ *809/556-5565*).

BY BUS

Privately owned air-conditioned buses are the cheapest way to get around the country. Be forewarned that the bus-music will be Dominican-loud and the a/c, if the bus has it, will be cranked up to the max.

Frequent service from Santo Domingo to the town of La Romana is provided by Express Bus. Buses depart from Ravelo Street in front of Enriquillo Park every hour on the hour from 5 AM to 9 PM; the schedule is exactly the same from La Romana, where they leave from Camino Avenue. In Santo Domingo, there's no office and no phone, but a ticket-taker will take your $4 just before departure. There's general chaos, a crazy kind of congestion (allow time in a taxi), horns blowing, and diesel fumes, but it all comes together. Also, watch your back, or rather your wallet and purse. Travel time is about 1¾ hours, and if luck is with you, the bus may show a first-rate American movie. Once in La Romana, you can take a taxi from the bus stop to Casa de Campo ($18) or Sunscape Casa del Mar ($25) or Iberostar Dominicus ($30).

BY CAR

While we generally do not like driving in the D.R., the Southeast Coast, though congested and unnerving around rush hour, is not too bad. However, we urge you not to drive at night. In the Bayahibe/Dominicus area, the Impagnatiello Rent Car and Yaset Rent a Car are reputable and may be cheaper than the major rental agencies. Budget, with an office at Casa del Mar, is one of the more reasonable major agencies; you can expect to pay between $45 and $80 for a small car; SUVs can be double.

Avis, which has offices in Juan Dolio and La Romana, is a good choice and it has 24-hour roadside assistance. You can choose a Volkswagon Fox for as low as $32, but a large SUV is $130. All companies deliver cars to the hotels.

Information **Avis** (☎ *809/688-1354 for reservations, 809/526-2344 in Juan Dolio, 809/550-0600 in La Romana*). **Budget** (☎ *809/566-6666 in Juan Dolio*). **Impagnatiello Rent Car** (☎ *809/906-8387*). **Yaset Rent a Car** (☎ *809/258-9340*).

BY GUA-GUA, MOTOCONCHO & TAXIS

Local buses are called *gua-guas,* and although not pretty or classy, they'll get you where you're going—not necessarily quickly, but certainly cheaply. You'll marvel at what people bring on the bus; we've seen a musician's kettle drum, Haitian paintings, or a 25-pound sack of rice. From Playa Juan Dolio near Plaza Oasis, you'll pay about RD$30 to go to San Pedro de Macoris, RD$65–RD$80 to La Romana, and RD$80 for Santo Domingo (be sure to take the express). You'll pay extra for luggage. Though crowded and frenetic, using a gua-gua is doable, and since the typical taxi fare is $50 for an hour trip, the gua-gua will be much easier on your wallet.

Motoconchos (motorcycle taxis) are usually found at the gua-gua stops. Ride at your own risk.

If you're staying at a hotel, you can arrange a taxi there. If you're an independent traveler, there are a couple of recommendable companies you can call. And if you find a driver you like, get his cell number so you can call him directly.

Taxi Companies **Juan Dolio Taxi** (⊠ *Playa Juan Dolio* ☎ *809/526–2227*). **Santa Rosa Taxi** (⊠ *La Romana* ☎ *809/556–5313*).

TOUR OPTIONS

All-inclusive resorts have their own tour desks, and if you're staying in a resort, you can reliably use the company that runs the tour desk. It makes sense to use your hotel's tour operator unless you hear negative comments from other guests or if the company doesn't offer the tour you prefer.

The primary tour operator on the Southeast Coast is Tropical Tours (with headquarters at Casa de Campo in La Romana), whose prices are even less than some nonpros and the cruise-ship excursions. Their vans are new or nearly new and well-maintained. If you've ever been on a Dominican excursion when a vehicle breaks down with no mechanic to come to the rescue, you can appreciate this. Also, most of their staff speaks English as well as other languages. They can take you to caves, on quads, on outback safaris, or even out to a ballgame. The company also operates boat tours to the islands.

Information **Tropical Tours** (⊠ *Casa de Campo, La Romana* ☎ *809/556–5801* ⊕ *tropicaltoursromana.com.do*).

Punta Cana

WORD OF MOUTH

"In Punta Cana, walking on the beach with the only goal of 'let's just walk until we get to that point over there' is a daily routine."

—kep

By Elise Rosen   **AS THE SUN RISES ON** Hispaniola, Punta Cana awakens to the lapping ocean, its clear, unspoiled blue brushing up against the pristine stretches of sugar-white sand, and swaying coco palms in the backdrop.

The region commonly referred to as Punta Cana actually encompasses the beaches and villages of Juanillo, Punta Cana, Bávaro, Cabeza de Toro, El Cortecito, Arena Gorda, Macao, and Uvero Alto, which hug an unbroken stretch of the eastern coastline.

A thriving tourism industry fuels the region, and—with such ripe ingredients as sun (the average daily temperature is 82°F; any downpours tend to be short bursts that give way to more sunshine), sand (35 mi of uninterrupted powder) and sea (opportunities for water sports abound)—it's no wonder. For Punta Cana, it was only a matter of time.

In 1969, when the terrain was covered in jungle, a group of North American investors purchased some land along the eastern coast. They put up a small hotel and an air strip (which spawned an international airport) and—voila!—tourism in Punta Cana was born. Their visionary project, now the PuntaCana Resort & Club, spreads out lavishly across 15,000 verdant acres. Club Med opened its doors as the first all-inclusive in the area, and following its lead dozens of others popped up within their own spacious enclaves along the coast. More recently, a fresh crop of boutique hotels has sprung up. Many resorts, including those on beaches as far north as Uvero Alto and as far south as Juanillo (Cap Cana), tag on the moniker "Punta Cana" although they're in their own distinct geographical areas. But the name "Punta Cana" is now a recognized draw for the swarms of visitors who arrive through Punta Cana International Airport. Indeed, the privately owned and operated airport is the second most heavily trafficked in the Caribbean, behind only Cancun, and 51% of all visitors to the D.R. now pass through its gates.

A hot destination for golf, Punta Cana lures players with its abundance of spectacular courses—crafted by renowned designers—and posh clubhouses. The area's growth shows no signs of slowing. Major new development projects include Cap Cana and Rōco Ki, and a handful of other megaresorts peppering the coastline. More than 5,000 new rooms are planned for the area by 2010.

Higüey, capital of the Altagracia Province (which includes Punta Cana) sits 21 mi (34 km) to the west. The site of three visits by Pope John Paul II, Higüey is notable for its towering, arched concrete cathedral. Its open-air market bustles in the morning when local shoppers flock in to buy produce and meat. Though poverty is visible here, Higüey is home to a large segment of the support staff at the resorts, about an hour's commute. It's also the site of the only post office that services Punta Cana, and a transit hub for buses bound for Santo Domingo and elsewhere.

Everywhere you turn, you can encounter friendly, smiling people. English is widely spoken by guest relations staff in the hotels. Though not necessary, knowing a few phrases of Spanish to communicate with support staffers—for example, housekeeping and maintenance—goes a long way.

EXPLORING PUNTA CANA

Nestled along a 35-mi contiguous stretch of sand along the east coast, Punta Cana and its tentacles extend from the south at Juanillo (Cap Cana) to the north at Uvero Alto. Within the alluvial plains that stretch inland toward Santo Domingo, the terrain is characterized by lush, green countryside, mostly flatlands with mangroves and some swampy areas. Pastures and ranches dot the landscape, and it's common to see horses and cattle grazing in the fields—and dogs along the roads, especially farther north in Macao and Uvero Alto. School kids amble along the shoulder—there are no sidewalks and barely any traffic lights in the region. Motoconchos, motorcycle taxis with one (legal) or more (illegal) passengers, are common and pose a driving nuisance.

A new highway—the so-called "Tourist Boulevard"—is being constructed from the airport to Uvero Alto and should significantly reduce the traveling time along that stretch, from about one hour to 25 minutes, as well as improve driving safety conditions.

Throughout the region, main roads (*carreteras*) are mostly paved country roads with two-way traffic but no dividing lines. There are many potholes, which are particularly hazardous after heavy rains, when the larger ones fill up with water and drivers have to avoid—or slog through—the big puddles. It's extra tough around the bends, but drivers adhere to a set of commonsense unwritten rules of the road—basically, choose the path of least obstacles, dodge potholes, and get out of the way when facing an oncoming vehicle.

As of this writing, there were scarce traffic signs or road-name labels on the roads throughout the region; resort billboards at junctions and landmarks give clues to point you in the right direction, but driving can be confusing. However, it seems better driving conditions in some areas aren't too far down the road. New pavement was being laid down in some spots, and a new signage deal was in the works—look for street labels, lane markings, traffic lights, and road maps to follow in the next year or two.

ABOUT THE RESTAURANTS

Punta Cana's mushrooming growth in recent years has spawned a smattering of new restaurants that might entice you to venture off the grounds of your all-inclusive resort and eat at least some meals elsewhere. Although the options are still limited outside of the resorts, there's a much broader array of eateries than ever before, ranging from oceanfront cafés to top-notch restaurants on the grounds of boutique hotels that are open to outside visitors. Familiar American chains like Hard Rock Cafe and Tony Roma's Steakhouse are also among the choices.

Still, the majority of visitors to the region are guests at all-inclusives, and eat most—if not all—of their meals at the resort where they are staying, for reasons of convenience and/or budget. Generally, a variety of options are included in all price plans at any given resort, always including a main buffet open for all daily meals. In addition, many all-inclusive resorts offer at least one or two à la carte restaurants included with the standard package; the largest resorts may have five or more. In cases where a "VIP" package is offered, there's usually at least one exclusive restaurant for guests on this plan. For any of the à la carte restaurants in the resorts, dinner reservations are usually necessary, especially in high season.

> ## PUNTA CANA: ORIGIN OF THE NAME
>
> The easternmost tip of the island was originally dubbed "Punta Borrachón," that is, Drunken Point. But with its blatant negative connotations, Frank Rainieri, the visionary co-founder of PuntaCana Resort & Club, knew that simply wouldn't work to reel in the jet-setting crowd. So, inspired by the *Palma Cana*—the D.R.'s national tree that grows abundantly in the region—he coined the much more pacifying name "Punta Cana," thereby setting the stage for the burgeoning tourism industry here.

A dinner dress code barring shorts, tank-tops, and beachwear is fairly standard at the à la carte restaurants. Although jackets are not typically expected, some restaurants require long pants and collared shirts for men. Check ahead at your resort if you're looking for more casual options.

ABOUT THE HOTELS

With its sweet trifecta of pearl-sand beaches, pleasant climate, and palm trees, Punta Cana has no trouble enticing visitors. It has become the so-called Cancun of the D.R., and despite having more than 25,000 hotel rooms, the region's resorts are often filled to the brim. Even in the heart of hurricane season (late August through October), when you can usually get a room somewhere, booking far in advance is advisable for the best properties.

The initial burst of popularity for Punta Cana as a tourist destination spawned a plethora of all-inclusive resorts. And while these are still exceedingly popular, a trend toward ultraluxury accommodations has emerged, evident both in the increasing prevalence of boutique or premium hotels (definitely *not* all-inclusive) and in the spruced-up exclusive offerings within the existing all-inclusive resorts.

Playa Uvero Alto, the northernmost developed area of the region, has four resorts and three underway along its idyllic beach shaded by coconut groves. In its more remote setting, about 24 mi (39 km) from the airport, the area is less crowded than Punta/Cana Bávaro, but hotels still fill up quickly despite the longer trip to the airport. Traveling time to and from this area should improve markedly once the new "Tourist Boulevard" is completed.

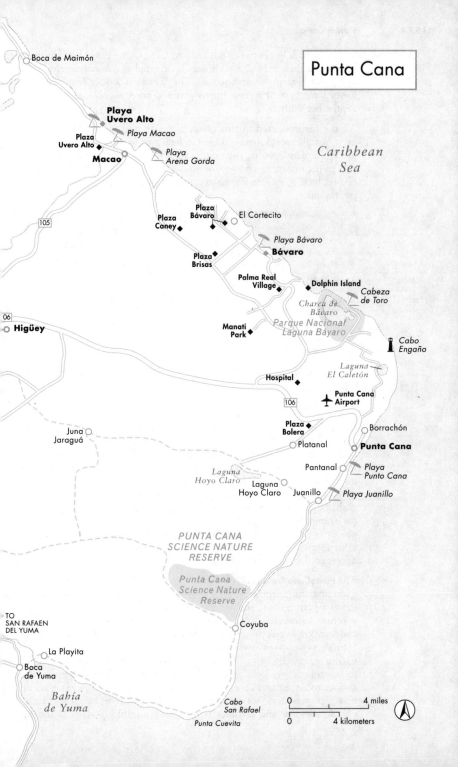

Punta Cana

Boca de Maimón

Playa Uvero Alto

Playa Macao

Plaza Uvero Alto

Macao

Playa Arena Gorda

105

Caribbean Sea

Plaza Bávaro

El Cortecito

Plaza Caney

Playa Bávaro

Bávaro

Plaza Brisas

Palma Real Village

Dolphin Island

Cabeza de Toro

Charca de Bávaro

06

Higüey

Parque Nacional Laguna Báyaro

Manati Park

Cabo Engaño

Laguna El Caletón

Hospital

106

Punta Cana Airport

Juna Jaraguá

Plaza Bolera

Platanal

Borrachón

Punta Cana

Laguna Hoyo Claro

Laguna Hoyo Claro

Pantanal

Playa Punto Cana

Juanillo

Playa Juanillo

PUNTA CANA SCIENCE NATURE RESERVE

Punta Cana Science Nature Reserve

TO SAN RAFAEN DEL YUMA

La Playita

Boca de Yuma

Coyuba

Bahía de Yuma

Cabo San Rafael

Punta Cuevita

0   4 miles

0   4 kilometers

Macao, which lies between Bávaro and Uvero Alto, is another charmed spot and is the site of phased luxury residential and resort development along the beachfront at Rōco Ki. The Westin Rōco Ki Beach & Golf Resort, the first of several hotels planned here, was slated to open in September 2008.

All the resorts listed in this chapter are along the beachfront; however, not all rooms are right on the beach (a feature factored into the price). In many resorts, you might face a several-minute walk or shuttle ride to the ocean, so choose your accommodations accordingly. Many resorts have spas offering an assortment of therapeutic and indulgent treatments.

WHAT IT COSTS IN DOLLARS					
	¢	$	$$	$$$	$$$$
Restaurants	under $8	$8–$12	$12–$20	$20–$30	Over $30
Hotels*	Under $80	$80–$150	$150–$250	$250–$350	Over $350
Hotels**	Under $125	$125–$250	$250–$350	$350–$450	Over $450

*EP, BP, CP **AI, FAP, MAP Restaurant prices are per person for a main course at dinner and do not include the 15% V.A.T. and 10% service charge. Hotel prices are per night for a double room in high season, excluding 15% V.A.T. and 10% service charge. All-inclusive rates include tax.

PUNTA CANA

5 mi (8 km) east of Punta Cana International Airport.

Playa Punta Cana is where the thrust of tourism in the entire region began with the opening of the first hotel in the 1970s. Nowadays development continues in PuntaCana Village, which is a draw for visitors from around the area, with its quaint stores where you can shop or dine. There's plenty to do, too, on the grounds of the PuntaCana Resort & Club, including fine dining, golf, a Metamorphosis spa, a tennis club, an ecological park, and a marina, making it an appealing day-trip (or evening) destination for anyone not staying here, but the resort does not offer any kind of a day- or night-pass to nonguests, so in order to take part in an activity here, you must make prior arrangements to get access to the resort grounds.

The **PuntaCana Ecological Foundation** sits on a 1,500-acre private reserve, encompassing tropical forest, natural lagoons, cold water springs, gardens, a petting zoo, and an iguana habitat. Among its missions is to promote sustainable development throughout the country by fostering cooperation between economic development and environmental protection, as well as involving the community. The foundation works with various research institutions to document all of the island's biodiversity to inform management practices regarding sustainable tourism. It also maintains an organic vegetable garden, which started as an experiment; now, its produce—for example, arugula, tomatoes, peppers, basil, chives, melons, and *auyama* (Dominican pumpkin)—is sold locally,

All-Inclusive: The Concept

All-inclusive resorts are the most common type of accommodations you'll find in Punta Cana. Here's a primer for anyone unfamiliar with this style of lodging.

Meals: At least one buffet restaurant serves breakfast, lunch, and dinner. Often, at least one and usually more à la carte specialty restaurants are included (e.g., Mexican, Italian, Japanese, Asian Fusion, and Dominican). A few restaurants such as premium steak houses might carry an extra charge. Snack bars will get you through the interim periods.

Beverages: Soft drinks, bottled water, alcoholic beverages (generally non-premium brands, whether domestic or international), and domestic beer are included, as well as a stocked minibar in all guest rooms. Some resorts even have liquor dispensers in the rooms.

Room Service: Policies vary. Where available, it may cost extra, have limited hours, or be an option only on upgraded packages.

Kids' Clubs: Most resorts have special programs for kids, typically geared to ages 4–12; a few hotels stand out with offerings in an extended (or more limited) range. Babysitters cost extra.

Activities: Nonmotorized water sports are generally included. Some resorts include one diving lesson in the pool. Diving and motorized sports are extra. There's always a slew of arranged activities going on—usually by the pool or in a games area. These might include dance lessons, Spanish lessons, stretching, yoga, water aerobics, volleyball, or pool tournaments. Some places have extras like skating, rock-climbing, or a trapeze.

Animation Teams: These are the folks who enthusiastically run the activities and try to generate a buzz among guests.

Tips: Though usually included, additional tipping for good service is not uncommon and is highly appreciated. Carrying extra $1 bills comes in handy.

Gym & Spa: Use of the gym is included; personal trainers cost extra. Most resorts have a spa. Sometimes use of steam rooms, saunas, and hot tubs is included. Massages and other treatments cost extra.

Nightlife: Some resorts are renowned for a show that stands out; generally, nonresort guests can attend by purchasing a night-pass. Entertainment usually rotates on a 7-day or 14-day cycle. Discos are standard; a few of the better ones are open to nonguests.

Casino: Many resorts have casinos with slot machines; some offer roulette and a few card tables with blackjack and assorted poker games. Texas Hold'em tables are not in abundance.

Excursions: Off-site excursions are not included.

Medical Care: Care is available 24 hours at on-site clinics. Charges for doctor services and medications are not included. International health insurance is accepted, but you must have the appropriate coverage.

Bracelets: When you arrive, most resorts will band you with a bracelet that identifies you as a guest and indicates your package level.

4

PUNTA CANA TOP 5

Sun, sand & sea. Sinking your toes in the cool sand at water's edge and soaking up the sun as you watch the white-capped tide roll in. Punta Cana has a well-deserved reputation for having some of the best beaches in the Caribbean.

Great golf. Punta Cana is quickly becoming a destination of choice for serious golfers. Playing a round at any of the area's renowned golf courses—for example, La Cana or Punta Espada—is a worthy endeavor for your family's golf fanatic.

Vibrant music & dance. Taking a merengue or bachata lesson and hitting the dance floor at your resort's

disco or at a local club like Montecristo. The nightlife doesn't get any better than at Pacha, in Bávaro's Riu resort complex.

Natural landscape. Exploring the regional flora and fauna, the sugarcane fields and the country lifestyle on any of the popular guided safari jeep tours can be a fun day for families. Just be aware that some companies keep the rum flowing during these trips; so be sure to ask if a particular excursion is family-friendly.

Activities enhanced by your surroundings. Horseback riding along the beach, especially on the night of a full moon, is a special experience.

including to some area restaurants. Etymology exhibits—butterflies, moths, and beetles—are an encyclopedia of life in the area. Guided tours of the reserve are available by appointment. Proceeds benefit the nonprofit foundation. ⊠ *PuntaCana Resort & Club* ☎ *809/959-9221* ⊕ *www.puntacana.org* ✉ *$10 for nonhotel guests* ☉ *Daily 8:30–5.*

BÁVARO

15 mi (24 km) northeast of Punta Cana International Airport.

Bávaro is centrally located along the eastern coast and is a hub of tourist activity. Many of the region's all-inclusive resorts are on Playa Bávaro, and shopping plazas, restaurants, nightlife, and services have sprung up nearby to accommodate the burgeoning number of visitors.

El Cortecito is a charming fishing village within Bávaro. It's home to a vibrant and colorful artisan market, where you can browse for souvenirs in the open-air stalls, as well as snack bars, restaurants, and vacation apartments. Also within Bávaro, farther north along the coast is a stretch of beach known as **Arena Gorda**, literally "fat sand." About 20 mi (32 km) from Punta Cana International Airport, it's an area replete with coconut groves and is home to several resorts.

At **Dolphin Island,** the adventure starts with a short boat ride as you leave the beautiful shore of Bávaro in the background, where you can spend some of your day lingering on the beach if you choose, before or after a swim with the dolphins or sea lions. The main program includes instruction, a show, and a 25-minute swim in calm, protected waters with the adorable dolphins (little Sasha and Juancho and their mom, Vicki) or sea lions. You must be 8 or older to swim, and no pregnant women are allowed, but no special skills are required. A flotation vest is provided. A DVD capturing your experience will be available for purchase as a souvenir. Sessions are at 9 AM and 2 PM daily; in high season, there's an additional session at 4 PM. Reservations must be made at least one day in advance. Free shuttles depart from the hotels. ✉ *Carretera Manatí, Bávaro* ☎ *809/221–9444* 🌐 *www.dolphinislandpark.com* 🎫 *$110 for dolphin swim; $65 for sea lion swim* 🕓 *Daily 9–5:30.*

ABOUT DOLPHIN SWIM PROGRAMS

Several organizations, including Greenpeace, have spoken out against captive dolphin encounters, asserting that some water parks get dolphins from restricted areas and that the confined conditions at some parks put the dolphins' health and safety at risk. Only you can decide whether you want to pay the $100-plus fee toward interacting with a captive dolphin. For some it's a positive, life-changing experience; for others, it's a traumatic one.

★ **Manatí Park** showcases local animals in its zoo, which includes iguanas, crocodiles, and tropical birds. A half-day tour (9 AM–1:30 PM or 1 PM–5:30 PM) includes a Taino cultural show, a horse show, and a dolphin and sea lion show. Ducks roam the gardens, where there's Dominican art on display. A brief swim or encounter with the dolphins is an option; bring your swimsuit and a towel (Dolphin Island, run by the same owner, offers a more extended swim). Free shuttles depart from the hotels. (✉ *Carretera Manatí, Bavåro* ☎ *809/221–9444 or 809/552–6100* 🌐 *www.manatipark.com* 🎫 *$30; $85 for admission and dolphin swim* 🕓 *Daily 9–5:30*).

NEED A BREAK?

Drop in for tapas and wine tastings at Latasca Wine & Food Sensations (✉ *Palma Real Shopping Village, Bávaro* ☎ *809/350-0239*) whenever you need a break from the sun, from shopping, or from the same old routine at your resort. It's open daily from 10 AM to midnight.

MACAO

20 mi (32 km) north of Punta Cana.

Macao is a pastoral village replete with pastures and ranches. Its striking beach, with dramatic headlands, inspired the most recent tourist inflow, and the latest resort development, which is ongoing at Rōco Ki.

PLAYA UVERO ALTO

7 mi (12 km) north of Macao, 24 mi (39 km) north of Punta Cana.

Ranches and rustic living characterize this little beach village, which has coconut groves and a stunning beach where development is continuing to press north of Macao. A couple of newer, small boutique hotels have popped up here. A new road being built from the airport

CLOSE UP

Saona Island

This scenic, secluded island with a beautiful beach is off the southeastern end of the D.R., near Bayahibe (see ⇨ Chapter 3, The Southeast Coast, for more information). Saona is part of a government-protected nature reserve replete with tropical wildlife and exotic birds in their natural habitat. It's off the southern coast of the Parque Nacional del Este and known for its exquisite beauty. The island's resplendent blue waters are teeming with various species of marine life, most notably the area's indigenous starfish. And protective sandbars keep the sand sparkling white. The breathtaking beach is a popular day-trip destination for tourists from the resorts in Punta Cana and La Romana. Most tours sail here by catamaran from Bayahibe (about 90 minutes from Punta Cana by tour bus), and you can spend the day kicking back on the beach or swimming. Extra features, like a stop at a natural pool, are included with some tours, which cost about $85 to $90 for a full day, including lunch and beverages. Bring suntan lotion, towels, a swimsuit, a camera, and some cash for souvenirs or extra drinks.

should cut down the hourlong trip by car. Nevertheless, to the most exclusive outposts, there's always the option of coming by helicopter.

HIGÜEY

37 mi (60 km) west of Punta Cana.

Meaning "place where the sun rises" in the language of the indigenous Taino Indians, Higüey was one of the first areas to be settled by the Spanish conquistadors in 1502. Capital of the Altagracia Province (which encompasses Punta Cana), the city is considered by Catholics to be a Holy Land because of a vision of the Virgin Mary there, and a litany of reported miracles in the area. Higüey was the site of three visits by Pope John Paul II (in 1979, 1984, and 1992), and nowadays the cathedral near the central square is the main draw for tourists. An open-air market within walking distance reveals a not-so-pretty slice of life and is a point of interest rather than a shopping destination. On the cluttered city streets, motorcycles are a heavy presence and zip around from every which way, so be alert whether driving or on foot. The Espresso Bávaro Bus Terminal, a hub of transit between the region, Santo Domingo, and elsewhere in the country, is here, as is the Altagracia Province post office, which services Punta Cana and the surrounding areas.

Many people employed by the hotels along the east coast beaches are residents of Higüey, with a commute of about an hour each way.

Basilica de Higüey Nuestra Señora de la Altagracia, Higüey's concrete basilica, was built in 1972 and is characterized by its representations of oranges, symbolic of the nearby orange grove where a vision of the Virgin Mary has become legend. There's a shrine depicting an orange tree and stained-glass windows with cut-outs shaped like oranges inside the cathedral, where you can climb the stairs of the sanctuary and touch the encased icon of the Virgen de la Altagracia, patron saint of the Dominican Republic. Outside, you can light a candle or purchase religious memorabilia. The pinched arches of the facade stretch 250 feet (75 meters) high. The basilica is the site of annual pilgrimages on January 21 and August 16. ⊠*Agustin Guerrero 66* ☎*809/554–4541* ⊠*Free* ☉*Daily 5 AM–7 PM; masses daily at 5, 8, and 10 AM, and noon; also Sat. at 6 PM and Sun. at 5 PM.*

Produce and meat are laid out for display at dozens of stalls at the open-air **Mercado Publico de Higüey.** With dogs roaming around, flies abuzz and slabs of meat strung up and strewn about in wheelbarrows—sometimes bloody and never refrigerated—this market is not the best place to seek out a snack, but nonetheless it's a captivating slice of life to see while you're in the area. If you want to purchase anything, nonperishables are the safest; if you do buy produce, make sure you wash it before eating. ⊠*Plaza Central, Av. Libertad* ☉*Mon.–Sat. 8–5.*

On the outskirts of Higüey, as you head into town along Carretera Higüey–La Otra Banda, you can find **Plaza Higüeyana**—an artisan market that draws busloads of tourists—on the right-hand side of the road. Here you can browse through racks and shelves full of souvenirs, like mamajuana, rum, T-shirts, jewelry, crafts, and ceramics.

Inside the Plaza Highüeyana, you can take a free tour (in English) of the **Museo Vivo Del Tabaco** (☎*809/551–1128* ⊕*www.museedutabac. com*), where you can see how tobacco is planted, harvested, and rolled into cigars. Near the entrance to the museum, you can also purchase hand-rolled cigars. ⊠*Carretera Higüey–La Otra Banda, at east end of Higüey* ☉*Daily 9 AM–7 PM.*

EN ROUTE Along the drive between Higüey and Punta Cana, the town of La Otra Banda is notable for its colorful, traditional homes. With its local flavor and picturesque setting 30 to 40 minutes inland from the beachside resorts at Punta Cana and Cap Cana, the area is poised to continue its recent real estate investment boom.

WHERE TO EAT

Many restaurants outside of the resorts that cater to international tourists are in and around Bávaro and Punta Cana. However, even the more remote areas have at least a few local restaurants beyond those listed here that are worth seeking out if you are adventurous. You might find good food, good value, and friendly service, but the farther you go off the beaten track, the more unlikely it is that English will be spoken.

$–$$$$ ✕**Capitan Cook's.** Lobster, king crab legs, and lots of fish are what's cooking at this seafood specialty house on the sand, where the fresh catch is stashed on ice in a fiberglass vault and grilled before your eyes. An à la carte menu is hand-scrawled on a jumbo bulletin board, with prices given in pesos, but U.S. dollars are accepted, too. Despite naysayers who object that the quality of the food has gone downhill, the bazaarlike atmosphere on the waterfront keeps reeling in the tour-

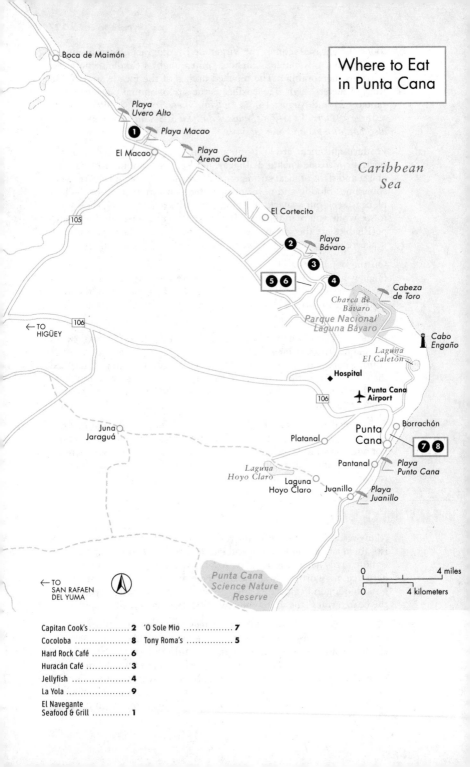

Where to Eat in Punta Cana

Boca de Maimón

Playa Uvero Alto
1
Playa Macao
El Macao
Playa Arena Gorda

Caribbean Sea

El Cortecito

2 Playa Bávaro

3

5 **6** **4**

Cabeza de Toro

Charca de Bávaro
Parque Nacional Laguna Bávaro

← TO HIGÜEY

105

106

Cabo Engaño

Laguna El Caletón

◆ **Hospital**

✈ **Punta Cana Airport**

106

Juna Jaraguá

Platanal

Punta Cana

Borrachón

7 **8**

Pantanal
Playa Punto Cana

Laguna Hoyo Claro
Laguna Hoyo Claro

Juanillo
Playa Juanillo

← TO SAN RAFAEN DEL YUMA

Punta Cana Science Nature Reserve

0   4 miles
0   4 kilometers

ist crowds. The restaurant offers free round-trip transportation by water taxi from the area hotels (daytime only). Some resorts offer a prix-fixe excursion (around $40) to the restaurant that includes drinks and the *parrillada mixta* (a mix of seafood—mussels, baby lobsters, fresh fish, squid, shrimp) with fries and salad, followed by coffee, fruit, and shots of fiery *mamajuana* (an herbal liqueur). Sit in the sand at the water's edge and watch as the fishermen hang their catch up by the tail. It's wild and crazy as mariachis play *Ai, yai, yai,* vendors hawk Haitian and Dominican art, and waiters sprint to the beach tables delivering sizzling metal cauldrons of the signature dish. ⊠*El Cortecito, Bávaro* ☏*809/552–0645* ♠*Reservations essential* ▤*MC, V.*

> ### BIRDS OF PUNTA CANA
>
> Within the diverse natural habitats of the area—beaches, fields, forests, and mangroves—more than 100 species of birds have been spotted. Among them are nectar-slurping hummingbirds, gliding frigatebirds, plunge-diving royal terns, fish-engulfing brown pelicans, singing mockingbirds, and wintering Cape May warblers. Hiking through a nature preserve or walking along Madre de los Aves Beach, you might see or hear 20 to 30 species in a single day. The Cornell Biodiversity Laboratory at the PuntaCana Ecological Foundation studies the region's unique birds and biospheres to help protect and conserve them.

4

$$-$$$ ✕**Cocoloba.** A feast of the senses begins with the eye candy at this
★ Oscar de la Renta–decorated Asian-fusion restaurant in the Punta-Cana Resort's distinguished clubhouse. The tableware—with colorful geometric plates—is so fetching that it makes the food, already stellar, taste even better. Waken your palate with an appetizer of sea bass and crabmeat cakes with mango chutney. For a main course, the pork tenderloin confit atop a yucca cake with cherries is irresistibly good. The extensive wine list complements the cuisine. To satisfy a sweet tooth, try the almond biscuit with chocolate sauce over caramelized pineapple. ⊠*PuntaCana Resort & Club, Punta Cana* ☏*809/959–2262* ♠*Reservations essential* ▤*AE, MC, V* ☉*No lunch.*

$$-$$$ ✕**Hard Rock Café.** There's nothing that takes a bite out of the blues like
☺ this familiar American standby, with all the namesake rock-and-roll memorabilia adorning the walls, and the café's standard fare: 10-ounce certified Angus beef burgers, hickory-smoked chicken wings, white-cheddar smashed potatoes, "twisted" mac and cheese, sandwiches, salads, and the like. Memorabilia on display here includes Madonna's black teddy with pink feather trim from her "Blond Ambition" tour and original Jimi Hendrix drawings and lyrics scrawled on a 1968 copy of the *New York Times.* Top off your meal with a visit to the gift shop, and take out a souvenir HARD ROCK PUNTA CANA T-shirt. Free shuttles are available from many Punta Cana hotels. ⊠*Plaza Palma Real, Carretera El Cortecito 57, Bávaro* ☏*809/552–8820* ▤*AE, MC, V.*

$$-$$$ ✕**Huracán Café.** A thatched-roof palapa over a wooden deck in the sand
★ shelters diners from the elements at this tony outdoor eatery set back a few paces from the ocean on a prime stretch of beach. Pastas and other Italian dishes dominate the menu, but a few Tex-Mex options

will please some palates. A prix-fixe dinner is a popular choice; for about $25, you get an appetizer, main course, mixed grill, wine, and coffee. By prior arrangement, the chef will also prepare special dishes according to your tastes. After dinner, kick back with a Cuba Libre and enjoy the starlight ambience. The place turns lively on Saturday nights, with weekly theme parties and a DJ spinning jams. If your timing's right, the full-moon parties are rollicking. ⊠*El Cortecito, Bávaro* ☎*809/221–6643* ▭*MC, V.*

$–$$$$ ✕**Jellyfish.** Shaped like a double-deck yacht, this sophisticated open-

Fodor'sChoice   air restaurant on the sand is a charming hotspot for lunch and dinner.

★   Tables are on light wooden platforms, sheltered by thatched roofing but not fully enclosed. When weather demands it, sheer white linens are secured to the wooden railings to protect against sun, wind, or rain without obstructing the exquisite beachfront views. At night, soft lighting creates a romantic effect, and lounge music enhances the ambience. Fresh seafood caught by local fishermen is the focus of the menu, but chicken and beef dishes are also available, as is a special children's menu. Lobster lovers can look forward to sinking their claws into the oven-baked *langosta de la casa* (house lobster). For a more diverse shellfish meal, try the seafood grill for two, which included crawfish, lobster, shrimp, conch, and octopus. One special option is the De Leon Cigar smoking lounge, where you can arrange a private dinner and showing with the owner, who will talk about the process of creating the specialty smokes; or you can simply light up and sample different cigars for sale. If you eat dinner, the restaurant offers free transportation back to your hotel (though not free transportation *to* the restaurant). Some resorts, like Paradisus Palma Real and the Barceló Bávaro complex, are within walking distance. The space is sometimes closed for private parties and weddings, so it's best to call ahead for reservations. ⊠*Bávaro* ☎*809/840–7684 or 809/868–3040* ⚑*Reservations essential* ▭*No credit cards.*

$$–$$$$ ✕**La Yola.** As if you were aboard a *yola* (a small fishing boat), you

Fodor'sChoice   will feel the gentle breeze blow over the harbor as you dine on a deck

★   overlooking the PuntaCana Marina. Using thatched cane for overhead shelter, and the ocean as a backdrop, the restaurant's decor blends elements of the region's natural marvels to achieve an utterly gratifying open-air dining ambience. Delicious cuisine—with both Mediterranean and Caribbean influences—and attentive service enhance the exceptional experience. Seafood and fish dominate the menu, but you'll also find beef and chicken selections. The chef will accommodate special dietary needs. For an appetizer, the spicy tuna tartare with guacamole relish starts you off with a pleasing burst of flavor and satisfying texture. Main plates, including the catch of the day—usually red snapper, grouper, or mahimahi—are artfully prepared and presented. Baked Chilean sea bass with clam and cherry tomato risotto is a savory special. ⊠*PuntaCana Resort & Club* ☎*809/959–2262 Ext. 8002* ⚑*Reservations essential* ▭*AE, MC, V* ✆*Closed Tues.*

$$–$$$ ✕**El Navegante Seafood & Grill.** Dig your toes in the sand or dine on the sheltered wooden porch as you savor your seafood at this local beachfront favorite. A tasty *parillada* (mixed grill) for two ($55) includes

baby lobster, shrimp, octopus, conch, and fillet fish. For those favoring turf over surf, there's also steak and chicken on the menu. To get here, from Carretera Uvero Alto turn on the unpaved beach access road at billboard south of Excellence Resort and drive about ¾ mi (1 km) to the end. ⊠*Playa Uvero Alto* ☎*809/468–0166* ⊟*AE, MC, V.*

$–$$$ ✕*'O Sole Mio.* Tucked away on a nondescript street, with no sign posted
★ outside, this delicious secret of a restaurant looks like any ordinary house; you really have to know where you're going to find it. Once you do, you'll likely encounter the owner, Nino, who's catered to an exclusive set of Punta Cana admirers (including Oscar de la Renta) with scrumptious Italian cooking since the early 1990s. There's seating for 50 people on an outdoor sheltered patio. Diners return time and again for the homemade pastas—linguine, spaghetti, penne, and rigatoni—and savory sauces. Many vegetables and herbs used here, including arugula, spinach, onion, and basil, come straight from the garden of the PuntaCana Ecological Foundation. Meat is imported from the U.S. There's a small menu, including highlights like baby lobster in wine sauce, plus daily specials. Foods are prepared simply— boiled or grilled rather than sautéed—and the chef will address any special dietary needs. Choose from an extensive list of imported wines to complement your meal. Sometimes organic homemade ice creams are offered for dessert. To get here from Punta Cana, take Carretera Punta Cana-Bávaro to Carretera Verón-Punta Cana; drive west along Carretera Verón-Punta Cana toward Higüey. In about 3 mi (5 km) you will come to a traffic light (not necessarily working); the junction is the turnoff toward Bávaro to your right. There will be a gas station on your left. Go past the light; the first gated entrance on your right is the restaurant. ⊠*Carretera Verón-Punta Cana, Verón* ☎*809/455–1143* ⚑*Reservations essential* ⊟*AE, D, DC, MC, V* ☉*Closed Sun.*

$–$$$ ✕**Tony Roma's.** Sink your teeth into succulent ribs—imported from the United States—at one of the newest outposts of this internationally renowned meatery, which opened here in early 2007. Juicy baby backs and other types of ribs smothered in your choice of signature sauce (e.g., original, honey, smoke, and hot) head up the menu, which also includes steaks, seafood, chicken, burgers, and salads. For starters, the onion loaf—giant and deep-fried to a golden crisp—is another favorite. ⊠*Palma Real Shopping Village, Suite 31, Bávaro* ☎*809/552–8880* ⊟*AE, MC, V.*

WHERE TO STAY

Most hotels in the region are clustered around Punta Cana and Bávaro, where more than 90% of the existing properties are all-inclusive. But development continues to press outward—northward to the more remote locations of Macao and Uvero Alto, and southward to the nearby Juanillo—and several of the newer offerings are ultraluxury non-all-inclusive resorts.

With development mushrooming in and around Punta Cana, several resorts were still under construction as this book was being written and

Rōco Ki

Translated from Taino language as "honoring the land," the multibillion-dollar development at Rōco Ki is a heavenly world set on the charmed Macao Beach. Its 2,700 acres on the east coast enchant with dramatic cliffs, palm trees, mangroves, and jungle. The theatrical backdrop is like nature's equivalent of a laser light show: green vegetation, turquoise sea, fuchsia flowers, blue sky, white sand. The blueprint for the 15-year phased development project maps out plans for posh hotels (seven to nine total), golf courses, a marina, a sports training complex, and various styles of luxury residences, all exuding an easygoing affluence in an environment at peace with nature. The magnificent undertaking strives to achieve the perfect balance between low-density, low-environmental-impact design and high-end comfort. With buildings and villas spread out among lagoons, mangroves and coastline, and weaved around ample conservation areas teeming with wildlife, the development is conceived with respect toward preserving the natural habitat while exceeding the most indulgent dreams of opulent living.

First to go up in phase one are the Westin Rōco Ki hotel and branded villas and the championship 18-hole, Nick Faldo–designed course, with its striking 17th-hole on a sculpted cliff, both set to open in September 2008. The developers are working in cooperation with the government to preserve and curate Taino artifacts unearthed during excavation at the Rōco Ki site, which will be displayed at a museum slated to open in fall 2009.

could, therefore, not be reviewed. The Westin Rōco Ki Beach & Golf Resort was expected to open in September 2008. In earlier stages of construction were Moon Palace in Macao (with 1,768 rooms planned), and two Eden H properties in Bávaro. Also, two hotels that changed hands in 2007—Dreams Punta Cana Resort & Spa and Sunscape Punta Cana—were undergoing major branding and management transitions and therefore could not be reviewed. However, all these hotels were expected to be major players in the Punta Cana theater.

VILLAS & CONDOS

With its allure as a residential area growing, Punta Cana and surrounding region have seen an ever-increasing number of villa and apartment enclaves marketed as second homes, vacation residences, or real estate investments spring up. Most of these enclaves have units for rent when the owners are not in residence. The Trump Farallon Estates at Cap Cana will *not* be part of the rental pool, however.

Palma Real Villas Golf & Country Club (⊠ *Cocotal Golf & Country Club, Bávaro* ☎ *809/730–6767, 809/221–1290 Ext. 5555, or 877/213–5002* ⊕ *www.palmarealvillas.com*), by Sol Melia, is an upscale ownership community with several different styles of two- to four-bedroom villas and condominiums, all with membership privileges at the Cocotal Golf Course—including discounted green fees, access to the club house and golf academy—special discounts and benefits at the Meliá Caribe

New & Noteworthy Resorts

Several resorts were in various stages of completion as this book was being written. You may wish to consider the following resorts when making your Punta Cana plans for 2008 even though we were not able to fully review these hotels since they were not open when this book was being researched.

Dreams Punta Cana Resort & Spa. With a fresh face after a multimillion-dollar renovation, this all-inclusive resort—formerly Sunscape the Beach—was rebranded and has been known under its new moniker since December 2007. In the remote setting near pastures and farmland, vacationers can find everything under the sun, including a plethora of à la carte restaurants and a buffet, 10 bars, and a large, inviting pool that winds around the grounds. Kids' club (for ages 3–12) activities include sand-castle building, arts and crafts, and rock-climbing. ✉ *Uvero Alto* ☎ *809/682–0404 or 866/237–3267* ⊕ *www.dreamsresorts.com.*

Majestic Elegance. This luxury all-inclusive is being built right next door to its sister, the Majestic Colonial and was slated to open in the fall 2008. Some facilities and grounds will likely be shared, but there's no word yet on the details of shared access and/or exclusive facilities. ✉ *Macao* ☎ *809/221–9898* ⊕ *www.majestic-colonial.com.*

Sunscape Punta Cana. This hotel, formerly the Occidental Allegro Punta Cana, was purchased in late 2007 and was undergoing major changes, including rebranding and renovations in early 2008. On a beautiful beach, the resort's 540 guestrooms are tucked into nine three-story buildings with red-tile roofs. The landscaped grounds are nicely maintained, but the jury is still out on how well guest expectations will be met in all areas of hospitality. For family-oriented vacations, you can find activities for kids ages 3–12, with supervised options for kids to explore the area, and beepers to keep you in touch. Guests can enjoy all activities and amenities without having to wear the ubiquitous all-inclusive wristbands. ✉ *Cabeza de Toro* ☎ *809/552–6000* ⊕ *www.sunscaperesorts.com.*

Westin Rōco Ki Beach & Golf Resort. Rising up dramatically at the edge of a cliff that juts out into the sea, this grand Spanish Renaissance–style resort is visible from some beaches many miles farther south along the coast. At this writing, the resort was expected to open in September 2008, the first imprint of true luxury (non-all-inclusive) hospitality in Macao. The complex includes not only the hotel but also Westin-branded condominiums and villas, seven restaurants, 24-hour room service, bars, a spa, tennis courts, a wedding gazebo, a marina, a gourmet market, and a conference center. The new, spectacular Nick Faldo–designed golf course (set to open simultaneously) is steps away, and guests here have privileged packages. ✉ *Macao* ☎ *954/624–1771 or 800/937–8461* ⊕ *www.westin.com* ⚒ *In-room: safe, kitchen (some), refrigerator (some), Wi-Fi. In-hotel: 7 restaurants, room service, bars, golf, tennis courts, pool, gym, spa, beachfront, water sports, children's programs (ages 3–12), laundry service, concierge, public Internet, public Wi-Fi, no-smoking rooms* ▭ *AE, D, DC, MC, V.*

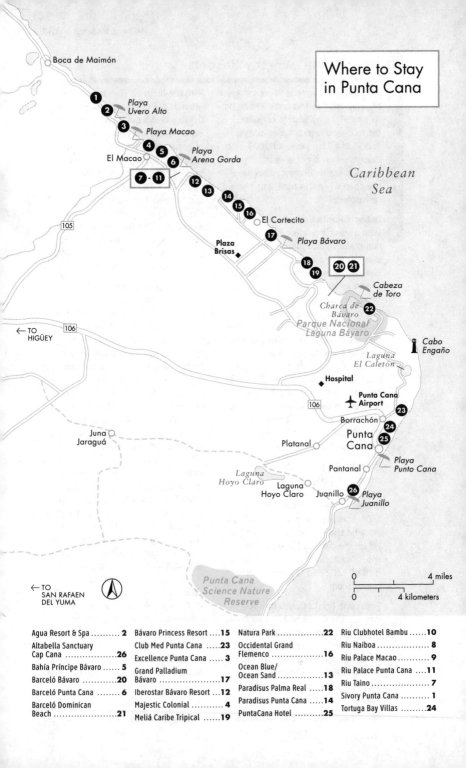

Where to Stay in Punta Cana

Boca de Maimón

1

2

3 *Playa Uvero Alto*

Playa Macao

4
5
El Macao **6** *Playa Arena Gorda*

7 - 11

12

13

14

15

16
El Cortecito

17
Playa Bávaro

Plaza Brisas

18
19

20 **21**

Cabeza de Toro

Charca de Bávaro
22
Parque Nacional Laguna Bávaro

Cabo Engaño

Caribbean Sea

105

← TO HIGÜEY

106

Laguna El Caletón

Hospital

Punta Cana Airport

106

Borrachón

Punta Cana

23

24
25

Playa Punto Cana

Juna Jaraguá

Platanal

Pantanal

Laguna Hoyo Claro
Laguna Hoyo Claro

Juanillo
26 *Playa Juanillo*

← TO SAN RAFAEN DEL YUMA

Punta Cana Science Nature Reserve

0 _____ 4 miles
0 _____ 4 kilometers

Other Hotel Choices

Punta Cana is awash in hotels. Those recommended in this chapter are our favorites, but there are others worth considering, such as: *$$ ($270–$350)* **Catalonia Bávaro** (⊠*Bávaro* ☎*809/412-0000* ⊕*www.cataloni-abavaro.com*) offers 711 rooms from this Spanish chain and draws a heavily European clientele.

$$ ($225–$325) **Hotel Grand Oasis Punta Cana** (⊠*Cabeza de Toro* ☎*809/686-9898* ⊕*www.hotelesoasis.com*) is a handsome, English-Caribbean style all-inclusive resort with 450 rooms along Cabeza de Toro beach. The lobby is bright and inviting, with an ivory-tone, marbleized floor, buttercup yellow walls and elegant, spiral staircases with iron railings. A similar palette of color is in the guest rooms, which have four-post beds, Jacuzzi tubs and a balcony or terrace. There's a pretty pool and the beach is fetching with its white sand and palm

trees sprouting up everywhere. The Metamorphosis Spa, with its meditation garden, offers a sleek sanctuary; conversely, there's a fun casino and a disco. There's also a gym, tennis courts and activities for the kids.

$$ ($236–$276) **LTI Beach Resort Punta Cana Golf & Spa** (⊠*Carretera Arena Gorda, Bávaro* ☎*809/221-6640* ⊕*ltibeachresort.com*) offers up a full basket of all-inclusive services, four restaurants, and several bars to appease guests. There are all sorts of daytime activities, with boogie boarding and catamarans among the nonmotorized water sports included. One highlighted extra is the wellness program in the Metamorphosis Spa. In the evenings, nightly shows, a disco and a casino (with a free shuttle), are among the options. Within the resort, the 47 junior suites at the Cayena Beach Club offer an exclusive level of luxury.

4

Tropical Hotel, and 24-hour security. Residents enjoy proximity to the Palma Real Shopping Village. The complex is a 20-minute drive from the airport. A managed property rental program is offered.

The **PuntaCana Estates** (⊠*PuntaCana Resort & Club, Punta Cana* ☎*809/959-7325* ⊕*www.puntacana.com*) are comprised of Corales, Hacienda, and Arrecife communities of exclusive Dominican-style estates that blend elegant architecture with the inherent beauty of the natural environment. Within sublime surroundings that include a 5-mi stretch of pearly beach and skyscraping palm trees, homeowners in these private retreats enjoy top-notch amenities and services, including a private VIP terminal at the Punta Cana International Airport, access to highly acclaimed golf courses designed by P. B. Dye and Tom Fazio (Corales only), elite clubhouses, the mesmerizing Six Senses Spa, an ecological preserve with natural springs, a full-service marina, tennis courts, housekeeping and nanny services, and all of PuntaCana Resort's restaurants and facilities. Owners can rent out their homes through a managed property rental program. Oscar de la Renta and Julio Iglesias, among the partners in the PuntaCana Resort & Club, as well as Mikhail Baryshnikov, have vacation homes in the ultra-exclusive Corales neighborhood.

Rōco Ki (✉*Macao* ☎*809/731–2800 or 888/476–2654* ⊕*www.rocoki. com*) is a huge development project including villas, bungalows, and gigantic luxury estates, with either beach or jungle views. Some Westin-branded condos and villas, from studios to three-bedrooms, are nestled between the striking Nick Faldo–designed golf course and the Westin Rōco Ki Beach & Golf Resort. The architectural styles draw inspiration from Taino culture. Superlative amenities, designed to meet the needs and desires of the most discerning residents, include room service, a concierge, and housekeeping. Rental plans are available.

HOTELS & RESORTS

$$$$
Fodor's Choice
★

Agua Resort & Spa. A thatched-roof, open-air lobby welcomes you to this serene oceanfront resort, where rustic natural beauty and high architectural style blend seamlessly. The design shows Dominican and Balinese influences, utilizing materials like *coralina* stone, cane, wicker, and wood. All rooms have four-post beds with a firm mattress and Frette linens, a furnished terrace, a large flat-screen TV, and artfully tiled floor lamps; some have dramatic ocean views. The remarkable stone bathrooms have porcelain basins and Korres amenities, plus such thoughtful extras as a toothbrush, toothpaste, and insect repellent. Second-level villas are enormous, with soaring thatched-cane roofs. For a small resort, the pool is quite large, but most guests will be drawn to the impeccable beach. Beyond the beach is an amazing coral reef that can turn bright red by night when the light is just so. Service is super-attentive, and the resort can organize horseback riding or helicopter tours, or simply lend you a DVD. This is an adult-oriented resort, but organized kids' programs serve ages 5–9. Meal plans are available. **Pros:** Serene and remote location, attentive staff, rustic luxury. **Cons:** Mosquitos, limited nightlife, no clock in room. ✉*Playa Uvero Alto* ☎*809/468–0000* ⊕*www.aguaresort.com* ⇄*40 rooms, 5 2- or 3- bedroom villas* ⌂*In-room: safe, DVD. In hotel: 2 restaurants, room service, bars, tennis court, pools, gym, spa, beachfront, water sports, no elevator, children's programs (ages 5–9), laundry service, concierge, public Internet, public Wi-Fi, airport shuttle, no-smoking rooms* ▤*AE, MC, V* ⊙*EP.*

$$$$
Fodor's Choice
★

Altabella Sanctuary Cap Cana Golf & Spa. With its awe-inspiring, palatial main lobby, this is the area's first hotel south of Punta Cana. Its gorgeous stone facade is reminiscent of the 16th-century Alcázar de Colón in Santo Domingo. The interior, influenced by Dominican colonial-style mansions, has enormous stone columns stretching up to the second floor, which is bedecked with intricate iron balconies and keystone arches. Light pours in through a stained-glass ceiling enveloping the spacious main hall, where you can find upscale shops and a resplendent stone water fountain. Near the lobby, peach-toned villas spread out along the waterfront. Within are the suites, each with an ocean view, a balcony, or a terrace. Some royal suites hover right over the water, with a Jacuzzi that opens fancifully onto the water. Round-the-clock butler service is an option in the high-end suites. When complete, four swimming pools will serve the hotel; one was ready at this writing. **Pros:**

Exquisite colonial-style design, top-notch golf, ultraposh accommodations. **Cons:** Continuing development all around at Cap Cana, some facilities not ready. ⊠*Juanillo* ☎*809/562–7555 or 800/785–2198* ⊕*www.capcana.com* ⇆*176 suites* ♿*In-room: safe, kitchen (some), refrigerator (some), Wi-Fi. In-hotel: 8 restaurants, room service, bars, golf courses, tennis courts, pools, gym, spa, beachfront, water sports, children's programs (ages 2–12), laundry service, concierge, public Wi-Fi, no-smoking rooms* ▭*AE, D, DC, MC, V* ⦿*EP.*

$–$$ ▨**Bahía Príncipe Bávaro Resort Spa & Casino.** A huge property—you have to be shuttled to the beach and the buffet—this resort feels impersonal, but guests don't seem to mind since there are plenty of pleasing choices for food and fun. All rooms are outfitted with Jacuzzi tubs, satellite TV, and a balcony or terrace. You can request a sea view if you opt for any of the premium club packages, which also offer perks such as a concierge, private check-in, 24-hour room service and upgraded amenities. In the Caribbean village replica, you'll find shops, à la carte restaurants, a karaoke–piano bar, a casino, pool tables and the disco, which cranks up around 1 AM. Three sister hotels (Bahía Príncipe Punta Cana, with 708 junior suites, Bahía Príncipe Bávaro, with 450 junior suites, and Bahía Príncipe Premier, with 288 junior suites) are part of the complex, sharing access to facilities. Well-managed, Bahía Príncipe has a dependable international staff. **Pros:** Polished international staff, golf nearby, good upgrade packages. **Cons:** Impersonal, limited access to à la carte restaurants, extra charge for use of in-room safe. ⊠*Playa Arena Gorda, Bávaro* ☎*809/552–1444* ⊕*www.bahia-principe.com* ⇆*1,536 suites* ♿*In-room: safe, refrigerator, Ethernet. In hotel: 8 restaurants, bars, pools, gym, spa, beachfront, water sports, no elevator, children's programs (ages 4–12), laundry service, public Internet* ▭*AE, MC, V* ⦿*AI.*

$ ▨**Barceló Bávaro Beach Resort.** On verdant grounds nestled up against
☺   a luscious beach, this expansive complex includes five hotels at various budget and service levels. The showcase Bávaro Palace is at the high end, but sister hotels—Bávaro Beach, Bávaro Caribe Beach, Bávaro Casino, and Bávaro Golf—share access to most facilities of the complex (all but the restaurants, amenities, and activities of the Palace, which are exclusive to guests staying there). Each hotel has its own buffet restaurant and unique features; for example, the Casino hotel is home to the 24-hour adult-only casino and to the large cabaret theater. The Golf hotel is quieter, with no organized activities. All resort guests get a half-price discount on green fees at the 18-hole golf course, which sits amid lush tropical vegetation. Neither the Casino nor the Golf hotels face the beach; others have ocean views but cost more. Among the diversions are minigolf, horseback riding, baseball and soccer fields, and a weekly movie night. A free shuttle transports guests around the complex. **Pros:** Beautiful golf course, enormous range of entertainment and activities, fun production show. **Cons:** Limited room-service hours, pool gets crowded and noisy, resort draws large conventions and groups. ⊠*Carretera Bávaro, Bávaro* ☎*809/686–5797* ⊕*www.barcelo.com* ⇆*1,921 rooms, 100 suites* ♿*In-room: safe, refrigerator, Ethernet. In-hotel: 13 restaurants, bars, golf course, tennis courts,*

pools, gym, spa, beachfront, diving, water sports, bicycles, children's programs (ages 4–12), laundry service, concierge, executive floor, public Internet, public Wi-Fi, no-smoking rooms ▭AE, DC, MC, V ❨◎❩AI.

$ ★ ▦ **Barceló Dominican Beach.** An exceptional value, this well-managed resort has been infused with upgrades since it was purchased from Ocean Hotels in 2007, and it now exudes appeal rivaling the higher-tier Barceló properties. Many guest rooms have been renovated and all have been outfitted with pillow-top mattresses; all rooms have balconies, satellite TV, and coffeemakers, and the minibar is restocked daily. The gym has all the standard machines—treadmills, stair-steppers, and stationary bikes—and free weights to get (or keep) you in top form. The wonderful Metamorphosis Spa looks out over the ocean, adding another dose of soothing to the mix of treatments. The Spanish restaurant El Mesón serves commendable meals in a charming setting, and the Brazilian rodizzio also gets accolades from guests; a coffee bar will pick you up in the afternoon. Basketball, archery, dance lessons, and Spanish lessons are among the full plate of daytime activities. For nightly fun, two theaters feature a schedule of entertainment on a 14-day rotation; weekly beach parties, a casino, and a disco round out the entertainment options. Wi-Fi is available in all rooms (rare in Punta Cana), although there is an extra cost. **Pros:** Attention to detail, Wi-Fi throughout, great coffee bar. **Cons:** Beach parties can get loud, extra cost for Wi-Fi. ✉*Bávaro* ☎*809/221–0714 Ext. 1801* ⊕*www. barcelo.com* ☞*638 rooms, 94 suites* ♿*In-room: safe, refrigerator, Wi-Fi. In-hotel: 9 restaurants, room service (some), bars, tennis courts, pools, gym, spa, beachfront, diving, water sports, bicycles, children's programs (ages 4–12), laundry service, public Internet, public Wi-Fi, no-smoking rooms* ▭AE, DC, MC, V ❨◎❩AI.

$ ☾ ▦ **Barceló Punta Cana.** White Spanish-style buildings with large pillars and red-tile roofs add to the spectacular vistas at this resort, where from ocean-facing balconies you can see towering palms swaying in the breeze on the sand. If you choose the standard package, it's worth it to pay extra for the new deluxe rooms in buildings 1, 2 and 3, which—after top-to-bottom renovations in late 2007—have fresh, sophisticated decor and are now nicer than some of the costlier, but older, suites. But the Premium Club suites also include upgraded amenities, such as a club room with bar and snacks, free Internet access, and preferred restaurant reservations. The Japanese and Dominican restaurants are top choices among the varied options for international dining; some menu items at à la carte restaurants have a surcharge. Plenty of activities, including a trapeze and rock-climbing wall, are fun for the whole family. Golf packages are available at nearby courses. One swimming pool caters to activity-seekers, a second is quiet. Two theaters and a large casino offer nighttime diversions. A basic wedding ceremony—with cake, sparkling wine and flowers—is included (upgrades are available). **Pros:** New quiet pool, helpful staff, deluxe rooms renovated in 2007. **Cons:** Unrenovated room interiors are tired, uninspiring hallways, extra charge for room service. ✉*Carretera Macao, Playa Arena Gorda, Bávaro* ☎*809/476–7777* ⊕*www.barcelopuntacana.com* ☞*751 room, 47 suites* ♿*In-room: safe, refrigerator, Ethernet (some).*

In-hotel: 7 restaurants, room service, bars, tennis courts, pools, gym, spa, beachfront, diving, water sports, bicycles, children's programs (ages 4–12), public Internet, public Wi-Fi, no-smoking rooms ▭AE, DC, MC, V †☉|AI.

$ ⊞**Bávaro Princess Resort.** Certain aspects of this Princess (one of four hotels within this kingdom) make you feel like you're in a fairy tale. The endless pool is one, with its palm-studded islets and swim-up bar; the graceful lobby with lush tropical plants and white pillars is another. This is one resort where advancing to a higher level is worth the charge. Be Queen for the Day and marry in the white-domed rotunda with the azure sea as your photographic backdrop—it's included in the fabulous Magical and Royalty packages. The Chopin international restaurant is a favorite among diners. There's a casino on the complex, as well as a popular disco, which is open to nonresort guests. Sister properties are Punta Cana Princess (adults only, 270 suites), Caribe Club Princess (355 rooms and suites) and Tropical Princess (310 rooms). **Pros:** Good disco, majestic decor, beautiful pool. **Cons:** Room upkeep is failing, with mustiness in some rooms. ⊠*Bávaro* ☎*809/221–2311* ⊕*www. princessbavaroresort.com* ⇝*686 suites, 82 junior suites* ⟁*In-room: safe, refrigerator. In-hotel: 7 restaurants, room service, tennis courts, gym, bars, pools, beachfront, water sports, public Internet* ▭AE, MC, V †☉|AI.

$$$ ⊞**Club Med Punta Cana.** Return visitors will surely recognize the playful whimsy and camaraderie that are hallmarks of this family-friendly resort. However, Punta Cana's first all-inclusive has a shiny new face after a $34-million renovation in early 2008 that has infused spark and savvy into this tried-and-true hostelry. Among the upgrades: flat-screen TVs and spiffy new bathrooms in every room, not to mention a brand-new spa with 10 treatment rooms plus special palapas for oceanfront massages. Also set to make a debut were expanded kid's clubs for all age groups, as well as 32 new 750-square-foot oceanfront family suites. Interactive parent and infant learning workshops are among the offerings at the new Baby Club, the only one of its kind in the region. At the teen center, a create-your-own-soda bar is a bubbling hit, and a new skate park gives boarders a venue to show off those ollies and slides. As always, cheery staffers (G.O.s) do their best to ensure there's never a dull moment, with yoga, merengue lessons, and circus programs. **Pros:** Inspiring animation staff, something for all ages. **Cons:** Limited dining options, constant bustle. ⊠*Provincia La Altagracia, apartado postal 106, Punta Cana* ☎*809/686–5500 or 800/258–2633* ⊕*www.clubmed. com* ⇝*539 rooms, 32 family suites* ⟁*In-room: safe, refrigerator. In-hotel: 3 restaurants, bars, tennis courts, pools, gym, spa, beachfront, diving, water sports, children's programs (ages infant–17), laundry service, public Internet, public Wi-Fi, airport shuttle* ▭AE, MC, V †☉|AI.

$$$$ ⊞**Excellence Punta Cana.** A sumptuous lovers' lair, this adults-only all-inclusive resort exudes romance and sensuality, with particular appeal to honeymooners or wedding parties. The open-air, tropical lobby looks onto grounds enveloped by a palm grove, where wedding ceremonies are held at the dainty gazebo or on the heavenly beach. A gorgeous spa—with a Zen fountain, indulgent massages and other treatments, and hot-and-cold water tubs—attends to soothing body and mind. Adorned with light pink-painted wood furnishings, all the spacious suites have double Jacuzzis (some with a second outdoors); most have king beds with a choice of pillows, robes, and slippers, a coffeemaker, and DVD player. Excellence Club rooms have perks such as concierge service; swim-out suites open directly onto the lazy river pool that snakes around the grounds. Honeymooners may appreciate round-the-clock room service, but if you're inclined to step out, there's a full range of activities and water sports to choose from, including private guided horseback rides. After the nightly entertainment, you can head to the disco to dance the night away or visit the casino that's open only to hotel guests. **Pros:** Adults-only getaway, gorgeous setting for weddings, waiter service at pool and beach. **Cons:** Definitely couples-oriented, distant from shopping and other restaurants. ⊠*Uvero Alto* ☎*809/685–9880* ⊕*www.excellence-resorts.com* ⇋*452 suites* ♿*In-room: safe, refrigerator, DVD. In-hotel: 8 restaurants, room service, bars, tennis courts, pools, gym, spa, beachfront, diving, water sports, bicycles, laundry service, concierge, executive floor, public Internet, public Wi-Fi, airport shuttle, no-smoking rooms* ▤*AE, DC, MC, V* ۞*AI.*

$$–$$$ ⛱**Grand Palladium Bávaro Resort & Spa.** The middle sister of the Fiesta Hotel triumvirate in Bávaro (and the largest of the three), the Grand Palladium is part of a megaresort and is, therefore, somewhat cold and impersonal (the theater seats 1,400). Although the resort is on an impressive stretch of white sand, only a few guest rooms have sea views. However, deluxe rooms and junior suites are nicely done, with arches and pillars, marbleized coral stone and hydro-massage tubs; exclusive family suites are an added bonus. A coral reef near the shore makes for exceptional snorkeling and diving. The soothing spa—right on the beach—is a professional operation. Both the Asian and Spanish restaurants are noteworthy for their authentic ambience and cuisine. The clientele is predominately European; Americans make up only a small percentage of the package groups. Another 425 rooms and 26 junior suites are at the **Grand Palladium Punta Cana Resort & Spa** within the same complex, with shared access to facilities, which include a casino and a minigolf course. For extra pampering (and about $120 more per room per night), you can stay at the adults-only, 504-room **Grand Palladium Palace Resort Spa & Casino,** the crown jewel of the empire; the so-called "royal suites" here all have ocean views, and guests get private check-in, room service, minibar restocked every day, and have access to the facilities of all the hotels. **Pros:** Excellent off-shore snorkeling, food specialty restaurants, nice spa. **Cons:** Few rooms have ocean view, no room service for standard rooms, minibar restocked three times per week. ⊠*Bávaro* ☎*809/221–8149* ⊕*www.fiesta-hotels.com* ⇋*636 rooms* ♿*In-room: safe, refrigerator. In-hotel: 11 restaurants, bars, tennis courts, pools, gym, spa, beachfront, diving, water sports, no elevator, children's programs (ages 4–12), laundry service, public Internet* ▤*AE, DC, MC, V* ۞*AI.*

$$ ⛱**Iberostar Bávaro Resort.** Like its two sister resorts, this Spanish doña
☾   has panache, evidenced in its lobby, an artistic showpiece. It's one of the more desirable Punta Cana properties, though not one of the newest,

and a good value. The dramatic public spaces segue into grounds crisscrossed with lagoons that lead to a broad, beautifully maintained white-sand beach. Although rooms don't compare with the public spaces, the Bávaro's are the sweetest (and most expensive), with a separate sitting area. True to Iberostar's emphasis on quality food and beverages, there are 11 restaurants, including Cajun and gourmet dining rooms. The shows are better than the norm, with house dancers, a band, and vocalists. The Iberostar Punta Cana and Iberostar Dominicana share facilities in the complex, but only guests at the more expensive Bávaro can dine at that resort's restaurants. **Pros:** Variety of good dining options, fun entertainment, dramatic lobby and grounds. **Cons:** Not singles-oriented, no Internet access in rooms. ⊠*Bávaro* ☎*809/221–6500 or 888/923–2722* ⊕*www.iberostar.com* ⇘*590 rooms, 8 apartments* ⌂*In-room: safe, refrigerator. In-hotel: 11 restaurants, room service, bars, tennis courts, pool, gym, spa, beachfront, diving, water sports, no elevator, children's programs (ages 4–12), laundry service, concierge, public Internet, public Wi-Fi* ⊟*AE, MC, V* ⏣*AI.*

\$\$\$
☺
★
Majestic Colonial. You'll feel like royalty in your roomy quarters, where special touches include jetted tubs, bathrobes, and slippers, a furnished balcony or terrace, and satellite TV. A special room-service closet ensures your privacy when you order in (room service, however, costs extra). But with so many choices outside your room, you might not spend much time tucked away. Picturesque grounds are punctuated with red and pink *coralillo doble* flowers lining cobblestone walkways. Nine bars, including a sports bar, pool, and beach bars, and a piano bar, accommodate drastic mood swings and engender bonhomie among guests. Get fitted out with a new look at the tattoo or hair-braiding parlors, then hit the nightly show (the Michael Jackson show gets raves), the disco, or the casino. By day, you can take aerobics or dance lessons, play baseball or soccer, archery or Ping-Pong. For the kids, there's a 9-to-5 club with plenty to keep them occupied, whether outdoor activities or indoor games, including Nintendo. Golfers get special rates at the nearby Punta Blanca course. Free wedding packages are offered. **Pros:** Room service closet for privacy, some suites have outdoor Jacuzzis, great Michael Jackson show. **Cons:** Two-beer per day limit in minibar, no coffeemaker in standard rooms. ⊠*Macao* ☎*809/221–9898* ⊕*www.majesticcolonial.com* ⇘*641 rooms, 17 suites* ⌂*In-room: safe, DVD (some), Ethernet. In-hotel: 8 restaurants, room service, bars, tennis courts, pool, gym, spa, beachfront, diving, water sports, laundry service, concierge, children's programs (ages 3–14), public Internet, public Wi-Fi, no-smoking rooms* ⊟*AE, D, MC, V* ⏣*AI.*

\$–\$\$
☺
Meliá Caribe Tropical. At this enormously popular, American-friendly resort, service has been restored and prices have leveled out, making it once again a good value. For an extra \$90 per night you can bump up to the VIP Royal Service, which gets you a true apartment-suite with butler service, a pillow menu, room service, a stunning pool with a "Grecian ruin," and a private beach area with luxe Indo beds. The restaurant-bar has a delightful breakfast and other repasts. For drinks and appetizers or to get online, swing over to the clubhouse. At least

one round of golf is included at the adjacent Cocotal Golf Club, and you get preferred tee times. Know that for most, it's a shuttle or train ride to the beach. Flintstone-theme kids clubs are a hit, with programs for infants to tweens. **Pros:** Proximity to golf course, adjacent to Palma Real Shopping Village. **Cons:** Most rooms far from the beach, many extra charges. ⊠ *Bávaro* ☎ *809/221–1290 or 800/336–3542* ⊕ *www. solmelia.com* ⇶ *1,144 suites* ☖ *In-room: safe, refrigerator, Ethernet. In-hotel: 15 restaurants, room service, bars, golf course, tennis courts, pools, gym, spa, beachfront, water sports, no elevator, children's programs (ages 4 months–13), public Internet, public Wi-Fi* ⊟ *AE, DC, MC, V* ⊖ *AI.*

$–$$ **⌖ Natura Park Eco-Resort & Spa.** You can feel good about being here as you dine on meals made from wholesome, all-natural ingredients. Carved from a former coconut plantation in 1997, the resort retains a mangrove forest and a natural lake, and exotic birds roam the gardens. The eco-sensitive architecture incorporates cut cane, coco palms, local wood, and unearthed stones into the furniture, walkways, and footbridges. Buildings occupy only 10% of the property, and the beach is rather small. This resort appeals to a niche group that prefers low-key, if any, activities. A loft area above the lobby is the designated reading room. Give your body a treat, and take it to the Health Center and Beauty Farm. Comedy and music shows start after dinner, followed by dance music until 1 AM. **Pros:** Healthful food, eco-friendly philosophy and architecture. **Cons:** Limited activities and dining options, small beach, little nightlife. ⊠ *Bávaro* ☎ *809/221–2626* ⊕ *www.blau-hotels. com* ⇶ *490 rooms, 20 suites* ☖ *In-room: safe, refrigerator. In-hotel: 3 restaurants, bars, tennis courts, pool, spa, beachfront, water sports, no elevator, children's programs (ages 2–12), public Internet, no-smoking rooms* ⊟ *AE, D, MC, V* ⊖ *AI.*

$$–$$$ **⌖ Occidental Grand Flamenco Punta Cana.** Plenty of choices for food and
ⓒ fun at this gigantic resort are likely to impress both families and night
★ owls. Most of the tastefully designed, spacious rooms (all of which have a balcony or terrace) got brand-new furnishings in early 2008. A graduated pool—one of the largest in Punta Cana—winds through the handsome grounds, with a swim-up bar that's a hub of activity; a separate quiet pool has no activities nearby, and with so many things going on all day, you may want to escape from time to time. The activity-packed children's program includes a mini-disco every evening, special entertainment for the kids, painting, family games, and theme parties. An ever-popular steak house, a Chinese restaurant, and sports bar serving American-style fast food are among the dining options. The disco, Mangú, draws crowds until the wee hours. The nightly show rotates on a seven-day cycle. Royal Club guests have an exclusive section of beach, private check-in, a private lounge, free Internet access, and an exclusive à la carte restaurant in a delightful air-conditioned space overlooking the beach. **Pros:** Nightlife is excellent, late-night pizzeria, fun for the whole family. **Cons:** No wheelchair-accessible rooms, no room-service for standard rooms. ⊠ *Bávaro* ☎ *809/221–8787* ⊕ *www. occidentalhotels.com* ⇶ *840 rooms, 25 suites* ☖ *In-room: safe, refrigerator. In-hotel: 9 restaurants, room service (some), bars, tennis courts,*

pools, gym, spa, beachfront, diving, water sports, no elevator, children's programs (ages 4–12), laundry service, concierge (some), executive floor, public Internet, public Wi-Fi, no-smoking rooms ⊟AE, D, MC, V ⑩AI.

$$–$$$ ⚄ **Ocean Blue/Ocean Sand Golf & Beach Resort.** This moderately priced ★ megaresort has a world of charm and exceeds expectations on many fronts. A free trolley traverses the expansive grounds, which are especially pretty at night. All rooms have a balcony or patio, but you pay extra to be near the exquisite beach; some room interiors could use a facelift. Premium suites, offering oversize marble bathrooms, Jacuzzi tubs, room service, and a VIP lounge, are worth the extra cost. The pool is divided into two sections, with one designated for activities and the other for relaxation. Food at the main buffet is exceptional; house wines are served from bottles. The resort's authentic Dominican restaurant is modeled after a traditional home, but if you're craving Americana with a side of fries, try the retro Route 66 diner. Mike's Coffee Shop serves made-to-order frappucinos and other hot and cold java drinks and herbal teas. Guests pay special reduced rates at the White Sands Golf Course; the resort itself has a bowling alley and casino. Service everywhere is prompt and friendly, yet there are some lapses, mainly attributable to linguistic misunderstandings. **Pros:** Free trolley every 10–15 minutes, Mike's Coffee Shop, bowling alley. **Cons:** Limited Internet access even for premium package, some drab interiors. ⊠ *Playa Arena Gorda, Bávaro* ☎ *809/476–2326* ⊕ *www.oceanhotels. net* ⇆ *436 junior suites, 272 suites* ⌂ *In-room: safe, refrigerator. In-hotel: 9 restaurants, bars, golf, tennis courts, pools, gym, spa, beachfront, diving, water sports, bicycles, no elevator, children's programs (ages 4–14), laundry service, public Internet, public Wi-Fi, no-smoking rooms* ⊟AE, MC, V ⑩AI.

$$$$ ⚄ **Paradisus Palma Real.** The cream of the crop among Punta Cana's lux-
⟳ ury all-inclusives, this resort is a show-stopper. The average suite, with
Fodor'sChoice flat-screen TV, CD player, balcony or terrace, and semi-open marble
★ bathroom with jet showers and a Jacuzzi for two, is extraordinary. You won't need to upgrade, but if you choose the Royal Service (available for adults only), you'll get a personal butler at your beck and call, private check-in, a private lounge with daytime snacks and evening cocktails, and customized turndown service. Family concierge plans lavish attention on your kids, who get their own check-in, kids' amenities in the rooms, and mini-size robes and slippers. Balinese sunbeds—some with thatched roofs—are cozy for lounging beside the glorious pool. The restaurants are around a central plaza and are opulently decorated, though admittedly the decor may outshine the food, as is the case in the Mediterranean room. Play at the nearby Cocotal Golf Course is complimentary, but nongolfers will be won over by horseback excursions or the so-called "Scuba Doo," which is basically underwater biking with an oxygen supply. **Pros:** Personalized attention, enticing outdoor spa, complimentary golf. **Cons:** Internet access costs extra, pool chairs and palapas get reserved early. ⊠ *Bávaro* ☎ *809/688–5000 or 800/688–5000* ⊕ *www.paradisuspalmareal.com or www.solmelia.com* ⇆ *554 suites* ⌂ *In-room: safe, refrigerator, DVD, Ethernet. In-hotel: 7*

restaurants, room service, bars, tennis courts, pools, gym, spa, beach-front, diving, water sports, bicycles, children's programs (ages 5–12), concierge, executive floor, public Wi-Fi, no-smoking rooms ▤*AE, D, DC, MC, V* ⦿|*AI.*

$$–$$$ ▦**Paradisus Punta Cana.** Big-league improvements have been made in recent years at this seasoned tropical getaway, as it has struggled to keep pace with the newer competition. One addition is the Reserve, an ultra-exclusive resort within the resort, with 192 suites, separate pools, and first-rate amenities that include an exclusive lounge, as well as concierge and butler service. On the main grounds, the pool complex is like a Hollywood set, with sculptures spouting water and Balinese sunbeds; the beach is alluring. An abundance of restaurants—few all-inclusives in Punta Cana offer so many—means you won't go hungry. You can show your more gregarious side at the karaoke bar—one of the more convivial spots to mingle—before retreating to your room, where 24-hour room service is available. The venue for the nightly show was being reconstructed as this writing; there's also a casino. A batting cage, rock climbing wall, and an archery range make up an action park. Or you can head for the links with unlimited green fees included at the Cocotal Golf Course. **Pros:** Large selection of dining options, 24-hour room service included with standard package, good golf packages. **Cons:** Not recommended for solo travelers, older rooms show signs of wear. ⊠*Bávaro* ☎*809/687–9923 or 800/336–3542* ⊕*www. paradisuspuntacana.solmelia.com* ⇨*500 suites, 192 royal suites* ⊘*In-room: safe, refrigerator. In-hotel: 10 restaurants, room service, bars, golf course, tennis courts, pool, gym, spa, beachfront, diving, water sports, bicycles, no elevator, children's programs (ages 5–12), laundry service, public Internet, public Wi-Fi, no-smoking rooms* ▤*AE, D, DC, MC, V* ⦿|*AI.*

$$$ ▦**PuntaCana Hotel.** The classy granddaddy of all resorts in Punta Cana,
☽   this charismatic hotel built in the 1970s spearheaded the area's tourism
★   industry and has kept pace with the times. Innovations and renovations consistently delight the well-heeled clientele, who can rely on top-notch service from a polished, attentive staff. A plethora of amenities—not to mention meticulously kept grounds and world-class golf—await guests. All rooms, with dark wood furnishings, stone floors, and floral bedding, have a balcony or terrace. Specialty restaurants are decorated with chic detail, as in Cocoloba, with the incomparable touch of Oscar de la Renta; La Yola charms with its setting overlooking the marina and its sophisticated seafood menu. Housed in the alluring golf club, the Six Senses Spa is a holistic oasis offering marvelous treatments using lemongrass, aloe vera, and tropical fruits grown locally. Zipping along the shore paths in a rented golf cart is an enjoyable way to get where you're going on the grounds, where you can explore hiking trails, swim at a freshwater spring, or visit the petting zoo. Kids' club activities include stretching classes, crafts, mini-bowling, Nintendo, Spanish lessons, and pony rides. Beachfront family casitas are equipped with baby video monitors. In the nearby PuntaCana Village, you'll find a Portuguese restaurant, a much-adored bar, an Oscar de la Renta outlet, an art gallery, and more shops. Meal-plan options are available. **Pros:** Expansive

and beautiful grounds, spectacular golf and spa. **Cons:** Limited night-life on-site, alienating for solo travelers. ⊠*PuntaCana Resort & Club, Punta Cana* ☎*809/959–2262 or 888/442–2262* ⊕*www.puntacana. com* ⇨*175 rooms, 16 junior suites, 11 suites, 38 casitas* ⟁*In-room: safe, refrigerator (some). In-hotel: 9 restaurants, bars, golf courses, ten-nis courts, pools, gym, spa, beachfront, diving, water sports, bicycles, no elevator, children's programs (ages 4–12), laundry service, public Internet, public Wi-Fi, airport shuttle, no-smoking rooms* ⊟*AE, MC, V* ⊺⊙⎮*BP.*

$$ ⊞**Riu Clubhotel Bambu.** The most upbeat resort in the giant Riu com-

⟳ plex, this bungalow-style, pastel-color caravansary is equally popular among activity-seeking young couples and families. Pumped up pool-side activities and nightly entertainment at the sheltered open-air the-ater keep guests' spirits and the energy level high. Among the diverse kids' club offerings are water polo, minigolf, badminton, and bowl-ing, as well as a special minidisco every evening, with face painting once a week. Guests here share access to the facilities of three sister Riu properties (all but the Riu Palace Punta Cana) and the unique Caribbean Street shopping and entertainment village. The Pacha disco and casino within the complex provide some of the best nightlife in the area. Golf packages are available for Riu guests at the nearby Punta Blanca course. Room furnishings are standard and simple (no king-size beds are available here). **Pros:** Lively hub of activity day and night, good kids' club, good golf packages. **Cons:** No king-size beds, no special views, not recommended for solo travelers. ⊠*Playa Arena Gorda, Bávaro* ☎*809/221–7575* ⊕*www.riu.com* ⇨*552 rooms, 8 suites* ⟁*In-room: safe, refrigerator. In-hotel: 5 restaurants, bars, ten-nis courts, pools, gym, spa, beachfront, diving, water sports, no eleva-tor, children's programs (ages 4–12), laundry service, concierge, public Internet, public Wi-Fi* ⊟*AE, D, MC, V* ⊺⊙⎮*AI.*

$–$$ ⊞**Riu Naiboa.** Simple, cozy rooms with basic furnishings and access to the facilities of three sister properties make this a pleasant choice for an economical family getaway. The standard main buffet restaurant is complemented by several à la carte choices throughout the complex. This hotel is close to the hub of activity at the complex's Caribbean Street, with shops, the ever-popular Pacha disco, and a medical clinic. Domestic beers and a liquor dispenser are included, but the minibar is only officially restocked every other day. (If you run out sooner, though, just ask and you'll likely get a resupply.) A complete water sports oper-ation on the beach is where you can gear up to windsurf, snorkel, body board, dive, or even try the latest Scuba-Doo, an underwater motor-ized bike that lets you get up close to marine life (oxygen is supplied through your domed helmet). Special rates are given to Riu guests at the nearby Punta Blanca golf course. **Pros:** Access to facilities at three resorts, near disco and shops, good golf packages at nearby course. **Cons:** Long walk to beachfront, minibar restocked every two days, dated room decor. ⊠*Playa Arena Gorda, Bávaro* ☎*809/221–7115* ⊕*www.riu.com* ⇨*364 rooms, 8 suites* ⟁*In room: safe, refrigerator. In hotel: 3 restaurants, bar, tennis courts, pools, gym, spa, beachfront,* *diving, water sports, no elevator, children's programs (ages 4–12), laundry service, public Internet, public Wi-Fi ▤AE, D, MC, V ⦾AI.*

$$$–$$$$ ▥ **Riu Palace Macao.** A beautiful water fountain beckons you into the pool at the heart of this resort, one of the prettiest spots in the sprawling Riu complex of five hotels. Victorian architecture with Caribbean touches sets a sophisticated tone for this three-story building, matched by the room decor with its elegant dark wood furnishings and crisp white walls. Nightly turn-down, room service, and premium liquors in the in-room dispensers set this hotel apart from the three more basic sister properties with which it shares facilities, and liken it more to the top-of-the-line RIU Palace Punta Cana. The Jacuzzi suites are roomy and comfy, giving extra living space, two satellite TVs, and two balconies, plus a view of the beach and its towering palms. Splurge for a third-floor suite, with its indulgent rooftop Jacuzzi enclosed in a white cupola. Sometimes the resort's gardeners will come around with fresh coconuts and offer to prepare them for guests on the spot. A free shuttle transports guests throughout the Riu property each evening, but the casino is in this hotel, from which it's a short stroll to the complex's shops on Caribbean Street and the popular Pacha disco. **Pros:** Great Jacuzzi suites, good minibar offerings, near casino. **Cons:** Buffet outshines à la carte restaurants, no ATM. ⊠*Playa Arena Gorda, Bávaro* ☎*809/221–7171* ⦿*www.riu.com* ⬗*328 rooms, 36 suites* ⌂*In-room: safe, refrigerator. In-hotel: 5 restaurants, bars, tennis courts, pools, gym, spa, beachfront, water sports, laundry service, public Internet, public Wi-Fi, no-smoking rooms* ▤*AE, D, MC, V* ⦾*AI.*

$$$–$$$$ ▥ **Riu Palace Punta Cana.** On a moonlight night, this megaresort deco-
★ rated with Arabian-style domes looks like a fairy-tale palace. A grand staircase winds up to the vast, dazzling lobby, which exudes opulence with a crystal chandelier, faux-gold gilt trimmings, replicas of Rubens paintings on the walls, and a wrought-iron lobby bar where a pianist plays at night. The megasize junior suites are more low-key, with dark wood against sunny yellow walls, achieving a look more akin to old Havana. Each has a jetted tub and a balcony or terrace. The buffet has flavorful, diverse choices and is more satisfying than the stand-alone restaurants. A negative is that the only Internet connection is in the sports bar, which can get noisy and smoky. In the pool, four Jacuzzis and semi-submerged lounge chairs add a special touch. Guests here have access to facilities of all five Riu resorts in the complex, including free admission to the casino at Riu Palace Macao. Resort guests get special rates at the Punta Blanca golf course. **Pros:** Access to all Riu facilities in 5 resorts; dazzling lobby, Pacha disco. **Cons:** No ATM at hotel, alcoholic beverages not included in casino. ⊠*Playa Arena Gorda, Bávaro* ☎*809/687–4242* ⦿*www.riu.com* ⬗*584 junior suites, 28 suites* ⌂*In-room: safe, refrigerator. In-hotel: 6 restaurants, bars, tennis courts, pools, gym, spa, beachfront, water sports, children's programs (ages 4–12), laundry service, public Internet, public Wi-Fi, no-smoking rooms* ▤*AE, D, MC, V* ⦾*AI.*

$$ ▥ **Riu Taino.** Surrounded by palm and banana trees, this sprightly colored bungalow colony within the convivial Riu complex lures a large contingent of Europeans, who make an annual trek and stay for at least two weeks. You'll find a peppering of Americans and Canadians at peak travel times, too. The single-level units each have one exterior wall painted in shades of berry, yellow, green, pink, orange, or blue. Rooms, decorated simply, have two or three beds, a patio or balcony, a minibar, and the ubiquitous liquor dispenser refilled every other day; adjoining rooms can accommodate families or groups. This resort is generally quiet, but a pizza place and a friendly bar with music at night—and occasionally a live band—keep the social scene alive. With access to all the facilities of the sister Riu hotels, there are plenty of activities to choose from, including two water sports stations at the beach. **Pros:** Shares facilities within the Riu complex, in-resort pizzeria. **Cons:** Lots of shady areas obstruct view of ocean, minibar restocked every two days. ⊠*Playa Arena Gorda, Bávaro* ☎*809/221–2290* ⊕*www.riu. com* ⤶*600 rooms, 12 suites* ⚬*In-room: safe, refrigerator. In-hotel: 7 restaurants, bars, tennis courts, pools, gym, spa, beachfront, diving, water sports, no elevator, children's programs (ages 4–12), laundry service, public Internet, public Wi-Fi* ☰*AE, D, MC, V* ⋈*AI.*

$$$$ 🏨**Sivory Punta Cana.** The promise of utter tranquillity and ultra-atten-
★ tive personal service lures visitors seeking a do-nothing itinerary to this boutique hotel and spa, which was among the pioneers of non-AI lodging in the area. Handsome suites, adorned with East Asian and Caribbean influences, set a tone of laid-back luxury; all have satellite plasma TVs, DVD players, CD players, stocked wine coolers, and minibars with soft drinks; the oceanfront Ysla Club suites have private plunge pools and their own bar. You can start your day with free coffee and pastries delivered to your door. At the communal infinity pool, chaise lounges are outfitted with comfortable cushions; waiter service is available for light bites and beverages. The resort's restaurants, which include Tau for Asian-fusion and the fancier Gourmond for French bistro fare, are open to nonguests; an 8,000-bottle wine cellar and a knowledgeable sommelier bestow a worldly touch. At night, a bar with live entertainment offers a spot to savor a cocktail under the stars. An all-inclusive plan (with high-end amenities) is available for an extra charge. **Pros:** Relaxing ambience, remote setting, extensive wine cellar, gay-friendly. **Cons:** Far from off-resort nightlife and shopping, limited on-site dining options. ⊠*Uvero Alto* ☎*809/552–0500* ⊕*www.sivo-rypuntacana.com* ⤶*55 suites* ⚬*In-room: safe, refrigerator, DVD. In-hotel: 3 restaurants, bars, room service, tennis court, pool, gym, spa, beachfront, water sports, no elevator, laundry service, concierge, public Wi-Fi, airport shuttle, no-smoking rooms* ☰*AE, MC, V* ⋈*CP.*

$$$$ 🏨**Tortuga Bay Villas.** Shuttered French windows opening to grand vistas
FodorśChoice of the sea and a cotton-white private beach are hallmarks of this lux-
★ ury-villa enclave within the grounds of PuntaCana Resort & Club. Personal attention is of the essence here; your every desire will be granted, if not anticipated, by your own villa manager, who is accessible by a cell phone provided to you. While privacy is paramount, there is a simultaneous sense of community. Oscar de la Renta designed the classy colonial-Caribbean rooms, which exude contemporary, understated elegance with a soft palette of colors and plush bed linens. The *coralina* stone bathrooms are breathtaking and include a Jacuzzi for

Punta Cana: Then & Now

In 1972 the area that spawned Punta Cana was nothing but wilderness. Through the jungle, a trip by four-wheel-drive vehicle would take six to eight hours from Higüey, the nearest city (now the route takes about an hour by regular car). "When we arrived, the country did not believe in tourism," says Frank Rainieri, a co-founder of PuntaCana Resort & Club. At the time, there were only 962 hotel rooms in the entire Dominican Republic. Partnering with Club Med, the pioneer developers built the first hotel in the region, with a mere 20 rooms, followed shortly thereafter by an air strip, thereby opening a window to the world beyond and planting the seeds of Punta Cana's emergence as the premier vacation destination

that it has become. In 1999 Grupo PuntaCana teamed up with Cornell University to form a biodiversity laboratory with an ecological reserve on its grounds; now, it's not only a hub of research on the area's ecosystems and sustainability but also an indicator of the founders' ongoing commitment to these causes. Grupo PuntaCana also established a polytechnic institute to help teach the area's potential workforce the skills necessary to do the jobs that are widely available within, and in support of, the tourist industry. "It is not simply a resort, it is a community," says PuntaCana co-founder Ted Kheel. Indeed he, along with partners Rainieri, Oscar de la Renta, and Julio Iglesias, all have homes at PuntaCana.

two; amenities include robes, slippers, and Gilchrist & Soames toiletries. The minibar is stocked with premium liquors, and there's a huge flat-screen TV. A golf cart is included to help you get around, and you can rent a laptop. Villa guests have an exclusive restaurant plus access to all the facilities of the main resort, notably the impeccable La Cana golf course designed by P. B. Dye and the glorious Six Senses Spa. **Pros:** Personal attention, gorgeous sprawling grounds, outstanding golf, VIP check-in at airport. **Cons:** Little nightlife, too isolated for singles. ⊠ *Punta Cana* ☏ *809/959–8229 or 888/442–2262* ⊕ *www.puntacana. com* ⌂ *15 1- to 4-bedroom villas* ⚿ *In-room: safe, kitchen, refrigerator, DVD, Ethernet. In-hotel: 9 restaurants, room service, bars, golf courses, tennis courts, pools, gym, spa, beachfront, diving, water sports, bicycles, no elevator, children's programs (ages 4–12), laundry service, concierge, public Internet, public Wi-Fi, airport shuttle, no-smoking rooms* ▤ *AE, D, MC, V* ⧠ *BP.*

NIGHTLIFE

With the predominance of all-inclusive hotels, nightlife in Punta Cana tends to center on whatever resort you are staying at. But there's more out there than first meets the eye. Some clubs, casinos, and shows at other resorts have very good reputations and are open to outsiders. Cover charges at the discos vary, ranging from none when it's early on an ordinary night to $10 or $20 during peak hours, especially when there's live entertainment. Don't forget your ID; when nonguests are allowed into the disco on a resort's grounds, security keeps a close eye on who is coming and going. Some resorts even offer nighttime excursions to a local disco, where you can go with a group and return at a scheduled hour.

An atmospheric lounge with big-screen TVs, **High Wave Café** (⊠ *Plaza Bávaro Shopping Center, Bávaro* ☎ *809/309–0500*) is a pleasant spot to drop by for cocktails after dinner and is easily accessible from the hotels on Bávaro. Early birds can grab a swinging love seat on the front porch.

★ Even if their night begins elsewhere, sooner or later many party-scene insiders wind up at **Mangú** (⊠ *Occidental Grand Flamenco Punta Cana, Bávaro* ☎ *809/221–8787*), with two floors of pulsating rhythms to keep club goers charged. Upstairs, techno is pumped nonstop, while the downstairs dance floor tends toward reggaeton, hip-hop, urban, and international beats, mixed up with salsa, merengue, and bachata. The dance club, on the grounds of the Occidental complex, allows guests from off-property, and you'll find a mix of tourists and locals at all hours of the night. Things don't get hot here until after midnight, and they keep on going all night long, until it's time to wrap up with an after-hours bite at the resort's pizzeria, open until 6:30 AM. One draw before things heat up on the dance floor: the club's big-screen TV is good for watching sporting events. There's usually a cover charge, ranging from $10 to $20 depending on whether there's live music.

★ **Montecristo** (⊠ *Palma Real Shopping Village, Carretera Cortecito-Bávaro, Bávaro* ☎ *809/552–8999*) is a trendy spot that evolves from a bar to a pulsating disco as the night goes on. The head bartender makes great mixed drinks with a flourish, and the manager is generally accessible to guests—tourists and locals alike. A big video screen serves as the backdrop for the dance floor, which mixes up DJ-spun international club music with merengue, bachata, and salsa rhythms—and sometimes live music. The club has arrangements with several local hotels for transporting groups. There's no cover charge here, and there's special pricing for various sponsored drinks on different nights.

Still called affectionately by its former name, Areito, which means "party" in Taino, the **News** (⊠ *Bávaro Princess Resort, Bávaro* ☎ *809/221–2311*) is one of the hot dance spots in Punta Cana, where tourists and locals let everything go on the dance floor, as the DJ spins international club beats.

A favorite among many locals, **Pacha** (⊠ *Riu complex, near Riu Naiboa entrance, Bávaro* ☎ *809/221–7575*) plays more merengue and bachata than most of the other dance clubs. Drinks here are cheaper, too. For a beer, expect to pay about 80 pesos (or about $2.50); the price can be double in some of the other clubs. Cover charges apply when live bands perform; otherwise it's free to enter, and nonresort guests are welcome.

SPORTS & THE OUTDOORS

FISHING

Big-game fishing is big in Punta Cana, with blue and white marlin, wahoo, sailfish, dorado, and mahimahi among the most common catches in these waters. Several fishing tournaments are held every summer. The PuntaCana Resort & Club has hosted the ESPN Xtreme Billfishing Tournament every year since 2003. Blue marlin tournaments are held at La Mona Channel in Cabeza de Toro. Several tour operators offer organized deep-sea fishing excursions.

At **PuntaCana Marina** (⊠ *PuntaCana Resort & Club, Punta Cana* ☎ *809/ 959–2262 Ext. 8004* ⊕ *www.puntacana.com*), on the southern end of the resort, half-day, deep-sea fishing excursions are available for $95 per person, with a minimum of two people, $70 for observers. For a Bertram 33-footer to go after tuna, marlin, dorado, and wahoo, it's $575 for four hours. It costs the same to charter a 45-foot Sportfisherman. Also, ask about the *yolas,* fishing boats with outboards.

GOLF

With comfortable climate year-round, abundant greenery, and stunning natural backdrops, Punta Cana is a highly desirable location for golf. Indeed, the region has some of the best golf courses in the Caribbean, designed by top golf architects including Nick Faldo, P. B. Dye, Tom Fazio, Jack Nicklaus, Jose "Pepe" Gancedo, Nick Price, and Alberto Sola. The region's pitch as a golf hot spot shows no signs of slowing, with the major resort community developments at Rōco Ki, Punta Cana, and Cap Cana each adding new, premier links to the field in the next few years.

The **Barceló Bávaro Beach Golf & Casino Resort** (⊠ *Bávaro* ☎ *809/686– 5797*) has an 18-hole, par 72 course, open to its own guests and those of other hotels. The course, with numerous water obstacles, was designed by Juan Manuel Gordillo, and was the first in the Bávaro area. The rate for those not staying at Bávaro is $120, which includes green fees, golf cart, and a day pass to the resort, which covers food and beverages for the day.

Cabeza de Toro (⊠ *Catalonia Bávaro Resort, Bávaro* ☎ *809/412–0000* ⊕ *www.cataloniabavaro.com*), a 9-hole, par-35 resort course, was designed by Alberto Sola. Green fees are $65 for 18 holes, $45 for 9 holes.

Both challenging and affordable, **Catalonia Caribe Golf Club** (⊠ *Catalonia Bávaro Resort, Bávaro* ☎ *809/412–0000* ⊕ *www.cataloniabavaro. com*) is an 18-hole, par-72 course spread out on greens surrounded by five lakes and an abundance of shady palms. Alberto Sola was the designer. Green fees are $75. Named for the coconut plantation on which it was built, **Cocotal Golf Course** (⊠ *Bávaro* ☎ *809/687–4653* ⊕ *www.cocotalgolf.com*), designed by Spaniard José "Pepe" Gancedo,

CLOSE UP

Cap Cana

One of the most ambitious new development projects in the Dominican Republic, Cap Cana is a resort and villa complex spread out over 30,000 acres (5 mi) of precious beach on bluffs 200 feet above sea level and about 10 minutes south of the Punta Cana airport. In time it will have at least four luxury hotels with 3,000 rooms, 5,000 residential units, 6 golf courses, a 5,000-seat amphitheater, casinos, a marina with yacht clubs and deep-sea fishing fleet, beach clubs, polo grounds, spas, and tennis and squash courts.

The flagship hotel, the Altabella Sanctuary Cap Cana Golf & Spa, opened in 2008, although some facilities were not complete at this writing. The pioneer of the golf courses, Punta Espada—one of three Jack Nicklaus signature courses planned for the complex—opened in 2006 and is the site of a new PGA Champions Tour event. The second, Las Iguanas, was preparing to open in late 2008. Also already up and running is the exclusive Caletón Beach Club, with its palapa roof and spectacular pool

carved into a coral base. Cap Cana Marina is being built in three phases; it's destined to be the Caribbean's largest, with 500 slips capable of docking yachts of more than 150 feet. Just off the treasured fishing grounds of the Mona Passage between the Dominican Republic and Puerto Rico, the marina will have a port authority and customs, restaurants, shops, and nightclubs. Phase one of the marina was slated to open by May 2008.

Coming soon is the Ritz-Carlton, a billion-dollar mixed-use complex with a 220-room hotel, residences, a spa, private beach club, five restaurants, and lounges, slated to open in early 2010. Also underway is Donald Trump's $2-billion real estate project, Trump at Cap Cana, which when complete will have a luxury resort, golf course, golf villas, estate lots, a beach club, condo hotel, and residences. Kicking off the first phase of development are the Trump Farallon Estates at Cap Cana, which generated record sales of its lot sites but which are, alas, not part of the rental pool at Cap Cana.

4

---

has 18 championship holes and 9 regular holes. It's a challenging par-72 course in a residential community dotted with palm trees and lakes. There's also a driving range, club house, pro shop and golf academy. Green fees are $135 for 18 holes, $80 for 9 holes, including cart.

Corales Golf Course (⊠ *PuntaCana Resort & Club, Punta Cana* ☎ *809/ 959–4653* ⊕ *www.puntacana.com*), designed by Tom Fazio, is a dramatic 18-hole course (members only) that at this writing was set to open in 2008. Laid out along cliffs and coves within a private enclave of luxurious homes, these links are on the grounds of the PuntaCana Resort & Club. Since the resort owns and operates the Punta Cana International Airport, flight paths were detoured so as not to disturb the peace for golfers here.

At this writing, **Hacienda Golf Course** (⊠ *PuntaCana Resort & Club, Punta Cana* ☎ *809/959–4653* ⊕ *www.puntacana.com*), designed by P. B. Dye, was set to open in 2009, representing another challenging addition to the spectacular setting at PuntaCana Resort & Club.

Popular Excursions

Beyond the gates of your resort, there are many opportunities to leave your chaise longue behind and explore the surrounding area. The following excursions are all extremely popular and variations are generally offered by several different tour companies (prices cited are just examples, and most charge tax on top of the fee):

■ **Aquatic Speed Boat Tour:** Cruise along the coast in a speedboat to a magnificent snorkeling spot (Apple, $62).

■ **ATV Tour:** Get off the beaten path in a four-wheeler for an insider's view of the local countryside for a half- or full day (Apple $65–$80).

■ **Bavaro Runners:** Tour the local countryside for the full day, with stops at sugarcane fields, cocoa plantations and a typical Dominican home, and eat an authentic Dominican lunch (Apple $80, Vacaciones Barceló $80).

■ **Catalina Island:** Sail out to this uninhabited, pristine 6-square-mi island off the coast of La Romana for an ultrasecluded retreat that's a fabulous spot for snorkeling and diving. It's an all-day tour (9 hours) that starts by bus from the hotels to Bayahibe (90 minutes); from there, you take a boat to the island (Colonial $80, with lunch, water, and soft drinks).

■ **Horseback Riding Tour:** Trot along the beach for an afternoon ride or for a moonlight tour, which might include a barbecue and a bonfire, as with the El Pat Ranch tour (Apple, $50).

■ **Kontiki Party Boat:** Hop aboard the party cruise and enjoy dancing, snorkeling, and lots of cold beer (Apple, $62).

■ **Manatí Park:** Exploring the park (see ⇨ Manatí Park *in* Exploring Punta Cana, *above*).

■ **Marinarium:** Snorkeling among nurse sharks and sun rays on a coral reef (Apple, $70).

■ **Outback or Jurassic Safari:** A half-day or full-day adventure takes you through the back roads to visit a cocoa plantation, local craft stores, a typical Dominican home, cigar factory, and a secluded beach for some boogie boarding (Apple, $65–$80).

■ **Samaná Whale Watching:** From January through March, head out to watch the wintering humpback whales that return to Samaná in droves for their mating and birthing season (Colonial $120, 9-hour tour includes flight and buffet lunch).

■ **Santo Domingo:** Full-day tour of the capital (Apple, about $68, includes lunch at Hard Rock Cafe; Vacaciones Barceló, $65).

■ **Saona Island:** See ⇨ Isla Saona *in* Exploring Punta Cana, *above* (about $85 to $95 for a full day, including fuel surcharge, lunch and beverages).

★ **La Cana Golf Course** (⊠ *PuntaCana Resort & Club, Punta Cana* ☎ *809/ 959–4653* ⊕ *www.puntacana.com*) is a breathtaking 18-hole championship course designed by P. B. Dye, with spectacular ocean views— 4 holes play right along the water. For resort guests, green fees are $71 for 9 holes, $115 for 18 holes, with cart included; for nonguests, fees are $96 for 9 holes, $156 for 18 holes, and $40 for a golf cart. Reserve two weeks in advance from November through April. Lessons and clinics are offered at the Punta Cana Golf Academy.

Punta Blanca Golf Course (⊠ *Carretera Arena Gorda, near Majestic Colonial Resort, Bávaro* ☎ *809/257–7360*) is a beautiful 18-hole, par-72 course designed by Nick Price. Green fees start at $120.

Fodor'sChoice **Punta Espada Golf Course** (⊠ *Cap Cana, Carretera Juanillo, Juanillo* ★ ☎ *809/688–5587*) is a par-72 Jack Nicklaus signature golf course characterized by striking bluffs, lush foliage, and winding waterways. There's a beach view from most of the holes, and half of them play right along the ocean. It's the first of three Jack Nicklaus signature courses planned at Cap Cana, and the site of a new PGA Champions Tour event that debuted in 2008. Green fees are $175, which includes golf cart, caddy, tees, two bottles of water, and practice on the driving range.

Fodor'sChoice **Faldo Legacy Golf Course** (⊠ *Rōco Ki, Macao* ☎ *809/731–2800 or* ★ *888/476–2654* ⊕ *www.rocoki.com*), designed by Nick Faldo, has challenging tees with dramatic views of the countryside and the beach, spread out over 7,000 yards of green. The spectacular, much-photographed 17th hole sits on a cliff with the ocean waves spraying up against the rocks. Faldo calls this area of the course "Los Dos Rezos" ("The Two Prayers") because even the greatest golfers might need more than finesse to get through it. Another area of the course is named "Lord of the Rings," a reference to its twisted mangrove shrubbery. The course was designed to be entirely eco-friendly.

White Sands Golf Course (⊠ *Near Ocean Blue Golf & Beach Resort, Bávaro* ☎ *809/552–6750* ⊕ *www.oceanhotels.net*), designed by Spanish champion Jose "Pepe" Gancedo—who's nicknamed the "Picasso of Golf"—is a handsome and challenging addition to the golf spectrum. At a pace of play of 4½ hours, the 9-hole inland course is par 72. The general admission cost is $130 for 18 holes plus $30 to rent equipment, but some nearby resorts offer reduced-rate packages. Another 9 holes were readying to open.

HORSEBACK RIDING

The **Rancho PuntaCana** (⊠ *PuntaCana Resort & Club, Punta Cana* ☎ *809/959–2262* ⊕ *www.puntacana.com*) is across from the main entrance of the resort. A one-hour trail ride winds along the beach, the golf course, and through tropical forests. The two-hour jungle trail ride has a stopover at a lagoon fed by a natural spring, so wear your swimsuit under your long pants. You can also do a three-hour full-moon excursion or take riding lessons. The stock are Paso Fino horses.

TENNIS

Most resorts have tennis courts where you can play for free during the day. Some have night lighting, but there's usually an extra charge to play after dark. If you're looking for a club atmosphere, PuntaCana Resort & Club has a tennis center open to nonguests; at this writing, there's also a racket center under construction at Cap Cana that will have tennis and squash courts open to the public. **PuntaCana Resort & Club** (⊠ *Punta Cana* ☎ *809/959–2262 Ext. 7158*) has six courts and gives tennis clinics on Tuesday and Thursday. There's also an exhibition stadium. Nonguests can play for two hours for $26; the courts close at 7 PM.

SHOPPING

Souvenirs and crafts are the focus of shopping in Punta Cana, and there are few outlets for high-end clothing or accessories. As in the whole country, the regional specialty products are cigars, coffee, larimar and amber jewelry, *mamajuana* (an herbal liqueur) and rum (especially the locally made premium Brugal).

Most resorts have a few retail shops, but prices tend to be higher than what you would pay for similar goods in the nearby shopping plazas or at kiosks on the beach. Many vendors sell crafts and goods from the neighboring Haiti, too, so if you're looking for something specifically Dominican, make sure that's what you're getting.

Shopping in the plazas with outdoor kiosks is like an inverted game of musical chairs. The soundtrack is the constant hum of greeting, searching, and haggling. Shopkeepers hope that when a shopper hits pause, they're standing in their store. Vendors thus tend to be persistent when trying to lure you in but are generally friendly. In regular stores, prices are not negotiable, but bargaining is expected at the kiosks.

SHOPPING CENTERS

The colorful bazaarlike atmosphere at **Bi2JH2O Artisanal Shopping Plaza** (⊠ *El Cortecito, Bávaro*) pronounced *bibijagua,* makes it fun to browse through the rows of shopping stalls laid out in the sand on Bávaro Beach. Here you can find handicrafts, cigars, mamajuana, handmade musical instruments, paintings, sculptures, wood carvings, amber, larimar and coral jewelry, and other novelties. Expect the spirited shopkeepers to beckon you into their kiosks; don't hesitate to look around before you settle on a purchase, as you might find a few pearls in what may at times seem like a sea of trinkets. Break out your bargaining tactics, as prices are not set in stone. There's a snack bar with Dominican munchies and restrooms nearby. The plaza is accessible on foot along the beach from a few hotels. Otherwise, grab a cab, and a camera.

Fodor'sChoice The **Galerias at PuntaCana Village** (⊠ *PuntaCana Resort & Club, Punta Cana*) lie within a still-blossoming shopping, dining, and residential complex built on the road to the airport, initially to house employees of PuntaCana Resort & Club and now also a tourist draw. Four banks are planned in the village, which is already home to a church and a school. The commercial square has an Oscar de la Renta shop, a Portuguese restaurant, a beauty parlor, and an art gallery where you can find locally crafted objets d' art on display, including an exquisite wooden chess set with giant pieces carved to resemble classical musicians on one side and Dominican pop stars on the other. Free transportation is provided to guests at PuntaCana Resort & Club.

Fodor'sChoice A standout among the region's shopping centers, **Palma Real Shopping**
★ **Village** (⊠*Bávaro* ☎*809/257–6382*) is a swanky, partially enclosed
mall designed with an eye toward light and space. Water fountains
and tropical plants infuse life into the bright and airy interior areas
beneath the blue-tile roof. Music pipes through the stone-floor plaza in
the center, where seating is available, and security is tight. Upscale retail
shops, which sell beach wear, clothing, skin care products, jewelry, and
more, line the walls. Several restaurants give visitors welcome dining
alternatives beyond the gates of their resorts. There are two banks,
ATMs, and a money exchange outlet. Store hours are open 10–10, but
the restaurants stay open later. Shuttle buses run to and from many of
the hotels with pickups every two hours. A new movie theater, the first
in Punta Cana, was being built here at this writing.

The sprawling **Plaza Bávaro Shopping Center** (⊠*Bávaro* ☎*No phone*)
has dozens of shops spanning two sides of the main street that cuts
through its center. On the side closest to the beach you can find clothing stores, jewelry, cigars and crafts, as well as three money-exchange
spots, a DHL shipping station, and a pharmacy, all laid out in a square;
in the middle is a bar where you can take respite from the bustle. Across
the street, most of the booths sell artwork and handicrafts, and if your
hair is long enough, you'll likely be approached by women offering to
braid it on the spot.

You won't find brand-name shops at **Plaza Uvero Alto** (⊠*Carretera
Uvero Alto, Uvero Alto*), but it's a convenient shopping center for the
hotels in the remote Uvero Alto area, with a bank and outdoor ATM,
money exchange, Internet access, small pharmacy, gift shops, and two
mini-markets (one in the front, the other tucked away in the back row
of booths) that sell sundries like suntan lotion and deodorant at prices
much cheaper than in the hotels. Behind the first row of enclosed stores,
peruse the colorful kiosks full of handicrafts, paintings, ceramics, and
other gift items; most shopkeepers here, although very friendly, don't
speak much English, so knowing even a few words of Spanish will
come in handy. **Jazmin** in Booth No. 1 will help you sift through myriad
artisan crafts with a smile. For beautifully designed pieces of larimar
and amber, and other locally made novelties, visit **Tesoro Caribeño**
(No. 5, front row of stores), where the owner speaks fluent English.
There's also a branch of the Politur (tourist police) in the plaza.

SPECIALTY STORES

CIGARS

Hand-rolled cigars are available everywhere you turn in Punta Cana.
Cigar lounges, where you can sample the aromatic flavors of the different tobaccos, are common, too. Dominican cigars—proudly touted
as even better than Cubans—make great gifts for aficionados and are
legal to bring back to the United States (100 per person max). Look for
sellers with expertise and, of course, authentic products.

Before 6 PM, you can watch cigars being handmade at **Cig's Aficionados**
(⊠*Palma Real Shopping Village, Bávaro* ☎*809/552–8754*), a repu-

table outlet for Dominican cigars. You can sample varieties at the shop, too, which is open daily, including Sunday, from 10 AM to 9:45 PM.

Near the airport, **La Tabaquería Cigar Club** (⊠ *La Plaza Bolera, Suite 10A, Punta Cana* ☎ *809/959–0040*), is a haven for cigar lovers, who can watch the handmade production process or relax at the bar with a drink. Fine Dominican and Cuban cigars are for sale, as are humidors and related accessories, from 9 AM to 9 PM daily. You can call the store to arrange transportation.

JEWELRY

Two types of stones are unique to the Dominican Republic, and make exquisite pieces of jewelry. Larimar is a rare blue pecolite that's only known presence in the world is in the southwestern D.R. The larimar mines unearth a story of the island's emergence from solidifying rock beneath the ocean floor about 100 million years ago. Dominican amber, about 25 million years old, in some cases encapsulates life forms and gives a peek into the past. Jewelers in Punta Cana showcase these stones as well as other precious gems.

★ It's hard to walk by the windows of **Harrison's Fine Jewelry** (⊠ *Palma Real Shopping Village, Bávaro* ☎ *809/552–8721*) without stepping in to admire the sparkling collection of jewelry, including a large selection of larimar and amber pieces in striking settings, as well as diamonds and other classic gems. Outlets of this renowned chain are also in several resorts of Punta Cana.

★ Browse through the museum showcases and panels depicting the fascinating history of the D.R.'s unique stones at **R&R Amber & Larimar Museum Jewelry** (⊠ *Palma Real Shopping Village, Bávaro* ☎ *809/552–8710*), before stopping at the jewelry shop on the way out.

Samai Factory Jewelry (⊠ *Plaza Bávaro, Store 39, Bávaro* ☎ *809/304–3770*) has some interesting amber and larimar pieces, as well as diamond and zirconium rings. Custom pieces can be made if you like a stone and want to change its setting.

Tesoro Caribeño (⊠ *Plaza Uvero Alto, Local 5, Uvero Alto* ☎ *809/707–3355*) has a fine selection of amber and larimar jewelry and other stones amid the colorful shelves full of souvenirs and crafts. Unique pieces are crafted by the same designers who create jewelry for the Harrison's chain, but are sold at generally lower prices. The owner speaks fluent English.

PUNTA CANA ESSENTIALS

TRANSPORTATION

BY AIR

The following airlines provide service from the United States (or connections through San Juan): American Airlines/American Eagle, Continental, Delta, United, and US Airways. Many visitors fly nonstop on charter flights to the D.R. direct from the East Coast, the Midwest, and Canada—particularly into Punta Cana. These charters are part of a package and can only be booked through a travel agent.

AIRPORTS & TRANSFERS

Punta Cana International Airport is the busiest of the Dominican Republic's international airports, handling some 1.5 million passengers a year. During the winter months more than 250 international flights arrive weekly in Punta Cana; in the summer months, about 100 per week.

Upon arrival, after a welcome by greeters in traditional Dominican dress, every visitor must purchase a "tourist card" for $10 at the Immigration Desk (U.S. currency only). American citizens do not require a visa to enter the country, only a valid passport.

> ## PUNTA CANA INTERNATIONAL AIRPORT
>
> With its thatched-roof hangars blending seamlessly into the tropical landscape, the Punta Cana International Airport has grown from humble beginnings. In the 1970s a private airstrip served the first wave of visitors and investors. But when that proved insufficient, a private development group built Punta Cana International Airport (symbol PUJ), which opened in 1984. It is now one of the largest and busiest airports in the Caribbean and is the port of entry for more than half of all passengers arriving by air to the D.R.

If you book a package through a travel agent, your airport transfers will almost certainly be included in the price you pay. Look for your company's sign as you exit baggage claim. If you book independently, then you may have to take a taxi or rent a car.

When you leave the D.R., anticipate long lines, and be sure to give yourself a full two hours for international check-in.

Information **Punta Cana International Airport** (*PUJ* ☎ *809/686–8790*).

BY BUS

Public buses service Punta Cana and Bávaro, but it's not easy to coordinate travel from point to point. Schedules are sporadic, and stops are not clearly marked.

From Santo Domingo, Espresso Bávaro buses depart from Avenida Máximo Gómez–Plaza Los Girasoles; the buses are not the best, but the price is right and the American movies current. If you're going to one of the Punta Cana resorts, you get off at the stop before the last and take a cab waiting at the taxi stand.

Information **Espresso Bávaro** (☎ *809/682–9670*).

BY CAR

If you're visiting or arriving by air into another region of the country, it's possible to drive to Punta Cana, but difficult. Drivers must take into account not only distance but also the condition of the roads, which are patchy at best. Some stretches may be paved straightways with lane demarcations signaling two-way traffic (and these *are* increasing in number as the government has invested millions of dollars in the infrastructure); other roads, however, may be unmarked curvy switchbacks replete with gaping potholes in some stretches. Drainage in many areas is poor and may slow down passage, particularly after heavy rains. Drivers avoiding potholes and large puddles tend to swerve in and out of their lanes into those of oncoming traffic, and the abundance of motorcycles and trucks in some areas adds to the obstacles. There are lots of unwritten rules of the road, but common sense is always at the top of the list. If you do drive, take it slow in unfamiliar areas and let faster-moving traffic pass when it's safe to do so.

It's reasonably easy to get from Santo Domingo to La Romana area, and the highway from Casa de Campo to Punta Cana is also a fairly smooth ride. In the eastern region, a new highway, *La Carretera Turistica* (Tourist Boulevard), is being built between the airport and Uvero Alto and adheres to all international standards of highway safety and construction. Huge sums—at least $100 million—had been invested in the project at this writing, but construction was not complete; the Dominican government was paying the lion's share of the total, but about 30% was to be contributed by local hotels in the form of taxes.

Few vacationers choose to rent cars in Punta Cana, but rental cars are available. Several major car rental companies have outlets at the Punta Cana airport as well as in Bávaro. Most will deliver cars to area hotels and bring you back to the office to complete the paperwork.

Free parking is available at all of the resorts. When you venture out, free parking is also common, including at the shopping plazas and local restaurants—and generally easy to find, except perhaps on the cluttered streets of Higüey.

Car Rental **Avis** (⊠ *Punta Cana International Airport, Punta Cana* ☎ *809/688–1354* ⊠ *Carretera Arena Gorda, Plaza Caney, Bávaro* ☎ *809/688–1354*). **Budget** (⊠ *Carretera Veron-Barceló, Bávaro* ☎ *809/696–6401*). **Europcar** (⊠ *Carretera Friusa-Melia, Friusa, Bávaro* ☎ *809/686–2861* ⊕ *www.europcar.com.do*). **National** (⊠ *Carretera Bávaro, Bávaro* ☎ *809/466–1083*).

Gasoline **Texaco** (⊠ *Intersection of Carretera Friusa and Carretera Riu-Arena Gorda, Friusa, Bávaro*).

BY TAXI

Fares in Punta Cana are high, and it's not uncommon to be charged US$40 for a 20-minute ride if you book through your resort's concierge. At Plaza Bávaro shopping center, where many taxis are standing around—and especially if you can negotiate in Spanish—you can get one for a fraction of that price. There are no meters, so confirm the rate with the driver before beginning your trip.

Information **Asotatupal 24-Hour Taxi Service** (☎ *809/688–8978* ⊠ *Uvero Alto*). **Siutratural Taxi Service** (☎ *809/552–0617* ⊠ *Plaza Meliá, Bávaro* ☎ *809/221–2741* ⊠ *Carretera Friusa, Bávaro*).

CONTACTS & RESOURCES

BANKS & EXCHANGE SERVICES

You may need to change some money, particularly if you're not staying in an all-inclusive resort, where dollars are usually accepted. Prices quoted in this chapter—and virtually all hotel rates in Punta Cana—are in U.S. dollars unless noted otherwise. The currency of the realm is the Dominican peso (written RD$); at this writing, the exchange rate was approximately RD$32.50 to US$1, and the rate is fairly stable. Most resorts will exchange money at the front desk (from U.S. dollars or euros to pesos, but not the other way). There are also money-exchange storefronts at all of the main shopping plazas. ATMs can be found on the grounds of many resorts and at the shopping plazas (note: ATMs dispense money in pesos only). At the Acce Caribe Express Exchange Center in Bávaro you can also send and receive money and use DHL shipping services.

Information **Acce Caribe Express Exchange Center** (⊠ *Plaza Bávaro, Bávaro* ☎ *809/552–0862*). **Banco Popular** (⊠ *Palma Real Shopping Village, Bávaro*). **Banco Popular** (⊠ *Plaza Uvero Alto, Uvero Alto*). **Globo Cambio Money Exchange** (⊠ *Palma Real Shopping Village, Bávaro*).

EMERGENCIES

Many resorts have a medical clinic on-site with general hours and 24-hour on-call emergency care. Note that medical coverage is not part of the all-inclusive packages, and care is expensive. A basic five-minute visit with a doctor may cost $50 or more; medications are extra. International insurance is accepted, but you must make sure you're covered internationally, for both medical services and pharmaceuticals.

For health problems that require more advanced medical attention or hospitalization, there are two area hospitals, both of which offer round-the-clock quality medical services and accept health insurance (again, if you're covered internationally; otherwise, you'll have to pay out of pocket). Pharmacies in every area rotate their 24-hour services; check with your hotel for the schedule.

Hospitals **Hospiten** (⊠ *Bávaro* ☎ *809/686–1414*). **Centro Médico Punta Cana** (⊠ *Carretera Bávaro, Friusa, Bávaro* ☎ *809/552–1506*).

Pharmacies **Farmacia Estrella** (⊠ *Plaza Estrella, Friusa, Bávaro* ☎ *809/552–0344*). **Farmacia Manglar** (⊠ *Plaza Punta Cana, Bávaro* ☎ *809/552–1533*) is open daily from 8 AM to midnight. **Farmacia Melo** (⊠ *Palma Real Shopping Village, Bávaro* ☎ *809/552–8737*). **Farmacia Uvero Alto** (⊠ *Plaza Uvero Alto, Uvero Alto* ☎ *809/468–0068*). **Pharma Cana** (⊠ *PuntaCana Village, Punta Cana* ☎ *809/959–0025*) is open daily from 9 AM to 10 PM.

HEALTH

Changes in climate and diet are the main culprits of health problems for visitors to Punta Cana, but it's important to protect yourself from water-borne illnesses. Always drink bottled water in the Punta Cana region and use it even to brush your teeth; if you have a coffeemaker in your room, use bottled water to make coffee. And drink bottled water regularly to avoid dehydration; it's readily available and included in all-inclusive packages. Ice in beverages is generally safe to consume, as are cooked foods and salads, since large resorts use purified water for cooking, washing vegetables, and ice-making.

Increasing food-safety standards have made broad inroads in the Punta Cana resorts, and food-safety issues are significantly less serious than they were in the early to mid-1990s. The best way to protect yourself against potential norovirus infection—a risk in any crowded environment like a vacation resort—is through good hygiene and frequent hand-washing; use a bottled hand sanitizer regularly as well. If you do experience stomach upset or diarrhea, don't hesitate to seek out the medical clinic at your resort.

Mosquitoes are common all over this tropical region, and you may encounter them in even the most luxurious hotels. Use a repellent, especially at dawn and after dark. A few resorts supply repellent in your room; otherwise, bring it with you or buy it once you arrive. Dengue fever has been reported in the Dominican Republic, though the highest incidence of infection occurs in the far western reaches of the country, along the border with Haiti. Malaria has been reported in the Punta Cana region in past years after hurricanes or serious tropical storms, but the CDC has no current warning about malaria in Punta Cana at this writing.

The most likely problem you'll encounter is sunburn. Protect yourself—and especially your children—against sunburn by using a sunscreen with an SPF of at least 15.

INTERNET, MAIL & SHIPPING

Internet access is generally available in the resorts, typically at an Internet café or business center, and less frequently in the guest rooms. Public Wi-Fi is often available in the lobby or in communal spaces. Often you must purchase an access code, even if you have your own laptop. Upgraded packages, however, sometimes include free wireless. In the hotels, service is expensive, and Internet cafés tend to charge $3 to $4 for 15 minutes.

The closest post office is in Higüey, about an hour west of the Punta Cana airport. However, all resorts have mail drop-boxes, and mail is picked up at least twice a week. Expect a typical letter or postcard to take about two weeks to arrive in the United States. If time is of the essence, consider using a private shipping company.

Post Offices Instituto Postal Dominicano (Provincia La Altagracia Post Office) (⊠ *Msr. Nouel 8, Higüey* ☎ *809/746–1040*).

Shipping Companies DHL (⊠ *Carretera Riu-Arena Gorda, Friusa, Bávaro* ☎ *809/552–0816*) is open weekdays 9–noon and 1–6, and Saturday 9–noon.

Federal Express (⊠ *Caribe Express, Calle Duverge 80, Esq. Mella, Higüey* ☎ *809/ 554–2330*).

PROSTITUTION

If you're looking for prostitution in Punta Cana, you can find it, but it's not a problem that surfaces—at least not blatantly—at the resorts. Although officials have made strides at curbing the D.R.'s reputation as a destination for sex tourism, if you venture off resort grounds onto local streets, you might encounter "gentlemen's clubs," where it's no secret that sex services are available.

At the hotels, one scenario (though reportedly less common these days) to be aware of involves Punta Cana's co-called "sanky panky" boys—often waiters, bartenders, and animation staff—who prey on single female guests, especially older ones, lavishing attention on them. A flirtatious "meet me in the disco" might be a precursor to a suggestion to rendezvous in a seedy motel, with payment expected for the gigolo's services and the room.

SAFETY

Violent crime against tourists in the D.R. is rare, and the island has a history of being safe. Punta Cana remains one of the safest regions, Uvero Alto even more so. However, poverty is everywhere in the country, and petty theft (particularly of cell phones), pickpocketing, and purse snatching does happen, particularly in Higüey.

Security at the all-inclusive resorts is very good, but it's important to take precautions against petty theft. As everywhere, common sense rules apply. Leave your valuables in the hotel when you walk along the beach. Use the safe in your hotel room or at the front desk; hide your laptop if it doesn't fit in the safe. It's safe to rent a car and drive yourself around the Punta Cana area, but when driving, always lock your car and don't leave valuables inside. Take hotel-recommended taxis at night. Don't buy or bring drugs: know that the penalties in this country are extremely tough—jail (not pretty), fines, and no parole.

There's a special branch of the police department dedicated to protecting the safety of tourists, called Politur, with branches in Friusa and Uvero Alto. Politur officers maintain a presence in the hotel areas and also monitor excursions. For emergencies, dial 911.

Information Politur (⊠ *Carretera Friusa-Arena Gorda, near Sitrabapu Bus Terminal, Friusa, Bávaro* ☎ *809/688–8727 or 809/754–3073*).

Politur (⊠ *Plaza Uvero Alto Shopping Center, Uvero Alto* ☎ *809/754–3044 or 809/754–2985*).

TOUR OPTIONS

Visitors to Punta Cana have a plethora of excursions to choose from, with many tour companies offering similar packages. Clients traveling on a tour company package tend to book excursions with the same company, or through the company affiliated with their resort (e.g., Vacaciones Barceló). Amstar is well-managed and reliable and is associated with Apple Vacations. Go Golf specializes in golf packages, with services tailored to clients seeking to make golf part of their getaway—whether it's the primary focus or just a one-time outing; the company will help arrange tee times, golf instruction, and transport to courses.

Information **Amstar DMC–Apple Vacations** (✉ *Carretera Bávaro, Bávaro* ☎ *809/221–6626* ⊕ *www.amstardominicana.com*). **Colonial Tours & Travel** (✉ *Plaza Brisas de Bávaro, Bávaro* ☎ *809/687–2203* ⊕ *www.colonialtours.com. do*). **Go Golf** (☎ *809/688–2978* ⊕ *www.tee-off-times.info*). **El Pat Ranch** (☎ *809/ 223–8896*). **Jurassic Safari** (✉ *Carretera Meliá, Bávaro* ☎ *809/552–1364* ⊕ *www. jurassic-safari.com*). **Takeoff Destination Service** (✉ *Plaza Brisas de Bávaro, Bávaro* ☎ *809/552–1333* ⊕ *www.takeoffweb.com*). **Turinter** (✉ *Carretera Bávaro, Km 5, Punta Cana* ☎ *809/221–0619* ⊕ *www.turinter.com*). **Vacaciones Barceló** (✉ *Barceló Bávaro, Bávaro* ☎ *809/686–5797 Ext. 1396* ⊕ *www.vacacionesbarcelo. com*). **VIP Travel Services** (✉ *Plaza Cueva Taina, Carretera Bávaro-Arena Gorda, Bávaro* ☎ *809/552–1001* ⊕ *www.viptravelservices.com*).

Samaná Peninsula

WORD OF MOUTH

"[Cayo Leventado] is a very small island . . . nice for a day-trip . . . but you'd be better off on the mainland if actually planning on staying over there."

—oldhippy

By Michael de
Zayas

"ONE OF THE AUTHORS OF the King James Bible traveled the Caribbean, and I often think that it was a place like Samaná that was on his mind when he sat down to pen the Eden chapters. For Eden it was, a blessed meridian where mar and sol and green have forged their union."   —Junot Díaz, *The Brief Wondrous Life of Oscar Wao*

You need only squint a bit in the sun to imagine a tropical paradise of Biblical proportions—a dramatically beautiful peninsula of coconut trees stretching into the sea like an island unto itself. It's something of a microcosm of the Dominican Republic: here you'll see poverty and fancy resorts, good and bad (and really bad) roads, verdant mountainsides, tropical forests, tiny villages lined with streetside fruit vendors, secluded beaches, and the radiant warmth of the Dominican people.

The green mountains teem with coconut trees and dramatic vistas of sea, full of hidden beaches reachable only on foot or by sea, protected coves, and undeveloped bays. There are also a number of all-inclusive resorts that claim territory to themselves, as well as quaint and low-key beachfront hotels and restaurants where you can find complete relaxation and tranquillity. Samaná (pronounced sah-mah-NAH) is the name of both the peninsula and its biggest town, as well as the bay to the south. It's worth noting that to locals, *Samaná* denotes only the biggest town, Santa Barbara de Samaná, which makes a great departure point for whale-watching or an excursion to Los Haitises park across the bay. The bay is home to some of the world's best whale-watching from mid-January to late March. If you're here during that time, don't miss it.

A visit to Samaná is really about two things: exploring its preserved natural wonders and relaxing at a small beachfront hotel. The latter is most readily accomplished in Las Terrenas, the only true tourist center, where you can find picturesque restaurants, accommodations of all types, and great beaches. Reach it by taking a winding road through the mountains from the town of Sánchez. At Las Terrenas you can enjoy peaceful *playas,* take advantage of the vibrant nightlife (including a casino), and make all your plans for expeditions on the peninsula. The other pleasures are solitary—quiet beaches, the massive national park Los Haitises, and water sports and hiking.

EXPLORING SAMANÁ

From the mainland Dominican Republic, Highway 5 runs along the southern coast of the peninsula, passing the westernmost town of any size, Sánchez, along to the biggest (and only real) town on the peninsula, Santa Bárbara de Samaná (called simply Samaná) in about an hour. From this main artery, a few roads cut north along winding, poorly maintained roads to the north shore, which is where you can find all the public beaches. Off the southeastern corner of the peninsula lies the small island of Cayo Levantado, accessible only by boat. The road continues to the northeastern beach outpost of Las Galeras. From here you'll want to rent a boat to reach the islands best, and most secluded, beaches.

ABOUT THE RESTAURANTS

You can stay busy finding your favorite restaurant at Las Terrenas, the town where you can find almost all the best restaurants on the peninsula. Particularly memorable is the collection of eight shoulder-to-shoulder restaurants on the beach called Pueblo de los Pescadores. These are on stilts above the sand, a few paces from the water.

Although you'll be able to get meat, fish is the island specialty here, and is available far and wide. Mero (grouper) and dorado (mahimahi) are the most abundant—you can find the traditional Dominican preparation of *pescado al coco* (coconut fish) virtually everywhere. Shrimp and lobster also readily available. Passion fruit, called *chinola,* is an abundant staple, as well as banana (*guineo*), orange (*naranja*), and giant papaya (*lechoza*). Chinola makes a great fresh-squeezed breakfast juice, especially mixed with pineapple (*piña*).

All restaurants have bars and serve as the nightlife focal points. Expect to pay around $8 to $15 for most entrées in this chapter; restaurants in the D.R. always charge in pesos, but you can sometimes pay in dollars.

ABOUT THE HOTELS

The quintessential stay, the one that has the most local flavor and puts you in contact with the people and spirit of Samaná, is in a small beach hotel run by expats. These were the region's first tourist outposts, and the oldest were opened in the mid- to late 1990s. In these small hotels you can find complete tranquillity: no TVs or phones, just a quiet, lush cabana haven with a footpath leading to the water. These hotels range from $50 to $140 per night and are mainly concentrated in the town of Las Terrenas and Las Galeras; rates in small hotels are often set in pesos, but you can sometimes pay in dollars. On a hill high above playa Cosón is Peninsula House, one of the world's great luxury B&Bs. It's new and almost unknown, and it's well worth the money if you can afford it.

There are seven all-inclusive resorts in Samaná, with rates ranging from around $100 to $150 per person (AIs in the Dominican Republic almost always charge in U.S. dollars). Bahía Príncipe, a Spanish all-inclusive chain, has four resorts scattered across the peninsula. These are of a higher caliber than the two all-inclusives at Las Terrenas's Cosón Beach, where there are two Viva properties, including a Wyndham; the Bahí Príncipe resorts are also newer than the Casa Marina Beach Resort at Las Galeras.

In Las Terrenas, Playa Bonita and Playa Cosón are the best places to stay and are removed from the louder nightlife of Las Terrenas beach. Be sure to ask if your room has air-conditioning if that's important to you (or phones or TVs for that matter). The weather is breezy and wonderful, and you may not find a/c to be a necessity (many smaller hotels don't offer it), but if it's important, you'll want to clarify ahead of time.

WHAT IT COSTS IN DOLLARS AND DOMINICAN PESOS				
¢	$	$$	$$$	$$$$
Restaurants in dollars	under $8	$8–$12	$12–$20	$20–$30	Over $30
Restaurants in pesos	under RD$275	RD$275–RD$410	RD$410–RD$680	RD$680–RD$1,000	Over RD$1,000
Hotels*	Under $80	$80–$150	$150–$250	$250–$350	Over $350
Hotels**	Under $125	$125–$250	$250–$350	$350–$450	Over $450

*EP, BP, CP **AI, FAP, MAP Restaurant prices are per person for a main course at dinner and do not include the 15% V.A.T. and 10% service charge. Hotel prices are per night for a double room in high season, excluding 15% V.A.T. and 10% service charge.

LAS TERRENAS

22 mi (35 km) northwest of Santa Bárbara de Samaná.

Las Terrenas is the main tourist base on the Samaná Peninsula. It, rather than Santa Barbara de Samaná, the peninsula's biggest town, is the true center of a visit to the region. The main roads from the southern part of the peninsula end up at the busy center of town along the water, where you can find lots of bars and shopping. Some visitors looking to get away from civilization may find it overcrowded, but others will enjoy the variety of restaurants and nightlife.

The center of town is split by a river outlet to the sea. To the east the beach is known as Playa Punta Popy, and this is the least desirable of the five big public beaches in Las Terrenas. To the west of the river in the middle of town is where much of the action is—you'll know you're here when you pass the Kick'n Ass Bar and Grill. A short distance later—beyond this partly Americanized section—the commercial flows into the charming at a conglomeration of restaurants along the beach called Pueblo de los Pescadores. The beach here is called Playa Las Terrenas. There's a casino farther along the road. Beyond this, the beach becomes even less commercial and more attractive, stretching to where the road ends: this is Playa Ballenas, named for the offshore rock islands that appear to resemble humpback whales.

As nice as Playa Las Ballenas is, Playa Cosón and Playa Bonita offer are even quieter and less trafficked since they're farther away from the town. At Playa Bonita you can bounce between the golden beach and one of the hotels directly across the rough road, where you can have lunch. Hotel Acaya is one of these hotels and has an open-air restaurant and bar.

Playa Cosón is an unspoiled 12-mi stretch of white sand, the best beach in Las Terrenas. At the time of this writing there were no finished developments along the main beach, but a number of condos were under construction. You can add a pool and drinks to your stay here by buying a day-pass at one of two all-inclusive resorts, which have long private beaches along the Bahía Cosón.

★ One mile southwest of Las Terrenas on the mountain road to Sánchez, **Ecotopia,** a private botanical park fills a vital role in a region without a public botanical garden. In the 70-acre preserve you can hike along trails, learning about the many varieties of exotic plants. Highlights of the hikes include a panoramic lookout where you can see across mountains to a view down over Cosón and Bonita beaches. There's also a natural pool you can swim in. The real pleasure is just walking past valleys full of heiconia and other tropical flowers. (⊠ *Hoyo de Cacao, Las Terrenas* ☎ *809/350–4820 or 809/299–4820* ⊕ *www. ecotopia-dr.com* ☞ *$2* ⊙ *Mon.–Sat. 8–5, Sun. 9–noon* ⊙ *Closed Mon. Jan.–May).* Provided that you're fit and willing to deal with a long and slippery path on horseback, an adventurous guided trip to the spectacular **Salto el Limón Cascade** is a delight. The journey is done mostly on horseback but includes some walking down rocky, sometimes muddy trails. You'll have to cross two rivers en route. Horse paths are slippery, and the trek is strenuous. The well-mannered horses take you across rivers and up mountains to El Limón, where you can find the 165-foot waterfall amidst luxuriant vegetation. Some snacks and drinks are usually included in the guided trip, but a grilled chicken lunch is only a few more pesos. The outpost for the trek, a local guide service called Santi Rancho, is relatively subtle; it's best to ask your hotel for detailed directions. The trip to the waterfall by horseback takes 40 minutes each way; the entire excursion lasts about three hours. ⊠ *Santi Rancho, El Limón.*

WHERE TO EAT

$–$$$ ╳ **L'Atlantico.** Prystasz Gerard, honorary French consul and former pri-
★ vate chef to François Mitterand, has camped out at this relaxed, thatch-roofed outpost right on the beach at the far end of Playa Bonita. The vibe is casual, the food a cut above. Gerard can prepare food that no one else in Samaná can, including a shrimp in cacao and whisky sauce and house-smoked fish. Dorado in champagne sauce? Mais oui—the fine local fish meets its fancy French fate, and you'll be glad for it. ⊠ *Playa Bonita, Las Terrenas* ☎ *809/240–6111* ▤ *AE, MC, V.*

$ ╳ **The Beach.** You might hear whispers of a "secret restaurant" on Playa
★ Cosón. There is indeed one—and only one—restaurant on this 12-mi stretch of virgin beach, and it's hidden behind a grove of coconut trees. After a long, torturous drive, you'll see a tiny sign with an arrow that's very easy to miss. Don't miss it. Open just for lunch, this is a splendid mix of fancy and relaxed beach club: an old plantation-style hut has an outdoor patio in the back. The regularly changing menu is based on what fresh ingredients and fish are available. Cooking is refined whether you opt for a hamburger or something a bit more elaborate like beef fillet with pepper sauce. Expect service on cotton linens and crystal glassware. Best of all, have a great meal and enjoy the virgin beach to yourself. ⊠ *Playa Cosón, Las Terrenas* ☎ *809/962–7447* ⊲ *Reservations essential* ▤ *No credit cards* ⊙ *Closed Mon. No dinner.*

Samaná
Peninsula

Playa
Las Ballenas

Playa
Cosón

Playa
Bonita

**Las
Terrenas**

El Portillo

Punta
Bonita

Barbacos

Las Yayales

*Monte
Las Canitas*

◆ **Ecotopia**

Monte
Negro

**El Catay
International
Airport**

La Majagua

5

Majagual
Adentro

El Catay

Sánchez

Las
Garitas

Punta
Gorda

5

Majagual

Los
Róbalos

Trujilo del Yuna

Río Barracote

*PARQUE NACIONAL
LOS HAÏTISES*

0   4 miles

0   4 kilometers

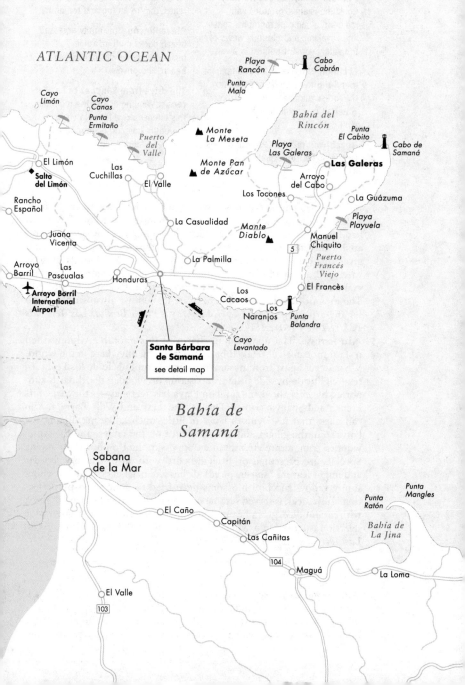

ATLANTIC OCEAN

*Cayo
Limón*

*Cayo
Canas*

*Punta
Ermitaño*

El Limón

◆ **Salto
del Limón**

*Rancho
Español*

*Juana
Vicenta*

*Arroyo
Barril*

*Las
Pascualas*

✈ **Arroyo Borril
International
Airport**

Las
Cuchillas

El Valle

*Puerto
del
Valle*

▲ *Monte
La Meseta*

▲ *Monte Pan
de Azúcar*

La Casualidad

*Monte
Diablo* ▲

La Palmilla

Honduras

Los
Cacaos

*Playa
Rancón*

*Punta
Mala*

🗼 *Cabo
Cabrón*

*Bahía del
Rincón*

*Playa
Las Galeras*

*Punta
El Cabito*

🗼 *Cabo de
Samaná*

Las Galeras

*Arroyo
del Cabo*

Los Tocones

La Guázuma

*Playa
Playuela*

*Manuel
Chiquito*

5

*Puerto
Francés
Viejo*

El Francès

Los
Naranjos

🗼

*Punta
Balandra*

**Santa Bárbara
de Samaná**
see detail map

*Cayo
Levantado*

*Bahía de
Samaná*

Sabana
de la Mar

El Caño

Capitán

Las Cañitas

104

Maguá

*Punta
Ratón*

*Punta
Mangles*

*Bahía de
La Jina*

La Loma

El Valle

103

SAMANÁ TOP 5

Boating to Parque Los Haitises. Coastline islands, grottoes with indigenous Taíno pictographs, coastline kayaking, and glorious views of the wildly verdant peninsula await.

El Limón Waterfall. A three-hour round-trip foray by horseback into the forest culminates in a dazzling waterfall cascading into a natural pool.

Beachfront meal at Pueblo de los Pescadores. Eight quality eateries sit chockablock on the water at Terrenas: they're all fun and romantic.

Playa Rincón. This rarely accessed beach packs it all in: a river, unspoiled mountainside, perfect beach, and privacy.

The drive from Sánchez to Las Terrenas. Winding across the mountain, this intense drive takes in views of the entire bay and beyond to Los Haitises National Park.

¢–$ ✕**Color Café.** This is the most inviting and stylish place to eat or have a drink on Bonita beach. Note the contemporary decor? It was all handmade by the owner, Josy Miklas, including the long lanterns created from palm roots collected nearby. It's this attention to detail that gives this café an elevated sense of languorous chic. Florals in glass vases add an air of sophistication. And yet lounge chairs and settees make it inviting to curl up with a book, too; it's a beach, after all. The menu offers typical Samaná fare; it's almost always right to go for the grilled fresh fish. ⊠*Hotel Acaya, Playa Bonita, Las Terrenas* ☎*809/240–6161* ▤*MC, V.*

¢–$ ✕**La Terrasse.** The unassuming charm of this adorable whitewashed
Fodor'sChoice   restaurant can rival relaxed beachfront dining anywhere in the world.
★   What sets it apart from its similar brethren on Pubelo de los Pescadores—eight side-by-side restaurants set up on wooden floorboards supported by stilts above the sand on Playa Las Terrenas—is the care of its French and Spanish owners Denise Cheynesy and Willy Barrera. You can guess that it's Denise's hand in little touches like perfume in the bathroom, the ginger and bougainvilliea on the tables, and the white wooden trim, a rare attempt at daintiness in the Dominican Republic. Specials are presented on a chalkboard with an ornamental border and might feature "sun-inspired" dishes like beignet de flores zucchini, sunny yellow zucchini blossoms deep-fried to golden, crispy perfection. Tuna steak is served sesame-crusted with a soy-based sauce, along with ratatouillee, green beans, and white rice. A surprisingly good wine selection is stored in a wine refrigerator. ⊠*Pueblo de los Pescadores, Las Terrenas* ☎*809/240–6730* ▤*No credit cards.*

WHERE TO STAY

¢   🖼**Coyamar.** Coyamar is the most inexpensive of the peninsula's lan-
★   guorous gems. If you don't mind going without a/c, it's hard not to love the hyper-relaxed atmosphere of this family-run small hotel on Playa Bonita. A path wends its way across the yard of orange trees, coconut

palms, and bamboo, to the beach at the end of lawn, which has the feel of a small seafront botanic garden. The restaurant, under an enormous thatch roof, serves fresh fish and is a wonderful place to read a book. Coyamar is the creation (the name, in fact, is an invention) of German expat owners Peter and Judith, who designed the environmentally sensitive hotel in the 1990s. Expect to see a shirtless Peter reading the papers while young son Tao cavorts with his two chow chows, Madox and Balu. Rooms are bright, with peach and light greens. Red floor tiles extend from spacious terraces to the comfortable interiors, which have high ceilings and colorful art. There is no air-conditioning, TV, or phone, but the shutters ensure breezy nights (there are also ceiling fans). Don't like the overhead fluorescent lighting at night? Light the candle in your room, and take in the sounds of the surf by flickering light. Life doesn't get simpler. ⊠*Playa Bonita 1, Las Terrenas* ☎*809/240–5130* ⊕*www.coyamar.com* ⇱*10 rooms* ⌂*In-room: no a/c, no phone, safe, no TV, Ethernet, Wi-Fi. In-hotel: restaurant, bar, pool, beachfront, no elevator, public Wi-Fi, some pets allowed* ⊟*MC, V* ⍒*CP.*

¢ ⛰**Hotel Acaya.** Ten steps from Playa Bonita, Acaya has a cosmopolitan beach bum vibe, mixing a casual setting with touches of surprisingly tasteful decor—and the addition of air-conditioning, a rarity in these parts. Rooms are simple, with white-tile floors and queen beds with pastel linens; but high ceilings, light colors, and wood shutters create a feeling of lightness and space. Stay closer to the restaurant; doubles in the next building aren't quite as nice. Josy Miklas, a former French fashion designer, opened the hotel in 1998. She has designed many of the furnishings, including lamps made from gourds collected on property and ensures a high standard of cleanliness. A full breakfast, included in the price, is made fresh each morning, even if you sleep in until 3. You get beach chairs and cushions for a day on the sand, and if you're feeling ambitious, there's a shop on-site to rent kite boards. Bathrooms are spacious, with two sinks, and are painted a cheery cerulean. The stylish restaurant and bar have hammocks and games that make it a relaxing place to hang out. **Pros:** Inexpensive, stylish, bright. **Cons:** The tide sometimes covers up the small beach. ⊠*Playa Bonita, Las Terrenas* ☎*809/240–6161* 🖷*809/240–6297* ⊕*www.hotelacaya. com* ⇱*16 rooms* ⌂*In-room: no phone, refrigerator, no TV, Wi-Fi. In-hotel: restaurant, bar, beachfront, water sports, no elevator, laundry facilities, laundry service, executive floor, public Internet, public Wi-Fi* ⊟*MC, V* ⍒*BP.*

¢–$ ⛰**Hotel Playa Colibri.** With full kitchens, a big pool, and big balconies
⟳ overlooking the beach, friendly and relaxed Colibri is the best bet for families on Playa Las Ballenas. Rooms overlook the pool and the ocean from very large balconies (they're actually larger than the bedrooms) and are equipped with a table and chairs for outdoor dining. The interiors suffer from overhead fluorescent lighting and generally artlessly assembled furnishings, but all rooms have full beach and pool views. The pool is one of the biggest and best pools in Samaná (it has a small kids section and a whirlpool, too). Rooms come in three basic layouts (type C save only a few dollars cheaper and face the rear, so focus on A or B rooms). The hotel has a bar directly on the beach under a thatched

5

roof and provides beach towels for guests. **Pros:** On the quieter end of Las Ballenas beach. **Cons:** Most rooms do not have a/c. ⊠*Playa Las Ballenas, Las Terrenas* ☎*809/240–6434* ⊕*www.playacoibri.com* ➥*41 rooms* &*In-room: no a/c, no phone, safe, kitchen, refrigerator, DVD, VCR, no TV, Ethernet, Wi-Fi. In-hotel: restaurant, room service, bars, tennis courts, pool, gym, spa, beachfront, diving, water sports, bicycles, no elevator, children's programs (ages 2–14), laundry facilities, laundry service, executive floor, public Internet, public Wi-Fi, some pets allowed, no-smoking rooms* ⊟*AE, MC, V* ⏏*EP.*

$$$$
Fodor's Choice
★

The Peninsula House. If you can afford it, a stay here will reset your thinking on what a small luxury property can be; this is one of the best B&Bs in the Caribbean, if not the world. The gorgeous Victorian-style plantation house with wraparound verandahs overlooks miles of coconut palms down to the ocean. It's family-run and showcases generation's worth of museum-quality sculptures, paintings, and objects d'art, many of which were acquired from the Far East and the Middle East. The art elevates the rooms and common areas to a fascinating visual experience. Dinner, available only to guests, takes place in the central open-air brick courtyard. Dishes, linens, even the stationery you find here is refined; not to mention that rooms come with flat-screen TVs (the only ones on the Samaná Peninsula at this writing) would be missing the point. No expense has been spared. For heaven's sake, the pool house has a world-class collection of African masks. Is $600 a lot for a room? It's not a full-fledged "resort," but we'd recommend that you consider saving now. In terms of international high-end travel, this is a real steal. The house opened in 2007, doesn't advertise, and the secretive entrance is unmarked from the road. **Pros:** Quiet and remote, luxurious, impeccable guest attention. **Cons:** Expensive, but that's the only drawback we can find. ⊠*Camino Cosón, Las Terrenas* ☎*809/307–1827 or 809/882–7712* ⊕*www.thepeninsulahouse.com* ➥*6 rooms* &*In-room: safe, DVD, Wi-Fi. In-hotel: bar, pool, spa, no elevator, laundry service, public Wi-Fi, no kids under 18* ⊟*AE, D, MC, V* ⏏*BP.*

NIGHTLIFE

Cacao Beach Casino. (⊠*Cacao Beach Hotel, Playa Bonita, Las Terrenas* ☎*809/240–6000*) is the only casino in Las Terrenas. On Playa Bonita, it's open daily from 7 PM to 4 AM. You'll find about two dozen tables offering blackjack and roulette, as well as slot machines. There's always a crowd.

El Mosquito (⊠*Pueblo de los Pescadores, Las Terrenas* ☎*809/877–8374*) is the main bar at Pueblo de los Pescadores. It opens nightly at 6 PM and offers a small food menu; there's occasionally live music. Mainly it's a wonderful place to enjoy drinks on the beach and gaze up at the stars.

El Toro Sobre El Techo (⊠*Pueblo de los Pescadores, Las Terrenas* ☎*809/240–6648*), another Pueblo de Pescadores favorite, is the busiest and most crowded scene in Las Terrenas, relative to its small size. Expect pulsing music and a singles-bar type crowd.

Kick'n Ass Bar & Grill (⊠*Playa Bonita, Las Terrenas* ☎*No phone*), run by an American expat, is a lively place for drinks and friendly conversation.

Syroz Bar (⊠*Calle Principal, Las Terrenas* ☎*809/866–5577*) is a consistent nightlife favorite, known for its live jazz.

SPORTS & THE OUTDOORS

BEACHES

On **Playa Bonita** (⊠*Las Terrenas*) you can bounce between the golden beach (BYO towel—no chaises) and one of the hotels and restaurants directly across the rough road, where you can have lunch. The beach can disappear in flooding and high tides. It's a quiet stretch of gold sand with leaning coconut trees.

Playa Cosón (⊠*Las Terrenas*) is a long, wonderful stretch of white sand and best beach close to the town of Las Terrenas. At the time of this writing it was completely undeveloped, but there are a dozen condo developments under construction, so that sense of solitude is not going to last. One restaurant, the Beach, serves the entire 15-mi shore.

Playa Jackson (⊠*Approximately 10 km (6 mi) from Las Terrenas by boat*)a secluded beach with a coral reef just offshore can be reached by hired boat from Las Terrenas or Las Galeras. It's a popular destination for snorkeling.

Playa Las Ballenas (⊠*Las Terrenas*) is the westernmost of the three beaches at the town of Las Terrenas (the others are Terrenas and Punta Popy; these three, in fact, are really a continuous stretch of beach with different names). It's the nicest stretch in town since it's the quietest section. The western edge is undeveloped. Moderate hotels across the street provide chaises to their guests, and the Hotel Playa Colibri runs a little bar on the beach.

Playa Punta Popy (⊠*Las Terrenas*) is basically an undistinguishable continuation of Playa Terrenas to the east; this section is slightly cleaner and less crowded the further east you travel.

Playa Terrenas (⊠*Las Terrenas*) is the most crowded (and dirtiest) of all the peninsula's beaches. As you approach the ocean from the town of Las Terrenas, a fork divides the road. To the west is Playa Las Ballenas, and to the east is this beach.

BOATING & FISHING

Boats are a great way to see more secluded beaches. Playa Escondida, for example, is the best spot in the area for snorkeling and can be reached only by boat. There are two boats serving Las Terrenas; one is particularly good for day trips.

Cap Ocean (⊠*Playa Las Ballenas, Las Terrenas* ☎*809/803–5595* ⊕*capocean.site.voila.fr*) has a 35-foot catamaran in the water across from Cacao Beach hotel. Captains Fabrice and Christian specialize in expensive fishing excursions. **Tortuga Excursiones** (⊠*Playa Las Ballenas, Las*

Terrenas ☎*809/913–6913*) operates a huge yellow catamaran that fits 80 people and heads to all nearby beaches. A Friday sunset cruise is particularly noteworthy. Departures are at 4:15 PM; the $20 fee includes drinks. Day-trips range from $30 to $80; kids are half-price.

DIVING

In 1979 three atolls disappeared following a seaquake off Las Terrenas, providing an opportunity for truly memorable dives. Also just offshore from Las Terrenas are the Islas Las Ballenas ("The Whale Islands"), a cluster of four little islands with good snorkeling. A coral reef is off Playa Jackson, a beach accessible only by boat.

Las Terrenas Divers (⊠*Playa Bonita, Las Terrenas* ☎*809/889–2422*) offers diving lessons and trips; diving equipment rentals start at $30, snorkeling equipment at $15. The shop is closed Sunday.

HORSEBACK RIDING

Rancho La Isabella (⊠*Behind Hotel Las Cayenas, Playa Las Terrenas, Las Terrenas* ☎*809/804–8960*) offers rides on Playa Bonita for $18 and Playa Cosón or Las Terrenas for $45.

SURFING

Surfing, windsurfing, wakeboarding, and kite surfing are popular in Las Terrenas. Playa Cosón has the best breaks. Playa Bonita is another popular spot, since like on Cosón there are no rocks. Two-hour lessons are $35, and a one-day board rental runs $25; it's usually $15 for half a day.

Pura Vida (⊠*Hotel Acaya, Playa Bonita, Las Terrenas* ☎*809/915–7750 or 809/878–6640* ⊕*www.puravidacaraibes.com*) rents surf boards and offers lessons. The company also rents mountain bikes and leads biking tours.

Las Terrenas Divers (⊠*Playa Bonita, Las Terrenas* ☎*809/889–2422*) rents surf and boogie boards and gives surfing lessons.

SHOPPING

Shopping isn't a big draw in Samaná in general, but Las Terrenas has the most shops, which mainly sell trinkets aimed at tourists. The closest thing to a mall is a collection of small shops called Plaza Taino.

Haitian Caraïbes Art Gallery (⊠*Calle Principal 233, Las Terrenas* ☎*809/240–6250*) is the main source for Haitian art in all the peninsula.

SANTA BÁRBARA DE SAMANÁ

22 mi (35 km) southeast of Las Terrenas.

The official name of the city is Santa Bárbara de Samaná; but these days it's just called "Samaná." An authentic port town, it's just getting its bearings as a tourist zone. It has a typical *malecón* (seaside promenade), ideal for strolling and watching the boats in the harbor. A small

Expats in Paradise

If you spend any amount of time on the Samaná Peninsula and you'll meet a gaggle of unaffiliated expatriate entrepreneurs who have made Samaná their homemade paradise and who have created most of its tourism infrastructure. In this way a tour of the peninsula is like an encounter with a series of delightful personalities. Here are three of their stories.

In the late 1990s, two young Germans, Peter and Judith, decided they wanted to start a new life in a tropical setting. They ranked all the warm-weather nations of the world, considering critical factors like political stability and crime rates. "This was before the Internet, and involved a lot of dedicated research," said Peter. "The DR was at the very top of our list." Then they built their hotel in Las Terrenas. Today a visit to the beachfront Coyamar Hotel—which exudes a breeziness that's decidedly romantic—is a trip into their world. You'll probably meet soft-spoken Judith at reception, and you'll see a barechested Peter and their son, Tao, who was born here in 2001, playing with their chow chow. "It's almost impossible to make a profit, but we enjoy our life," Peter said.

French-born Yvonne Bastian arrived in 1998 from the Central African Republic, where she'd run a restaurant that had served presidents and dignitaries. Revolution brought her to the Dominican Republic, and she's been the guiding gastronomic light in the main town of Santa Bárbara de Samaná sever since. In 2007 the restaurant Xamana opened, and suddenly there were *two* good restaurants in town. Yvonne's grown-up son runs the front of the house. The duo's care is evident in the tranquil, oasislike interior.

In 2005 a blended family of three hailing from South Africa, France, and the United States, were in search of a new life project and a new place to live. Cari Guy had grown up in the kitchens of his family's Colorado restaurants and later found success operating a luxury B&B in Provence. There he met Marie-Claude Theibault, whose Parisian family had imported antiques from the Far East for generations. Her son Thomas Stamm grew up in the United States and South Africa. The three had sought out locales in Croatia, Spain, and beyond. "We came to the Dominican Republic visiting friends, and knew we'd found our place when we saw Samaná," said Thiebault. "It was beautiful, and nothing like this had ever been done." The Peninsula House—their ultra-refined six-room hilltop property overlooking huge swaths of coconut forest to the sea—was built from scratch, using a French architect. Thomas handles guest relations, Marie-Claude the gardens, and Cari the cooking. The result is one of the world's most unique small-property experiences.

5

but bustling town, Samaná is filled with friendly residents, skilled local craftsmen selling their wares, and a handful of outdoor restaurants.

A big all-inclusive Bahía Príncipe Cayacoa, is on one end of the bay road on a hill. Day passes are available (and the resort has the only beaches in town). The hotel also operates a block of new and colorful gift shops and a casino. This is, obvious to all, the first and only attempt to capture cruise-ship passenger money in town. Along Avenida del Malecón is

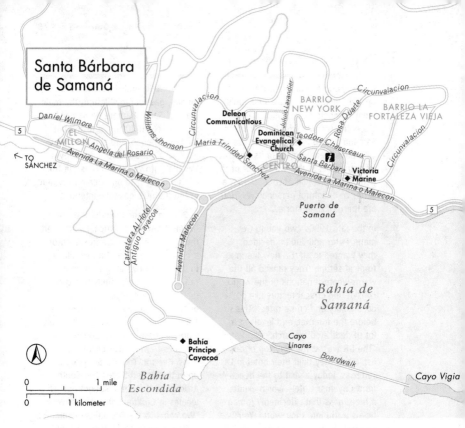

Santa Bárbara
de Samaná

Victoria Marine, ground zero for tours to see whales from January until late March, as well as the Los Haitises park across the bay.

Though there are no public beaches in Samaná town, but you can hire a boat to take you to **Cayo Levantado**, which has a wonderful white-sand beach on an island in Samaná Bay. Today, the small island has largely been turned into a commercial enterprise to accommodate the 1,500 cruise-ship passengers who dock here each day; it has dining facilities, bars, restrooms, and lounge chairs on the beautiful beach. Unfortunately, it's also a tacky tourist trap, especially when there's a ship in port. The company that runs cruise-ship services on the island also operates the public section of the island and is guilty of some bad decisions, including importing sea lions and charging tourists $8 to take a photos with them. It's this sort of practice that can make Cayo Levantado an unpleasant experience, though the beaches are undeniably beautiful. The new Grand Bahía Príncipe Cayo Levantado, an upscale, all-inclusive resort, claims the eastern two-thirds of the island for its private use and sells one-day passes that allow you to use the resort's facilities and get food and drinks for about $70. Day trips to Los Haitises often stop here for some beach time before returning to Santa Bárbara de Samaná. ⊠*Samaná Bay,* ☎*No phone* ☜*Public beach free* ☉*Daily dawn–dusk.*

Back in 1824, a sailing vessel called the *Turtle Dove,* carrying several hundred escaped American slaves, was blown ashore in Samaná. The historic **Dominican Evangelical Church** is the oldest original building left in Samaná. It actually came across the ocean from England in 1881 in a hundred pieces and was reassembled here, serving the spiritual needs of African-American freedmen who emigrated here from Philadelphia, Pennsylvania in 1824. ⊠*Calle Chaseurox, in front of Catholic church* ☏*809/538–2579* ✉*Donations appreciated* ☉*Daily dawn–dusk.*

En route to the Cayacoa hotel, the tiny **Whale Museum & Nature Center (Centro de Naturaleza)** is dedicated to the mighty mammals of the sea. Samaná has one of the largest marine mammal sanctuaries in the world and is a center for whale-watching in the migration season. The CEBSE (Center for Conservation and Ecodevelopment of Samaná Bay and its Environment) manages this facility, which features a 40-foot humpback skeleton. ⊠*Av. La Marina, Tiro al Blanco* ☏*809/538–2042* ⊕*Samana.org.do* ✉*RD$50* ☉*Daily 8–noon and 2–5.*

Los Haitises National Park. One of the premier highlights of a trip to the Dominican Republic—and probably the most extraordinary part of a visit to the Samaná Peninsula—is a chance to explore Los Haitises National Park. Los Haitises (pronounced High *tee* sis), which is across Samaná Bay from the peninsula, is famous for its karst limestone formations, caves, and grottoes filled with pictographs and petroglyphs left by the indigenous Taïno, who inhabited this area before Columbus' arrival.

The park is accessible only by boat, and a professionally guided tour is highly recommended—especially so you can kayak along the shoreline. Another option is to hire a fisherman to take you over on a small boat, but then you'll miss the guidance that an experienced operator can provide.

On a trip you'll sail around dozens of the dramatic rock islands and spectacular cliff faces. Swirling around are hundreds of beautiful coastal birds from 121 different species, including Louisiana the magnificent American frigate birds, brown pelicans, brown booby, and varieties of egrets and herons. The sight of dozens of different of birds continually gliding past the boat at any time is enough to make a birdwatcher out of anyone.

A good tour will let you visit the many caverns. Your flashlight will illuminate Taino and pre-Taino hieroglyphs, and learn how the forest slowly consumes the caves. But the best experience is being able to kayak here. Unlike mangrove kayaking trips in, say, the Florida Everglades, the mangroves here are dramatically flanked by the karst formations. It's a continual sensory delight. The islands rise dramatically and have wild growths of plant life and birds swooping around. The area was used as a local in a half-dozen international versions of the *Survivor* television series. ⊠*Samaná Bay* ☏*No phone* ✉*Admission included with guided tour (required)* ☉*Daily dawn–dusk.*

WHERE TO EAT

¢–$ ✕**El Sabor Samanés.** Although not as inexpensive as it should be, if you want local food, this corner restaurant across from the bay beneath is your best bet in town. It's also across the street from the bay and easy to locate with its blue awning. Sit at a range of plastic chairs and tables, or order from the glass display of Dominican dishes like mofongo. Most fish dishes are RD$300. Cocktails are $5. There are also sandwiches, tacos, and burgers. ⊠*5A Av. Malecón* ☎*809/538–2225* ⊟*No credit cards.*

$ ✕**La Mata Rosada.** Next door to El Sabor Sabanés, La Mata represents more than a step up in comfort and gastronomic complexity. The French owner-chef Yvonne Bastian has been luring local expats and foodies since the late 1990s. She sets tables up with white linens in an all-white interior including an army of ceiling fans to keep you cool; breezes sneak in from the bay across the street. There's a plentiful array of choices, starting with a sea and country salad of conch, potatoes, greens, and bacon; or the "gourmet" plate, a mix of grilled lobster and other shellfish. Ceviche, a specialty of this port town, is made with dorado (mahimahi) and conch. Whether you go local or international, order the creole shrimp or a substantial salad, and you should leave satisfied. But save room: desserts are presented with pride. ⊠*5B Av. Malecón* ☎*809/538–2388* ⊟*AE, MC, V* ⊗*June–Nov., closed Tues.*

$–$$$ ✕**Xamaná.** Xamana is a collection of firsts, the most important being
Fodor'sChoice   that it's the first restaurant in Samaná to take itself seriously. Believe it
★   or not, this is the only air-conditioned restaurant on the entire peninsula—and the only one with imported meat on the menu. Yes, someone has invested money in the attempt to draw comfort seekers. The owners, as well as general manager Franco Bianchimani, come from Santo Domingo's Caffe Bellini, one of the country's most reputable establishments. Come for the floor-to-ceiling glass window views of the bay from the second-floor dining room. Sleek black-and-white chairs and stylish settings raise the bar, and leave the thatch-roof clichés in the dust. Start with a regional specialty, lambí sautéed with lime, white wine, garlic and fresh ginger. Entrées include Mediterranean-style mahimahi. The homemade tiramisu is hard to beat on the dessert menu. And at meal's end, savor a shot of the complimentary *chinolacello* or *mangocello* liqueurs mixed with seasonal passion or mango fruit. ⊠*20 Av. Malecón* ☎*809/538–2129* ⊟*MC, V.*

WHERE TO STAY

$$ 🏨 **Bahía Príncipe Cayo Levantado.** This all-inclusive resort—the most
★   expensive and highest rated of the four Bahí Príncipes in Samaná—hogs two-thirds of the gorgeous island for itself. Whether that's good or bad, you can't deny that it has the best beaches, pools, and recreational choices of any resort in the area. Twice-daily ferries shuttle you to the island from the mainland; you're welcomed with a beverage at reception and given a bracelet. Unfortunately, if you tire of foreigners in Hawaiian shirts and bad food, you're stuck here until the next morning. Well, at least you've got a nice room to wait it out in: each has a balcony or terrace that looks out over the ocean with a big canopy bed

and a whirlpool bath separated by a glass partition from the bedroom. Service is a high point—and you will be endeared to the hard-working local Dominican staff. The peppy "animation" team puts on shows each night. **Pros:** Beautiful beach, new rooms with ocean views. **Cons:** Bad food, expensive for this region, ID bracelet required, removed from reality. ⊠*Cayo Levantado* ☎*809/538–3232* ⊕*www.bahiaprincipe. com* ⇆*195 rooms* ⌂*In-room: safe, refrigerator. In-hotel: 5 restaurants, room service, bars, pools, gym, spa, beachfront, diving, water sports, laundry service, public Internet, public Wi-Fi* ⊟*AE, D, DC, MC, V* ⦿*AI.*

$$ 🏨**Bahía Príncipe Cayacoa.** As you might expect of an all-inclusive built in the middle of a setting of immense natural beauty, this place combines the best and worst of everything Samaná has to offer. Of the four Gran Bahía's on the peninsula, only this one doesn't make you feel like a prisoner (although you're still wearing a plastic ID bracelet) since town (and the good food you can find there) is a five-minute walk away. Best are the mesmerizing views: the ocean, the town, and the rolling green landscape all lie before you from this hilltop perch on the bay. It's also the only hotel in the town of Samaná (the next closest, Gran Bahía Samaná, is 10 minutes away but feels unpleasantly isolated). Day visitors can purchase a pass for $70 that includes all food, drinks, and recreation (an excellent choice for cruise passengers). You need to stay a minimum of three nights to dine at the nonbuffet restaurants. Cayacoa has its own spa and disco. Snorkeling and kayaks are included. **Pros:** Beautiful views, fun activities. **Cons:** Bad food, forced to wear ID bracelet. ⊠*Puerto Escondido, Santa Bárbara de Samaná* ☎*809/538–3131* ⊕*www.bahiaprincipe.com* ⇆*209 rooms, 86 suites* ⌂*In-room: safe, refrigerator. In-hotel: 5 restaurants, room service, bars, pools, gym, spa, beachfront, diving, water sports, laundry service, public Internet, public Wi-Fi* ⊟*AE, D, DC, MC, V* ⦿*AI.*

$$$$ 🏨**Hotel Las Ballenas Escondidas.** Looking for a truly relaxing and peaceful setting with a private beach? The French couple who run this place have created a small utopia of gardens and thatch-roofed bungalows sloping down to the sea. An infinity-edge pool is in the middle of it all. Ballenas Escondidas is 15 minutes east of Samaná port, nearly halfway to Las Galeras. This means it's essentially in the middle of nowhere. But where the remoteness and the nice pool and restaurant might seem to imply an all-inclusive experience, there are no forced good times here. At night the ocean is the only music you'll hear. In the day time, a private terrace with two bamboo chairs overlook the hibiscus, bougainvillea, coconut trees, and colorful pastels of the other bungalows; a few cats roam the grounds. The hotel offers boating excursions directly from its small beach. All bungalows have ceiling fans but no a/c. **Pros:** Private, quiet, beautiful. **Cons:** Remote location, thin sheets, older mattresses, no credit cards. ⊠*Los Naranjos* ☎*809/495–0888* ⊕*www. ballenas.free.fr* ⇆*12 bungalows* ⌂*In-room: no a/c, no phone, safe, refrigerator, no TV. In-hotel: restaurant, bar, pool, beachfront, laundry service* ⊟*No credit cards* ⦿*BP.*

FodorsChoice ★

5

SPORTS & THE OUTDOORS

BEACHES

Although Santa Bárbara de Samaná has no public beaches, there is one private beach near town and one reachable by ferry.

Puerto Escondido (✉ *Puerto Escondido, Santa Bárbara de Samaná*)is the beach at the Bahía Principe Cayacoa, and day visitors can enjoy the sands if they buy a day-pass at the resort. Though crowded with guests, the beach offers great views of the bay, plenty of drinks, and the best strand on the south side of the peninsula.

To reach **Cayo Levantado** (✉*Samaná Bay* 🎫*Free* 🕙*Daily dawn–dusk)* you must hire a boat in town or take an excursion to Los Haitises that stops here. The beaches are overly commercialized but beautiful, though on days when cruise ships are in port they are packed with passengers.

SPAS

The peninsula's only true public spa is run by the Bahía Príncipe Cayacoa hotel, across from the hotel's entrance in a separate building. **BahíaSpa** (✉*Bahía Príncipe Cayacoa, Carretera Camino Playa, Samaná* 🕾*809/538–3131 Ext. 1298* ⊕*www.bahia-principe.com*), offers 50-minute "Caribbean Relaxing" massages for RD$1,800. The spa also offers a wide range of other body treatments, waxing, facials, and a hot stone therapy.

WHALE-WATCHING & MARINE EXCURSIONS

Humpback whales come to Samaná Bay to mate and give birth each year for a relatively limited period, from approximately January 15 through March 30. Samaná Bay is considered one of the top 10 destinations in the world to watch humpbacks. If you're here during the brief season, this can be the experience of a lifetime. You can listen to the male humpback's solitary courting song and witness incredible displays as the whales flip their tails and breach (humpbacks are the most active species of whales in the Atlantic).

Victoria Marine/Whale Samaná (✉*Across street from cement town dock, beside park, Samaná* 🕾*809/538–2494* ✐*kim.beddall@usa.net* ⊕*www.whalesamana.com*) is owned by Kim Beddall, a Canadian who is incredibly knowledgeable about whales and Samaná at large, having lived here for 20-some years. Her operation is far and away the region's best, most professional, and environmentally sensitive. On board the *Victoria 11,* a 50-foot motor vessel, a marine mammal specialist narrates and answers questions in several languages. Kim herself conducts almost all the English-speaking trips. The $50 price does not include the RD$100 Marine Mammal Sanctuary entrance fee. Kim also welcomes cruise passengers but requires advance reservations. You must be able to arrive on shore by 9 AM for the morning trip and by 1:30 PM for the afternoon trip.

She also conducts trips to Los Haitises National Park on Tuesday, Thursday, and Saturday on the *Mistral,* a 45-foot catamaran. Tours, which cost $25 per person, include a terrific lunch and last four to five hours. Kim's boat has a dozen kayaks in which teams of two explore the shoreline.

Kim Saves the Whales

Samaná Bay is considered one of the top destinations in the world to watch whales. If you're here in season—humpback whales come to mate and give birth from mid-January for about 60 days—this can be the experience of a lifetime. Humpbacks are the most active species of whales in the Atlantic (Melville called them "the most lighthearted and gamesome of all the whales" in *Moby-Dick*). You can witness incredible displays as the whales breach over and over, spouting a column of air and water with each surface, and then sink with a graceful arc terminated by their beautiful and distinctive tails. If you're lucky, the humpbacks will sometimes leap out of the water acrobatically or slap their tails. You'll witness and learn about other maneuvers, too, like "logging" and "spy-hopping," when the whales submerge themselves for about five minutes at a time. Playing scout and being the first to spot the site of the next breach is part of the fun. The real advantage of whale-watching in Samaná is the reliability—the sighting rate is 95% between January 20 and March 20, so you're practically guaranteed to see whales.

The first official whale watch was conducted in Samaná in 1983 and was led by a Candian named Kim Beddall, who is now the peninsula's recognized whale expert and tireless advocate for natural causes and responsible growth. Kim arrived in 1983 from Toronto to teach diving. She got a look at the whales during her stay and was hooked: "The local fisherman told me that whales came here to drink fresh water. Nobody knew what species they were or really why they came to Samaná, but they were here and I was hooked."

Kim is responsible for the co-management process of whale-watching to ensure responsible activity (and thus to make sure the whales keep returning). There are now 43 official permits for whale-watching, a number that's now fixed in perpetuity. The fewer the boats, and the larger the size of the boats, the less stress on the whales. (The effect of large cruise ships that frequent the area on mating whales is still unknown.) The rules that Kim helped formalize (a continual bureaucratic and political process) includes minimum boat sizes, minimum distance from whales, viewing order, length of time each boat can be with a whale, and a ban on swimming with the whales.

Now a certified marine mammal specialist, Kim leads the regions' best trips. Her company is Victoria Marine/ Whale Samaná.

LAS GALERAS

northeast of Santa Bárbara de Samaná.

Las Galeras is the endearingly unkempt north coast sister of Las Terrenas. Despite its tucked-away location in eastern end of the Samaná Peninsula, the town maintains a lively rhythm—thanks, mostly, to the hubbub created at the epicenter of the town, which abuts the shoreline. El Kiosko, a barebones grouping of local food merchants beneath a roof thatched with coconut fronds, serves up Presidentes for crowd of equal parts locals, resident expats, and onlooking tourists. The beach itself is rocky and uneven, but you can bring your own towel and rent a white plastic chaise for RD$100 (about $3), accept the syncopated merengue blaring out of a parked car, and stare out toward the keys dotting the horizon. Or, better yet, hire a boat from the beach. The fellow manning the push cart stacked with glossy conch shells can make arrangements for a local fisherman to guide you on a wooden charter out to some of the most pristine beaches the peninsula has to offer, Rincón, Frontón, and Madama. You should be able to get a boat to Playa Rincón for about $15 per couple.

WHERE TO EAT

¢–$ ✕**Coconut Roy's Paradise Restaurant.** John Bomare of East Texas constructed a big grill on the main corner of town, a block from the beach, gave it a catchy name, and with his French wife Audrey offers smoked baby back ribs, steaks, grilled lobster, and seafood to hungry foreigners. The bar here also functions as the nighttime center of town, so if you're spending a night in Las Galeras, you're probably having a drink at Roy's. Expect to make friends with a young waitress from, say, New Zealand, and other folks making their way around the world—bungalows on property are offered at rock-bottom prices. ⊠*Calle Principal, Las Galeras* ☎*No phone* ▤*MC, V.*

$–$$ ✕**El Kiosko.** Expect Yaquelín to come out and solicit you when she sees you trying to figure this place out. That's the charm of the kiosks, the collection of outdoor eateries that's the soul of Las Galeras. The amiable Yaquelín is the proprietress and most outgoing of eight small kitchens that run independently (each represented by their own hand-painted wooden signs, with names like Cafeteria Coco Loco). Kiosko is the big straw hut at the end of the road just before the beach. All the local vendors who all pretty much offer the same thing: beer, squid, pork, shrimp, and fish. Lobster served in the native coconut style runs RD$500 and is served with rice, potatoes beans, and a salad. ⊠*Calle Principal, Las Galeras* ☎*No phone* ▤*No credit cards.*

WHERE TO STAY

¢ ▦**Todo Blanco.** This is the kind of place—just a few people, beautiful beachfront, cheap, not much to do, a couple of gazebos with heavenly ocean vistas, a lawn overtaken by coconut trees, hammocks—where reading a good book is your highest priority. There's one housing structure here, a two-story white building with five rooms on each floor. Each room has a balcony of white wood (indeed, all is white, the eponymous *todo blanco*). The set-up is simple: a couple beds of average quality, a wicker chair, a dresser, ruddy tiles. Nothing luxurious: no phones, a TV in the lobby. But, oh, that view—and suddenly all the time in the world to finish that book. You pay $15 extra for a/c, and breakfast is an additional $5. Todo Blanco is the second hotel to the right on the beach when you reach Las Galeras. **Pros:** Simple, relaxed beachfront setting. **Cons:** Not luxurious, few on-site activities. ⊠*Playa Las Galeras, Las Galeras* ☎*809/538–0201* 🖷*809/538–0064* ⊕*www.*

hoteltodoblanco.com ⬛10 rooms ⬛*In-room: no phone, no TV, no a/c (some). In-hotel: bar, beachfront, no elevator, laundry service, some pets allowed* ⬛MC, V.

$ ⬛**Villa Serena.** The best hotel choice in eastern corner of the peninsula, ★ Villa Serena makes a wonderful, relaxed vacation in Samaná a breeze. You'll love the secluded location removed from the hubbub of the main beach; but you'll appreciate being able to walk over to the main street to mix with locals and day-trippers. Included in the price are kayaks, bicycles, and snorkeling equipment—you can paddle out to a perfect little island not far off shore, snorkel around the perimeter, and pack a picnic lunch. Sensational room 17 has two balconies and a hammock overlooking the beach. Rooms have bamboo canopy beds with covering scrims. Excursions directly from the premises including the "dream beach" package for a reasonable RD$1,800 per couple—get a tour of all the area's secluded beaches and be dropped off for as long as you like at your favorite. Rooms are available with and without a/c. Prices include a full breakfast. **Pros:** Private beachfront, quiet and secluded property, fine staff. **Cons:** 10-minute walk to town. ⬛*Las Galeras* ☎809/538–0000 ⬛*www.villaserena.com* ⬛21 rooms ⬛*In-room: no a/c (some), no phone, no TV. In-hotel: Restaurant, room service, bar, pool, beachfront, water sports, bicycles, no elevator, laundry service, public Wi-Fi* ⬛MC, V ⬛*BP.*

¢ ⬛**Villa La Plantación.** Remi Catinot is the exuberant owner and keeper of this castle—two two-story buildings set around a pool he constructed in early 2008. He is rightly proud. While the location is not beachfront—you're about a block from the beach—these simple rooms provide a home base from which to explore Las Galeras for a song. Try for a second-floor rooms; they have their own terraces. Most rooms have brand-new mattresses and happen to provide the best sleep in town, regardless of the cost. Although rates are quoted in euros for the convenience of the mostly European clientele, you will actually pay in the equivalent of either pesos or U.S. dollars. **Pros:** Pleasant, exuberant owner onsite, good mattresses for sleeping. **Cons:** Not on the beach. ⬛*Las Galeras* ☎809/538–0079 ⬛*www.villalaplantacion.com* ⬛12 rooms ⬛*In-room: no a/c (some), no phone, no TV. In-hotel: bar, no elevator* ⬛No credit cards ⬛*EP.*

SPORTS & THE OUTDOORS

BEACHES

Playa Escondida is, as its name (Hidden Beach) implies, a hard beach to find on your own. You'll need to hire a boat from Las Galeras (or perhaps Las Terrenas). It's a great destination for snorkeling and solitude.

Playa Las Galeras (⬛*Las Galleras*) is within this tiny coastal town, a 30-minute drive northeast from the port. It's a lovely, long, and uncluttered beach. The sand is white, the Atlantic waters generally calm. It has been designated a "Blue Flag" beach, which means that it's crystal clean with no pollution, though there are several hotels here. This is a good snorkeling spot, too.

Playa Rincón (✉ *5 km [3 mi] by boat, 15 km [9 mi] by road from Las Galeras*), a beautiful, white-sand beach, is considered one of the top beaches in the Caribbean. It's relatively undeveloped, and at the far-right end is a sheltered area, where you can snorkel. At the other end, cliffs segue way into the turquoise water of Caño Frio, an ice-cold river that runs down from the mountains and forms a splash pool, ideal for rinsing off the salt water. There are no facilities per se, but local ladies will sell you the freshest lobster and fish in coconut sauce with rice, and other creole dishes as well as cold drinks. You can reach Playa Rincón by boat or bus from Las Galeras. A boat is preferable; expect to pay about $15 (*See* ⇨ *Boating*).

BOATING

It would be a fine thing if, immediately arriving at Las Galeras, you headed straight to the beach, and the many small fishing boats lined there. "Take me to the beaches," should be enough to get you a wonderful tour of the remote beaches here, the best on the peninsula. **Excursiones Melo** (✉ *Playa Las Galeras, Las Galeras* ☎ *829/333–1805*) has a boat at the ready and will skiff two people off to Playa Rincón for RD$1,200. You can be dropped off there and asked to be picked up at any time. A more complete tour of the areas other beaches will be slightly more money, but worth every penny.

SAMANÁ PENINSULA ESSENTIALS

TRANSPORTATION

BY AIR

American offers connections to El Catey airport in Samaná from San Juan. All other flights come from other points in the Dominican Republic. Flights from other airports are relatively cheap and frequent.

The peninsula has two airports with regular service: El Catey (AZS), which is a 30-minute drive from Las Terrenas and a 40-minute drive from Samaná town; and El Portillo (EPS), which is just a few miles east of Las Terrenas.

AeroDomca flies three times daily from Las Isabella domestic airport in Santo Domingo to El Portillo and back for $75 each way. AeroDomca offers charter flights to all airports in the D.R., as well as helicopter transfers to all Dominican airports.

Another small domestic airline, Takeoff Destination Services, flies daily from Punta Cana to El Catey (AZS) for $129 and El Portillo for $99. Takeoff also flies to El Portillo (EPS) from Santo Domingo (SDQ) for $69 and from La Romana (LRM) for $99. From Las Americas, Takeoff also offers three inexpensive flights ($69) to El Portillo at 10 AM, 3 PM, and 5 PM; there's also an evening flight from Las Americas to El Catey for $129. All costs are for one-way service.

Also served from Santo Domingo by Aeronaves Dominicanas and Air Santo Domingo.

Information **AeroDomca** (⊠*Plaza El Paseo, Las Terrenas* ☎*809/240–6571* ⊕*www.aerodomca.com*). **Takeoff Destination** (☎*809/552–1333* ⊕*www. takeoffweb.com*).

BY BUS

Caribe Tours offers a four-hour bus service form the capital. There are stops in Sá nchez, Las Terrenas, and Santa Bárbara de Samaná. There are six departures in each direction daily. (The time to reach the Samaná Peninsula was recently cut in half, when a new highway from the capital opened in summer 2008, so you can expect some schedule changes to accommodate the shortened trip.)

From Santiago, Transporte PEPE runs four buses daily to Samaná, starting at 8 AM, with the last, at 3 PM, a nonstop route to Las Terrenas.

From Puerto Plata, Transporte Papagayo is a private bus service leaving Puerto Plata at 6:45 AM from in front of the hospital. It goes as far as Sánchez, returning at 2 PM.

Information **Caribe Tours** (⊠*Av. 27 febrero, corner of Leopoldo Navarro, Santo Domingo* ☎*809/221–4422*). **Transporte PEPE** (⊠*Calle Pedro Francisco Bonó, Santiago* ☎*809/582–2134 or 809/582–5709*). **Transporte Papagayo** (⊠*Puerto Plata* ☎*809/749–6415*).

BY CAR

Renting a car is the best way to get around the island, though driving in the D.R. can be a hectic and even harrowing experience. Get a four-wheel drive if at all possible; you'll need to go through serious mud, puddles, and countless potholes.

Javier Inversiones Rent-a-Car, a local agency in Samaná, can put you in a Jeep or even a Toyota Camry, although there is not a large inventory of automatics. You can expect to pay at least $50 a day—more for an automatic—but that does include insurance.

In Las Terrenas, consider Indianapolis Car Rental, which often has the best prices. Daihatsu Terios, which are rugged mini-SUVs, go for RD$2,300 a day or RD$1,800 a day based on a one-week rental. If you dare, you can also rent a scooter for RD$900 a day or RD$550 a day based on a week's rental.

Another inexpensive option in Las Terrenas is SAINAR.

Information **Indianapolis Car Rental** (⊠*Av. Playa Popy, Las Terrenas* ☎*809/875–6015*). **Javier Inversiones Rent-a-Car** (⊠*7 Francisco Rosario Sánchez, Samaná* ☎*809/249–5937*). **SAINAR** (⊠*Calle Duarte 238, Las Terrenas* ☎*809/252–9826*).

BY TAXI

Negotiate prices, and settle before getting in the taxi. To give you an idea of what to expect, a minivan that can take eight people will normally charges $90 for the round-trip from Samaná to Las Terrenas, including a two-hour wait while you explore or enjoy the beach. Similarly, you'll pay $80 round-trip to travel from Samaná to Las Galeras or Playa Rincón. Many of the drivers speak some English. Within Samaná, rickshaws are far less costly and are also fun. Called *motoconchos de carretas,* they are not unlike larger versions of the Thai tuk-tuk, but can hold up to six people. The least you will pay is RD$10. They're fine to get around town, but don't even think about going the distance with them. If you are based in Las Terrenas, you can call Eddy's Taxi.

Information **Eddy's Taxi** (☎ *809/252–7888* ⊕ *www.eddystaxi.com*).

CONTACTS & RESOURCES

BANKS & EXCHANGE SERVICES
The most common foreign bank in the Dominican Republic is Scotia-bank, with 54 branches throughout the country, including two in the Samaná peninsula. This is the most reliable place to change money or use an ATM. The branches are open weekdays 8:30–4:30 and Sat. 9–1. Note that you won't find any ATMs at all anywhere east of Santa Barbara de Samaná, including at Las Galeras, so if you're heading there, money up in Samaná first.

EMERGENCIES
Hospitals **Centro Medico Vicente**(⊠ *Calle Maria Trinidad Vicente, Santa Bárbara de Samaná* ☎*809/538–2535*).

Pharmacies **Farmacia Giselle** (⊠*Santa Bárbara 2, Samaná* ☎*809/538–2303*).

INTERNET, MAIL & SHIPPING
You'll find several convenient Internet cafés in Santa Bárbara de Samaná, Las Galeras, and Las Terrenas. The cost to go online ranges between RD$30 and RD$80 per hour, inexpensive to be sure. Almost all hotels have at least Wi-Fi in their lobby areas.

Internet Cafés **Centro Llamada Edwards** (⊠*4 Francisco Rosario Sánchez, Samaná* ☎*809/538–2476*) has five computers and charges only RD$30 an hour to connect. **Deleon Communications** (⊠*13 Maria Trinidad Sánchez, Samaná, across from landmark Palacio Justicia* ☎*809/538–3538*) has six computers and four phone booths.

TOUR OPTIONS
There are a number of tour operators based in Las Terrenas. One of these is Sunshine Service, which will help you book all possible trips, rentals, and tours, including Los Haitises and snorkel trips to Playa Jackson.

If seeing the sights from the air is more your style, AeroDomca offers 15-, 30-, and 45-minute helicopter tours from El Portillo Airfield (just east of Las Terrenas). Flights are inexpensive, starting at $25.

Samaná Tourist Service is a local travel agency that arranges flights, transportation, excursions, and hotel stays.

Information **AeroDomca** (⊠*Plaza El Paseo, Las Terrenas* ☎*809/240–6571* ⊕ *www.aerodomca.com*). **Sunshine Service** (⊠*Calle del Carmen 151, Las Terrenas* ☎*809/240–6164* ⊕ *www.sunshineservice.ch*). **Samaná Tourist Service** (⊠*Av. La Marina 6, Samaná* ☎*809/538–2740*).

The North Coast

PUERTO PLATA, PLAYA DORADA, SOSÚA,
CABARETE & CABRERA

WORD OF MOUTH

"Both kite and windsurfing are very popular [in Cabarete] because of the windiness of the area. While our husbands enjoyed those sports, we found the area and sand perfect for lounging. Also, you can walk along the beach at night and pick which bar/restaurant you want to enjoy."

—kacollier

"Playa Dorada all the way. Have a great time folks."

—cvdoj

THE DOMINICAN REPUBLIC'S NORTHERN COAST, with mountains on one side, is also called the Amber Coast or the Amber Riviera because of the large quantities of golden amber found in the area. The sands on its 75 mi (121 km) of beach are also golden. As the area moves up on the luxury scale, the Riviera moniker seems more appropriate all the time.

Puerto Plata was founded by the island's first governor, Nicolás de Ovando, in 1502. Subsequently, in the colonial days, there were pirates, also called corsairs, skulking around almost every cove, to the degree that the city had to be abandoned in 1606. Nonetheless, because of that threat tourists have San Felipe, an attractive fort, to tour. Puerto Plata is a typical Dominican city, but it has some tourist appeal, mainly because of the wooden houses with gingerbread fretwork from the Victorian era, which was its halcyon age.

Nearby, the beaches of the Costa Dorada are along Puerto Plata's principal highway, where there are two large all-inclusive resorts; Playa Dorada is the nearby, long-established resort area, where the D.R.'s first all-inclusive resorts were built. If you want R&R and a tan, you don't have to leave the golden beach. When you want to explore, within a two-hour radius are a plethora of towns, including Sosúa, Cabarete, Cabrera, and even Santiago (*see ⇨ Chapter 7, Santiago & the Cibao Valley*). Each offers its own magical mix of Caribbean character and characters. The fun quotient is high in Sosúa and particularly Cabarete, where strong ocean breezes create the ideal conditions for kite- and windsurfing.

The north country is like Eden when you venture out to more remote areas and discover the beaches and the rich, tropical vegetation that grows up the hillsides to the cliffs. Cabrera is a new hot spot, and it's helping to redefine the Domincan vacation, with its upscale rental villas. And visitors are now beginning to discover the glorious, often unpopulated beaches between Rio San Juan and Cabrera. With a wide mix of visitors (from backpackers to high-end tourists), the North Coast is whatever you want it to be.

EXPLORING THE NORTH COAST

Most visitors to the North Coast fly into the International Gregorio Luperon Airport (POP) in Puerto Plata and either base themselves in Playa Dorada, from which they set forth to explore, either by rental car or on guided tours. Others head straight to the established resort town of Sosúa. The young and sporty keep going until they hit Cabarete, renowned for its surfing—kite- and windsurfing, too—and its hot nightlife. More recently, the Cabrera area, a 60 minute-drive due east from Cabarete, is being discovered by those who want a more tranquil and upscale villa experience. A few travelers even head to the Samaná Peninsula, but the new airport there makes the trip from Puerto Plata less necessary.

ABOUT THE RESTAURANTS

Restaurants run the gamut here, from lovely, fine-dining experiences down to good surf-camp chow downs. And there are the local joints selling rice and beans, often with some indeterminate meat component. You can find more independent establishments in Cabarete and Sosúa, which draw a larger contingent of independent travelers. Since Playa Dorada is primarily an all-inclusive compound, there are not too many choices outside the resorts, but we list a couple of good ones and fun cafés as well.

The price of food here keeps escalating, and that is as true in grocery stores as much as in restaurants. Generally, restaurants in Cabarete are priced higher than those in Sosúa. The good news is that the quality of the food on the North Coast is on the rise. Not all restaurants take credit cards, so be sure to ask in advance if that matters, and if they do take credit cards, there's usually a 4% or 5% surcharge. The tax and service (which usually totals 26%) are often not included in the menu prices, so be sure to ask about that as well. This is one place where you can leave your Amex card at home; most restaurants do not accept it unless they're in hotels.

In the supermarkets you'll pay 16% tax on most of your purchases. If you shop the *colmados,* tax is not usually added, but prices are higher. The D.R. is no longer a cheap place to dine out; now, as in the rest of the Caribbean, you'll save greatly on your food bill by staying at an all-inclusive resort, especially if the food there is good.

ABOUT THE HOTELS

Playa Dorada was one of the first resort areas in the D.R. to be developed, and it still has a dozen or so all-inclusive resorts, along with one deluxe boutique hotel, Casa Colonial. What's interesting is how these older resorts are evolving in order to compete with their increasingly upscale competition to the east. Barcelo, wanting a presence in this region, purchased the Occidental Grand Flamenco in November 2007 and has renamed it Barcelo Puerto Plata; the company is in the midst of a major renovation, adding a gym and spa. A sexy new redo of a 20-some year-old Blue Bay Villa Dorada as an adults-only resort is also a major happening; it's spa-oriented and well-priced. Holiday Village Golden Beach (formerly Jack Tar Village) has taken the club-within-a-club concierge concept to a budget resort. And perched on a mountain ridge, the new Tubagua Plantation Village appeals to budget travelers and groups.

Cabarete and Sosúa were once proud to say that they were the strongholds of the small, casual hotel. Nowadays there are as many rooms in all-inclusive resorts as in the small independents. Condos have also come to Cabarete in particular, and many are luxurious complexes on the ocean front. Farther out, in Cabrera and Abreu, luxury villas in exclusive gated communities are the draw.

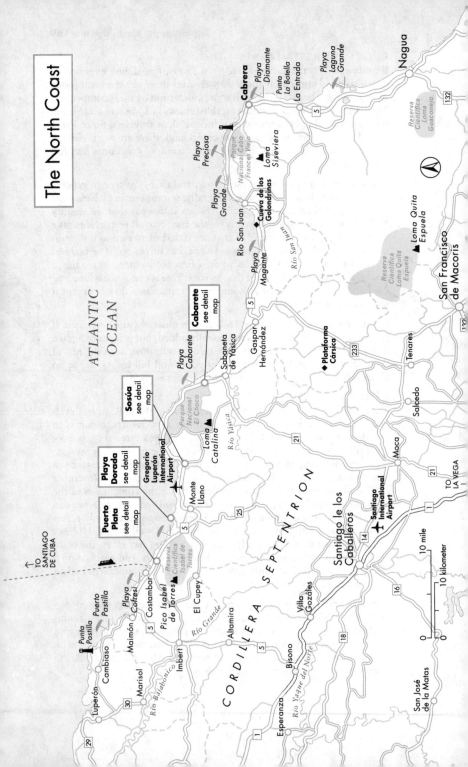

The North Coast

NORTH COAST TOP 5

Beach It. Take yourself to one of the less populated beaches in Cabarete or as far afield as Playa Preciosa in Rio San Juan.

Kite surfing. Try an adventure sport like kite surfing, or if you cannot physically participate, watch the kites and take the pictures. The sails are a form of flowing art.

Play 18 holes. Playa Dorada's Robert Trent Jones–designed course is moderately priced, and its renovated clubhouse is a convivial experience.

Love the Nightlife of Cabarete. The night here starts early with Happy Hour at one of the beachfront restaurants. After dinner, when the dancing cranks up, it's another whole party. Sosúa is another popular destination for nightlife.

Experience Ocean World. Swim with the dolphins, see white tigers close up, and watch the sea lions perform at this world-class marine adventure park.

WHAT IT COSTS IN DOLLARS					
	¢	$	$$	$$$	$$$$
Restaurants	under $8	$8–$12	$12–$20	$20–$30	Over $30
Hotels*	Under $80	$80–$150	$150–$250	$250–$350	Over $350
Hotels**	Under $125	$125–$250	$250–$350	$350–$450	Over $450

*EP, BP, CP **AI, FAP, MAP Restaurant prices are per person for a main course at dinner and do not include the 15% V.A.T. and 10% service charge. Hotel prices are per night for a double room in high season, excluding 15% V.A.T. and 10% service charge.

PUERTO PLATA & PLAYA DORADA

Puerto Plata is 18 km (11 mi) east of Gregory Luperon International Airport; Playa Dorada is 13 km (8 mi) east of Puerto Plata.

A port founded in 1502, Puerto Plata's name was inspired by the shimmering silver (*plata*) color of its coast at sunset. The city is cradled between the colonial harbor and Mt. Isabel de Torres, which provides a dramatic backdrop. The largest city on the North Coast, its charm is the extent and variety of its Victorian architecture, unrivaled by any other Dominican city. The gingerbread fretwork and pastel colors of its houses and public buildings convey the romantic aura of an earlier time. These vestiges of its halcyon days now house mostly tourist-oriented businesses—galleries, shops, bars, restaurants, and clubs.

Although Puerto Plata seems to have been sleeping for decades, this was a dynamic city both in colonial times and the Victorian Era, and it's on the way back up now. You can get a feeling for this past in the magnificent Victorian gazebo in the central **Parque Independencia**; the beautification of the park and its gazebo is a work in progress. The **Fortaleza de San Felipe** protected the city from many a pirate attack

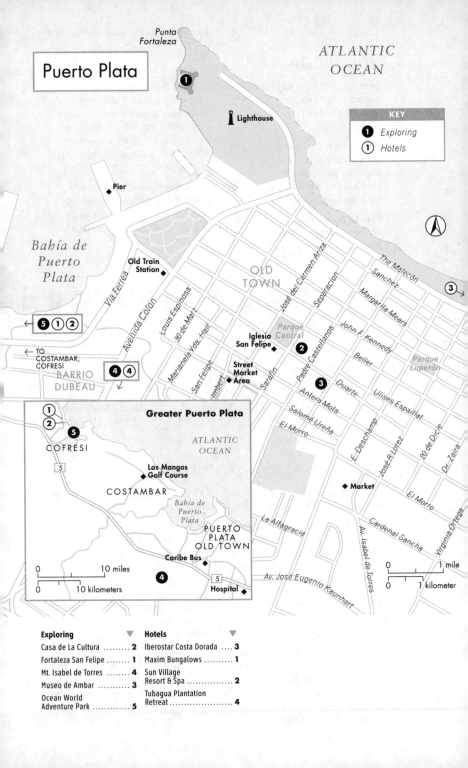

Puerto Plata

ATLANTIC OCEAN

Punta Fortaleza

Lighthouse

KEY
① Exploring
① Hotels

Pier

Bahía de Puerto Plata

Old Train Station

OLD TOWN

The Malecón

José del Carmen Ariza
Separación
Sanchez
Margarita Mears

Parque Central

John F. Kennedy

Beller

Parque Luperón

Iglesia San Felipe

Street Market Area

Casa Castellanos
Padre Castellanos
Antera Mota
Salomé Ureña
El Morro

Duarte
Ulises Espaillat

E. Deschamp
José-R-Lorez
20 de Dicie
Dr. Zaira

Via Ferrea
Avenida Colón
Louis Espinosa
30 de Marz
Marianela Vda. Hall
San Felipe
Imbert
Sarafin

⑤①②

← TO COSTAMBAR, COFRESI

BARRIO DUBEAU

④④

Market

La Altagracia

El Morro
Virginia Ortega

Greater Puerto Plata

①②⑤
COFRESI

ATLANTIC OCEAN

Los Mangos Golf Course

COSTAMBAR

Bahía de Puerto Plata

PUERTO PLATA OLD TOWN

Caribe Bus

④

Hospital

Cardenal Sancha

Av. Isabel de Torres

Av. José Eugenio Kaunhart

0   10 miles
0   10 kilometers

0   1 mile
0   1 kilometer

Exploring ▼	**Hotels** ▼
Casa de La Cultura **2**	Iberostar Costa Dorada **3**
Fortaleza San Felipe **1**	Maxim Bungalows **1**
Mt. Isabel de Torres **4**	Sun Village Resort & Spa **2**
Museo de Ambar **3**	Tubagua Plantation Retreat **4**
Ocean World Adventure Park **5**	

and was later used as a political prison. The nearby **lighthouse** has been restored, which it desperately needed. On the Malecón, new street lights have been erected and the construction here and on the main highway is finally finished. Organization has come to the Malecón, and the many food carts are being replaced by a more hygienic *parador* (which in the D.R. is a small, roadside restaurant serving up local specialties). Similarly, the vendors selling souvenirs and crafts now congregate in a *modelo* (market).

Big changes are afoot in this town, which is realizing what it needs to do to become a tourist destination. The Office of Cultural Patrimony, which has done an admirable job of pulling Santo Domingo's Zona Colonial from the darkness, is at work on Puerto Plata. Simultaneously, a group of private business owners and investors have developed a long-term plan for beautifying the city to take advantage of its hundreds of classic, wooden gingerbread buildings. Mansions are slowly being restored; a Victorian mansion on Calle Jose del Carmen is now a gallery and coffee shop. A new museum for the country's heroes will be in the former family home of Independence hero, Gregory Luperon, in the old town. Most of these houses, painted in pastels with wooden, gingerbread fretwork, are found around the central park—to the northeast and for about eight blocks east and down to the ocean.

6

Numbers in the margin correspond to points of interest on the Puerto Plata map.

WHAT TO SEE

② **Casa de La Cultura.** Drop by here when you're strolling through the park. An art gallery has revolving exhibits that will help you understand how much talent there is in this country. You may even wish to buy from a budding artist. This Victorian building also has workshops for those talented in dance and music. ⊠*Parque Central, Calle Separación, near Duarte* ☎*809/261–2731* ⊠*Free* ☉ *Weekdays 9–noon and 3–5.*

① **Fortaleza de San Felipe.** The only remaining vestige of the colonial era ☾ in Puerto Plata was built in the mid-16th century to defend the city against pirates bent on pillaging the growing wealth from its shipping port. In 1605 the fort was dismantled and rebuilt in 1739. It has a moat and a small museum with some historical artifacts—nothing fascinating, though there are relics from the period. The thick walls and interior moat made it ideal for use as a prison, which is exactly how the fort was utilized. Kids will enjoy the opportunity to run around and explore, but it's not a must-see attraction, certainly for adults. The views of the bay are excellent, and a grassy knoll provides a pleasant place to set. The fort is included on most city tours. A restored lighthouse is adjacent, and is included in the entry fee for the fort. ⊠*At eastern end of Av. Circunvalación, on peninsula in Bahía de Puerto Plata* ☎*No phone* ⊠*RD$50* ☉ *Daily 9–5.*

④ **Mt. Isabel de Torres.** Southwest of Puerto Plata, this mountain soars 2,600 feet above sea level and is notable for its huge statue of Christ.

Up there also are botanical gardens that despite efforts, still are not memorable. You can choose to hire a knowledgeable English-speaking guide for $5 per person. A cable car takes you to the top for a spectacular view. The cars usually wait until the cars are filled to capacity before going up—which makes them cozy; and should the electricity happen to go off, there's no backup generator. You should do this in the morning, preferably around 9; after noon, the cloud cover rolls in and you can see practically nothing. The vendors here who want you to buy their jewelry and crafts are really tenacious; if you really are not interested, let them know this unequivocally. ⊠ *Off Autopista Duarte, follow signs* ☎ *No phone* ☒ *Cable car RD$250* ☉ *Thurs.–Tues. 9–5.*

❸ **Museo de Ambar Dominicano** *(Dominican Amber Museum).* In a lovely old galleried mansion, this museum both displays and sells the D.R.'s national stone, semiprecious, translucent amber, which is actually fossilized pine resin that dates from about 50 million years ago, give or take a few millennia. Shops on the museum's first floor sell amber, souvenirs, and ceramics. Dominican amber is considered to be the finest in the world. If you buy from street vendors for a low price, you're probably buying plastic. ⊠ *Calle Duarte 61* ☎ *809/586–2848* ☒ *RD$15* ☉ *Mon.–Sat. 9–5.*

❺ **Ocean World Adventure Park.** This multimillion-dollar aquatic park in Cofresi has several interactive marine and wildlife programs, including dolphin and sea lion shows and encounters, a tropical reef aquarium, stingrays, shark tanks, a rain forest, and a Tiger Grotto inhabited by Bengal tigers. Looking out to the sea, a buffet lunch is delightful but not included in the entrance fee. You don't have to come on a tour, but you must make advance reservations if you want to participate in one of the swims or encounters, which carry an additional charge. For example, if you're brave enough for the shark encounter for $15 extra, you'll feed them and touch them in the shark lagoon; a stingray encounter is included with this option as well. If you're staying in the Puerto Plata or Cabarete area, ask at your hotel for tour schedules; if you're at nearby Sun Village, transfers are free. Children must be six to do the dolphin swim, and a photo lab and video service can capture the moment. A private beach, locker room, a splashy marina, a Las Vegas–style casino and fine-dining restaurant, make for a fascinating mix. *(See Casinos and Boating.)* ⊠ *Calle Principal, down hill from Sun Village Resort & Spa, Cofresi, Puerto Plata* ✛ *Turn off Carretera Turistica to Santiago, at sign for Ocean World* ☎ *809/291–1000 or 809/291–1111* ⊕ *www. oceanworld.net* ☒ *$55* ☉ *Daily 9–5.*

NEED A BREAK?

Colorful flying flags from many a country, that's to let you know that "fureners" are welcome. Sam's Bar & Grill (⊠ *Jose del Carmen Ariza 34* ☎ *809/586–7267*). The place has character, and many Caribbean characters. Sit down, have a cold one, and some "familiar" food like a Philly steak sandwich and get the latest skinny on the goings on around town.

WHERE TO EAT

$–$$$ ✕**Al Fresco.** An intimate restaurant where you can dine on a terrace embellished with hanging plants, Al Fresco is just behind Hemingway's Café, a popular night spot owned by the same good family. The sushi and grilled lobster are reason enough to come. But you may return—even if you have paid for an all-inclusive package—because this is a sanctuary away from that frenetic pace, with heady music and fine wine. Ondina, a professional manager and caring owner, will see that your order is well-served, be it the penne putanesca or porcini risotto, whether you truly dine alfresco or inside with a/c. If you want to keep it light, the salads are exceptional, especially the house salad with goat cheese, arugula, grilled shrimp, and nuts. ✉*Playa Dorada Plaza, Calle Duarte at Avenida 30 de Marzo, left of Hemingway's Café, Playa Dorada, Puerto Plata* ☎*809/320–1137* ▤*AE, MC, V* ⊘*No lunch.*

> ### FOOD SAFETY
>
> The Cristal Program is a certificate of achievement that has rigorous criteria of hygiene in the kitchen and in all food-service areas. Most hotels that graduate from the program proudly hang their diploma in plain view. UHS is a similar program. European based, it's subscribed to by some of the Spanish-owned hotels. It's smart to ask when trying to select a resort. These programs have cut down on stomach and intestinal problems immensely.

$–$$$ ✕**Lucia.** New life has been breathed into Lucia by one of the most well-
★ respected, innovative chefs in the country, Rafael Vasquez. The setting is now as artistic as a gallery, with orchids galore, crisp white linens, and attentive waiters in white guayabera shirts. Although Vasquez is not as perfect as he was when he was behind the stove (he is now a corporate executive chef for three resorts in the area), the menu is comprehensive and contemporary. Guests love the fresh tuna tartare with soy and sweet chilli dipping sauces and a smoking wasabi-lime sorbet. The rich foie gras with apples and a spiced chocolate sauce is as sensual as you find in French territory. Simple carnivores can order an Angus fillet. The molten chocolate volcano with vanilla ice cream is the dessert you want. When the digestif cart is rolled over, be daring with a Brunello grappa or a local Brugal Unico. ✉*Casa Colonial, Playa Dorada, Puerto Plata* ☎*809/320–3232* ▤*AE, MC, V.*

WHERE TO STAY

¢–$ ▦**Blue Bay Villa Doradas.** This redo of a 1980s-era resort exceeds your expectations. The stunning, grand entrance (a Sara Garcia design) with its slender, white pillars utilizes white fabric to shelter the lobby from tropical rainfalls. The cushy, woven lounge furniture with bright and floral pillows, the boutique with its tropical whites, the staff in their tropical whites, all make for one attractive island scenario. It provides the backdrop for the weekly manager's party that may be the country's best: a stellar five-piece band, mimosas, and delicious hors d'oeuvres. The exuberant management leads the way to an admirable display of

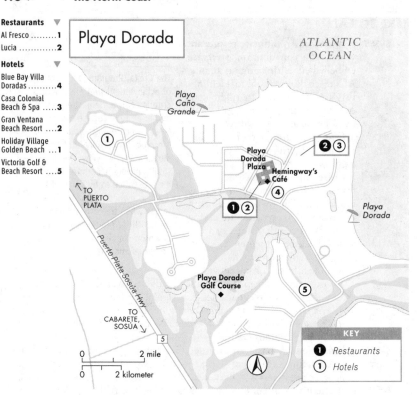

abundance that represents all the à la carte Asian and seafood restaurants as well as the international buffet, from raw oysters to a real turkey dinner. P.S.: This is an adults-only resort—no children allowed; upgrade your room if you can afford it. **Pros:** Great spa, handsome beach club and stellar beachfront, yoga and golf classes included. **Cons:** Mosquitoes are a constant problem, the animation staff and the music are just too loud some days, standard and standard-plus rooms are not luxurious. ⊠*Playa Dorada, Puerto Plata* ☎*809/320–3000, 809/320–1600 for reservations* ⊕*www.bluebayresorts.com* ⬠*245 rooms, 4 suites* ⬡*In-room: safe, refrigerator. In-hotel: 4 restaurants, bars, tennis courts, pools, gym, spa, beachfront, water sports, bicycles, no elevators, laundry service, concierge, executive floor, public Internet, public Wi-Fi, no-smoking rooms, parking (no fee)* ⊟*AE, D, DC, MC, V* ❘⊙❘*AI.*

$$$$
FodorsChoice
★

🏨 **Casa Colonial Beach & Spa.** Rivals say "over the top" isn't superlative enough to describe this exquisite, all-suites boutique hotel designed by Sara Garcia Cassoni, the first in the D.R. to join the lofty Small Luxury Hotels of the World. White stucco buildings have columns and wrought-iron balustrades and most guests think that it's a restoration of a colonial mansion. Suites are outfitted with the finest Frette linens. The lobby feels more like a lounge, with a stellar bar; Lucia's, the

Sarah Garcia—A Dominicana Role Model

Sarah Garcia is revered as an architect, considered by many to be the top designer on the North Coast, if not in the entire country. She has become the architect of choice for the moneyed owners of Sea Horse Ranch. Her contemporary homes are showpieces in their exclusive, gated communities. But she also designs resorts, and a prime example is the boutique hotel Casa Colonial, which was challenging because of its odd-shape oceanfront setting in Playa Dorada.

Garcia is one of five daughters of Don Isidro Garcia, a poor boy from rural Rio San Juan. When he was a boy, her father sold small packets of rice to neighbors, traveling on horseback. But from these humble beginnings he grew up to become a land baron, making his fortune in cacao and cattle; in 1986, he began to invest in resort properties. Don Isidro recently passed away at the age of 82, leaving his daughters to manage his estate. As Sarah says: "My father was my hero. I couldn't believe that he could die. We were all girls, and he raised us to be proud and to be strong together, as well as individuals. This is a country of

men, and I worked so hard to develop myself. In New York it is difficult to make a name for yourself; imagine here? Dominican women use their 'weapons' (sensuality); I let my work speak for itself. People say that I am the best, but the most important thing is to compete with yourself. Thanks God, the clients come to me now. I don't have time to knock the doors!" Garcia's advanced education took her to the United States, England, France, and finally Italy, and it was in the latter where she became accredited in interior design and where she met her husband, Roberto Casoni, who is the vice-president for the Victoria Hotel Group. "As for Roberto," she says, "we have love and we are partners, too. I was lucky to find the other half of my orange! He understands my desire to work and to continue to reinvent myself. I feel that makes me both a better wife and mother."

At present, Garcia is volunteering her services to redesign the family home of Independence hero Gregorian Luperon, to create a museum for national heroes. It's in the old town of Puerto Plata, the city of her birth.

designer gourmet room, is worthy of this boutique hotel. Upscale spa devotees will savor the Baqua Spa, with its Vichy showers, body wraps, inventory of massages and facials, and refreshing juices. The rooftop sundeck is close to heaven—an infinity pool and four warm Jacuzzis provide several agreeable alternatives to the golden beach. It has also served as a venue for wedding reception and for private dinners for two. **Pros:** Luxury boutique experience, glorious spa, this is how you would like to live. **Cons:** Can feel empty during the low season, quiet even in the high season, service not as sharp as you would expect for these prices (and few speak good English). ⊠*Playa Dorada, Puerto Plata* ☎*809/320–3232* ⊕*www.casacolonialhotel.com* ⇗*50 suites* ⌂*In-room: dial-up, refrigerator. In-hotel: 2 restaurants, bar, pool, gym, spa, beachfront, concierge, laundry service, public Wi-Fi* ☒*AE, MC, V* ⏿*EP.*

$–$$ 🏨 **Gran Ventana Beach Resort.** This resort is characterized by a sophisticated style that sets it apart from the nearby competition. The lobby, with pottery and local drums suspended from the walls, is a contemporary study in Caribbean colors with a fountain. The beach is on a point with unobstructed views to the left. Families are a good share of the market, and this resort is solid as far as the tour operators are concerned, with service and food improving each season. Many couples prefer the larger rooms (sans good ocean views, unfortunately) that surround the quiet pool. A Victorian-style wedding gazebo is popular for nuptials. **Pros:** Consistently good food and service for this price point, plenty of activities for the whole family. **Cons:** Feels busy year-round, the buffet is often better than the freestanding dining rooms. ⊠*Playa Dorada, Puerto Plata* ☎*809/320–2111* ⊕*www.vhhr.com* ⌘*499 rooms, 2 suites, 1 penthouse* ⌂*In-room: safe, refrigerator. In-hotel: 5 restaurants, bars, tennis court, pools, gym, beachfront, water sports, bicycles, no elevator, children's programs (ages 4–12), public Internet* ▤*AE, MC, V* ⎮◎⎮*AI.*

$ 🏨**Holiday Village Golden Beach.** One of Playa Dorada's first resorts (formerly the Jack Tar Village) has changed its name and concept, taking the budget-oriented property to an entirely new evolutionary level. Having been selling solely to groups from Canada and the United Kingdom (primarily families), the resort still has good kids facilities, including water slides and three kids' clubs. Now G.M. Jose Mariá Espart, who for a decade made Flamenco's Michaelangelo Club special, has brought the same level of service to the 44 newly renovated accommodations in the Royal Club section, which are being advertised and sold in the U.S. market. Only ambience music plays at the adults-only Royal Club pool, while the other guests and kids get revved up by the British MC at the big pool. A $6.5-million redo in late 2006 also added the handsome, cylindrical Lotus Asian restaurant. **Pros:** Four good specialty restaurants including a Caribbean one on the beach, well-known public casino and disco, price is very right. **Cons:** Infrastructure is not top-drawer, only a precious few of the villa accommodations have water views, food is not generally memorable in the buffet. ⊠*Playa Dorada, Puerto Plata* ☎*809/320–3800* ⊕*www.occidentalhotels.com* ⌘*179 rooms, 37 deluxe rooms, 38 family rooms, 10 family suites, 7 suites* ⌂*In-room: safe, refrigerator, DVD (some). In-hotel: 5 restaurants, bars, tennis courts, pools, beachfront, water sports, no elevator, children's programs (ages 4 months–16), laundry facilities, laundry service, concierge, executive floor, public Internet, public Wi-Fi (some), parking (no fee)* ▤*AE, D, DC, MC, V* ⎮◎⎮*AI.*

$–$$ 🏨**Iberostar Costa Dorada.** This resort will dazzle you with its sprawl-
★ ing lobby, its hardwood benches and sculptures, and its curvaceous pool with a central Jacuzzi encircled by Roman pillars. As you swim along you can see the mountains and the beach. Other all-inclusives could learn from Iberostar's excellent buffet; of the à la carte restaurants, the Brazilian is the standout and the Mexican quite authentic. This resort does a lot right, and yes, there is a spa. Newly repainted, the rooms are somewhat dated but attractive, with their woven wall hangings and bright colors. Many staffers speak English here, and the resort itself is close to Puerto Plata, so you can have more contact with real Dominican life. At night, you can watch the show (the music is

especially good) from the outdoor seating in the garden. **Pros:** Good management makes for a happy staff and a fun resort, blue-flag beach, top-shelf liquor in the lobby bar. **Cons:** Popularity translates to high-occupancy year-round, no Wi-Fi, pool can be very noisy. ⊠*Playa Costa Dorada, Carretera Luperon, Km 4, Marapica, Puerto Plata* ☎*809/320–1000 or 888/923–2722* ⊕*www.iberostar. com* ⤴*498 rooms, 18 suites* ⚬*In-room: safe, refrigerator. In-hotel: 4 restaurants, bars, tennis courts, pools, gym, spa, beachfront, diving, water sports, no elevator, children's programs (ages 4–12), public Internet, public Wi-Fi* ⊟*AE, MC, V* ⦿*AI.*

> **DIVE SHOP TIP**
>
> The dive shop at Iberostar, a Dressel Divers International operation, is a five-star PADI center. The Spanish director runs a fun ship, with creative dives and international instructors; safety is always a priority. If ever you wanted to learn to dive or to take it to the next level, this is your chance. Nonguests can take dive trips from here as well as guests from the resort.

$$$$ 🛏**Maxim Bungalows.** On a hillcrest overlooking its sister resort, Sun Village, this is unequivocally a level above the luxury in most of the Puerto Plata area resorts. The "bungalows" here are actually luxurious condominiums, which look like sexy bachelor pads. Characterized by dark hard woods, they are strikingly chic, sleek, and uncluttered with lots of leather and modern art. It's all quality and cutting-edge, from the shiny metal kitchen surfaces to the flat-screen TVs, iPod docks, and surprisingly, a retro Murphy bed in the living room. Guests can chill in the communal lounge with top-shelf liquors, play in the private pool, or work out with a trainer. Larger units can be created by combining two or more larger units. **Pros:** The restaurant and its 24-hour room service are top-notch, VIP treatment at the airport and complementary transfers in new SUVs, guests can dine at any of the Sun Village restaurants for free. **Cons:** The private beach, beachside pool, and spa are not on-site, pretty pricey for the region, minimalist decor will not appeal to everyone. ⊠*Paradise Dr. 1, Cofresi, Puerto Plata* ☎*809/970–3377 or 888/446–4695* ⊕*www.maximbungalows.com* ⤴*36 studios, 36 1-bedroom condos, 36 2-bedroom condos* ⚬*In-room: safe, kitchen (some), refrigerator, Wi-Fi. In-hotel: restaurant, room service, bar, pools, gym, laundry service, concierge, public Wi-Fi, airport shuttle, parking (no fee), no-smoking rooms* ⊟*AE, D, DC, MC, V* ⦿*AI.*

$$ 🛏**Sun Village Resort & Spa.** Like a sprawling Mediterranean hill town
☺ (be comfortable in your shoes) with an aqua labyrinth of pools, Sun Village keeps climbing higher. It's no longer just a family resort catering to the adjacent Ocean World; it's a fun, happening place for sophisticated couples and incentive groups. November's annual film festival attracts an interesting international crowd and is an exciting time to visit. An alluring spa and fitness center features a distinctive pool and Asian garden, plus 205 spa suites with sea views (most regular rooms have no view). Don't opt for less than a superior room, though all guest rooms will benefit from a modest renovation, which was in the works for 2008 at this writing (ask for a renovated room). The newest offer-

A D.R. Film Festival

Mid-November guests at the all-inclusive Sun Village Resort & Spa in Puerto Plata can have the singular experience of coupling a Caribbean beach vacation with the stellar excitement of attending a film festival and hobnobbing with award-winning actors, directors, and filmmakers. During the four-day Dominican International Film Festival (⊕ *www.dominicaninternationalfilmfestival.com*) guests can relax on the terrace with a rum cocktail during the grand-opening ceremony, leave the pools to watch a feature screening in the wide-screen theater lounge, or catch a panel discussion after lunch. By night the VIP parties, live entertainment, and lavish buffets are enough to have guests reserving for next year's event, as many repeat fans have done in past years.

ings, Maxim Bungalows, overlook the property and are exceptional. **Pros:** Great spirit and large fun quotient, the buffet is definitely a notch above, the management and staff go that extra mile to please. **Cons:** Steep hills and stairs here, feels isolated (and is a sizable cab fare if you go somewhere). ✉ *Cofresi Beach, Cofresi, Puerto Plata* ☎ *809/970–3364 or 888/446–4695* ⊕ *www.sunvillageresorts.com* ⇄ *300 rooms, 8 suites, 3 villas* ⚒ *In-room: safe. In-hotel: 5 restaurants, bars, tennis courts, pools, gym, spa, beachfront, diving, water sports, bicycles, children's programs (ages 4–12), public Internet, public Wi-Fi* ⊟ *AE, MC, V* ⍟ *AI.*

¢ 🏨**Tubagua Plantation Retreat.** Called a Plantation Village Retreat, this 12-acre property is dedicated to eco-tourism and sustainable development. It operates as a base camp for groups and mission trips, offering rustic, palapa-style accommodations on a mountainside with a spectacular ocean view. The Village can accommodate up to 48 people with flexible meal plans and logistical support. Set back from the coast, it's on the first inland ridge some 1,000 feet above sea level. Santiago is less than an hour's drive along a spectacular, winding mountain road. There are private lockers, shared bathroom facilities, a game room, and hiking trails; beach access is 15 minutes away. **Pros:** Authentic rural setting that's still 15 minutes from Puerto Plata airport, all the necessary facilities and services including clean water, power, and even Wi-Fi, spectacular views. **Cons:** You have to book the entire retreat, sleeping and bathing facilities are shared, limited public transportation options due to remote location. ✉ *Km 18, Carretera Turística, Tubagua* ☎ *809/586–7923* ⊕ *www.Tubagua.com* ⇄ *1 longhouse with 18, 3 palapas sleeping 2 to 6, 2 cabins sleeping 2 to 6* ⚒ *In-room: no a/c, no phone, no TV. In-hotel: restaurant, bar, pool, public Wi-Fi* ⊟ *No credit cards* ⊗ *Closed Dec. 25–Jan. 1 and Easter wk* ⍟ *EP.*

$-$$ 🏨**Victoria Golf & Beach Resort.** Victoria's public spaces are filled with
★ eye-catching Indo-Caribbean furnishings, including a Chinese bed in the lobby, where the reception desk is backed by two oversize zebra-print mirrors. Coral stone and travertine are seen throughout. Victoria's niche has been etched: couples, honeymooners, and golfers—the

The Elliott Foundation

Fred Elliott, the founder and chairman of Sun Village, created his foundation in 1994 to give humanitarian support to the people of the Dominican Republic. The Elliott Foundation focuses on the wellness and education in the local communities, thus giving children a chance for change. In collaboration with the D.R. government and other Humanitarian Organizations, it has accomplished remarkable results in establishing and improving locals schools, an orphanage, medical clinics, and hospitals.

The foundation encourages Sun Village guests to bring suitcases full of used clothing and medical supplies, visit the orphanage while on vacation, and donate to the cause in any way they can. Employees are equally involved, like Elmond Jean, a Haitian who selflessly aids those not as fortunate who live in his Haitian *batay* (a destitute barrio).

You can read more about the foundation at the Sun Village resorts Web site (⊕ *www.sunvillageresorts.com*).

resort overlooks the golf club. While you can get a breakfast-only plan, you can go all-inclusive for just $20 more, so that makes more sense, especially since the buffet is better than the norm and service is super. Upstairs, the gourmet restaurant has been contemporized, and the adjacent Lotus Club serves as a cool, sophisticated lounge. A flashy boutique sells enticing jewelry and white resort wear. New is the spa suite where guests can enjoy massages and other services. Victoria's strip of sand has its own upgraded beach club with an à la carte menu; though the resort is not on the beach, you can get there in five minutes or less by fast shuttle. Weddings can be amazingly affordable here. **Pros:** Has a Cristal Certificate for food hygiene, two great pools, including a "chill" pool with a soothing cascade. **Cons:** Not on the beach, needs another stand-alone restaurant, might be too quiet for some. ⊠*Playa Dorada, Box 22, Puerto Plata* ☎*809/320–1200* ⊕*www.vhhr.com* ⇋*164 rooms, 26 suites, 3 2-bedroom villas* ⌂*In-room: safe, refrigerator. In-hotel: 3 restaurants, 3 bars, tennis court, pools, gym, diving, water sports, bicycles, no elevator, public Internet* ⊟*AE, D, MC, V* ⊗*AI.*

NIGHTLIFE & THE ARTS

BARS

Café Cito (⊠*Carretera Luperon, Marapica, Puerto Plata, ¼ mi [½ km] west of Playa Dorada's main gate, ¼ mi [½ km] east of Iberostar, next to Avis* ☎*809/586–7923*) is a fun, unpretentious place to feed and hang out, a fave of Canadian expats and *turistas*. It's owned by a cool guy, Tim Hall, who is from Canada. For a low price you can have a simple meal from the grill (using imported meat). But it's the good times, the camaraderie, the sports on a big screen (via satellite), and the music from the jukebox that make this a welcome break from the Costa Dorada or Playa Dorada resort compounds. On sale are Tim's boxes of select cigars, each a different brand.

Tim Hall—A Quintessential Expat

Tim Hall first came to the D.R. in 1983 as a journalist to write a feature for the *Toronto Star* about Playa Dorada, the new tourist destination in Puerto Plata. He was a young Canadian lad, who, like so many who have chosen the expat life, came back again and again until he finally stayed.

Tim began by writing for the country's only English-language newspaper, *Santo Domingo News*. He went on to publish a local Spanish-language newspaper and to produce a tourism-related TV show. Although his talents as a scribe are still sought after, Tim has learned the lesson of the Caribbean: survival depends on wearing more than one hat. Now, he is the North Coast's Canadian Honorary Consul, explaining, "I was appointed in 1988, after a phone call that woke me up on my 30th birthday. It's been 20 years now and lots of stories to tell."

The main hat he wears these days is as proprietor of Café Cito, an open-air Caribbean restaurant near the Iberostar Costa Dorada. Since the late 1990s, Café Cito has become known as a funky, fun expat hangout with a menu that promises a taste of home. Sitting at his table, he reminisces: "In 1982, charter flights started bringing planeloads of tourists to Playa Dorada, and some of the country's first all-inclusive resorts. During that first tidal wave of tourists, local fishermen were getting pulled off their boats to wait on tables, delivering dinners like surf

'n' turf, and getting raked over coals because a steak wasn't medium-rare. At the time, nobody knew about medium-rare. Yet Dominicans have amazing resilience, and the ability to smile whether the tip is 10 pesos or 10 dollars."

New tax benefits are starting to draw more expat retirees, including a strong contingent of boomers, and Tim is there to provide for them, as well as the more casual tourists. "One of the things I enjoy is sharing things that I've discovered. For example, Café Cito organizes pub crawls for the tourists in the compounds to get out for a taste of real life. We drive them from bar to bar in Sosúa and Cabarete and we drink rum and smoke my cigars." (Hall has his own cigar label, Artisan Selection.)

Tim lives with his Dominican wife, Beatriz, and their four children on a 12-acre mountaintop farm overlooking the coast. He has built Tubagua, a plantation retreat with thatch-roof cabanas with 14-foot mezzanines for budget groups. As he says, "Living in the islands doesn't provide your typical security, such as a pension to look forward. And I haven't owned a BMW, but my life pretty much belongs to me." And his future plans? "This plantation is going to be as funky and fun as Café Cito—but with a spa and cabanas and a knock-out view. Now that it's up and running I might drop a few hats."

Hemingway's Cafe (✉*Playa Dorada Plaza, Calle Duarte at Av. 30 de Marzo, Playa Dorada, Puerto Plata* ☎*809/320–2230*) has long been the rockin' spot for the young at heart who love to party. There's rock or reggae by DJs or live bands, but only big-name merengue bands elicit a cover charge. On Saturday night there's a Latin fiesta, and on Thursday the mike is taken over by karaoke singers. The kitchen closes at 2 AM and serves American-style, fun food and good 'burgers, with fajitas a specialty.

CASINOS

On the north coast, the Holiday Village Golden Beach in Playa Dorada and Occidental Allegro Playa Dorada both have popular American-style casinos. Breezes in Cabarete has its Casino Carnival, which received a glamorous redo in late 2007. Ocean Sands is in Cabarete.

The extravagant **Ocean World Casino** (⊠ *Calle Principal, Cofresi, Puerto Plata, 4.3 mi west of town center* ☎ *809/291–1111* ⊕ *www.ocean-world.net*) was constructed within the Ocean World complex in 2006 and rivals its counterparts in Las Vegas. The whimsical decor and furnishings are from a fantasy world, and windows offer sea views. The Octopus Bar overlooks the spiffy new marina and its flotilla of yachts. A nocturnal tour of the Ocean World complex can include a sunset happy hour at the Lighthouse Lounge, dinner at Poseidón, and then a Las Vegas–style review, *Bravissimo,* which is a flurry of beautiful dancing girls and guys with incredible voices. If you want the night to continue even later, there's the Lighthouse Disco.

DANCE CLUBS

Crazy Moon (⊠ *Paradise Beach Club & Casino, Playa Dorada* ☎ *809/ 320–3663*) is a mega dance club that's often filled to capacity. Latin music and hip-hop mixed with Euro sounds are popular. Rest up from time to time at the horseshoe bar, so that you can keep the pace until the wee hours of the *mañana.* The negativo here is that this worn-out resort and its casino are anything but high-brow.

Gravity (⊠ *Playa Nacho Resort, Playa Dorada* ☎ *809/320–6226*) doesn't crank up until after midnight, but it keeps rolling until 4 AM. Locals and tourists hip-hop together.

Mangú Disco (⊠ *Holiday Village Golden Beach, Playa Dorada* ☎ *809/ 320–3800*) is a happening, late-night disco in Playa Dorada, that *turistas* should check out during their stay. What's novel is that choreographed dancers perform, but they're not exactly Vegas quality. On ladies' nights, geared to women whose husbands are at the casisno tables, the emcee and on-stage dancers keep the crowds laughing and learning the local dance steps. The muscular disco kings may peel off their shirts, but they don't go much further. *Putas* (not to mention some *putos*) do hang here, but the action is not as bad (or as obvious) as at many places. Signs warning against bringing in weapons or drugs may make some leery, but know that the government mandates those signs, and the policy is for your safety.

BEACHES

Many beaches on the North Coast are accessible to the public (in theory, all beaches in this country, from the high-water mark down, are open to everyone) and may tempt you to stop for a swim. That's part of the uninhibited joy of this country. Do be careful, though: some have dangerously strong currents, which may be the reason why they're undeveloped.

Cofresi Beach (⊠ *Calle Pincipal, Cofresi, Puerto Plata, 4.3 mi west of town center*) offers a long stretch of golden sand that's good for swimming, but with some wave action as well. It's mainly used by the public until the stretch where Sun Village's facilities are. On the other side of the public area is Ocean World and its marina.

Playa Dorada (⊠ *Off Autopista Luperon, Puerto Plata, approximately 10-min drive east of town*), is the primary beach destination on the North Coast and one of the D.R.'s most established resort areas. Each hotel has its own slice of the beach, which is covered with soft sand, nearly white now thanks to its participation in the $6 million beach rejuvenation. Lots of reefs for snorkeling are right offshore. Gran Ventana Beach Resort, which is on a point, marks the easternmost end of the major hotel development. If you're not staying at one of the resorts in the Playa Dorada complex then it's best to enter the beach on the before this point. Zealous hotel security guards try to keep you off "their" stretch of beach, but by law they cannot if you walk along the water's edge. They can keep you off the chaise lounges and from coming into the resort's property. The Atlantic waters are great for windsurfing, waterskiing, and fishing.

SPORTS & THE OUTDOORS

BIKING

A number of resorts in Playa Dorada have bicycles available for no charge. They are often not the best wheels you'll ever spin, but it's really delightful to cruise around Playa Dorada on two wheels. It's safe enough since cars go slowly, and you can wave to the drivers of the horse carriages as you pass them by.

BOATING

Ocean World Marina (⊠ *Calle Principal, Cofresi, Puerto Plata, 4.3 mi west of town center* ☎ *809/970–3373 or 809/291–1111* ⊕ *www. oceanworldmarina.com*) is a new state-of-the art marina, strategically positioned between the heavily traveled Florida–Bahamas region and the Puerto Rico–eastern Caribbean region. It has filled a large 300-mi (480-km) void on the North Coast where no full-service marina previously existed. The new 35-acre complex has 120 slips that accommodate sailboats of up to 200 feet (each slip has full service including cable TV, electricity, and telephone). It's a port of entry with its own immigration and customs office, concierge, laundry and shower facilities, a duty-free shop, food-liquor store, car-rental service (even hourly rentals), marina store with fishing supplies, as well as an entertainment clubhouse, nightclub, casino, and first-class dining facilities.

DIVING

Dressel Divers (⊠ *Playa Costa Dorada, Carretera Luperon, Km 4, in front of Iberostar, Marapica, Puerto Plata* ☎ *809/320–1000 Ext. 1364* ⊕ *www.dresseldivers.com*) is one of the best of the area dive centers.

Spanish-owned, it has an international staff and PADI five-star rating. Dressel offers it all, from one- and two-tank dives in the region's best dive spots, such Sosúa Bay, to night dives, instruction and certification—even for PADI Advanced instructor. Snorkeling gear can be rented by nondivers. The company will arrange a pick-up at resorts other than Iberostar.

GOLF

Los Mangos Golf Course (✉ *Carretera John F. Kennedy 2, Costambar, Puerto Plata* ☎ *809/970–3073 or 809/696–2858*) is about 5 km (3 mi) west of Puerto Plata and is much less crowded and more tranquil than many of the large resort areas, even more so than Cofresi, which is a bit farther west. Costambar is right off the Puerto Plata–Santiago Highway. You'll see a large overhead sign on the right. Go to the security gate and say you're coming to check out the golf course. Green fees at Los Mangos Golf & Beach Resort are $30 for 18 holes, $20 for 9, and you can enjoy a couple of cold ones at the little club house. The course is open from 9 to 6 daily.

Golf Digest has named **Playa Dorada Golf Club** (✉ *Playa Dorada, Puerto Plata, next door to Victoria Resort* ☎ *809/320–3472* ⊕ *www.playadoradagolf.com*) one of the top 100 courses outside the United States. It's open to guests of all the hotels in the area, though Victoria guests receive a discount. Green fees for 9 holes are $50, 18 holes $75; caddies are mandatory for foursomes and will cost about $12 for 18 holes, $7 for 9; carts are optional, at $20 and $15. The clubhouse was refurbished with contemporary style for the Salvatore Ferragamo Golf Tournament.

TENNIS

Occidental Tennis Academy (✉ *Occidental Club on the Green, Playa Dorada, Puerto Plata* ☎ *809/320–1111 for hotel's main switchboard* ⊕ *www.occidentalhotels.com*) was the first tennis academy in the Caribbean. It's equipped with seven Har-Tru clay and hard courts (nightlighted), as well as a gym, pool, social club, and pro shop. Classes are given and supervised by pros. Programs are for adults and children five and over. You can get private ($13 an hour) or group classes ($8), in English or Spanish, for beginners to professionals. Courts can also be rented by nonguests.

Playa Naco Resort & Spa (✉ *Playa Dorada, Playa Dorada* ☎ *809/320–6226 Ext. 2568*) allows nonguests to play on its four clay courts for $10 an hour by day, $20 at night. Lessons from the pro cost $23 an hour plus the cost of the court.

SHOPPING

Puerto Plata is not a shopping mecca, but you can find enough interesting stores to both quell your shopping urge and pick up a few funky gifts, like mamajuana, the Dominican herbal liqueur.

In Puerto Plata, a popular shopping street for costume jewelry and souvenirs is **Calle Beller. Playa Dorada Plaza,** on Calle Duarte at Avenida 30 de Marzo, is a 26,000 square foot commercial complex with more than 70 retail shops, plus food outlets, a children's playground, and more. A shopping center in the American tradition, its stores sell everything from cigars, rum, coffee, and herbal remedies to ceramics, trinkets, American clothing brands, Oscar de la Renta tops, Gottex bathing suits. The seven showrooms of the **Tourist Bazaar,** on Calle Duarte, are in an old mansion with a patio bar.

DISCOUNT STORES

Discount Plaza (⊠ *Playa Dorada Plaza, Calle Duarte at Av. 30 de Marzo, Puerto Plata* ☎ *809/320–6645*) is the local equivalent of Wal-Mart, though on a small scale. The clothes you can find here are of the same caliber—bathing suits, flip-flops, baseball caps, and the like. You can choose from a pretty good selection of toiletries if you have forgotten anything, as well as rum. There are also cheap Dominican souvenirs. You can buy phone cards here, as well as make long-distance calls in private booths and exchange currency.

HANDICRAFTS

Collector's Corner Gallery & Gift Shop (⊠ *Playa Dorada Plaza, Calle Duarte at Av. 30 de Marzo, Puerto Plata* ☎ *No phone*) has souvenirs, including many made of amber.

JEWELRY

Harrisons (⊠ *Playa Dorada Plaza, Calle Duarte at Av. 30 de Marzo, Puerto Plata* ☎ *809/586–3933*) doesn't sell trinkets but rather high-end jewelry, most likely at better prices than in your hometown. For quality larimar and amber with well-designed settings, many in platinum, this is it. Branches can be found in many touristic zones, including Cabarete and Sosúa.

SOSÚA

16 mi (25 km) from Puerto Plata.

This small community was settled during World War II by 600 Austrian and German Jewish refugees. After the war many of them returned to Europe or went to the United States, and most who remained married Dominicans. Only a few Jewish families reside in the community today, and there's only the original one-room wooden synagogue.

Sosúa is called Puerto Plata's little sister and consists of two communities—El Batey, the modern hotel and expat residential neighborhood, and Los Charamicos, the Dominican quarter—separated by a cove with one of the island's prettiest beaches. The sand is soft and the color of light amber, the water clear and calm. The walkway above the beach is packed with tents filled with souvenirs, pizzas, and even clothing for sale. The town developed a reputation for prostitution in the 1990s, but much continues to be done to eliminate that and to clean up the more garish elements.

With numerous supermarkets, banks, pharmacies, restaurants, schools, and all the necessities for day-to-day living, the town lends itself well to

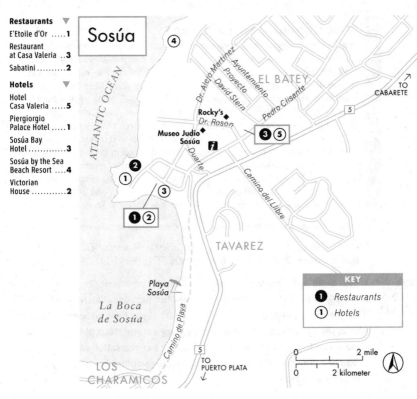

the expat lifestyle. Sosúa has the D.R.'s largest concentration of German residents and tourists, and it sometimes seems that you can get schnitzel here more easily than sancocho.

The up-and-coming Dominican families are coming back to the big houses on the bay, even as upscale condos and hotels are springing up to cater to higher-paying tourists. An example is Sosúa Ocean Village, a gated residential community that is destined to be the next prestigious address. On 100 acres, it's five minutes from El Centro and is filled with million-dollar beachfront homesites and resort-style amentities (Gold's Gym and Sanctuary International Day Spa); the community also has a rental pool of villas, town houses, and apartments.

EXPLORING SOSÚA

Sosúa is not a destination known for its sights. However, the **Museo Judio Sosúa** stands as an exception, chronicling the immigration and settlement of the Jewish refugees in the 1940s. This is a fascinating place, and depending on who is the docent, you may hear about the kinds of prejudices that met the Jewish settlers when they arrived here. The adjacent small, wooden synagogue hosts many marriage ceremonies

A Caribbean Jewish Refuge

Dictator Rafael Trujillo is an infamous character, but one of the best things he ever did for his country was to inaugurate an immigration plan for certain ethnic groups, including Jewish refugees fleeing Nazi persecution. In 1938 he granted visas to about 5,000 Jews from Nazi-occupied lands in Europe. In 1939 the Dominican Republic Settlement Association (DORSA) acquired land held by the United Fruit Company, and in 1940 the first refugees arrived and settled the land, followed by many others in the coming years. After World War II ended in 1945, many left the island for the United States, Mexico, or Europe to seek professional employment. Those who remained turned their attention to dairy farming, which was their primary means of employment in Sosúa. The families that stayed prospered, and a few of the families live on in Sosúa today.

for Jewish couples from abroad. ⊠ *Calle Dr. Rosen at David Stern, El Batey, Sosúa* ☎ *809/571–1386* ⊡ *RD$75* ⊙ *Weekdays 9–1 and 2–4.*

NEED A BREAK?

You could walk right past Rocky's (⊠ Calle Dr. Rosen, El Batey, Sosúa ☎ 809/571–2951), a little hole in the wall just past Casa Valeria, if it weren't for the come-hither aroma of barbecue ribs. If you have an apartment or a villa, you can even get takeout. Rocky's is not a pretty place, but it's a friendly place to hang out, especially if you strike up a conversation with the expats who like the price of beer here. *If* the public computer is working, you can check your e-mail.

WHERE TO EAT

$$ ✕**L'Etoile d'Or.** Behind the French doors, this intimate restaurant is draped with billowing white fabric and displays enough candle power to be ecclesiastical. The menu is now à la carte, and courses are artistically plated, the exception being the vegetables that are served family-style. One might begin with a classic like coquilles St. Jacques, followed by king prawns flambéed with Pernod. Service is discreet and professional, the wine list upscale. This is an ideal place for a proposal, and it can follow the traditionally impressive presentation of a Chateaubriand for two with Bernaise sauce, culminated with a "surprise" dessert, something sensually chocolate. ⊠ *Victorian House, Calle Dr. Alejo Martinez 1, El Batey,, Sosúa* ☎ *809/571–4000* ⊴ *Reservations essential* ⊟ *AE, MC, V* ⊙ *Closed Mon. (varies seasonally). No lunch.*

$ ✕**Restaurant at Casa Valeria.** A wave of pink adobe, sculpted in a Mexican hacienda design, is the Restaurant at Casa Valeria and the diminutive hotel of the same name. A palm tree snakes its way through the thatched roof, and a handpainted mural of a happy, local scene takes up one wall. From the tiny galley such classics like salad Niçoise and escargot provençales emerge, as well as inimitable pastas such as a carbonara with a splash of Ameretto as the secret ingredient. Guests brag about the filet mignon bordelaise with caramelized onions. Chill with the soothing CDs as you segue to crêpes with French bitter orange and Grand Marnier confit. Pricing is an incredible value for the peso. Breakfast is also very popular here. ⊠*Calle Dr. Rosen 28, El Batey, Sosúa* ☎*809/463–3710* ⊟*MC, V* ⊘*No lunch or dinner Wed.*

$–$$ ✕**Sabatini.** Your principal reason for being here is the panoramic vista of Sosúa Bay, which is *fabuloso* as the night lights dance across the rippling tide to create an appropriately romantic setting. Attempt to reserve one of the two tables in the corner Victorian turrets. An Italian classic like beef carpaccio can be your starter, or you can have something more innovative like grouper carpaccio or a mixed salad with shrimp, avocado, and pineapple. Similarly, there are classics like veal scallopine in white wine sauce or a luscious gnocchi in gorgonzola sauce with walnuts. The new Italian manager sees that the dishes are prepared as they should be, and the veteran waiters give laudable service. ⊠*Calle Alejo Martinez 1, El Batey, Sosúa* ☎*809/571–4000* ⌂*Reservations essential* ⊟*AE, D, DC, MC, V* ⊘*Closed Mon. (subject to change). No lunch.*

WHERE TO STAY

¢ ⊞**Hotel Casa Valeria.** In a sweeping, hacienda design—reminiscent of Mexico—this pink adobe, housing both a hotel and a restaurant, is a standout in this quiet neighborhood. Wrought-iron gates open to a courtyard, and most of the simple accommodations face the pool in the rear garden. The proud owners are a Dutch couple. Ärien, in a most efficient manner, has refurbished each of the rooms (some have hand-painted tropical murals), upgraded furnishings, and installed new a/c. Ärien's wife Diana adds the feminine touch and softened the courtyard, which is candlelighted by night. This inn may be cheap, but it's also a great value. Airport transfers are included if you stay a week. **Pros:** Nicely renovated, the owners will transfer you to the airport for half the price of a taxi, rooms have cable TV. **Cons:** These are not deluxe accommodations, service is limited, no views. ⊠*Calle Dr. Rosen No. 28, El Batey, Sosua* ☎*809/571–3536* ⊕*www.hotelcasavaleria.com* ⇱*9 rooms* ⌂*In-room: kitchen (some), no phone. In-hotel: restaurant, pool* ⊟*MC, V* ⓞ*EP.*

$ ⊞**Piergiorgio Palace Hotel.** Italian fashion designer Piergorgio has left his namesake Victorianesque inn for another world, but his widow is carrying on the dream without any major alterations. This Victorian-style inn, with its wraparound verandah and intricate fretwork, is a tribute to that halcyon era. Ask for the six newest rooms or the cliffside suite (No. 500s). Yes, they have the same white wicker furniture as other rooms, but colorful drapes and comforters from Europe adorn the beds instead of the pinks and florals. The hotel's location is superlative for weddings—the gazebo has breathtaking bay views, as does the pizzeria (with the wood-burning oven) and the main Italian restaurant. Honeymooners love its romanticism, fostered by the charming, strolling guitarist, and ladies appreciate the salon and spa services (men, too, for that matter). **Pros:** The alfresco breakfast is delightful, none of the aggravating elements of an all-inclusive, views are incredible, especially from the penthouse terraces. **Cons:** The furnishings and ambience are dated, most of the staff speaks little English, now lacking a strong, personable, authoritative figure. ⊠ *Calle La Puntilla 1, El Batey, Sosúa* ☎ *809/571–2626* ⊕ *www.piergiorgiohotel.com* ➾ *55 rooms, 3 apartments, 2 penthouses* ⚒ *In-room: safe, kitchen (some), refrigerator, Wi-Fi. In-hotel: 2 restaurants, bars, pools, spa, no elevator, public Internet, public Wi-Fi, no-smoking rooms* ☰ *AE, MC, V* ⊙| *BP.*

$$ 🏨 **Sosúa Bay Hotel.** Bellmen, who look snappy in their pith helmets, are stationed at the entrance of the handsome Carib-Indonesian lobby. The pools cascade into each other with awesome, panoramic views of Sosúa Bay; the oceanfront rooms in buildings 3 and 4 have the best views. The rotunda buffets are far better than the norm—particularly on Seafood Night—and even better than the stand-alone restaurants. At night, couples kiss under the gaslights to the words of "Bésame mucho," sung by a Dominican songbird posed against the magical backdrop of the moonlighted bay. The long-awaited Sosúa Bay Center was expected to open just across from the hotel in June 2008 with a casino, small convention center (capacity up to 600 people), gym with two squash courts, and an international anti-aging medical spa. **Pros:** Fun atmosphere, steps away from town but mercifully quiet, caring, efficient, and good-humored management and staff. **Cons:** No top-shelf liquors at the bag, balconies are small and have just chairs, no chaises, guest rooms not as attractive as lobby and public areas. ⊠ *Calle Dr. Alejo Martinez 1, El Batey, Sosúa* ☎ *809/571–4000* ⊕ *www.sosuabayresort. com* ➾ *193 rooms* ⚒ *In-room: safe, refrigerator. In-hotel: 5 restaurants, bars, pools, gym, beachfront, diving, water sports, bicycles, children's programs (ages 4–12), laundry facilities, public Internet, public Wi-Fi, no-smoking rooms* ☰ *MC, V* ⊙| *AI.*

$$ 🏨 **Sosúa by the Sea Boutique Beach Resort.** Proudly Canadian-owned, this once-dated hotel had a metamorphosis in 2007. Passed from father to son, it has now been completely refurbished with black, queen-size sleigh beds and handsome, minimalist black-and-white decor. The small, open-air lobby has comfortable couches and a coffee table in a sitting area. The central pool, dive shop, main restaurant, bar, and "private" beach are still inviting. Joseph's Grape & Grill specialty restaurant, under a white canvas big top, is on a promontory overlooking the crashing surf. The hotel continues to have a mainly returning clientele—older and Canadian—but according to the veteran manager, Americans are starting to discover its charms. **Pros:** AI plan is optional but an exceptional value, most meals served à la carte with good house wine, Wi-Fi is available throughout the property. **Cons:** No organized activities or nightlife at hotel, many rooms have no real closets (only a pole with hangers near the bathroom). ⊠ *Calle B. Philips, Sosúa* ☎ *809/571–3222* ⊕ *www.sosuabythesea.com* ➾ *58 rooms, 33 suites* ⚒ *In-room: safe, refrigerator (some), kitchen (some), Wi-Fi. In-hotel: 2 restaurants, bars, pool, beachfront, diving, laundry service, public Internet, public Wi-Fi, no-smoking rooms, parking (no fee)* ☰ *AE, MC, V* ⊙| *BP.*

$$$ 🏨 **Victorian House.** Roosted on a cliff above breathtaking Sosúa Bay,
★ this boutique hotel is a delightful replica of a Victorian gingerbread

house. It's much more low-key and not as densely populated as its sister property, the Sosúa Bay Hotel, next door. (You can pipe into its all-inclusive plan.) Check-in is at a white-pillared cottage, originally a settlement house for Jewish refugees in the 1940s. Multilingual concierges pamper independent travelers. Terraces have teak lounge chairs and ottomans, not to mention ever-changing knockout views. **Pros:** Bi-level penthouses are outstanding, consistently good service, small hotel that still offers tie-in meal plan with a nearby sister property. **Cons:** Lack of elevators can be hard if you're on a higher floor, not quite as spiffy as it was after its last redo. ⊠*Calle Dr. Alejo Martinez 1, El Batey, Sosúa* ☎*809/571–4000* ➷*32 rooms, 15 suites, 3 penthouses* ⚼*In-room: safe, kitchen (some), refrigerator. In-hotel: 5 restaurants, room service, bars, pools, gym, beachfront, diving, water sports, bicycles, concierge, no elevator, children's programs (ages 4–12), laundry facilities* ▭*MC, V* ⍑*BP.*

> ### LOCALLY MADE IN SOSÚA
>
> The dairy products that the early Jewish immigrants developed are still available today. Named Sosúa Productos, they include everything from unsalted butter, natural yogurt, and fruit-flavored yogurt drinks to cheese and even sausage. The quality is excellent, and they're available in every store of any size in the area, as well as in *colmados y supermercados* from Juan Dolio to Barahona.

NIGHTLIFE & THE ARTS

Nightlife in Sosúa consists of lolling around your hotel bar and lobby, as some, like Sosúa Bay Hotel, have live entertainment or music playing. Walking into town and hanging at one of the bars or restaurants, such as La Roca, or taking a coffee at one of the cafés, is another option. If you're here because you heard that the place was ripe for sex tourism, you'll find that the less savory elements of Sosúa are now relegated to the east end of town, including the infamous Merengue Bar, which has a popular disco upstairs.

The best expat bar was begun by a Canadian pop star who named it Voodoo Lounge; it's now owned by one of the original bartenders, Mélanie, who has renamed it Ruby's. Tourists sometimes motor on over to the little Casino at Playa Chiquita.

Club 59 (⊠*Pedro Clisante, corner of Calle Dr., Rosen El Batey* ☎*No phone*) is atop the infamous Merengue Bar, a red-light landmark, which has been cleaned up and gentrified, but is still essentially the same place. If you want to dance where the girls are, or at least gyrate to the Afro beat from your bar stool, then climb the stairs to 59. It has a long bar and is attractive, almost tasteful. There is usually no cover, but drinks cost more here than in other bars. Early on, around 10 PM, you'll see about 10 scantily dressed Dominican and Haitian *chicas* to each guy. As the night progresses, the men—mainly older Caucasians—come in ever greater numbers.

6

Ruby's Lounge (✉ *Pedro Clisante, corner of Calle Arzeno, last building of Sosúa Bay Complex, El Batey, Sosúa* ☎ *No phone*), formerly the Vodoo Lounge and Sosúa's most upscale bar, has a hip new French-Canadian proprietress named Mélanie, who is intent on keeping her two-story lounge–dance club at the same good level and decibel as in its previous incarnation. Each night has a different theme, be it karoke or Latin; well-known blues and jazz players perform often. On the weekends it might be a mix of live bands and DJ "Vegas Dave," who really knows how to animate a room! The good news is there is no cover charge, and if you start drinking early (before 8 PM), you'll enjoy discounted prices. No prostitutes are allowed to solicit here, but sometimes come in after work just to chill.

BEACHES

Playa Sosúa (✉ *Carretera Puerto Plata–Sosúa, El Batey, Sosúa*), the beach on gorgeous Sosúa Bay, is renowned for its coral reefs and dive sites and is about a 20-minute drive east of Puerto Plata. Here, calm waters gently lap at a shore of soft, golden sand. Swimming is delightful except after a heavy rain, when litter often floats in. But beware of sea urchins in the shallow water (they attach themselves to large rocks). From the beach you can see mountains in the background, the cliffs that surround the bay, and seemingly miles of coastline. Snorkeling from the beach can be good, but the best spots are offshore, closer to the reefs. (Don't bother going to "Three Rocks"—save your $20 and snorkel off the beach.) Unfortunately, the beach is backed by a string of tents where hawkers push souvenirs, snacks, drinks, and water-sports equipment rentals. Lounge chairs can usually be had for RD$60, so bargain.

SPORTS & THE OUTDOORS

DIVING

There's good snorkeling in Sosúa Bay right off the beach, but you can also take a dive boat to a sandy beach and have a look-see underwater at colorful gardens and reefs abundant in tropical marine life. The North Coast is dotted with numerous reefs, walls, wrecks, and caverns, making this a good destination for divers. In the waters off Sosúa alone you can find a dozen dive sites (for all levels of ability) with such catchy names as Airport Wall (98 feet) and Pyramids (50 feet). You can book a cavern dive for Gri Gri Lagoon and be transported by van to Rio San Juan.

Several dive schools are near Sosúa Beach, but you're always better off enjoying the quality and dependability provided by a PADI five-star dive shop. The Sosúa hotels have dive shops on-site or can arrange trips for you. Rental equipment, dive packages, and courses are available for every level from introductory to instructor.

Northern Coast Aquasports (✉ *El Batey, Sosúa* ☎ *809/571–1028* ⊕ *www. northerncoastdiving.com*) is a five-star, Gold Palm PADI dive center;

The Reef Ball Foundation

If you think the Reef Ball Foundation sounds like some annual charity event at a yacht club, it most assuredly is not. It's a nonprofit organization founded in 1993 to help restore and protect the natural reef systems throughout the world, including the reef in Sosúa Bay, by dropping reef-enhancing balls of concrete.

In September 2007 four Reef Ball workers were seen getting sweaty and sandy as they poured a concrete mixture into large round moulds on the beach at Sosúa Bay. Tourists and the young beach boys alike were spellbound by the goings on. The weighty balls looked like something that might have been dropped from outer space.

After deploying a reef ball, a team of trained divers known as a Coral Team, transplants imperiled corals on to the artificial reef. Eventually, coral growth covers the Reef Ball leaving nothing exposed except a healthy natural reef.

The foundation workers taught local dive operators and resort staff the art of constructing and deploying these balls to provide the infrastructure needed to rehabilitate coral habitats devastated by pollution, overfishing, and severe storms.

The **Reef Ball Foundation, Inc.** (⊕ *www.reefball.org*) is a publicly supported nonprofit group that has placed Reef Balls in 56 countries; projects are planned in 14 more. Their projects include artificial reefs, estuary restoration, red mangrove plantings, coral propagation, erosion control (often beach erosion), and education on preserving natural reefs.

it's also the only National Geographic Center in the D.R. Professionalism is apparent from the initial classroom and pool practice to their trips to legendary dive sites around beautiful Sosúa Bay, where you can explore the reefs, walls, wrecks, and swim-throughs, from 25 to 130 feet. Successful completion of a three-day course and $350 earns you a PADI Open Water Certification card. Classrooms have air-conditioning and DVDs. There's a fine retail shop in the front, with gear that includes Maui Jim sunglasses. Friday nights, the British owners host an authentic curry supper and beer party for their clients.

SHOPPING

If you need to know anything about anything in Sosúa, stop by and meet Patrick at **Patrick's Silvermithy** (⊠ *Calle Pedro Clisante 3, El Batey, Sosúa* ☎ *809/571–2121*). He has been here for decades and is kind about aiding gringos. He has a sense of humor and also makes tasteful silver jewelry if you are looking for a souvenir of your time here.

CABARETE

10 mi (15 km) east of Sosúa.

The North Coast's third well-known town is Cabarete. Although the main street is cacophonous, crowded, and smoky with the fumes of *motoconchos,* it's easy to ignore the annoyances when you're having so much fun. A hot destination, especially for the young—and more and more for retiring baby boomers—one of its main claims to fame is the wind. Nowhere on the island can you find such perfect conditions for windsurfing, kite surfing, and just plain surfing. It's the site for numerous international competitions like the annual Master of the Ocean competition, held on the last weekend in February, which encompasses all three sports. The competition only seems to grow in prominence each year.

> ### A SOSÚA HAIR SALON
>
> Almost right above Patrick's Silver-smithy is Andrea's beauty salon, **The House of Beauty & Fashion** (⊠ *Calle Pedro Clisante 3, 2nd fl., El Batey, Sosúa* ☎ *809/571–2597*). Andrea is German, and although this is not a chichi glamour salon, everyone here does what they do very well, be it haircuts, pedicures, or massages. The prices are good, too.

Those who are afraid to ride the waves or to soar like an eagle propelled by a piece of lightweight fabric can still watch and enjoy these colorful goings-on across the blue horizon and later chat-up the water adventurers as they bar hop and dance the night away at the many bars and restaurants that line the beachfront. Europeans adopted this town decades ago, followed by Canadians and now Americans, who are now both visiting and buying in; yes, condos have come to Cabarete, and in general the town is movin' on up.

NEED A BREAK?

Claro (⊠ *Calle Principal, just past Velero Beach Resort, at sign for* CASA BLAN-CA ☎ *809/867–8884*) is not the name of the proprietress of this five-table "brunch room" (that would be Sandy); instead, it means "of course" in Spanish. You can enjoy a variety of breakfast choices from 10 to 2 (though it's closed Monday). But if you're looking for lunch, have a wrap, the weekly special (which might be couscous), or the good cheeseburger. Claro has a kids' menu with surprising variety, from chicken fingers to pigs in blankets. Down a driveway, off the main drag, it's also away from the noise.

WHERE TO EAT

Americans tend to leave at least 10% over and above the 10% service charge (which goes to everyone working in the restaurant). Servers have become accustomed to that and are starting to expect it from English-speaking customers. So now with 16% tax, you should expect to pay a whopping 36% on top of the menu prices for your meals.

Many restaurants in Cabarete only take cash, or if they do take plastic will charge you 4% to 5% more for the privilege. Always ask, and come with money in your pocket. You can leave your American Express card home, because most restaurants won't take it unless they're real pricey or are within a good hotel.

$ ✕**Ali's Surf Camp.** You sit at long tables with a disparate group of strangers from at least three different countries, surrounded by bullrushes

Cabarete's New Age

A kite-surfing instructor was heard to say recently, "We were originally a two-star destination and now we have these five-star condo-hotels and villa complexes. What's happening?" Although the backpackers and surfers—from boarders to kiters—still come, and there are still a certain number of low-rent digs for them, many have had to move on to find the next cheap, windy destination. Other veteran expats are thinking of packing it in as well: "Why, they even paved the main street!" they say, "And what with the price of groceries and everything doubled in the last five years... well, maybe Ecuador is next."

Here's a story that illustrates how Cabarete's new age is finally starting to take shape. In 1968 Luis Noboa Batule had the vision to buy nearly 14 acres with almost 2,000 feet (600 meters) of beachfront between two points, Punta Goleta and Punta Cabarete, facing east. He had read in a tourism book that properties facing the sun would give tourists more hours of sunlight. He purchased some land from the Brugal rum family for $10,000 and later added 66 acres across the road encompassing a tropical lagoon, which is now within the El Choco National Park. Ironically, young Noboa was working at a rival rum factory, Bermudez, at the time, having dropped out of school to support his family following his father's death. This patriarch and his family now own 40% of the undeveloped beachfront left on Cabarete Bay. And their oceanfront property, now called Punta Goleta, will be the site for the first phase of the new Seawinds condominium project, which is expected to open in 2009. Starting with 82 units—including studios, one-, two-, and three-bedroom apartments— every *room* will have unobstructed ocean views.

A barometer of the town's evolution can also be read when you see what's happening with the long-established Windsurf Resort. In the late 1990s Canadian Gordon Gannon built it as a cheap haunt for young board boys. By 2006 attractive condos had been added, and the crowd had shifted to mostly couples, many of them baby boomers. Gordon's son, also Gordon, anticipated the new, upscale movement in Cabarete, began his own condominium project called Ocean Point on primo Kite Beach property. Now two of the three phases have come to fruition beautifully, and other high-end condos have sprung up nearby, including Ocean Dream, Harmony, and (soon) Symphony. Windsurf Resort itself is coming down, only to rise again like a phoenix as an upscale condo-hotel with five giant units directly on the beach as well as 80-some units on the current hotel's location. A stainless-steel bridge shaped like a windsurfing sail will soar over Cabarete's main street.

6

poking up from a lagoon. Many of your fellow diners will be kiters staying at the adjacent surf camp, considered Cabarete's best. You can have a good feed for around 10 bucks. Try grilled, sweet barbecued ribs with fries and a Dominican salad, or the house special churrasco— and always there's a shooter of mamajuana. The German owner, Ali, changes offerings often but at this writing, rotisserie chicken is the designated Saturday special; a wood-burning oven always puts out flavorful pizzas. The palapa roof gives the terrace shelter from the sun, you had

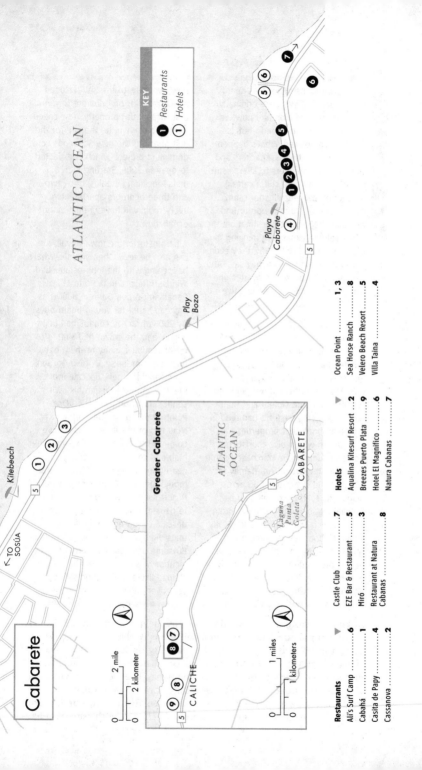

Cabarete

ATLANTIC OCEAN

← TO
SOSÚA

Kitebeach

Play
Bozo

Playa
Cabarete

KEY

| ● | Restaurants |
| ① | Hotels |

Greater Cabarete

ATLANTIC
OCEAN

Laguna
Punta
Goleta

CALICHE

CABARETE

Restaurants ▶

Ali's Surf Camp	6
Cabahá	1
Casita de Papy	4
Cassanova	2
Castle Club	7
EZE Bar & Restaurant	5
Miró	3
Restaurant at Natura Cabanas	8

Hotels ▶

Aqualina Kitesurf Resort	2
Breezes Puerto Plata	9
Hotel El Magnifico	6
Natura Cabanas	7
Ocean Point	1, 3
Sea Horse Ranch	8
Velero Beach Resort	5
Villa Taína	4

0   2 mile
0   2 kilometer

0   1 miles
0   1 kilometers

best douse yourself with mosquito repellent. You can call to make reservations, and you should if you have a large group. ⊠*Procab Cabarete, Cabarete* ☎*809/571–0733* ⊟*No credit cards* ☉*No lunch.*

¢–$ ✕**Cabahá.** The hip decor and the hot-pink wall paint at this diminutive café, illustrate the same good taste as the music, top-shelf liquor, fresh-fruit drinks, and healthy fare. For example, fresh mango juice with anejo rum and triple sec may be the best cocktail you'll have in the DR—unless you try the special-recipe mojitos with crushed ice. Breakfast can be anything from fresh smoothies or muesli. Organic salads and interesting sandwiches, such as smoked salmon and cream cheese on dark bread, are on the lunch menu. *Picaderas* (finger foods) and fish ceviches are on offer for dinner. A must-try is the hummus with a drizzle of house-made pepper oil. Most everything is healthy, and there are no fried foods on the menu; most dishes are even low-calorie, except for the desserts such as double chocolate cake. The Chilean chef–proprietress is Haudy (pronounced *Howdy*) Retamal, and she has a loyal following. ⊠*Paseo Don Chiche 14, across from Fred's, Cabarete* ☎*809/963–8397* ⊟*No credit cards* ☉*No lunch in low season.*

$–$$ ✕**Casita de Papy.** Cabarete Beach is awash in trendy beach restaurants, where you can see plenty of sexy, young customers but where the food falls short of mediocrity. The reason this decade-old family restaurant, owned by a retired French chef, has made the cut that a couple of its specialties are true palate pleasures. The food will help you overlook the dated polyester tablecloths and the service. They do try, but it's just not quite there. But here's the deal: order the sizzling cauldrons of either 16 large *camarones* (shrimp) or *langostinos* (small lobsters) in a creamy anise sauce. True, this is the most expensive thing on the menu, but two people can easily share a cauldron, and you can spread the wealth even wider if you order the fish quenelles, too. ⊠*Cabarete Beach, Cabarete* ☎*No phone* ⊟*No credit cards.*

$–$$ ✕**Cassanova.** This new player has spared no expense in creating this southeast Asian–inspired restaurant, which has lots of glitz and a large Buddha head at the entrance. On the beach are kite-shaped lights in the palms, a flaming torch, and Dominican musicians serenading. While the menu is extensive, few local residents brag about the food. The most popular items are the Thai red chicken curry and the shrimp with pastis. You can also order some tapas like the peanut chicken satay or the symphony of fish. Service is quite good. But if you hit the restaurant for happy hour or a late nightcap (the kitchen closes at midnight, but the crowd stays on), you can have your beers or blender drinks and people-watch. It's the scene you're here for, after all. ⊠*Cabarete Beach, Cabarete* ☎*809/571–0806* ⊟*AE, MC, V.*

$$$ ✕**Castle Club.** A man's home is his castle. In this one Doug Beers prepares creative lunches and dinners for guests who traverse the rocky

driveway to enjoy this one-of-a-kind experience. His wife, Marguerite, is the gracious hostess, who shows patrons their home and the artwork strategically positioned between the many open-air arches. Served on antique lace tablecloths strewn with bougainvillea, the well-orchestrated dinner might consist of canapés, carrot-ginger soup, Thai salad, grouper with a ginger–passion fruit sauce, fiesta rice, cold lemon soufflé, and coffee. After dinner Doug lights a fire in the great room and offers guests a liqueur to warm their interior. Advance reservations are required. ✉ *Mocha Rd., between Jamao and Los Brazos, 20 min from Cabarete* ☎ *809/357–8334 or 809/223–0601* ✐ *castleclub@hotmail.com* ⏛ *Reservations essential* 🖃 *No credit cards.*

> **THE LINEN NAPKIN STANDARD**
>
> Hope for linen napkins wherever you go. Some savvy diners make it a prerequisite in choosing their restaurant for dinner. Only the cheapest paper napkins are used in this country, and some diners judge a meal by how many napkins it takes to get through it. Five is not uncommon—eight becomes worthy of a mention. But wash it all down with a cold *cerveza* or a bottle of Chilean wine. Who's counting?

¢–$ ✕**EZE Bar & Restaurant.** This beach restaurant has a loyal following from breakfast to dinner, from wallet-watchin' windsurfers to wealthy capitaleño families. Dish names are taken from surfer jargon and includes such offerings as Bluebird's Salad (chicken tenders over mixed greens with a sweet chili salsa), the EZE Club Dude (curried grilled chicken), and the Rocker (grilled, marinated beef with onions, peppers tomato, and tzatziki on a soft pita). Frosty, tropical cocktails are excellent, and you can get an energy kick from yogurt and mango smoothies. The blenders also churn out healthy, organic veggie elixirs. Conversely, if you need a bacon cheeseburger fix, this be the place. Dinner is priced similarly to lunch, with more refined specials, like calamari or even lobster. The manager, Christos, is Bulgarian and so is the mezze platter. ✉ *Cabarete Beach, in front of Carib Wind Center, Cabarete* ☎ *809/880–8779* 🖃 *No credit cards.*

$–$$ ✕**Miró Gallery & Restaurant.** Chef-owner Lydia Wazana, a Canadian of Moroccan descent, is a queen-pin among the art set, too, and there's always artwork hanging as well as imaginative offerings like Morocco's chicken tagine or Asian-seared tuna. Grazers can share tapas such as the Middle Eastern hummus, baba ganoush, and grilled veggies. Look for items that pair with the incredible curry aïoli or spicy pineapple chutney and wasabi potato puree. The menu and master sushi-maker from Lydia's former restaurant, Wabi Sabi, with its classic sashimi and sushi, as well as some fab' innovations that include shrimp tempura rolls, are here now. Take a table on the beach (seating out there has been made lounge-y-er) or curl up with your buddies or beaus on the king-size Balinese sunbed, especially on nights when jazz man Roberto tickles the keyboard. ✉ *Cabarete Beach, Cabarete* ☎ *809/853–6848* 🖃 *No credit cards* ⊘ *Closed Oct. 15–Nov. 15. No lunch.*

$$–$$$ ✕**Restaurant at Natura Cabanas.** Seafood is at the heart of the menu here,
★ and appropriately so, for diners listen to the sounds of the waves crashing on coral rock as they fork the catch of the day with a buttery pistachio sauce. Start with the octopus in mint vinaigrette and then segue to a shellfish pasta in a pink sauce or lobster scampi. It all tastes so fresh. The filet mignon with mixed mushroom sauce is perfection. For dessert enjoy a classic such as a pear poached in red wine à la mode. The wines are French, Spanish, and Chilean (go for the *reservas*). Tables are set with geometric plates, laced linens, and oversize wine glasses. Service is warm, caring, and efficient, the international music atmospheric. ⊠*Natura Cabanas, Perla Marina, Cabarete* ☎*809/858–5822 or 809/571–1507* ⚓*Reservations essential* ▭*AE, MC, V.*

WHERE TO STAY

Each year the number of deluxe accommodations seems to be on the rise even as the less expensive lodgings, from surf camps to cheap hotels and apartment complexes, dwindle. Once Cabarete was one of the few hold-outs against all-inclusives, but the AIs now share the market with the small hotels. Villas and condominiums have become the preference of increasingly affluent visitors and second-home buyers.

VILLAS & CONDOS

$$$–$$$$ ⊡**Casa Colonial Villa 77.** An astounding renovation of one of Sea Horse Ranch's earlier homes, this sophisticated villa combines character with the latest in home decor and materials for a hip, yet traditional environment. The decor shifts between more traditional iron grillwork to dramatic contemporary art; the smoky-green, wood cabinets in the impressive kitchen and the sea-grass sleigh beds all combine to make this vacation rental feel more like a real home. The state-of-the-art home theater surrounds an Italian L-shape sofa. The creative pool complex has a dive rock, submerged basking platform, and Jacuzzi (not heated). Amid palms and birds-of-paradise is the palapa gazebo, which comes equipped with an iPod docking station. Both families and groups will adore this home. **Pros:** Flat-screen TVs in all the rooms, maid Carmen is one of Sea Horse Ranch's best, unique four-seater golf cart is included. **Cons:** It's close but not on the ocean, not one of the latest mega-mansions. ⊠*Sea Horse Ranch, Las Palmas, Cabarete* ☎*809/571–3880* ⊕*www.sea-horse-ranch.com* 🛏*4 bedrooms, 4 bathrooms* ♿*Safe, dishwasher, DVD, daily maid service, on-site security, pool, laundry facilities* ▭*AE, MC, V* ⦿*BP.*

$$$ ⊡**Ocean Point.** Five years in the making, the wait was worth it for the pizzazz of this new five-star condo complex in the dunes of Kite Beach. This is the good life, as one sits at the pool, shaded by a golden market umbrella and watching the parade of multicolor surf-kites in the big blue ocean. You can take out a kayak or boogie board or just bob around with a pool noodle. The stucco facade of these three-story buildings is attractive; all the condos have expansive terraces and outdoor dining areas. Yet the interiors outshine all, with the fully equipped, Italian designer kitchens being the best attribute, especially for those who want to stay in for dinner. The 4-bedroom/4-bath 4,000-square-

foot penthouses are tastefully luxurious and worth the extra money if you have a larger family. Mind you, the two-bedroom condos are 1,800 square feet. The two buildings are identical. The reception office and concierge for both projects is in the second phase, in a thatch-roof structure. The concierge can arrange pre-arrival grocery stocking and nanny service, too. **Pros:** Gorgeous views, quality building materials, elevators (!). **Cons:** A 20-minute beach walk to most restaurants, no breakfast or meals available on-site. ⊠ *Kite Beach, Carretera Principal, Cabarete* ☎ *809/571–0030* ⊕ *www.oceanpointdr.com* ⇥ *28 2-bedroom condos, 10 4-bedroom penthouses* ⚲ *Safe, dishwasher, Ethernet, Wi-Fi, daily maid service, on-site security, Jacuzzi, pool, beachfront, laundry facilities, no-smoking rooms (some)* ▭ *AE, D, DC, MC, V* ⦿ *EP.*

$$$$ 🏩 **Sea Horse Ranch.** Celebrities and other bigwigs frequent this luxury
★ residential resort, but with privacy paramount and security tight you can never get anyone to say whom you might see. The enclave has a relatively long history, having first opened in 1993, and has earned its enviable reputation. All the rentals have a private pool and a maid who cooks breakfast (you supply the groceries). A chef can be requested, but a month's notice is advised, even more for the Christmas holidays. One of the *negativos* of villa vacations is having to provision, a real chore when you don't know where to shop and may not speak the language. Sea Horse Ranch will provision your villa for $50, and even offers a nanny service. Within the rental villa inventory, there are some lovely older homes with character as well as spanking new, multimillion dollar Caribbean mansions that go beyond your fantasies. The beach club restaurant overlooking a dramatic cove delivers. The equestrian center is world-class. There's a two-night minimum stay (Christmas and New Year's is one week) but no check-in or check-out time. **Pros:** One of the most organized, well-managed villa enclaves in the country, potent security makes your vacation worry-free, location close to Puerto Plata and the airport. **Cons:** There's not much sense of place (you could be in an upscale neighborhood in Florida or Southern California), not all villas have Wi-Fi (and DSL is expensive). ⊠ *Cabarete* ☎ *809/571–3880 or 800/635–0991* ⊕ *www.sea-horse-ranch.com* ⇥ *75 villas* ⚲ *In-room: safe (some), kitchen, Wi-Fi (some). In-hotel: restaurant, bar, tennis courts, pool, beachfront, no elevator, parking (no fee)* ▭ *AE, MC, V* ⦿ *EP* ⇌ *2-night minimum.*

$$$$ 🏩 **Villa Catalina.** This 3½-acre, beachfront estate is the premier home-
Fodor'sChoice site in Sea Horse Ranch, having been designed by famed architect Sara
★ Garcia in 2006. The style might be best described as Tuscany meets Manhattan. The sprawling rose-color stucco mansion looks like an Italian palazzo, while the contemporary interior has more quality artwork than a dozen galleries in SoHo. An unexpected cartoon sculpture on the front lawn is just one of many whimsical art pieces, like an Adam and Eve on glass, a massive painting of a zebra pair, and a Sopranos' pinball machine, all framed by neutral and white furnishings. More color exists in the five bedrooms, including the blue-and-white room with its cobalt ocean views and yes, more art. **Pros:** Both a private (with cavern) and semi-private beach, so large that it would not feel crowded even if there were a crowd. **Cons:** Beach nearly dis-

appears when the tide is high, lacks a traditional warmth. ✉*1 Sea Horse Ranch, Los Corales, Cabarete* ☏*809/571–3880* ⊕*www.villa-catalina.com* ⬩*5 bedrooms, 6 bathrooms* ⬩*Safe, dishwasher, DVD, daily maid service, cook (breakfast only), on-site security, hot tub, pool, beachfront, laundry facilities* ⊟*AE, MC, V* ⎟⎛⎞*BP.*

$$$$ ⌗ **Villa Windsong 129.** Unique among the Sea Horse Ranch collectivo, this sprawling vacation home is not only on one of the most enviable beachfronts, it's Balinese in design, utilizing the most natural construction materials: palapa roofs, native coralina and fieldstone floors, round white stones, and hemp ropes on the high-ceiling rafters. Individual bedrooms flank the main building that has an open-air living room, which extends to a home-chef's dream kitchen in stainless steel. A wood-burning pizza oven is indicative that this is ideal for casual fun, especially good for family reunions. Past the infinity pool, an Asian-influenced gazebo looks onto the beach with its tidal pools. The indoor-outdoor environment provides a natural high. **Pros:** Sandals and pareos suit this villa, bedrooms have their own patios and one has a baby's nursery. **Cons:** Not as many cushy creature comforts as some expensive manses here, lacks a formality or elegance that some upscale clients desire. ✉*Sea Horse Ranch, Las Olas, Cabarete* ☏*809/571–3880* ⊕*www.sea-horse-ranch.com* ⬩*4 bedrooms, 4 bathrooms* ⬩*Safe, dishwasher, DVD, daily maid service, on-site security, pool, beachfront, water toys, laundry facilities* ⊟*AE, MC, V* ⎟⎛⎞*BP.*

HOTELS & RESORTS

$ ⌗ **Aqualina Kitesurf Resort.** Compared to the digs many surfers occupy, this small mid-rise hotel is a deluxe address. In fact, many of the occupants, particularly in low season and on weekends, are well-to-do Dominican families, who often take the units with kitchens or the penthouses. The young kite surfers usually live on breakfast, burgers, and burritos from the Dare2fly bar, right in front, where the kite school is. A small pool is to the left, and the tiny lobby has a free public computer. It's all modern and moderately priced. **Pros:** All rooms have balconies and incredible views of the sea and the kite action, excellent two-for-one rum cocktails during happy hour. **Cons:** More regular maintenance is needed due to heavy occupancy, everything feels small—the hotel, grounds, pool, beachfront, can be noisy, especially on weekends. ✉*Kite Beach, Cabarete* ☏*809/571–0787* ⊕*www.aqualina.com* ⬩*7 rooms, 8 studios, 4 jr. suites, 3 apartments* ⬩*In-room: safes, refrigerators, kitchen (some). In-hotel: restaurant, bar, pool, beachfront, water sports, no elevator, laundry service, public Internet, public Wi-Fi, parking (no fee)* ⊟*MC, V* ⎟⎛⎞*EP.*

$–$$ ⌗ **Breezes Puerto Plata.** This Super Clubs resort, one of the few 24-hour all-inclusives on the North Coast, is actually between Sosúa and Cabarete, on 62 expansive acres with an extensive beach and quietly removed from the highway noise by a long driveway. Rooms and villas have been completely gutted, and new white furniture has been moved in, accented by a yellow motif. Exteriors are now painted in the same cheery yellow. The newer hotel buildings 10 and 11 have had minor cosmetic improvements, but they were fine before, with bi-level master suites furnished with rough-hewn four-posters and woven wall hangings. The sprawling resort has the Lighthouse Spa that is consistently recommendable. Its Carnival Casino, one of the few locally, has also had a floor-to-ceiling redo. A Dominican family favorite on weekends and during low season, the resort is also frequented by Europeans and Americans, who prevail in the winter season. **Pros:** There are quiet spots even when the resort is full (such as on the beach in front of the spa's faux lighthouse), memorable breakfast buffet, tipping is simply not allowed. **Cons:** Internet is only accessed in the computer room and is expensive, other than the great breakfast the food is not super, clientele can be rowdy. ⊠ *Carretera Cabarete, Cabarete* ☎ *809/696–2858* ⊕ *www.superclubs.com* ➱ *436 rooms, 22 jr. suites, 8 2-bedroom suites* ♿ *In-room: safe, refrigerator. In-hotel: 5 restaurants, bars, tennis courts, pools, gym, spa, beachfront, water sports, no elevator, children's programs (ages 4–12), laundry service, public Internet, parking (no fee)* ☰ *AE, D, DC, MC, V* ⦿ *AI.*

$-$$ ⬚ **Hotel El Magnifico.** You'll find a healthy dose of unexpected luxury ★ at this stellar boutique condo-hotel just a gravel driveway from the dusty craziness of town. The open reception area, backed by an artistic screen, is flanked by a quiet seating or swinging area (there's a comfy hammock) that whispers tranquillity. The lush gardens hold a pair each of pools and Jacuzzis. For your accommodations, try to get the new building 6; building 3 has some of the best interior design, but no water views; building 1 has an artsy Caribbean design and lots of color. The stonework surrounding it and the walkways to the warm, oceanfront Jacuzzi, are eye-popping. Creator Gerhard Hebert, a charming French Canadian, came to the DR as a surfer in 1984, and he has built a following. **Pros:** Even when the hotel is full, the gardens and pools do not feel crowded, interior decor is chic contemporary, children under 15 years are complimentary. **Cons:** Steep spiral staircases and no elevators, no restaurant or bar on-site, no phones (and no way to communicate with reception), credit cards carry a ridiculous 16% surcharge. ⊠ *Calle del Cementario, Cabarete* ☎ *809/571–0868* ⊕ *www.hotelmagnifico. com* ➱ *7 rooms, 10 1-bedroom apartments, 12 2-bedroom apartments, 1 3-bedroom apartment* ♿ *In-room: no phone, kitchen (some), refrigerator, Wi-Fi. In-hotel: pool, hot tub, beachfront, no elevator, parking (no fee)* ☰ *MC, V* ⦿ *EP.*

$$ ⬚ **Natura Cabanas.** This oceanfront eco-paradise offers accommodations ★ in thatched-roof cabanas, such as the Africana, more sophisticated with bamboo, artistic brick, and stonework. The diverse clientele enhances this back-to-nature experience; you might find yourself next to a surfer, a young neurologist, or a yoga aficionado. Lole, the *dueña*, and her caring, bilingual staff promote camaraderie. Healthful breakfasts and lunches are served in one of the two waterfront restaurants, where the mellow music is the backdrop for backgammon and conversation. At night the seafood restaurant woos diners. The artistically designed Attabeyra Spa, is completely individualistic, and has services like chocolate wraps and massage on the beach. The splendid yoga pavilion is a *palacio*: it's the oceanfront setting for classes, retreats, and weddings. The pool palapa with its colorful Indian sarongs, is the setting for romantic dinners for two and VIP parties. ■ TIP → There's a special discount if you pay in cash.

✉Playa Perla Marina, Cabarete ☎809/571–1507 ⊕www.natura-cabana.com ➹11 bungalows &In-room: no a/c, no phone, kitchen (some), refrigerator, no TV. In-hotel: 2 restaurants, bar, pool, spa, beach-front, no elevator, parking (no fee) ▭AE, MC, V ❏CP.

$ ★ 🏨**Velero Beach Resort.** Laze in the hammock or swing on the palm that bends over the beach while you watch the kite surfers work to become airborne. They're the only thing between you and the horizon at this well-managed hotel and residential enclave with its own beachfront and manicured gardens studded with cacti, orchids, and

RAMILIFE—BREAK FOR A WELLNESS DAY

The staff of **RamiLife** (☎809/710–1221 ⊕www.RamiLife.com) offer a day of health for the area's resort guests to help them recover from many all-inclusive days of too much food and too many rum drinks. Treatments are structured around the RAM-Energy-Median massage (REM). Services are offered at Natura Cabanas every Monday and Friday in the glorious, outdoor yoga pavilion.

pottery. Well-heeled Dominicans, hip Americans, and other international guests appreciate that it's removed from the noise of town yet just minutes down the sand from the happening bars. The spacious two-bedroom suites and three-bedroom penthouses with full kitchens are the best deals and can be divided into smaller units, including standard rooms (without kitchens) if you're just a couple. Guests in standard rooms get a complimentary breakfast at the private beach restaurant. You might ask for the Art Deco Building 111, which has all been repainted. The views from the penthouses are knockout and an excellent value if three couples share. Ask about the 10% discount for cash. **Pros:** Blenders, microwaves and DVDs in the junior suites and above, new Balinese sunbeds at the pool are wonderfully hedonistic, a popular wedding and honeymoon venue. **Cons:** No elevators, all spiral staircases, standard rooms are not spacious. ✉Calle la Punta 1, Cabarete ☎809/571–9727 or 866/383–5376 ⊕www.velerobeach.com ➹56 suites &In-room: safe, kitchen (some), refrigerator, Wi-Fi (some). In-hotel: restaurant, pool, beachfront, no elevator, public Internet, public Wi-Fi ▭MC, V ❏EP.

¢–$ 🏨**Villa Taina.** Smack amid the action, steps down from the main drag, this small, German-owned inn encapsulates the original spirit of Cabarete. It caters to the independent traveler and the young and sporty who want more commodious digs than a surf camp. Enjoy an ample breakfast at Serenada, the beachside restaurant, which is sheltered from the wind by translucent kite boards borrowed from the kite-surfing center; your fellow coffee drinkers may be shielded by German and French newspapers. By night, the revamped restaurant serves international cuisine, with special buffet theme nights, cool sounds, and a fun crowd. The interiors may be a bit dated, but this beach hotel is an excellent value—it even has free in-room DSL lines. Request the quiet rooms (the second floor up to the penthouses) that front the beach. **Pros:** Right in the middle of things, efficient and caring German owner. **Cons:** Small pool, noise of town can be heard in the buildings closest to the street, rooms are on the small side. ⊠*Calle Principal, Cabarete* ☎*809/571–0722* ⊕*www.villataina.com* ⊅*56 rooms, 1 apartment* &*In-room: refrigerator, Ethernet. In-hotel: restaurant, bar, pool, beachfront, water sports, no elevator* ⊟*MC, V* ⦿*BP.*

NIGHTLIFE & THE ARTS

All around the country and in many foreign ports, the nightlife in Cabarete is known as the big beach party. And so it is. Bar-hopping is the name of the game here. The open-air bars and restaurants that line the beachfront mainly attract the young and restless, but anyone who is ageless is made welcome. It starts at happy hour, which, like at Onno's might include half-price tapas from 4 to 7; couple that with the half-price local drinks from 6 to 8. The best advice is to walk the beach and see which bars offer the best discounts (and when), then make your plans. Earlier curfews have moved closing at bars up to 3 AM on weekends, helping to curb after-party crime. ⚠ **Nevertheless, after midnight exercise your street sense on the beach. Watch your back as well as your purse or wallet. Even better, don't walk the beach alone after dark, especially deserted stretches.** Be wary of motoconchos, which zip down the streets with little notice of pedestrians. Men may be approached by prostitutes, or younger tourists by drug dealers. We recommend you avoid both. You don't want to hear the horror stories.

BARS & CAFÉS
Lax (⊠*Cabarete Beach, Cabarete* ☎*809/710–0569*) is a perennially popular, open-air bar that really comes alive by night. You can sit in the sand in lounge chairs or jump into the action under the palapa, where a DJ will be spinning madly or a live band will be rockin'. There's good grazing chow, too, and special theme nights like Thai (not bad, either). Drinks come from the blenders and in pitchers, but be patient, getting one can take time when the bar backs up. As it's next to a small hotel, it must close early now—1 AM.

DANCE CLUBS
Onno's Bar (⊠*Cabarete Beach, Cabarete* ☎*809/571–0461*), under new ownership since 2007, is promising many innovations and remains a serious party place. It's usually wall-to-wall and back-to-back as the young and fit pack the dance floor and groove to techno sounds while other multinational youth sit at the tables in the sand. It's easier to get served at the beach bar than the main one, and as you chill, people will pass by, introduce themselves, converse, and then move on. It's fun and friendly, although on Friday and Saturday nights, when it stays open until 3 AM, the scene can be too rowdy.

BEACHES

The wonderful expanse of Atlantic beach that is Cabarete has been made not only more aesthetically pleasing but more user-friendly since its beach rejuvenation. Morning is best for swimmers and children, when the wind is light and the water calmer. Most of the beaches are soft sand with few rocks. No motorized water sports nor scuba diving are allowed at any of these beaches, but since this is a prime windsurfing area, especially in front of Carib Wind Center, swimmers must be on guard for surfers of various kinds.

Kite Beach (⊠ *Sosúa–Cabarete Rd., 1.2 mi [2 km] west of town, Cabarete*) was so named because it's where kite surfing, the hot new sport taking over town, is practiced. The heavy kiting traffic makes swimming here fairly hazardous. On the sand you'll see instructors teaching new students how to work the lines that hold the wind foil—the colorful "kite." An experienced kiter is like poetry in motion, and it's mesmerizing to watch them. The windy month of March is prime time.

> **THE SANTIAGO ALTERNATIVE**
>
> Check out airfares to Santiago, which has numerous direct flights from New York, Newark, and Miami. JetBlue has rates as low as $150 one-way. The flight arrives around 4:30 AM, but now that the spiffy Courtyard by Marriott Santiago opened five minutes from the airport, you can bunk there, spend the day at Centro León, and take a bus or taxi to the North Coast towns of Puerto Plata, Sosúa, and Cabarete. Since JetBlue prices by segments, you could fly out of another destination without penalty.

Playa Cabarete (⊠ *Sosúa–Cabarete Rd., Cabarete*) is the main business district of this town. If you follow the coastal road east from Playa Dorada, you can't miss it. The beach, which has strong waves after a calm entrance, and ideal, steady wind (from 15 to 20 knots) is an integral part of the international windsurfing circuit. Segments of this long beach are strips of sand punctuated only by palm trees. The regeneration of Cabarete Beach was a $3 million engineering project that made the beach some 115 feet wider, adding an infusion of white sand. In the most commercial area, restaurants and bars are back-to-back, spilling onto the sand. The informal scene is young and fun, with expats and tourists from every imaginable country.

Playa Encuentro (⊠ *Sosúa–Cabarete Rd., 3.7 mi [6 km] west of Cabarete Beach, Cabarete*) is the area's main surfing beach because the waves here are large. Yes, the original ride-the-waves type of surfing on a fiberglass board is the ideal activity here. However, you need to be a strong swimmer, for currents are mighty, and you must be careful of the rocks.

SPORTS & THE OUTDOORS

BIKING & HIKING

Pedaling is easy on pancake-flat beaches, but there are also some steep hills in the D.R. Several resorts rent bikes to guests and nonguests alike. You can have a mountain-biking adventure for a half or full day through the interior of the Dominican Republic. A 3,000-foot downhill ride on winding mountain roads can be great fun for all levels of athletes. A guided ride that includes a support vehicle makes the trip safer and may help to alleviate the anxiety of the less experienced biker. Things look different from atop a bicycle seat and this is an exhilarating way to get into the heart of the country and learn about the Dominican culture and vegetation by biking through Dominican villages, refreshing yourself with tropical fruits, and taking an invigorating swim in the Jamao River.

Hiking offers another way to integrate with the Dominican countryside. You can explore one of the newest national parks in the country, El Choco, an incredible 77 square mi of jungle, lagoons, caves, forests, and open backcountry right outside Cabarete.

The more adventurous might want to make the cascade hike to the 27 Waterfalls of Damajagua, although this nontechnical climb is quite physically demanding, and you must be able to swim. You'll face a labyrinth of tunnels, caves, and natural pools. Water sliding and jumping down rock formations can be challenging but will give you a sense of pride when it's over.

★ **Iguana Mama** (⊠ *Calle Principal 74, Cabarete* ☎ *809/571–0908 or 809/571–0228* ⊕ *www.iguanamama.com*) is the original adventure-tour company on the D.R.'s North Coast. The company has traditional and mountain bikes and will take you on guided rides on the flats or test your mettle on the steep grades in the mountains. Downhill rides, which include a taxi up to the foothills, breakfast, and lunch, cost $85 for a full-day trip, $60 for a half-day trip. Advanced rides, on and off roads, are $40 to $50. Guided hikes cost $35 to $65. In addition, this well-established, safety-oriented company offers horseback riding on the beach and courtryside for $40 for two hours, canyoning, and a host of other adventure sports.

BOATING

★ **Carib Wind Center** (⊠ *Calle Principal, Cabarete* ☎ *809/571–0640* ⊕ *www.caribwind.com*) is a renowned windsurfing center (known for decades as Carib BIC Center) that also rents Lasers, 17-foot catamarans, boogie boards, and sea kayaks. It has an Olympic Laser Training Center with a former racer instructing. Experts even, champions in their own countries, come to train here. For the 2008 Beijing Summer Olympic games, 17 participants in the Laser windsurfing competition had their main training here.

HORSEBACK RIDING

Horseback riding is a delightful way to experience the beach and see the interior. It's best to go with an operation that maintains a certain caliber of mounts, equipment, and guides. Some of the local ad hoc guys will take you for less and let you gallop the beach, but if the tack breaks 10 minutes out and you bite the sand, don't expect to get your money refunded. Iguana Mama also offers horseback riding trips, both on the beach and in the countryside (*see* ⇨ *Biking & Hiking, above*).

Sea Horse Ranch Equestrian Center (⊠ *Cabarete* ☎ *809/571–3880 or 809/ 571–4462*) is a professional, well-staffed operation. The competition ring is built to international regulations, and there's a large schooling ring. An annual invitational jumping event is sanctioned by the Dominican Equestrian Federation. Lessons, including dressage instruction, start at $35 an hour, and endurance rides are $30 for 90 minutes, $50 for three hours, including drinks and snacks—but make reservations. The most popular ride includes stretches of beach and a bridle path across a neighboring farm's pasture, replete with wildflowers and butterflies. Feel free to tie your horse to a palm tree and jump into the waves.

TENNIS

Sea Horse Ranch (✉ *Cabarete* ☎ *809/571–2902*) has a tennis center with five clay courts, illuminated for night play and open to nonguests. Court time is $20 per person an hour, with an additional fee of $7 for night play. Instructions, available in four languages, cost $20.

WIND- & KITE SURFING

Fodor's Choice ★ Between June and October, Cabarete Beach has what many consider tobe optimal windsurfing conditions: wind speeds at 20 to 25 knots (they come from the side shore) and 3- to-10-foot Atlantic waves. This also makes Cabarete a safer alternative since the wind always blows toward the shore here, a plus for both novices and the weary, who will always drift back toward the beach rather than out to sea. The Professional Boardsurfers Association has included Cabarete in its international windsurfing slalom competition. The novice is also welcome to learn and train on wider boards with light sails.

In kite surfing, the board—smaller than a traditional windsurfing board—is attached to a parachute-like "kite." Those who are proficient can literally fly through the air. It's a heady, adrenaline-spiked ocean adventure. One fortysomething novice explained that if you have surfed, it should only take about three hours to get the hang of it. As for the fear factor, it's there, but you will learn to control your kite. The novice is welcome to learn and train on wider boards with lighter sails.

Many ask if kite surfing is an expensive proposition. Although one place offers an initial come-on for $20, which is just a trial run on the sand, the answer is that real lessons are not inexpensive. For private lessons, you should expect to pay $459 for 3 days (9 hours) or less; $612 or 4 days (12 hours). Group lessons can be cheaper; if you have a friend, you can take 3 days (9 hours) for $382 each, 4 days (12 hours) for $510 each.

Carib Wind Center (✉ *Cabarete* ☎ *809/571–0640* ⊕ *www.caribwind. com*), which has been in business since 1988 as the Carib BIC Center, has just changed its name, owner Ari Bashi explains, because BIC was the name of the boards that he bought exclusively. Now he carries a number of brands including many Olympic Laser boards. Equipment and instruction are offered and lessons are generally $30 to $35 an hour; boards rent for $20 an hour. A gem of a windsurfing club, this family-owned business has many repeat clients and is open year-round. In the complex is its beach bar, EZE, as well as a retail shop. It has all the paraphernalia for surfing and a good variety of sunglasses, includ-

ing Maui Jim's and some of the best
bikinis, cute miniskirts, and dresses
in town.

★ **Kite Club** (⊠ *Kite Beach, next to
Ocean Point, Cabarete* ☎ *809/571–
9748 or 809/972–6609* ⊕ *www.
kiteclubcabarete.com*), an International Kitesurfing Organization
(IKO) Certification Center, is a
fraternal sports club that has multilingual lessons, from beginner to
instructor certification. Prospective
students generally book in advance
online. Those kiters (and part-time
residents) who have their own
gear pay inexpensive, weekly dues
to belong, to use the beach furniture and the rescue boat if needed.
Equipment can be rented, too, and
the adjacent snack shop is open to
all. Credit cards are accepted.

Kitexcite (⊠ *Kite Excite Hotel, Kite Beach, Cabarete* ☎ *809/571–9509,
809/913–0827, or 809/914–9745* ⊕ *www.kitexcite.com*) operates a
large school for one of the Caribbean's newest popular sports.

★ **Kite Club Grill** (⊠ *Kite Beach, next to Kite Club, Cabarete* ☎ *809/571–
9748*) is run by Calin, an expert kiter and Columbia University grad,
and she keeps the prices down and the food level high. Have a late
breakfast here—excellent coffee with an egg, cheese, ham, and avocado
sandwich, or lunch, in the form of smoothies, wraps, tuna fillet sandwiches, or specials like couscous.

Laurel Eastman Kiteboarding (⊠ *Playa Bozo, in front of Ocean Dream,
Cabarete* ☎ *809/571–0564* ⊕ *www.laureleastman.com*) is one of the
best-known and respected schools, offering a free lesson with certified
instructors from 10:30 to 11 AM daily. In four days, beginners can learn
the theory of the wind and start using the smaller kite trainers.

SHOPPING

In Cabarete, shopping is mainly for trinkets and souvenirs, Dominican cigars, beachy resortwear, complementary jewelry, and surfing
paraphernalia.

ART GALLERIES

Lisa Kirkman Gallery (⊠ *Ocean One Plaza, next to Banco Santa
Cruz, Cabarete* ☎ *809/571–0108*) has a great selection of nationally
acclaimed contemporary masters, up-and-coming artists, and works
from the winners of the last art festival (held in Santo Domingo) and
of the Eduardo León Jimenez national competition for contemporary
artists. The gallery rocks when there's an art opening, and the Indo-

Caribbean furnishings (also for sale) create a loungelike atmosphere. Many of the artworks and accessories could be carried on a plane, or shipping can be arranged. At **Miró Gallery & Restaurant** (⊠ *Cabarete Beach, Cabarete* ☎ *809/571–0888*) you can find rotating exhibitions of contemporary art with an emphasis on Latino artists and photographers, especially from the Dominican Republic and Cuba. Opening soirees are social events.

CLOTHING

Mare (⊠ *Calle Principal, across from blue Victorian building with gingerbread fretwork, Cabarete* ☎ *809/571–0360*) sells some of the town's best swimsuits, as well as sundresses, pareos, and crinkly miniskirts. There's a large selection of quality flip-flops and sandals, men's swimsuits and jams, plus T-shirts. Come here for chic, straw sun hats (Panama-style and more), on down to baseball caps.

GIFTS

Gary's Gift Shop (⊠ *Calle Principal, across from Supermercado Albercito, Cabarete* ☎ *No phone*) is just one of the many no-name souvenir shops selling tschotkes. You may ask, "Where's the sign?" But if you find it, you can also find that among the better gift items are handmade candles in the shape of a dugout boat, key rings, pink shell necklaces, colorfully painted wooden turtles, photo albums and picture frames made with sand and fiber, flip-flops, and inexpensive "Panama" hats, caps, and visors. And this is where the locals go to buy their cigars.

JEWELRY

Beach Box Boutique (⊠ *Paseo Don Chiche 5, Cabarete* ☎ *809/571–0673, 809/399–7628 cell*), the sister shop to Fred Joyas, has colorful and utilitarian beach bags, pareos, organdy sun hats, shell jewelry, and wide silver bracelets. **Fred Joyas** (⊠ *Paseo Don Chiche #3; turn at green BHD sign for ATM, Cabarete* ☎ *809/571–0673 or 809/399–7628*). *Joyas* is Spanish for jewelry. Here it's silver jewelry coupled with the island's semiprecious stones—larimar, amber, and black onyx—as well as shells and beads. Fred is the proprietress, a savvy French woman with stylin' taste.

CABRERA

60 mi (96 km) east of Cabarete.

Cabrera, Abreu, Rio San Juan, and the Playa Grande area are largely unspoiled and pristine coastal areas. There's a raw beauty, with some beaches that are still completely undeveloped, soaring cliffs overlooking pounding ocean waves, and towering inland hills with sweeping vistas not seen elsewhere on the island. In addition, there are some of the most luxurious villa choices in the country. These high-end holiday homes are far away from the action and the *negativos* of Sosúa and Cabarete and will appeal primarily to those who wish to avoid the sometimes raucous nightlife scene in both Sosúa and Cabarete. Still, it's just an hour's drive to the east over a well-paved highway, making day trips a possibility. This area will appeal to a more moneyed crowd—baby boomers for the most part—who want a more relaxed, higher-quality lifestyle.

Though originally thought of as remote, this area is now booming. It has come full circle from being out in the *campo* (country), when most of the land was still held in small, family-owned farms, mainly a cattle-raising area. Now tucked into the pastoral landscapes and oceanfront vegetation are some of the most exclusive gated communities in the country.

Yet Cabrera itself is still a sleepy, dusty Dominican town centered on its central square, which is remarkably clean. Tourists can safely mingle with townies in the park and can stop for a drink at one of the adjacent restaurants like the thatched-roof Town Square Bar. In a land of warm, friendly people, Cabrerans are among the sweetest. Nearly 50 local and expat children now attend the new International Academy here, soon to expand to a secondary school.

Until recently, the area was very limited as far as such essentials as supermarkets, mainly just little local *colmados* (grocery stores) and farm stands on the Cabrera Road. Now, you can shop in the large, new Supermarket Ahorra on Calle Marie Gomez.

People now come to swim and sun, this stretch of the North Coast being famous for its fine beaches such as Playa Precioso and Playa Grande. And they come for the golf at the Playa Grande Golf Course, a famous Robert Trent Jones Jr. But you don't come here for sights because there aren't any; and other than the beaches and golf courses, you won't even find many activities, just beautiful surf and sand and lots of sun.

WHERE TO EAT

A quick synopsis of the Cabrera dining scene includes the most rustic Dominican outpost, Babanuco's, as well as the hilltop Hotel La Catalina's terrace dining room. In between, there are some recommendable, middle-of-the-road restaurants where you get a tasty Dominican meal with a full complement of seafood, including conch and octopus, for $6 to $15 for a main course.

The Carretera Río San Juan–Cabrera is lined with many other modest restaurants serving mainly Dominican food, as well as a few Italian spots. As most are open-air with thatched roofs, they can be noisy, even dusty, but welcoming. In town around the central park are another handful of local restaurants, and even a pizza place, where you can get your pie to go.

$ ✕ **Babanuco Bar & Restaurant.** You want rustic? This is genuine, funked-up Dominican rusticity. Furniture might be a tree stump, decoration a cow horn; tablecloths are raw burlap. The floor is dirt. In the primitive bar hang vintage license plates from French Canada, the United States, and the Netherlands. The food served up by chef–owner Juan Alberto is flavorful and authentic, with seafood a specialty of the *casa*.

Try langoustines and lambi, *pulpo* (octopus), land crab, and fillet of fresh, fresh fish. And Juan goes that extra mile, past the ubiquitous creole sauce, like conch in mushroom sauce with fried green bananas and salad. It's cheaper and even more fun if you come with a group. Make a party, and with some notice he can hire musicians for you. ✉ *Off Carretera Rio San Juan-Cabrera Entrada de Saltadero, Cabrera* ☎ *809/223–7928* ▭ *No credit cards.*

EN ROUTE Just past Babanuco Restaurant & Bar is El Salidero waterfall. You may see some of the local kids scooting down the embankment to swim in the icy pool at the bottom of the cascade. You, too, can attempt this, but proceed with caution as the moss makes the rocks slippery.

$–$$ ✕ **Restaurant at Hotel La Catalina.** This hotel restaurant does indeed offer a pleasant dining experience, especially if you arrive early enough to have a cocktail at the bar accompanied by house-made pâté and sway to international music as you gaze down the cliff to the ocean. This restaurant has gone through many incarnations and now with two international consulting chefs; it's definitely still on the way up. Still evolving, the menu offers chicken, fish, shrimp, pork, beef, and a vegetarian choice, and each day a chef's special (lobster one day, barbeque another) is added. Starters are particularly well-priced (as are desserts), with flavorful soups starting at $3.50. A meal here has an air of camaraderie and conviviality—so much so that it can sometimes feel like a house party. ✉ *Las Farallones, off Carretera Rio San Juan–Cabrera, 4 km (2.5 mi) east of Cabrera ⚓ Turn at sign for Catalina, go another 1.5 km (0.9 mi) up hill to sign for Catalina, and then turn left. Go straight into gated community of Las Farallones, where restaurant is on right* ☎ *809/589–7700* ▭ *AE, MC, V.*

WHERE TO STAY

In addition to a bevy of luxurious vacation villas, the Cabrera area has a clothing-optional resort that is making a good name for itself and a hillside hotel with condominiums that has an admirable history going back to the late 1980s and is popular with the embassy crowd in Santo Domingo. At this writing, the Cristal Beach Resort, a new condo-hotel, is expected to open on Orchid Bay in 2009. It will be the region's first true five-star resort, with a full-service restaurant, spa, tennis courts, and a beach club.

PRIVATE VILLAS

$$$$ 🏨 **Sunrise Villa.** Unique is the only way to describe this beachfront retreat. The luxurious villa compound designed in a Balinese style by architect Sara Garcia is a collection of individual structures that house five suites, with the main house as a focal point. Spread over two lush, tropical acres, the exotic architecture and interior design make it a romantic getaway destination, a photographer's dream, the perfect island wedding venue, or a super home for fun-filled family reunions, with each person or couple having an individual cabana. There are cribs and booster seats, a billiard room, and a giant chess set. This level of privacy makes it ideal for golf-guy getaways. The vacation atmosphere is laid-back, relaxing, and luxurious without being pretentious. There's even a house bar. The staff is well-managed by Chris Quinlyn, one of the American owners. Rates are based on the number of guest rooms you plan to use and include free use of Wi-Fi. The meal plan is an additional $50 per person per day, and airport transfers can be arranged. **Pros:** One of the best locations on Orchid Beach, meal plan includes one dinner at a great Cabrera restaurant, villa comes with a full staff. **Cons:** Most rooms are in separate buildings, so if it rains you better have an umbrella handy, the ocean air has aged the structures somewhat since they were built in 2002, meal plan is mandatory. ✉*Orchid Bay Estates 26, Orchid Beach* 🕭*Plaza Commercial Maria, Av. Maria Gomez 10, Carbrera* ☎*809/589–8083, 809/710–1078 cell, 610/429–9616 rental office in U.S., or 866/845–5210* ⊕*www.sunrise-villa.com* 🛏*8 bedrooms, 9 bathrooms* ♨*Safe, dishwasher, DVD, Wi-Fi, daily maid service, cook, on-site security, hot tub, pool, gym, beach-front, bicycles, water toys, laundry facilities, some pets allowed, no smoking* ▤*AE, MC, V* ⦿*EP* ☞*4-night minimum.*

$$$–$$$$ ▦**Villa Cantamar.** This low-rise, ultracontemporary, 11,000 square-foot home in a minimalist, Asian style, has a broad sweeping expanse of verdant lawn that ends abruptly at a rock cliff soaring above the beach below. A free-form, zero-entry swimming pool and Euro-style outdoor furniture are a knock-out. This luxurious oceanfront estate, which sits on 2.5 acres within a prestigious gated community, enjoys rare privacy since it's flanked by undeveloped land. If you love innovative design by a premier architect (Sara Garcia), and sleek, minimalist decor, all in a secluded, romantic setting, this could be your dream villa. While children are allowed, this home is remote and geared to adults. Airport pick-ups can be arranged. A meal plan of $55 per person per day is mandatory and additional to the rental cost. **Pros:** Staff are a cut above the norm, amazingly well priced, VIP airport reception available at Puerto Plata (POP). **Cons:** Some might not like the isolation, decor not glamorous or ornate, beach is beautiful but relatively inaccessible, so guests usually drive to one of the known beaches. ✉*Seatree Estates 1, Abreu* 🕭*Plaza Commercial Maria, Av. Maria Gomez 10, Cabrera* ☎*809/589–8083, 809/710–1078 cell, 610/429–9616 for reservations in U.S., or 866/845–5210* ⊕*www.villacantamar.com* 🛏*4 bedrooms, 5 bathrooms* ♨*Safe, dishwasher, DVD, Wi-Fi, daily maid service, cook, on-site security, hot tub, pool, beachfront, laundry facilities, some pets allowed, no smoking* ▤*AE, MC, V* ⦿*EP* ☞*4-night minimum.*

$$$$ ▦**Villa Castellamonte.** Italian for "little castle on the sea," this is the
Fodor's Choice   crown jewel in the string of lavish vacation homes collectively known
★   as Orchid Bay Estates. Its Italianate design, ceiling paintings, and original art by Guillermo Estrada raise it to the level of palazzo. Guests can swim in the hotel-size pool, bubble in the Jacuzzi, or descend the stairway that leads to a semi-private, golden beach. The home offers as many diversions and amenities as a beach resort (even a well-stocked wine cellar); the caring staff makes it feel like home. Kids are welcome and love the game room, karaoke, shuffleboard, and more. This is truly opulent and unforgettable, be it for a destination wedding, small conference, or a Big Chill reunion. With eight bedrooms, even these

The Villa Alternative

One of the hottest tropical destinations in the Caribbean, the Dominican Republic has always been known as a cheap date because of its many all-inclusive resorts, which began in Playa Dorada and really took hold in Punta Cana. The European crowd was the first to grab on to the all-you-can-eat-and-drink concept; Americans followed suit, and at first almost everyone was happy. But AI resorts are no longer the only show in town.

Villas now provide a popular alternative. You can have the services and amenities of a five-star hotel, as well as a well-trained staff dedicated solely to your needs. And you don't have to elbow your way through a throng of strangers to get a cocktail. Vacation villas are privately owned homes and may be moderately priced or luxurious. Most have three or more bedrooms (larger homes have as many as 10) and are perfect for group trips, including family reunions, corporate retreats, and destination weddings.

Villa vacations are best-suited for savvy travelers who seek a personalized vacation experience with privacy a priority, particularly around the pool and in dining areas. However, the D.R. offers many enclaves, gated communities with resortlike amenities and restaurants that offer the privacy of a villa with the services of a resort. Some villas are right in town, offering the opportunity to interact daily with local residents and have a more genuine experience in the country.

Price is always a factor, but while all-inclusive resorts offer savings on food and drinks, shared facilities are often crowded and both food and drink mediocre. If more people crowd into a room, the cost goes up while comfort goes down. A mid-range AI resort can still offer a tremendous value and is almost always cheaper than a comparable room in a luxury resort.

Villas typically offer a single price for the entire villa including its complement of staff, features, and amenities. If all of the bedrooms are occupied and the total costs shared, the cost of staying in a villa (even considering the added cost of provisioning) can be about the same as the cost of a room at a luxury resort, when all the expenses are figured on a per-person basis.

For example, a large beachfront villa in Cabrera's Orchid Bay Estates can accommodate 16 people and costs $2,600 per night. This is about $160 per person per night, which is the equivalent price of a upper mid-range all-inclusive resort in the D.R. but much less than a comparable luxury room at a resort on almost any other island. If you're willing to pay double that, you can have an ultra-luxurious contemporary villa, also right on the water.

While provisioning (meals, snacks, and beverages) are almost never included in the villa rental price, they often can be added for a moderate daily supplement. Many villas offer breakfast and even lunch preparation as a part of your maid's daily duties (some for a relatively small additional fee). Personal chefs can be engaged to prepare and serve dinner in most villas. And the cost of these services as well as food are usually considerably less than the cost of restaurant meals at a luxury resort.

rates are affordable when considered per person. Airport transfers are available from Puerto Plata; the mandatory meal plan is $65 per person per day. **Pros:** For all its grandeur and size it's as laid-back as a garden hammock, master suites are sumptuous indeed and have gas fireplaces, an English baker provides scones, fresh-baked cookies, breads, and cakes. **Cons:** The beach is rocky and requires reef shoes, two great Danes live on site, the staff of 8 can be a bit much. ✉ *Orchid Bay Estates 10, Orchid Bay* ☝ *Plaza Commercial Maria, Av. Maria Gomez 10, Cabrera* ☎ *809/589–8083, 809/710–1078 cell, 610/429–9616 for U.S. reservations office, or 866/845–5210* ⊕ *www.northcoastmanagement.com* ⇌ *8 bedrooms, 10 bathrooms* ♿ *Safe, dishwasher, DVD, Wi-Fi, daily maid service, cook, on-site security, hot tub, pool, gym, beachfront, bicycles, water toys, laundry facilities, no smoking* ⊟ *AE, MC, V* ⦿ *EP* ⊄ *4-night minimum.*

HOTELS & RESORTS

$$$–$$$$ 🏨 **Caliente Caribe.** This 130-acre clothing-optional resort, which has jokingly been called a naughty place, has turned out to be very nice indeed. Upon entering the reception–lobby, which flows into the main dining room, you'll first notice the naked people, but then you see the sweep of sand with primitive rock paintings. Though there are a few (nude) activities such as kayaking, snorkeling, pool volleyball, tennis, and aqua aerobics, guests are often content simply doing nothing and wearing nothing. Formerly Eden Bay, the property was purchased in 2005 by Caliente Resorts of Tampa, who brought in a praiseworthy chef and gave the property a major facelift, renovating all the rooms. Accommodations are in the main building as well as four tiers of one- to two-bedroom villas. The latter are spacious, with rattan furnishings and some tasteful, handpainted murals of palm trees. The meals, which are primarily served à la carte, are very impressive. If you want to sample this lifestyle, you can buy a day pass for $75. Airport transfers are included from either El Catey or Puerto Plata airports. **Pros:** The guests are amazingly friendly and the camaraderie contagious, caring and efficient staff (clothed), much repeat business. **Cons:** Fairly isolated (a $30 round-trip taxi from Cabrera), Seacliff rooms (least expensive) are a hike from the main facilities, guests can be nude at dinner. ✉ *Cabrera–Rio San Juan Hwy., Km 8, Abreu* ☎ *809/589–7750* ⊕ *www.calienteresorts.com* ⇌ *48 rooms, 12 studios, 62 1-bedroom villas, 4 2-bedroom villas* ♿ *In room: safe, kitchen (some), Wi-Fi. In-hotel: 2 restaurants, bars, tennis courts, pools, gym, spa, beachfront, water sports, no elevator, laundry facilities, laundry service, public Internet, public Wi-Fi, airport shuttle, parking (no fee), no kids allowed, no-smoking rooms* ⊟ *MC, V* ⦿ *AI.*

$$ 🏨 **Hotel La Catalina.** Some 4 mi from the ocean, this hillside retreat still enjoys a panoramic view of the ocean-blue. The adult-oriented getaway was carved from the cliffs in the 1980s by a French Canadian and has evolved over the years, with condominiums added gradually. However, it still retains an air of refinement and tranquillity. The hotel was purchased in 2007 by American cousins, and resident owner Tim Moller, after years of living in the D.R., communicates equally as well with his moneyed Dominican clients, the embassy crowds, Europe-

ans, and American golfers as he does with the local people. Reception is more like a boutique, where handsome jewelry and crafts, which were made by the courteous, long-term employees, are sold. Airport transfers (which can cost as much as $200) are included with a week's stay, as is a beach shuttle. Massages and pedicures can be arranged on-site. **Pros:** Rooms are pristine and clean, convivial bar serves top-shelf liquors, grounds are appealing with mature landscaping. Airport transfers (worth as much as $200) included with a week's stay. **Cons:** About 10 minutes from beaches and the golf course, decor is outdated, far (80 minutes) from Puerto Plata airport. ⊠ *Las Farrallones, Off Carretera Rio San Juan–Cabrera, 4 km (2.5 mi) east of Cabrera, Cabrera* ✛ *Turn at sign for Catalina, then continue 1.5 km, (0.9 mi) up hill to sign for Catalina, and turn left; go straight into gated community of Las Farallones* ☎ *809/589–7700* ⊕ *www.lacatalina.com* ↩ *36 rooms, 6 1-bedroom condos, 11 2-bedroom condos* ⚖ *In-room: No a/c (some), no phone, no TV, kitchen (some). In-hotel: restaurant, bar, tennis court, pools, no elevator, laundry service, public Internet, public Wi-Fi* ▤ *AE, MC, V* ⏀ *MAP.*

BEACHES

Independent travelers, true beach lovers, and those in the know have discovered the incredible beaches in this relatively isolated area west of Cabarete. Some travelers may even want to rent a car and take a day trip from the Puerto Plata, Sosúa, or Cabarete resorts, while others opt to stay in this pristine area.

Lago Dudu (⊠ *Carretera Río San Juan, Km 21, Cabrera*) is a large freshwater lake fed by an underground spring, just off the main road and hidden in the bush. The lake is so deep that scuba divers go down regularly, but rumor has it that no one has ever located the bottom. You'll be greeted by great rope swings and really cold water throughout the year. There are no facilities.

Orchid Bay Beach (⊠ *Carretera Río San Juan, Km 17, Cabrera*) is the large public beach within Orchid Bay Estates. It's seldom used by anyone but the residents of Orchid Bay villas. Very picturesque, it's swimmable in a couple of choice locations. It's also the site for the forthcoming Cristal Beach Resort.

Playa Caleton (⊠ *Carretera Río San Juan–Cabrera, Km 1, Rio San Juan*) has virtually no waves and is superb for snorkeling with caves nearby. It's a favorite for just playing around in the water. There are local food stands and souvenir shops on the beach as well.

☺ **Playa Diamonte** (⊠ *Carretera Río San Juan–Cabrera, Km 19, Cabrera*) is a very pretty beach that was formed from an estuary where an underground river sends fresh water into the ocean. The result is a broad beach that is very shallow for up to 200 feet into the ocean. This is an excellent beach if you have small children, and it has easy drive-up access.

Playa El Breton (✉ *Carretera Río San Juan–Cabrera, Km 14, Río San Juan*) is close to Cabrera within Parque Nacional Cabo Francis. It's the perfect beach for swimming, playing, searching for sea shells, and snorkeling. It has no facilities and is quiet and uncluttered.

Playa Entrada (✉ *Carretera Rio San Juan–Cabrera, Km 21, La Entrada*) is one of the longest beaches on the North Coast and has been too remote for many years. However, that means the beach is exceptionally pristine and unspoiled, the site of several move location shoots, which have taken advantage of its remoteness. Though technically in La Entrada, it's part of the municipality of Cabrera. You'll find a few beach shacks that sell cold drinks and Dominican snacks.

Playa Grande (✉ *Carretera Río San Juan–Cabrera, Km 12, Río San Juan*) next to the famous golf course of the same name. This beach has been named one of the top beaches in the world. It's a gorgeous stretch of sand with food stands and souvenir shops. Regrettably more development is on the table at this writing.

Playa Preciosa (✉ *Carretera Río San Juan–Cabrera, Km 12, Río San Juan*) is next to Playa Grande. It's a favorite of the locals because it's so beautiful. You have to descend a sandy bank to reach the completely open beach, which has excellent conditions for surfing (be careful). There are no facilities, though the views are stunning.

SPORTS & THE OUTDOORS

Those staying in and around Cabrera will have many opportunities to get out and enjoy the sporting life, whether it's on horseback or under the sea. Gri Gri Lagoon in Rio San Juan is a great diving and snorkeling destination. Most guests in the region will choose to make all arrangements through their villa management company. North Coast Management, the primary agent in these parts, has a reputation for knowing all the best local operators. Iguana Mama will allow guests staying in the Cabrera area to join their organized tours and activities, but they will not come out just for small groups. Other dive and activity outfitters in Sosúa and Cabarete offer trips to the Cabrera area.

DIVING & SNORKELING

Gri Gri Lagoon in Rio San Juan is the region's best dive and snorkeling destination. There are some exciting caves to explore, and most of the top dive operators out of Sosúa offer trips here, which you can join. Brianda Tours (*see ⇨ Tour Options, in North Coast Essentials, below*) also offers trips here. After snorkeling and/or diving near or into some sea caves and then visiting a beach and snorkeling in a quiet cove, your boat will return for a brief and quiet ride through the mangrove swamp, teeming with tropical sea birds. There are some 20 dive sites in the area with amazing coral, caves, and underwater mountains, as well as a wide variety of colorful sea life. Expect to pay $85 for two dives, $50 if you're just snorkeling. While snorkelers can also negotiate with the local boatmen to take them out into the lagoon, we don't recommend this as an option because of safety concerns.

GOLF

Playa Grande Golf Course (⊠ *Carretera Río San Juan–Cabrera, Km 9*
☎ *809/582–0860* ⊕ *www.playagrande.com*), between Río San Juan
and Cabrera on the North Coast, is sometimes described as the Pebble
Beach of the Caribbean, with 10 holes along cliffs overlooking the
Atlantic Ocean. It carries the signature of Robert Trent Jones Sr. In
December 2008 the course is expected to close for an extended, major
renovation. Upon reopening, the course will probably be restricted to
guests of a new hotel planned for the club and private members. Villa
guests may or may not have privileges at the reopened course, so be
sure to check with your rental agent. At this writing green fees to play
the 18-hole, par-72 course are $120 ($90 for 9 holes); all fees includes
the cost of a mandatory cart. Caddies, also mandatory, are an additional $15 for 18 holes, $8 for 9. Dress code dictates no tank tops,
bikinis, or cutoffs.

HORSEBACK RIDING

This is ranch country, and taking a horse through the countryside just
seems like the right thing to do. Local *ranchos* have horses on-site, but
to arrange a ride, you'll need to go through your villa management
company or contact Iguana Mama (*see* ⇨ *Biking & Hiking in Sports
& the Outdoors, in Cabarete, above*). Transportation will be included.
You'll trek through the countryside and rain forest on a two- to three-
hour horse ride (depending on your stamina), either in the morning
or late afternoon, with an English-speaking guide. Refreshments are
included; children under 12 must be accompanied by an adult. Expect
to pay about $35 for an adult, $25 for a child.

SHOPPING

In general you don't come to this remote location to shop; however,
you'll just find some local souvenirs, with the Dominican rum and
coffee always a good buy. There are fewer businesses in this part of
the North Coast than in the areas closer to Puerto Plata. The shopping is coming up fast, however, and new shopping plazas are under
development.

NIGHTLIFE

Most of Cabrera's bars are local places, not really aimed at *turistas*.
But since, contrary to what you may hear in the United States, dancing rather than baseball is the true Dominican passion, you'll be able
to shake your booty all night if you're willing to search out the latest
local hot spots. The restaurant at Hotel La Catalina has a vocalist on
Friday night, and you can have dinner and just drinks in the lounge.
Babanuco's also has a fun bar scene. (*For information on both of these
restaurants, see* ⇨ *Where to Eat, above*.) Every town in the D.R. has
a patron saint, and in Cabrera the annual **Patronales Festival** in late
September lasts for nine days. The whole town comes out for loud
music and live bands on a makeshift stage. The entertainment can be

top-notch, and there are also carnival rides and a festive atmosphere that will appeal to kids.

NORTH COAST ESSENTIALS

To research prices, get advice from other travelers, and book travel arrangements, visit www.fodors.com.

TRANSPORTATION

BY AIR

Visitors to the D.R.'s North Coast generally fly into Gregorio Luperon International Airport in Puerto Plata; most major airlines have flights here. It may be cheaper for you to fly into Cibao International Airport in Santiago (*see* ⇨ *Chapter 7, Santiago & the Cibao Valley*), but you may face a two-hour drive to and from the airport if you're staying in Cabarete. If you're staying in Cabrera, you may be able to fly into El Catey International Airport in Samaná (*see Chapter 5, The Samaná Peninsula*), though most regularly scheduled flights to that airport from the United States have been suspended.

It's also possible to take a domestic flight from Higuero Airport in Santo Domingo; there are also flights from La Romana and Punta Cana (either charter or regularly scheduled service). But given the added cost, it's rarely a good deal to make this kind of complicated connection.

AIRPORTS & TRANSFERS

Gregorio Luperon International Airport is about 7 mi (11 km) east of Playa Dorada. Cibao International Airport in Santiago receives an increasing number of international flights. El Catey is a new, impressive international airport about 25 mi (40 km) west of Samaná.

If you book a package through a travel agent, your airport transfers will almost certainly be included in the price you pay, and even some private villas can arrange airport transfers. If you travel independently, then you may have to take a taxi or rent a car.

Anticipate long lines and be sure to give yourself a full two hours for international check-in. Missing luggage, particularly if you're traveling American Airlines and making a connection in Miami, are common, but your bags will almost always be delivered to your hotel the next day, though theft can be a problem.

Information Cibao International Airport (*STI* ✉ *Santiago* ☎ *809/582–4894*). **Gregorio Luperon International Airport** (*POP* ✉ *Puerto Plata* ☎ *809/586–0107 or 809/586–0219*).

BY BUS

Privately owned air-conditioned buses are the cheapest way to get around the country and connect Puerto Plata with Santo Domingo. The one-way fare is about $7.50, and the trip takes 3½ hours. Just be aware that buses can be packed, especially on weekends and holidays. For more information on these buses, see ⇨ Chapter 2, Santo Domingo.

Information **Caribe Tours** (☎ *809/221–4422*). **Linea Gladys** (☎ *809/565-1223 in Santo Domingo, 809/ 539-2134 in Puerto Plata*). **Metro Buses** (☎ *809/566–7126 in Santo Domingo, 809/586-6062 in Puerto Plata, 809/587-4711 in Santiago*).

BY CAR

The major car-rental companies operate in Puerto Plata, which has the airport of choice for most independent travelers. Prices can be high (up to $600 per week). You'll save by making your car reservation in advance.

Major Agencies **Avis** (✉ *Gregorio Luperon International Airport, Puerto Plata* ☎ *809/586–0214* ✉ *Next to Café Cito, Carretera Luperon, Playa Dorada, Puerto Plata* ☎ *809/586–7007* ✉ *Playa Dorada Plaza, Calle Duarte at Avenida 30 de Marzo, Puerto Plata* ☎ *809/320–4888*). **Budget** (✉ *Gregorio Luperon International Airport, Puerto Plata* ☎ *809/586–0413*). **Europcar** (✉ *Gregorio Luperon International Airport, Puerto Plata* ☎ *809/586-7979*). **Hertz** (✉ *Puerto Plata* ☎ *809/586–0200* ✉ *Cibao International Airport, Santiago* ☎ *809/612–7000*).

BY PUBLIC TRANSPORTATION

Motoconchos are a popular, inexpensive mode of transportation in such areas as Puerto Plata, Sosúa, and Cabarete. You can flag down one of these motorcycle taxis along rural roads and in town; rates vary from RD$20 per person for a short run, to as much as RD$100 to RD$150 between Cabarete and Sosúa (double after 6 PM).

BY TAXI

Taxis, which are government regulated, line up outside hotels and restaurants. They're unmetered, and the minimum fare is about $4, but you can bargain for less if you order a taxi away from the major hotels. Though they are more expensive, hotel taxis are the nicest and the safest option. Freelance taxis aren't allowed to pick up from hotels, so they hang out on the street in front of them. They can be half the cost per ride depending on the distance. Carry some small bills, because drivers rarely seem to have change.

Information **Taxi-Cabarete** (☎ *809/571–0767 in Cabarete*). **Taxi-Sosúa** (☎ *809/ 571–3097 in Sosúa*). **Tecni-Taxi** (☎ *809/320–7621 in Puerto Plata*).

CONTACTS & RESOURCES

EMERGENCIES

Emergency Services **Ambulance & Fire** (☎ *911*). **Police Emergencies** (☎ *809/586-2804 in Puerto Plata, 809/571–2233 in Sosúa, 809/589-7305, or 809/582–2331 in Rio San Juan/Cabrera*).

Politur (*Tourist Police* ☎ *809/775–8854 in Puerto Plata, 809/589-2831 in Rio San Juan/Cabrera*).

Medical Clinics **Clínica Dr. Brugal** (✉ *Calle José del Carmen Ariza 15, Puerto Plata* ☎ *809/586–2519*). **Centro Médico Sosúa** (✉ *Av. Martinez, Sosúa* ☎ *809/571–3949*). **Servi-Med** (✉ *Plaza La Criolla, Sosúa* ☎ *809/571–0964* ✉ *Calle Principal, next to Helados Bon, Cabarete* ☎ *809/571–0964*).

Centro Medico Cabrera (✉ *Cabrera* ☎ *809/589–7410*).

6

24-hour Pharmacies **Farmacia Deleyte** (⊠ *Av. John F. Kennedy 9, Puerto Plata* ☎ *809/586–2583*).

INTERNET, MAIL & SHIPPING

At the Playa Dorada Internet Center computers cost US$4.99 for one hour, US$2.99 for a half-hour, US$1.99 for 15 minutes. It's expensive but cheaper than the others nearby. Also, there are two phones for calling long distance, at a low 25¢ a minute, about a third of what it costs at Discount Plaza. However, you have to get them to turn down the music (they sell popular Latin CDs), and the phones are not in private booths.

Alf's Internet Center in Sosúa is next door to Alf's Tours and run by the same good people. You can buy nice refreshing juices, coffee, and snacks, as you surf the Internet. Price wise, it's the going rate, about RD$60 per hour.

There are two FujiFilms in Cabarete, one where they sell camera gear and can do color prints from digital cameras, and this one, which has a bank of computers and several phones. The manager, Luis Zabala, is more savvy than most, although his English is minimal; happily, this café is not very noisy, though open to the street. But you can have your color prints run while you surf the Internet. Expect to pay RD$30 for a half-hour, RD$45 for 45 minutes, and RD$60 per hour; annoyingly, the computer just shuts off as your time lapses, but it can be easily reset so you don't lose anything you were writing.

Internet Cafés **Alf's Tours Internet** (⊠ *Calle Pedro Clisante, Sosúa* ☎ *809/571–1013* ⊕ *www.alftour.com*). **FujiFilm** (⊠ *Calle Principal, Cabarete* ☎ *809/571–9536*). **Playa Dorada Internet Center** (⊠ *Play Dorada Plaza, near children's playground, Playa Dorada*).

Post Offices **Post Office** (⊠ *Calle 12 de Julioat Separacion, 2 blocks north of Parque Central, Puerto Plata*).

Shipping Companies **Sosúa Business Services** (⊠ *Ocean Dream Plaza, Suite 8, Cabarete* ☎ *809/571–0668* ⊠ *Calle Pedro Clisante, Sosúa* ☎ *809/571–3451*).

TOUR OPTIONS

Most North Coast travelers arrange their activities and tours through the company that sold their travel package, such as Apple Vacations or Hotel Beds. Most do a decent job, but there are a few independent tour operators in the region.

In Sosúa, multilingual Alf's Tours has been a mainstay for years.

Iguana Mama, in Cabarete, specializes in adventure sports, having a reputation for being the most safety-oriented, reliable, and fun tour company.

A relatively new company, specializing in educational, adventure, and incentive programs for groups, is Tours, Trips, Treks & Travel, which was founded by its president, Richard Weber, a veteran Iguana Mama trip leader who adheres to the tenet of experiential learning; in addition to adventure tours, the company does cultural tours, including local experts.

Brianda Tours, in Abreu, services the area from Playa Grande all the way to Cabrera and will take smaller groups than Iguana Mama. The tri-lingual staff takes clients to Gri Gri Lagoon for diving and snorkeling, on horseback riding excursions, on fishing trips, and on sightseeing tours that might include stops at local villages where you can meet the locals. Prices are moderate and can be customized for groups.

Outback Safari in Puerto Plata operates the wildly decorated open trucks that take groups into the Dominican countryside, stopping at fruit plantations, schools, and local homes to see how the people live. This will get you out of the AI compound or your luxury villa and give you more of a feel for what the countryside is like. These touristy trips may not be to the liking of some more sophisticated travelers because these are booze buses with loud music, though kids seem to like these trips. Outback goes as far as the Playa Grande area, and villa guests staying in Abreu or Cabrera can meet up with them there. Given substantial advance notice, they may provide pick-up even in Cabrera. Tours leave at either 8 or 9 AM and return at 4 or 4:30 PM; expect to pay $79.

Private tours are another option. You should expect to pay $125 a day for a guide, and figure $100 for the transportation, which can be a reasonable cost for a group of four or more. Personalized tours can include beautiful waterfalls, freshwater lagoons, secret jungle paths, or almost any other adventure you can name. Your hotel or rental villa management company will be able to hook you up with good drivers and English-speaking guides.

Information **Alf's Tours** (⊠ *Calle Pedro Clisante 12, across from North Coast Dive Center, El Batey, Sosúa* ☎ *809/571–9904 or 809/571–1013* ⊕ *www.alftour.com*). **Brianda Tours** (⊠ *Carretera Cabrera–Rio San Juan, Km 8, Abreu* ☎ *809/707–6096* ⊕ *www.briandatours.com*). **Iguana Mama** (⊠ *Cabarete* ☎ *809/571–0908* ⊕ *www. iguanamama.com*). **Outback Safaris** (⊠ *Plaza Turisol, Local 7, Ave. Luperon km 2.5, Puerto Plata* ☎ *809/244–4886* ⊕ *www.outback-safaris.com*)

Tours, Trips, Treks & Travel (⊠ *Cabarete* ☎ *809/867–8884* ⊕ *www.4Tdomrep. com*).

VISITOR INFORMATION
Oficina de Turismo (⊠ *Jose del Carmen Ariza 46, Puerto Plata* ☎ *809/586–3676*).

Santiago & the Cibao Valley

SANTIAGO, LA VEGA VIEJA, JARABACOA,
CONSTANZA

WORD OF MOUTH

"We took a day trip to Santiago. There we visited
a cigar factory, and a ranch located in the mountains. We had lunch, went horseback riding, and
then sped down a river on an inner tube."
— Michel

By Eileen
Robinson
Smith

SANTIAGO, WHICH IS IN THE province of the same name, is in the agricultural heart of this developing Caribbean country. The Dominican Republic's second city, it's approximately 90 minutes south of Cabarete on the scenic Autopista Duarte. With a population of some 750,000, it's the intellectual, educational, and cultural center of the region. It's also the economic center of the fertile Cibao Valley, where most of the country's sugar, tobacco, and coffee are grown.

The city itself has many centuries-old buildings, architectural vestiges of its Victorian heyday, a dominating cathedral, an authentic fort cum museum, fascinating side streets, and a festive covered market dating from the 1940s. Visitors often take scenic horse carriage tours to soak up the atmosphere.

This charming provincial city can be home base for exploring the D.R.'s mountainous Cordillera Central, including the towns of Jarabacoa, Constanza, and the national park area of Valle Nuevo. Nearest to Santiago is La Vega, the somewhat quaint center of lower Cibao Valley. (La Vega Vieja was one of the oldest settlements in the New World.) If you head up to the mountains, plan on staying a couple of days in one of the atmospheric yet rustic lodges, and pack warm clothing for temperatures that can feel more like fall in New England. These mountains offer a respite from the island's hot temperatures and a complete change of pace. The air is crisp and pine-scented, and around every turn in the mountain roads is a panoramic view. It can be a glorious and unexpected experience in a Caribbean island best known for its beach resorts.

EXPLORING SANTIAGO & THE CIBAO VALLEY

This diverse area is a special part of the Dominican world, and if you have sufficient time, it's worth the effort to go here. You can fly directly into Santiago's airport or drive up from Puerto Plata or even Santo Domingo. The city is worth at least a day of exploring, but if you spend the night, you can then head for the hills in the morning. La Vega is 25 minutes by car from Santiago and is not a favored tourist destination, except during its annual *Carnaval* celebration. Beyond, and in the Cordillera Mountains are Jarabacoa, Constanza, and Valle Nuevo. Jarabacoa is 36 km (22 mi) southwest of Santiago, while Constanza is another 36 km (22 mi) south of Jarabacoa. From Constanza to Valle Nuevo and the cottage complex of Villa Pajon, you follow the carretera to San Jose de Ocoa, then take the turn-off to Valle Nuevo; the total distance is about 24 km (15 mi).

Many of the towns are reachable by *gua-guas*, the local public buses and minivans, but the trip will be much more pleasant if you have your own transportation (preferably four-wheel drive, which is an absolute requirement if you plan to visit Villa Pajon), so you can meander around and up the mountain roads. Even though the distances do not sound far, you have to allow twice as much time as you would normally because of the steep, winding mountain roads. But once you arrive, you will be glad you made the effort.

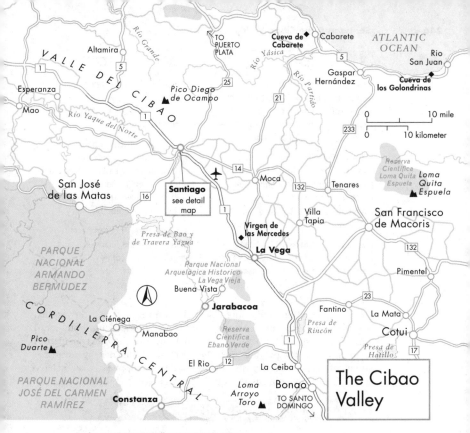

ABOUT THE RESTAURANTS

The dining scene in Santiago is not known for having a vibrant restaurant scene like Santo Domingo's. Even the city's few fine-dining establishments stick to the classics. The restaurant in Hotel Gran Almirante is generally recommendable, serving a good selection of tapas. More recently, a TGI Fridays has opened next door to the city's best hotel, emblematic of the local love of American chain restaurants. Many restaurants and cafés line the Calle del Sol, starting at the central Parque Duarte; most have outdoor seating that is great for people-watching. Similarly, down the Avenida de Monumento from the landmark Heroes monument, there are restaurants that are lively and fun, serving mainly Dominican or simple fare.

In the mountains the food ranges from the heavy Dominican specialties served at the simple *comedors* (local restaurants), to some better than basic, atmospheric restaurants, where rabbit and other game are specialties and fresh vegetables taste as if they came straight from the earth. This is strawberry country, so fresh strawberries are usually on the menu in some form.

SANTIAGO & THE CIBAO VALLEY TOP 5

Centro de Leon. Santiago's world-class art museum is worth several hours of your time, and your visit can include lunch and a tour of the replicated cigar factory, circa 1900.

Flow River Flow. An excursion to the D.R.'s mountainous Cordillera Central can include white-water rafting and visits to waterfalls, an adventure tour that is well worth your time.

Exploring Santiago. This can be done on your own, and you can use horse carriages to go the distances.

English-speaking freelance guides station themselves around the Heroes Monument. A guided city tour is another good option.

Carnaval in Santiago or La Vega. Like New Orleans' Mardi Gras, Carnival in Santiago or La Vega is one of the quintessential Dominican experiences. If you have the right spirit, it can be a fun, memorable party.

Factory Tours. This can be entertaining, when the factories produce rum, cigars, and coffee.

ABOUT THE HOTELS

In Santiago you can find a sophisticated city hotel and, near the airport, a recommendable American chain hotel. A restaurant cum hotel in an upscale suburb is of a better quality than most of the other properties in town, where the pickings are otherwise slim. In the nearby mountain towns of Jarabacoha, Constanza, and Valle Nuevo, one can really have a relaxing getaway in rustic lodges with fireplaces to take off the chill.

WHAT IT COSTS IN DOLLARS					
	¢	$	$$	$$$	$$$$
Restaurants	under $8	$8–$12	$12–$20	$20–$30	Over $30
Hotels*	Under $80	$80–$150	$150–$250	$250–$350	Over $350
Hotels**	Under $125	$125–$250	$250–$350	$350–$450	Over $450

*EP, BP, CP **AI, FAP, MAP Restaurant prices are per person for a main course at dinner and do not include the 15% V.A.T. and 10% service charge. Hotel prices are per night for a double room in high season, excluding 15% V.A.T. and 10% service charge.

SANTIAGO

145 km (90 mi) northwest of Santo Domingo, 55 km (34 mi) southwest of Puerto Plata, 60 km (37 mi) south of Cabarete.

The second city of the D.R., where many past presidents were born, is reached by the Autopista Duarte, the four-lane highway from Puerto Plata that follows a centuries old trade route that is even still dotted with sugar mills, many of which are being renovated by the Office of Cultural Patrimony and the Brugal Rum company. This industrial center has a surprisingly charming, provincial feel, and a gentility characterizes the entire city, which has a slower pace and less crime than the capital. The city is dominated by the families of sugar barons, who have been making their fortunes from rum for centuries, the cigar kings, and bankers; there is a hierarchy of moneyed families in this city, and their presence and influence is felt. The women of Santiago are said to be among the fairest and best-looking in the country, and the men are true *caballeros* (gentlemen), often donning Panama hats. Santiago's full name—Santiago de Los Caballeros—comes from the fact that it was founded by a group of 30 Spanish noblemen.

Generations of Italian and Cuban immigrants, including the famous Fuentes (the cigar Fuentes), have become successful in everything from the restaurant business to cigar manufacturing, adding flavor to the ethnic mix. Like Santo Domingo, real Dominicans live here—entire generations—not just the transplants who live in hotel housing in resort areas like Punta Cana, which never had an identity before it was developed.

Traditional yet progressive, Santiago is still relatively new to the tourist scene but already has several thriving restaurants and hotels. It's definitely worth setting aside some time to explore the city. Some colonial-style buildings—with wrought-iron details and tiled porticos—date from as far back as the 1500s. Others are from the Victorian era, with the requisite gingerbread latticework and fanciful colors, while more recent construction is nouveau Victorian. Old Town Santiago is roughly the area from the centralized park, Parque Duarte to the Fort and then to the Monument. It takes in Duarte Street, to Independence and includes Las Carreras Avenue Mella Street, San Luis Street, August 16, March 30, Sabana Larga, Luperon, Cuba streets, Salvador Cucurullo, and Benito Moncion streets and Avenida Monumento.

Santiago is also the center of the island's cigar industry, and the Arturo Fuente factory is in the free zone here. Cafés and restaurants abound on the Calle del Sol, and on weekends the outdoor cafés allow you to watch the world of Santiago go by. This is a great, feel-good city that is often underestimated. Inland, there are no pearl-white beaches, but in the nearby foothills and mountains of the Cordillera chain, there are icy rivers and little natural *balnearios* (swimming pools).

WHAT TO SEE

A relaxing and popular way to see the sights of Santiago is on a horse and buggy ride. This is definitely slow travel, but it's very atmospheric to be clicking along closer to street level and not locked up in a bus or taxi. You get a real sense of what life must have been life in a more genteel era. Horse and buggy drivers congregate around both Duarte Park and the Heroes Monument. Expect to pay about $15 for a 30-minute ride (bargain if your Spanish can take it) and settle on the price before you trot on.

Numbers in the margin correspond to points of interest on the Santiago map.

Bathroom Break

If you're coming to Santiago from Santo Domingo, all the *capitale-ños* stop at **Parador Jaracanda** (⊠*Autopista Duarte, between Santo Domingo and Santiago, at northern edge of Bonao* ☎*809/525–5590*) because it has the cleanest and most well-maintained restrooms on the highway. However, it's accessible whether you're traveling north (on the left) or south (on the right). You can also get food. Dominicans prefer their own heavy specialties from the buffet, but lighter eaters may prefer yogurt, cheese, fresh-baked goods, tea, or coffee to go. You can also get sandwiches. There's an attached hotel if you need to stop for the night, and it's a fine place for that, with the 22 rooms costing less than $40 a double. It's a possible accommodation for a Carnaval overnight, it you cannot secure lodging in Santiago.

❼ Bermudez Rum Distillery. This is a rum-making island, and some tourists look forward to the free booze that comes with a tour of one of the factories. One of the Dominican Republic's three Bs—Brugal and Barcelo being the other two major rum producers—Bermudez used to be numero uno, but it now, reputedly, holds the third-rated spot. On your tour you'll learn that there are three types of rum; first is white rum (the least expensive variety), then gold or amber, and finally *anejo* (aged rum, which is usually sipped like brandy and coupled with a choice Dominican cigar). It's easiest to tour this processing and bottling plant as part of a city tour because a visit is by appointment only. The tour itself is not very exciting unless someone on the line misses a beat and the bottles go crashing into each other and everyone claps. ⊠*Pueblo Nuevo* ☎*809/947–4201* ☒*Free* ☉ *Weekdays 9–noon and 2–5.*

❷ Catedral de Santiago Apóstol. Santiago's cathedral dominates the south side of Parque Duarte. The lovely pink stucco adds to the calming effect that the park has on this part of the old city. Its construction spanned decades from 1868 to 1895, and it replaced an earlier cathedral destroyed by an earthquake in 1842. The end result is a mix of Gothic and neoclassic architecture. The most noteworthy features are the stained-glass windows, which are actually contemporary designs by Dominican artist Dincón Mora. In the cathedral lies the remains (in a marble tomb) of a Santiago native son, Ulises Heureaux, a former president of the dictator sort. ⊠*Parque Duarte, Calles 16 de Agosto to Benito Monción* ☎*No phone* ☒*Free* ☉ *Mon.–Sat. 7–9 AM, Sun. 7 AM–8 PM.*

❾ Centro León. Without question, this is a world-class cultural center for the Dominican arts. A postmodern building with an interior space full of light from a crystal dome, the center includes several attractions, including a multimedia biodiversity show, a museum dedicated to the history of the D.R., a simulated local market, a dramatic showcase of Dominican art and sculpture, galleries for special exhibits, a sculpture garden, an aviary, classrooms, and a replica of the León family's first cigar factory, where a dozen cigar rollers are turning out handmade

Fodor'sChoice ★

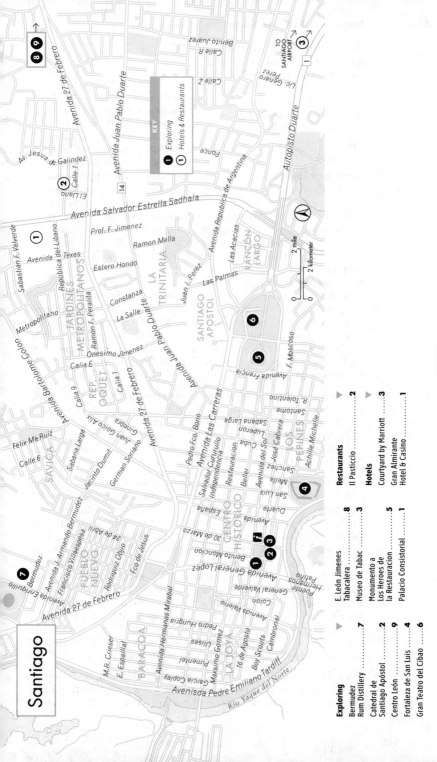

Santiago

KEY

- ● Exploring
- ① Hotels & Restaurants

Exploring ▶

Bermudez Rum Distillery	**7**
Catedral de Santiago Apóstol	**2**
Centro León	**9**
Fortaleza de San Luis	**4**
Gran Teatro del Cibao	**6**

E. León Jimenes Tabacalera	**8**
Museo de Tabac	**3**
Monumento a Los Heroes de la Restauracion	**5**
Palacio Consistorial	**1**

Restaurants ▶

Il Pasticcio	**2**

Hotels ▶

Courtyard by Marriott	**3**
Gran Almirante Hotel & Casino	**1**

cigars. There's even a first-rate cafeteria and a museum shop where you can buy high-quality, artsy souvenirs and jewelry. ⊠ *Ave. 27 de Febrero 146, Villa Progresso* ☎ *809/582–2315* ⊕ *www.centroleon.org. do* ⊠ *RD$50, RD$150 guides in English* ⊙ *Exhibitions Tues.–Sun. 9–6, public areas daily 9–9.*

❹ **Fortaleza de San Luis.** Newly opened to the public, the fort was a military stronghold from the late 17th century right up through the 1970s, when it became a prison. Its most recent reincarnation is as a museum showcasing Air Force weaponry from World Wars I and II, as well as weapons and artifacts

from the colonial days, including a collection of Spanish coins. The artwork is not stellar, but there are some Taíno artifacts and primitive art and even some Trujillo-era art from the 1950s. The Generalissimo apparently had an insatiable sexual appetite and for it was named "the goat"; there are some fascinating caricatures of him in that guise. The city's 19th-century clock tower is also here. ⊠ *Calle San Luis at Calle Boy Scouts* ☎ *809/724–7276* ⊠ *Free* ⊙ *Daily 9–5.*

❻ **Gran Teatro del Cibao.** Santiago's main performing arts theater was built in the 1980s and is often claimed to be a modern marvel of a theater. Not much happens in the mammoth landmark these days, and it's not so beautiful. Tours are not allowed, though you can always attend the occasional theater or opera production. ⊠ *Av. Monumento, across from Parque Monumento and Monumento a Los Heroes.*

❽ **E. León Jimenes Tabacalera.** You can gain an appreciation for the art and skill of Dominican cigar making by taking a tour of this company's cigar factories, which may be among the best offered. Also known as La Aurora Cigar Factory, it's a hard-working Dominican institution (since 1903) that is international and multinational, exporting some of the world's best cigars to the United States, Puerto Rico, Canada, Mexico, and Europe. It's owned by a premier Santiago family who run a classy tour. You will marvel as you watch the cigar rollers roll those leaves, glue, cut, tap, and then move on to the next one. The process can seem a bit repetitious, but nonetheless it's fascinating if you've never seen it done. Almost everyone ends up buying some beautifully packaged cigars in the factory store. The tour takes approximately 90 minutes. ⊠ *Av. 27 de Febrero 146, Villa Progresso* ☎ *809/563–1111 or 809/535–5555* ⊠ *Free* ⊙ *Tues.–Fri. 9–noon and 2–5:30.*

❸ **Museo de Tabac.** This museum, which is in an old tobacco warehouse, is a tribute to this cigar-producing region and a good historical introduction to an important Dominican business. Visitors will learn everything that they didn't know about tobacco, from when it's a leaf in the ground to when it's hand-rolled to create excellent cigars. It's not the greatest museum you have ever been to, but if you're in town and interested in the subject, it's worth the time. ⊠ *Parque Duarte, Calle 30 de Marzo, at Calle Aug. 16* ☎*No phone* 🖃*Free* ⊙*Tues.–Fri. 9–noon and 2–5:30.*

⑤ **Monumento a Los Heroes de la Restauracion** *(Monument to the Heroes)* is
Fodor'sChoice a huge attraction here. Vela Zanetti painted the murals that decorate
★ its walls, and they show the distinct influences of Diego Rivera. The topmost observation level gives an impressive view of the sprawling city. Recently completed, a multimillion dollar renovation is ingenious, with dioramas, a Carnaval costume display, and statues of the heroes done in a bronze-look-alike composition. Although it began its life as a monument to the dictator Trujillo, when it was erected in the 1940s, the government changed the name and focused on Trujillo's assassination, rededicating it to those heroes who died between 1863 and 1865 in the war to free the country from Spain. In the lovely park that surrounds the monument, the same kind of sculptures sit whimsically on park benches. ⊠*Av. Monumento* ☎*No phone* 🖃*Free* ⊙*Tues.–Sun. 9–6.*

① **Palacio Consistorial.** This is another tribute to Trujillo's love of opulence, and in this case the city is grateful to have such a grand example of European neoclassic architecture. The former town hall has become an integral thread in the fabric of life here. Old men sit outside and play dominoes, directing *turistas* into the building, which is the local headquarters of the Ministry of Culture and is a center for cultural programs. It hosts some fascinating contemporary art exhibits as well as a little museum that tells the story of the city. Annually during Carnival, winning masks are hung for all to see. El Palacio is one of the landmarks that sit smack on the tree-shaded central park and next to a revered, private social club, Sociedad Centro de Recreo, an old haunt of Trujillo's (established in 1894, it's still owned by the Bermudez Rum family). ⊠*Parque Duarte, Calle de Sol and Benito Monción* ☎*No phone* 🖃*Free* ⊙*Tues.–Fri. 9–noon and 2:30–6.*

**OFF THE
BEATEN
PATH**
Take a coffee break! Dominicans always do, and this one is free. The **Natura Bella** coffee factory is on the Autopista Duarte between Puerto Plata and Santiago, just south of town of Navarette on your right if you're headed toward Santiago (on the left if you're headed toward Puerto Plata). Take a break and have a sample of any of their organic (USDA certified) coffees or even an espresso. If you truly want to gain some coffee knowledge, call ahead—the Italian owner speaks English—and request a tasting (like a wine tasting). The South American, quality-control expert will teach you a thing or two, including how certain blends have a citrusy taste! Of course, they would like it if you would purchase a pound or two (though there is no pressure). And why not? Fresh organic coffee is a superior product, and the artsy packaging makes it an even better gift. When you call to make your tasting reservation, you can ask for more detailed directions. ⊠*Villa Gonzalez, Autopista Santiago-Navarrete, Las Lavas* ☎*809/880–4144* 🖃*Free* ⊙*Mon.–Sat. 9–5.*

A Cigar Family's Charitable Trust

What you see when you drive the dirt road to Chateau de la Fuente, the tobacco plantation of Arturo Fuente Cigars, looks like a dream vision. A pristine yellow-and-white complex rises from an uncultivated field with a primary school (through 11th grade), medical clinic, laboratory, pharmacy, multiuse community center, baseball stadium, basketball and volleyball courts, and more. At this writing, the Arturo Sandoval School of Music was slated to open in fall 2008. The Cigar Family Charitable Foundation built this rural miracle.

In 1992, when Carlos Fuente Jr. (Carlito) and his father, Carlos Fuente, bought these cow pastures, they were nothing but mud; the road was nearly impassable. Ragged children would run alongside the car and beg, an activity that continued right up until 2004, when the Fuente family charity and the Newman family, their distribution partners in the United States, built this complex.

Since 2001 additional donations have been received, including a bus from Metro Bus Company, a communal kitchen from a well-known restaurant group, and a baseball stadium, sponsored by Marvin Shanken, publisher of *Cigar Aficionado*. In a country where litter is omnipresent and schools characteristically are dirty and scrawled with graffiti, this one has still looks brand-new, with landscaping as attractive as that of a gated, residential community. The school houses 448 students, and will be adding a 12th grade.

The Foundation's generosity extends to the community, with an astounding litany of outreach projects already completed: construction of clean-water stations; extension of electricity to homes, new bridges over rivers; new sanitation programs; repairs to existing community health facilities and schools; nutrition, prenatal, and preventative medicine programs.

Unlike many other organizations, 100% of every dollar contributed goes directly to the charitable projects. The Fuentes and Newman families underwrite all administrative, legal, accounting, office, and marketing costs.

Carlito Fuente is a deeply caring, sensitive, and sincere person, who transmits his intensity, energy, passion, and dreams to those he encounters. "There is no greater love than that of family," Carlito says ardently. Now he has an extended family with two branches—his cigar family of friends and associates, who have helped make all this possible, and the children and families within some 11 communities who consider him their beloved patriarch.

WHERE TO EAT

$–$$ ✕ **Camp David Ranch.** This well-established landmark restaurant is in an upscale neighborhood in the hills about 20 minutes outside Santiago. The restaurant was opened in 1989 by Jose Ml. Bermudez, a visionary, businessman, collector, and newspaper writer. Though it was never a ranch, nor a camp, his son's name is David. You may be surprised by the urban chic decor, with ultrasuede couches and Wi-Fi. This surprising restaurant cum hotel is heralded for its delicious lunches, and this is the best time to see the magnificent views. Sit on the terrace, enjoy the sounds of sophisticated music, and experience the kind of seamless service you would expect in a fine-dining restaurant back home. Recommended on the menu are the authentic Caesar salad, filet mignon with Roquefort sauce (medium-rare), or a shellfish paella. Dominican specialties are present as well. The menu is the same at dinner, when the nocturnal view is spectacular—so many twinkling lights below. The tastefully decorated, oversize hotel rooms start at $40 a night. Be sure to see the vintage car collection, which once belonged to Trujillo. ⊠ *Carretera Luperón, Km 7.5 and follow signs, Guarboquery* ☎ *809/276–6400* ⊕ *www.campdavidranch.com* ▤ *AE, D, MC, V.*

> ### TRUJILLO'S CADDIES
>
> A magnetic attraction for Camp David—particularly for car-lovers and those who remember the 1950s—is a unique collection made up of Cadillacs and jeeps that once belonged to Dictator Trujillo and his son. Vintage models include Trujillo's renowned 1956 black Cadillac Fleetwood with two horns mounted on its left flank, and a smashing yellow and black Caddie, as well as his son Ramis's army jeep, a 1954 Willy's Jeep C63. (Ramis was commander in chief of the armed services) are parked right in the contemporary, cocktail lounge.

$ ✕ **Il Pasticcio.** Everyone from college students to cigar kings, presidents to politicos, movie producers to movie stars packs this eccentrically decorated culinary landmark. Tourists take photos of the new bathrooms with their ornate mirrors and Romanesque plaster sinks. Chef-owner Paolo, a true *paisano*, makes this bungalow a personality palace. (He's just added a new yellow Vespa to his collection on display.) His mouthwatering creations are authentic and fresh. Try the great antipasto selections, or commence with the Pasticcio salad, with smoked salmon, mozzarella, anchovies, capers, and baby arugula. Paolo couples fresh pastas with unexpected sauces, like gnocchi with puttanesca. Even the bread service comes with three sauces, one is like pesto, another Pomodoro, and the best is a creamy anchovy sauce (these sauces can be had on pasta, too). Finish with a pony of lemoncello and the best tiramisu outside of Venice. ⊠ *5, Calle 3, at Av. Del Llano, Cerros de Gurabo* ☎ *809/582–6061 or 809/276–5466* ▤ *AE, MC, V* ⊗ *Closed Mon.*

FodorsChoice ★

¢–$$ ✕ **Tipico Bonao.** Two similarly named sister restaurants stand on opposite sides of the highway outside Santiago so they can catch drivers coming from both directions. Savvy Dominican city-dwellers recommend the sisters, saying that they are the offspring of a caring family and that service is professional. The best news for travelers: the restrooms are clean and well-supplied. You can get a good breakfast here: Dominican (fried salami, cheese, eggs, etc.), American (pancakes), or French (croissants and cappuccino). The five-page menu includes nearly every typical Dominican dish, with highlights being roast pork and Asopao with crab claw meat. *Nueva* offerings are attempts to please foreigners, including Baskin-Robbins ice cream and fresh strawberries. ⊠ *Autopista Duarte, Km 90, Monseñor Nouel* ☎ *809/296–6000* ⊠ *Autopista Duarte, Km 83* ☎ *809/525–3941* ▤ *MC, V.*

WHERE TO STAY

¢ **Camp David Ranch.** In a suburban area 20 minutes outside Santiago, this hotel and restaurant complex offers gorgeous views of the Cibao Valley. And indeed it's modern, with all the creature comforts you would expect; you may be surprised by how upscale and urban chic the lobby is (there's even Wi-Fi). Though well-known as a restaurant not everyone tells you that it has three floors of hotel rooms, too. English is spoken, and overnight guests can have their breakfast at the adjoining restaurant. The tastefully decorated, oversize rooms have balconies, most with incomparable views of the city and the Valley. It's best to have a rental car here (the hotel is well signposted), but if you don't feel like driving, the sum you will save on accommodations will make the taxi fares worthwhile. **Pros:** Clean air and manicured grounds, no noise, excellent value. **Cons:** Fairly far from town, hotel has only the single restaurant, first-floor rooms do not have views. ⊠ *Carretera Luperón, Km 7.5, Guarbo* ☎ *809/276–6400* ⊕ *www.campdavidranch. com* ⟳ *35 rooms* ⚲ *In-hotel: restaurant, room service, laundry service, public Wi-Fi, no elevator, no-smoking rooms, parking (free)* ⊟ *AE, D, MC, V.*

$ **Courtyard by Marriott Santiago.** This squeaky-clean American hotel has a small lobby as attractive as a stateside J.W. Marriott. The plush bedding and bevy of pillows in the contemporary rooms are normally found only in the priciest resorts; the thick wall-to-wall carpeting is certainly not the norm, either. Bravo! Breakfast is an ample buffet, and the food in the restaurant is generally quite good, including great cheeseburgers with imported U.S. beef. Ten minutes from downtown, the hotel is convenient for business people, who fly into Santiago, catch the free shuttle, utilize the meeting rooms and 24-hour business center, taking out cash from the ATM here. **Pros:** Many staffers speak English, personalized service is the norm, discounted weekend rates, lovely pool area. **Cons:** Small compared to a grand hotel, no fine-dining restaurant, not in the middle of town. ⊠ *Autopista Duarte, Km 9, Santiago* ☎ *809/612–7000* ⊕ *www.marriott.com* ⟳ *138 rooms, 33 suites* ⚲ *In-room: safe, refrigerator, Ethernet, Wi-Fi. In-hotel: restaurant, room service, pool, laundry service, public Internet, public Wi-Fi, airport shuttle, parking (no fee), no-smoking rooms* ⊟ *AE, MC, V* ⦿ *EP.*

$-$$ **The Hodelpa Gran Almirante Hotel & Casino.** The best hotel in down-
★ town Santiago attracts business travelers with its great business center and executive level with panoramic city views, but the pool and sundeck, fitness room, and steam and sauna are equally attractive to tourists. Guest rooms are large but utilitarian and could use a cheery redecoration, but new bedding and plush pillows let you sleep with the angels. But it's worth the supplement to stay on the executive floor, where the rooms have been given a clean, modern look and where a 30-minute massage and a free nightly happy hour are among the extra perks. A most appealing breakfast buffet with excellent service is an option; by night, you can enjoy a meal or Spanish-style tapas in the same restaurant. You can have a calming Asian-inspired massage, and there's a sauna in the fitness center. A new contemporary lounge–disco offers some entertainment at night. **Pros:** The best hotel in town, fun

casino, great pool with warm Jacuzzi. **Cons:** Service from the friendly staff can be inconsistent, hotel lacks the elegance of a grand hotel. ✉*Av. Estrella Sadhala, corner of Calle 10, Santiago* ☎*809/580–1992* ⊕*www.hodelpa.com* 🛏*151 rooms, 4 suites* ⊘*In-room: safe, refrigerator. In-hotel: 2 restaurants, room service, bars, pool, gym, laundry facilities, concierge, executive floor, public Internet, public Wi-Fi, parking (free), no-smoking rooms* ⊟*AE, MC, V* ⦿*EP.*

EN ROUTE

About 3 mi (5 km) north of La Vega is Santo Cerro (the Holy Mount), site of a miraculous apparition of the Virgin and therefore many local pilgrimages. The Convent of La Merced is here, and the views of the Cibao Valley are breathtaking. The town's remarkable Concepción de la Vega Church was constructed in 1992 to commemorate the 500th anniversary of the discovery of America. The unusual modern Gothic style—all curvaceous concrete columns, arches, and buttresses—is striking.

NIGHTLIFE

Santiago does not have the number of nightspots that the capital has, but there are a few good ones, as Santiagoans like to dress up, go out, and feel their dances. The city is under the same curfew restrictions as Santo Domingo, so nightspots must close at midnight during the week and 2 AM on Friday and Saturday nights; casinos in hotels do not have to abide by the curfew. It's not unusual to see a bevy of cars, the majority late-model SUVs, beelining it to the Hotel Hodelpa Gran Almirante at 2 AM to play the tables at its casino. That hotel's Cosmopolitan Bar can sometimes stay open past curfew, and it will be a happening place on those nights.

As there are fewer places, those that are "in" are frequented by all age groups not just the young and good-looking. In addition to those listed, Il Pasticcio, reviewed here as a restaurant, is also a nightly gathering place. Patrons are open and welcoming, none more so than the Italian owner Paolo. People table hop, and it is easy to make new friends.

BARS

Cosmopolitan Bar (✉*Hotel Gran Almirante & Casino, Av. Estrella Sadhala, corner of Calle 10* ☎*809/580–1992*) is the latest reincarnation of the hotel's bar, redone in strikingly contemporary white and blue decor. It's one of the in-spots for the local in-crowd and, of course, hotel guests. Martinis are fashionable, perhaps because martini glasses are part of the graphic art.

Moma Bar (✉*Centro Plaza Internacional, Av. Juan Pablo Duarte at Calle Ponce* ☎*809/724–6781*) is named after the art museum in New York City and is a truly descriptive name because the design is modern and contemporary, just like the Jazz, Spanish rock, and electronic music that plays there.

CASINOS

The **Casino at Hotel Gran Almirante** (✉ *Hotel Gran Almirante & Casino, Av. Estrella Sadhala, corner of Calle 10* ☏ *829/582–7304*) is similar to a small Vegas casino, offering craps, poker, roulette, black jack, Texas Hold 'em, and slot machines. It's well managed, and service is particularly good; drinks are served to players. The casino stays open nightly until 5 AM. Special activities have included various casino promotions, live bands, and even dominoes competitions, and the latter are fun to watch since the game is a traditional Latin one, popular among older gentlemen.

DANCE CLUBS

La Dolce Lounge (✉ *Plaza Zona Rosa, Av. Juan Pablo Duarte at La Salle St.* ☏ *809/971–0415*) has modern decor and an excellent environment for partying, but on some weekend nights when live bands play on the expansive stage, the crowds can be wild and the atmosphere more suitable to the young.

LA VEGA

50 mi (80 km) south of Puerto Plata, 25 mi (40 km) southwest of Santiago.

Founded in 1495 by Christopher Columbus, La Vega is the site of one of the oldest settlements in the New World. Gold was discovered here by the Spanish in the 1490s, and they also established the first mint in the New World here. The original settlement, now referred to as La Vega Vieja, was destroyed by a hurricane. El Parque de Flores is the town's central park and has a delightful, contemporary water fountain. The brightly painted, centuries-old buildings surrounding it are being restored under a beautification project of President Leonel Fernandez. Plans are to have an ongoing exhibition of carnival masks in one of them.

A commercial center for the surrounding farms, it's not a tourist magnet except in February, when La Vegas is justly celebrated for its Carnival, reputed to be the best in the country. The celebration dates back to the first Spanish settlers, and at this time the normally reserved, hardworking townspeople can become rowdy, especially when joined by nearly 100,000 fellow Dominicans and tourists. The Presidente flows faster than the water in the fountain during Carnaval, so be careful when driving during this time since Dominicans are not known for being so disciplined about not driving while intoxicated. But in general, it's a pretty safe party, with good security, and it's fun. Just book accommodations far in advance since even Santiago is busy during this time with its own Carnaval.

Crowds sit in bleachers erected along the parade route or join the organized, costumed groups who are the official marchers. Costumes can be lavish, heavy, and wildly decorated—otherworldly, even. La Vega is known for its distinctively haunting devil masks. These creations are intricate, fanciful gargoyles painted in surreal colors; spiked horns and

Mask Maker

Just days before Carnaval, young mask maker Miguel Morine Morte was still working feverishly to finish some masks for a La Vegan troupe. His older brother and mentor, Melvin Antonio Morte, was off to get a visa for a European trip (he and his masks would be part of a contingent promoting the Dominican Republic as a tourist destination).

After Miguel dries the *diablo conjuelo* (limping devil) masks on a clothes line after they have been painted. (That particular name is the registered name for one of the local Carnaval groups, which has some 160 members, and each member would require a mask.) The devil had immense horns like barbed branches, an elongated nose, and a leering smile and rows of long teeth. The mask was painted in the colors of 2007, white and apple green. Such an art object costs US$1,030, which is not bad compared to the heavy, ornate costumes priced at more than US$4,000. The prices are high because each mask takes the artisan and his assis-

tants seven days to make. This is good money in a country where the poorest citizens don't make that much in an entire year.

The 20 year old, who had started painting for his brother when he was six, insisted that his business wasn't just about the money: "The *conetos* (masks typical of La Vega's Carnaval), are a cultural tradition, not just in my country but in many others around the world like Brazil, even Germany." He went on to explain the process of fabricating a mask. First a clay mold is sculpted and secured with nails through the head. Then a mixture of gesso (chalk) and acrylic is applied and allowed to dry. It's painted and dried again. Miguel even produced a set of dental work: "In earlier times, they would use real cows' teeth, but now we have a mold for them too."

How might a tourist acquire such a mask? Miguel says, "*Turistas* can ask a wearer when the parade is over if they would like to sell theirs. Some do, and the going rate is half of what it cost them, say $500."

cows' teeth (originally real but now simulated) lend an eerie authenticity. Several artisans work in dark, cramped studios throughout the area, their skills having been passed down for generations.

⚠ Before you dance wildly in the street, be forewarned that some of the young male marchers snap cowhide whips, so you need to stay clear. Their buddies wield hard-rubber, faux animal bladders and whack people in the butt.

JARABACOA

43 mi (70 km) south of Santiago.

Nature lovers should consider a trip to Jarabacoa, in the mountainous region known rather wistfully as the Dominican Alps (altitude 2,666 feet). Alas, the town is not pristine like a real Alpine village, though some of the buildings strive for the look. The clean mountain air is contaminated by the many *motoconchos* that scoot around the downtown.

It's far more hectic than you imagine it will be, and the only peace and tranquillity is found outside of town. Still, the buzz of activity and the European visitors all make Jarabacoa a fun place to visit. The central park is quite pleasant and is surrounded by some decent restaurants as well as a pretty Catholic Church.

> **DID YOU KNOW?**
>
> You may think that you have tasted new potatoes, but unless you live in Idaho, you probably have never tasted a really fresh potato until you have had one straight from the fields of Constanza and Valle Nuevo. It's an amazing difference.

But a lot of the joy of visiting Jarabacoa is the opportunity to take excursions on foot, horseback, or by motorcycle taxi to the surrounding waterfalls and forests—quite incongruous in such a tropical country. Other activities include adventure tours, particularly white-water rafting or canoe trips, canyoning, jeep safaris, and paragliding, trekking, and mountain-biking. Unless you plan to climb Pico Duarte, most of these excursions are more tourist adventures than solitary eco-tours. Accommodations in the area run the gamut from bare-bones to rustic-but-homey on up to one hotel of international standards.

WHERE TO STAY & EAT

$-$$ ✕ **El Bambu.** The region's rocky, fast-flowing rivers are much of the appeal of Jarabacoa. This social club along the Yanqui River, has a suspension bridge leading to terrace seating, walkways, inviting pools, and a bar, all along the river. In addition to the main restaurant, there's a large pavilion where a DJ plays, as well as a piano bar. Sunday lunch is the busiest time here, and if you like your music loud and parties fierce, this is the time to come. If you are looking for a more quiet repast, come midweek for a long lunch with a bottle of a Chilean *Reserva*, when you can enjoy the music of the river. The menu is largely upscale Dominican cuisine, and some of the standouts include pumpkin soup, yucca croquettes, sea bass in garlic sauce, and the house specialty—rabbit in red wine sauce. It's delicious indeed, although you may find as many bones as meat. Side dishes are extra! ⊠ *Carretera Jarabacoa, Manabao, Km 2½* ✛ *16 mi (26 km) north of Jarabacoa* ☎ *809/656–0026 or 809/501–3020* ⊕ *www.jarabacoariverclub.com* ⌘ *Reservations essential* ▤ *AE, MC, V.*

■ **TIP➔** The Jarabacoa River Club was also constructing 55 hotel rooms at this writing in early 2008. The first phase offers two tiers on a hillside; units promise to be spacious, if not a decorator's dream, with a motel look rather than the kind of atmospheric, natural materials like pine, bamboo, and thatching that were used for the attractive restaurant. Check the Jarabacoa River Club Web site for information on rates.

¢ ▦ **Hotel Gran Jimenoa.** On the river of the same name, this is an upscale hotel with a central pool that segues into gardens ornamented with a small waterfall that mimics the river's, and the river is overlooked by the hotel's restaurant, Piedras Del Río. A narrow suspension bridge leads to a palapa-roofed karaoke bar. The hotel's choice rooms are in the Río building, which are set back but offers river views; the primo ones are on the second and third floors. Rooms are large and are nicely decorated. Rates go up on Friday and Saturday nights, and in summer and holidays expect higher prices and mandatory meal plans. ■ TIP→ **River-view rooms are the same price, so request one.** Pros: Rooms have dated decor, staff and management both professional and caring, nice sauna. **Cons:** A sizeable conference center means that big business groups tend to take over midweek, 10 minutes from town. ⊠ *Av. Confluenzia, at entrance to Los Corrilitos, Jarabacoa* ☎ *809/574–6304 or 809/574–4345* ⊕ *www.granjimenoa.com* ⌁ *60 rooms, 1 suite, 2 apartments* ⓑ *In-room: safe (some). In-hotel: restaurant, room service, bar, pool, no elevator, laundry service, public Internet, public Wi-Fi, parking (no fee), some pets allowed* ⊟ *AE, MC, V* � ⎁*BP.*

ADVENTURE TOURS

Iguana Mama (⊠ *Cabarete* ☎ *809/571–0908* ⊕ *www.iguanamama. com*), the adventure-tour operator based in Cabarete, offers a large variety of tours and activities in the Jarabacoa area. This experienced, highly recommended company is a good choice if you're staying in Puerto Plata or Cabarete and do not wish to make the trip to Jarabacoa on your own since they will take care of all of the transportation details for you. *For more information, see* ⇨ *Biking & Hiking under Sports & the Outdoors in Cabarete in Chapter 5, The North Coast.*

In Jarabacoa, safety and professionalism can mean the difference between life and death in the mountains and on the rivers. The undisputed adventure operator adhering to that criteria is **Rancho Baiguate** (⊠ *La Joya, Jarabacoa* ☎ *809/574–4940* ⊕ *www.ranchobaiguate. com*). Their roster of activities runs the gamut, from canyoning to river rafting to mountain-biking, not to mention trekking on foot or horseback. The company will even help you do the strenuous climb up Pico Duarte, which is attempted by only a few hardy souls every year. The company even offers lodging on its ranch, but the facilities may be a bit too rustic for typical American travelers.

CONSTANZA

22 mi (36 km) south of Jarabacoa, 45 mi (72 km) south of Santiago.

The road south of Jarabacoa takes you higher up in the mountains until you reach Constanza, which has an altitude of 4,264 feet. However, since you are in the Cibao Valley you do not feel that high. The town is surrounded by farmland, which gives you the impression of being on level ground, interestingly enough. Although Constanza has approximately the same number of residents as Jarabacoa—slightly fewer than 30,000—it has a much more small-town feel, with a less crowded downtown. However, in some ways it's not as attractive as Jarabacoa, particularly because its central park is not as appealing. Town folk seem friendlier, however, with more time for you. Without the broad range of adventure tours offered by local operators, the real reason you go to Constanza is to breath in some fresh, cool mountain air and just relax, which you can do in a couple of nearby lodges.

NEED A BREAK?

If you're in Constanza and looking for a place for a nice drink, the Q Liquor Store (⊠ *Calle Antonio Maria Garcia 2, Constanza* ☎ *809/539–2680)* **is unexpectedly hip, carrying top-shelf brands like Grey Goose. A new adjacent café serves gourmet coffees, cocktails, and more.**

WHERE TO EAT

¢–$ ✕ **Mi Casa.** The Acosta family, Jose and wife Estela, have run this restaurant–hotel for decades. Papa is still on the floor, and Estela is still in the kitchen, but she now receives some help from their son. The interior is rustic, pine-paneled, and homey, and the comfort food on the menu is prepared with love. You can always have the flavorful chicken soup that will cure anything and a litany of fresh fruit juices, including strawberry and carrot. Dominican specialties prevail, even for breakfast, which has become a crossroads for locals and tourists to meet; the same is true during the busy lunch period. The Acosta's have 13 simple, inexpensive guest rooms, which were in the process of a renovation at this writing. ⊠ *Calle Luperon, corner of Calle Sanchez, Constanza* ☎ *809/539–2764* ⊟ *MC, V.*

$ ✕ **Restaurant Deligne.** Stop here when you're looking for something more healthful and with a bit more atmosphere than the locally popular *comedors,* the typical cinder block restaurants serving up enormous portions of hearty Dominican fare. This pleasantly rustic restaurant built from pine and love offers both indoor and outdoor seating. You can ask for a large salad with fresh, curly lettuce and an array of vegetables, or you can have your main meal, by day or night, including lamb in Creole sauce or a small rabbit or guinea hen in a red wine sauce. The owners are accommodating and use quality, fresh produce. Alas, it's a pity that the hotel rooms don't have the same feel-good ambience. ⊠ *Gaston Fernandez Deligne, corner of Reyes, Constanza* ☎ *809/539–2213* ⊟ *AE, D, DC, MC, V* ⊗ *No dinner Mon.*

WHERE TO STAY

¢   ▦ **Altocerro Villas, Hotel & Camping.** Close to town, this little rancho is in a bucolic setting, surrounded by planted fields and down a country road. The central communal areas are good-looking, done in a modified country motif and are squeaky clean, including the second-floor restaurant and 10 hotel rooms; the adjacent minimarket has a good selection but is pricey. The villas, which look more like two-story town houses are in tiers on a hillside, and the most desirable have working fireplaces. All have well-equipped kitchens and balconies and views of the Constanza Valley. You won't be roughing it here, not with cable TV and Wi-Fi, too. The more outdoorsy may choose to stay in the separate campground, but even it is commodious, with clean restrooms, BBQ, and bonfire areas, a playground, and rustic gazebos. **Pros:** Good value

CLOSE UP

Japanese Colonists and Constanza — A Success Story

In the foreground of a black-and-white photo of the first ship carrying Japanese colonists to their new home in the Dominican Republic in 1956, a father, Hitoshi Waki, holds his tiny son (Teruki, age one) while his little daughter (Yumiko, age two) plays next to them. The picture is the book *Más Relatos Sobre Constanza* by Constancio Cassá, his second book on the subject.

Generalissimo Rafael L. Trujuillo embarked on a program to bring in new immigrants to the D.R. in the 1950s. His invitation was extended to Japanese, Spanish, Hungarian, and Lebanese colonists; in the late 1940s, he had also invited Jewish refugees from Europe to settle in Sosúa. Japan, which was suffering from overpopulation and an economic and social crisis following World War II, sent a total of 1,282 colonists, who entered the D.R. between 1956 and 1959.

Trujillo's government scattered the settlers in different regions of the country, but 201 individuals from 30 Japanese families put down their roots in Constanza. Their mission was to make it a premier agricultural area, which it still is today. They were sold fertile land dirt-cheap. It's said, also, that while Trujillo wanted more "white blood" in his country, he later approved of the Japanese immigrants, as they proved themselves industrious, yet docile.

As is common in the Japanese culture, several generations of the Waki family live under the same roof, including Teruki's teenager daughter and son. The home itself is one of the largest and most attractive on the periphery of the original *Colonia Japonese* (Japanese Colony). Today it's the poorer Dominicans who live in the converted barracks originally constructed for the Colonia Japonese.

In Spanish, Choko Waki (Hitoshi's wife) explains that in order to be accepted into the country initially, a family had to have four adults capable of working, and they had to sign a work contract. Neither she nor her daughter Yumiko remembers any prejudice being shown against them. Yet their culture was so different from that of the local Dominicans. Initially, the Japanese married only among themselves and with others who they met at the island-wide reunions every year in the capital. Also, there were family-arranged marriages and "mail order" brides from the fatherland. However, as time passed, children were baptized in the Catholic Church and intermarriage with Dominicans began.

The Waki family lived in the colony housing for 12 long years; Hitoshi (now deceased) eventually owned a florist shop in Santo Domingo and commuted. This large, durable home was constructed in the late 1960s and looks out to fields planted with vegetables and strawberries and to a greenhouse. Teruki, assisted by his sister, makes their primary living by growing the greenery used by florists.

Surprisingly, there are no Japanese restaurants in Constanza, despite the long history. Yumiko interjects: "A relative and I have been thinking about opening a take-out place... What do you think?"

for money, bi-level two-bedroom villas are particularly attractive and spacious, you're in the country. **Cons:** Not a whole lot of personality or charisma, units have dated decor. ✉ *Colonia Kennedy, Constanza* ☎ *809/539–1553, 809/530–6192 reservations only* ⊕ *www.altocerro.com* ⇆ *10 rooms, 4 suites, 10 1-bedroom villas, 14 2-bedroom villas, 6 3-bedroom villas* ♿ *In-room: kitchen (some), Wi-Fi. In-hotel: restaurant, no elevator, public Wi-Fi, parking (no fee)* ▭ *AE, D, DC, MC, V* ⦿ *EP.*

¢ ⛄ **Hotel Vista Del Valle.** If you come into town and want something centrally located and inexpensive for

the night, you'll be safe, warm, and dry at this family-run hotel built in 2003. Some attractive rustic touches include rough-hewn furniture and hall lights fashioned from rope, twigs, and branches. Popular with European budget travelers on weekends, local business travelers dominate midweek. You do get some views of the surrounding countryside, particularly from the third-floor front rooms (back rooms have no views but are more removed from the street and scooter racket below). Do make advance reservations. **Pros:** Great location, cheap but not sleazy, interesting decor brings it above the bare bones. **Cons:** Rooms are small, stairs are steep, no amenities or restaurant. ✉ *Antonio María Garcia 41, corner of Matilde Viñas, Constanza* ☎ *809/539–2071 or 829/447–4010* ⇆ *12 rooms* ♿ *In-hotel: no-smoking rooms* ▭ *No credit cards* ⦿ *EP.*

¢ ⛄ **Villa Pajon.** With the smoke rising from the chimneys, this hideaway
★ could be in the North Carolina mountains. If it were, it might be used for a photo shoot in a country-home decor glossy. You'll find fieldstone fireplaces in the communal dining room and in each of the cabin, which have white-stucco walls crisscrossed by beams, lots of lodge pole pine, and gingham and plaid fabric. It has all been done in remarkably good taste, and you'll fling open your green shutters to reveal gardens of cala lilies, hydrangeas, and purple Agapanthus. This 1,000-acre property (at 7,150 feet elevation) was first a lumber mill, then a flower plantation. It's now a potato farm as well as a vacation haven for savvy urban dwellers, romantic couples, families, and tourists who want to experience the simple mountain life. Each cabin has a well-equipped kitchen with a gas range; there are dining tables on the front porches and BBQs. Transportation can be arranged if you don't have a car up to the task of the rough road, and cooking or maid service can be provided for an additional charge. The best rates can be found during midweek and in summer. **Pros:** The true simple country life, horses are available to take over logging trails, the owners speak English and are genuinely hospitable and fun. **Cons:** No electricity (though battery-operated

generators are promised), the dirt road from town requires a four-wheel drive, guests must bring all their own supplies. ⊹ *Take Calle de Constanza to San Jose Ocoa, 15 mi (24 km) from Constanza* ✉ *Valle Nuevo* ☎ *809/412–5210* ⊕ *www.villapajon.com* ⇆ *1 1-bedroom cabin, 3 2-bedrooms cabins, 3 3-bedrooms cabins* ♿ *In-room: no a/c, no phone, kitchen, no TV. In hotel: no-smoking rooms* ▭ *No credit cards* ⦿ *EP.*

SANTIAGO & THE CIBAO VALLEY ESSENTIALS

TRANSPORTATION

AIR TRAVEL

Cibao International Airport in Santiago is the gateway to the entire Cibao Valley. With service from JetBlue and others, it's definitely the best airport if you're visiting only this area. It's also possible to fly into the Gregorio Luperon International Airport in Puerto Plata, but that will add almost two hours onto your drive after arrival.

Airports **Cibao International Airport** (*STI* ✉ *Santiago* ☎ *809/582–4894*). **Gregorio Luperon International Airport** (*POP* ✉ *Puerto Plata* ☎ *809/586–0107 or 809/586–0219*).

BUS TRAVEL

Metro Bus and Caribe Tours have frequent service from both Puerto Plata and Santo Domingo to Santiago. Metro's service from Santo Domingo is hourly, between 6 AM and 7:45 PM, and the trip takes about 2 hours and costs about $8. Between Puerto Plata and Santiago, the trip takes about 1¼ hours and costs about $3. Schedules change, but for now buses leave Puerto Plata about every 2 hours, at 9, 11, 1, 4, and 6. Metro is a comfortable, upscale bus line.

Caribe Tours takes longer than Metro to get to Santo Domingo, 2½ hours with many local stops, but it also costs slightly less, about $6; there are about 25 runs daily between 6 AM and 8:15 PM. Caribe Tours also stops in La Vega, which takes another 45 minutes, where you can transfer for a bus to Jarabacoa for about $6. There are two bus stations in Santiago, so make sure your bus is leaving from Las Colinas Terminal. Caribe Tours service from Puerto Plata is good, too, hourly between 6 AM and 9:30 PM. The cost is about $3, and it takes 1¼ hours; that same bus continues on to Sosúa, which takes another 45 minutes and costs about $1 more.

Linea Gladys runs between Santo Domingo and Constanza from Santo Domingo.

Bus Companies **Caribe Tours** (☏ *809/576–0790 in Santiago, 809/221–4422 in Santo Domingo, 809/574–3796 in Jarabacoa*). **Linea Gladys** (☏ *809/565–1223 in Santo Domingo*). **Metro Buses** (☏ *809/582–9111 in Santiago, 809/566–7126 in Santo Domingo, 809/586–6062 in Puerto Plata*).

CAR TRAVEL

It's certainly easier to get around the area if you have your own transportation. Just remember that some places are only reachable with a four-wheel-drive vehicle, which can be very expensive in these parts.

Car Rentals **Avis** (✉ *Cibao International Airport, Santiago* ☏ *809/223–8153*).

Francis Rent A Car (✉ *Carretera a Salto Jimenoa Dos, Km 2, Jarabacoa* ☏ *809/574–2981*). **Hertz** (✉ *Cibao International Airport, Santiago* ☏ *809/612–3380*).

Honda (✉ *Cibao International Airport, Santiago* ☏ *809/233–8179*).

TAXIS

Taxi-Queen is the company that works through the Santiago hotels; drivers have passed security checks and wear their ID tags around their necks. Their cars are not wonderful, and they're unlikely to speak English, but their prices are especially reasonable. Taxi-Tourismo, the company that services the Cibao Airport in Santiago and has safer, more commodious vehicles (mostly SUVs and minivans) but higher rates.

Information **Taxi-Queen** (☏ *809/570–0000, 809/233–3333 in Santiago*). **Taxi-Tourismo** (☏ *809/829–3007 in Santiago*).

CONTACTS & RESOURCES

EMERGENCIES

Medical Clinics **Centro Medico De. Abad** (✉ *Calle del Carneb, near Gaston Fernando Deligne, Jarabacoa* ☏ *809/574–2431*). **Corominan Clinic** (✉ *Calle Restauracion 57, corner Cuba, Santiago* ☏ *809/580–1171*). **Hospital Metropolitana de Santiago HOMS** (✉ *Autopista Duarte, Km 2.8, Santiago* ☏ *829/947–2222*). **Union Medica del Norte** (✉ *Av. Pablo Duarte, in front of International Plaza, Santiago* ☏ *809/226–8686*).

24-hour Pharmacies **Pharmacy Carol** (✉ *Av. Estrella Sadhalá 29, corner Bartolomé Colón, Santiago* ☏ *809/581–3147*).

INTERNET CAFÉS

Camber Net, in Santiago, is quite a good place; its computers are newer than most, its prices better (RD$50 per hour), and some of the employees speak English. It stays open until 10 PM. Centro de Copiado y Papelería, in Jarabacoa, offers both Internet computers and some business services like photocopying and office supplies. It's also inexpensive at RD$45 an hour. Ciber Bibilotec Emy is in Constanza.

Information **Camber Net** (✉ *Calle Espana 41, near Av. Restauraccion, Santiago* ☏ *809/734–2232*). **Centro de Copiado y Papelería** (✉ *Calle Duarte, near Indepedencia, Jarabacoa* ☏ *809/574–2902*).

Ciber Bibilotec Emy (✉ *Opposite children's baseball field, Constanza* ☏ *No phone*).

POST OFFICE

Information **Post Office Jarabacoa** (⊠ *Av. Independencia W, Jarabacoa*). **Post Office Santiago** (⊠ *Calle del Sol at San Luis, 3 blocks up from central park, Santiago*).

TOUR OPTIONS

In Santiago, freelance guides hang out at the Heroes Monument and can give tours in English for about $20 for an hour. Vacation Tours, a travel agency with an office in the Hotel Gran Almirante in Santiago, can also arrange city tours.

Information **Vacation Tours** (⊠ *Hotel Gran Almirante & Casino, Los Jardines, Santiago* ☎ *809/825–1996 Ext. 252* ⊕ *www.vacationtours.com.do*).

VISITOR INFORMATION

Information **Oficina de Turismo Constanza** (⊠ *Calle Matilde Viná near San Miguel Andrés Abreu, 2nd fl., Constanza* ☎ *809/539–2900*). **Oficina de Turismo Jarabacoa** (⊠ *Plaza Ramirez, across from west side of central park, 2nd fl., Jarabacoa* ☎ *809/574–7287*). **Oficina de Turismo Santiago** (⊠ *Parque Duarte, Calle de Sol, Edificio Gu, 2nd fl. de Santiago, Santiago* ☎ *809/582–5885*).

7

Dominican Republic Essentials

There are planners and there are those who, excuse the pun, fly by the seat of their pants. We happily place ourselves among the planners. Our writers and editors try to anticipate all the issues you may face before and during any journey, and then they do their research. This section is the product of their efforts. Use it to get excited about your trip to Dominican Republic, to inform your travel planning, or to guide you on the road should the seat of your pants start to feel threadbare.

GETTING STARTED

We're proud of our Web site: Fodors.com is a great place to begin any journey. Scan Travel Wire for suggested itineraries, travel deals, restaurant and hotel openings, and other up-to-the-minute info. Check out Booking to research prices and book plane tickets, hotel rooms, rental cars, and vacation packages. Head to Talk for on-the-ground pointers from travelers who frequent our message boards. You can also link to loads of other travel-related resources.

▌RESOURCES

ONLINE TRAVEL TOOLS

All About the Dominican Republic In general, information on museums and national parks, eco-tourism, as well as the "lay of the land," can be found on the government's Web sites, under Visitors Information. Some other general and somewhat specialized sites follow.

Hispanola (⊕ www.hispanola.com) has paid advertisers with listings of hotels and real estate agencies but nonetheless is an excellent source of information on hotels, adventure tourism, and outdoor fun; the site also has good detailed maps.

VISITDOMREP (⊕ www.visitdomrep.com) is a Web site for Belgians wanting to learn more about the country; the site is in English, French, and Dutch and has brilliant photography and design.

Currency Conversion Google (⊕ www. google.com) does currency conversion. Just type in the amount you want to convert and an explanation of how you want it converted (e.g., "14 Swiss francs in dollars"), and then voilà. **Oanda.com** (⊕ www.oanda.com) also allows you to print out a handy table with the current day's conversion rates. **XE.com** (⊕ www.xe.com) is a good currency conversion Web site.

Safety Transportation Security Administration (TSA ⊕ www.tsa.gov)

Time Zones Timeanddate.com (⊕ www.timeanddate.com/worldclock) can help you figure out the correct time anywhere.

Weather Accuweather.com (⊕ www.accuweather.com) is an independent weather-forecasting service with good coverage of hurricanes. **Weather.com** (⊕ www.weather.com) is the Web site for the Weather Channel.

Inspiration Julia Álvarez's award-winning novel In the Time of the Butterflies tells the story of three sisters who Trujillo had desired and whose family tried to get out of the country. The author's second novel, How the Garcia Girls Lost their Accents is about Dominican immigrants in the United States.

Mario Vargas Llosasa's novel, Fiesta del Chivo is the story of an attractive girl whose own father gave her up to Generalissimo Rafael Trujillo. He relates the history of the infamous dictator and of those who killed him. The title comes from Trujillo's nickname, el chivo (the goat).

In Drown, Junot Díaz writes about growing up in the D.R. and New Jersey with dual nationality and a dual mind-set.

Sugarball: The American Game, The Dominican Dream by Alan M. Klein is a nonfiction account of the game nearly every young Dominican boy wants to play.

In the book, Why the Cocks Fight, Michele Wucker uses the country's most controversial sport as a metaphor to discover the unsettled and always controversial relationship between the Dominican Republic and Haiti.

Sanky Panky is a film about the young sexual predators—primarily male staffers at all-inclusive resorts—who prey on lonely and/or adventurous foreign women.

VISITOR INFORMATION

Information **Dominican Republic One** (⊕www.dr1.com) is a "trusted site" of the Secretariat de Turismo. It's written by bilingual staffers at the ministry and has the official word on the latest news, travel, and airline information. **Dominican Republic Tourist Office** (⊕www.godominicanrepublic.com ☎212/588–1012, 888/374–6361 in New York City, 305/444–4592, or 888/358–9594 in Miami).

▎THINGS TO CONSIDER

GOVERNMENT ADVISORIES

As different countries have different world views, look at travel advisories from a range of governments to get more of a sense of what's going on out there. And be sure to parse the language carefully. For example, a warning to "avoid all travel" carries more weight than one urging you to "avoid nonessential travel," and both are much stronger than a plea to "exercise caution." A U.S. government travel warning is more permanent (though not necessarily more serious) than a so-called public announcement, which carries an expiration date.

▎TIP➔ **Consider registering online with the State Department (https://travelregistration.state.gov/ibrs/), so the government will know to look for you should a crisis occur in the country you're visiting.**

The U.S. Department of State's Web site has more than just travel warnings and advisories. The consular information sheets issued for every country have general safety tips, entry requirements (though be sure to verify these with the country's embassy), and other useful details.

The Dominican Republic is one of the safer islands in the Caribbean. A first impression may make you think otherwise. Although the D.R. is a very poor country—and crime does happen—violent crime against foreigners is very rare. And even though you may hear warnings about pickpockets and purse snatching by motorcycle-riding thieves, both are relatively unusual. In fact, you may find Dominican honesty refreshing. The best tactic for dealing with the D.R. is not to be paranoid, just cautious, and as in New York City, only carry the credit cards and money that you actually need. Keep the rest in your hotel safe.

If you are the victim of a crime, you have to offer the police "gas money" and a reward to really get some help. Should you find yourself in that predicament, consult a savvy, English-speaking Dominican and ask what amount would be appropriate; this transaction always works best when you have a translator.

Each area in the D.R. has its own safety concerns. For example, avoid walking in Cabarete after midnight, as much to save yourself from speeding motoconchos as criminals. Prostitution can be an annoyance there, as can drug dealers. Wise tourists avoid both, particularly drugs; trust us when we tell you that you do not want to have to spend time in a Dominican jail.

In Punta Cana, which is one of the safest regions, muggings or robberies have occurred when *turistas* have come out of a casino stumbling drunk and bragging about their winnings.

As for Santo Domingo, even though it's considerably safer in the tourist zones now, it's still a large metropolitan city and has higher crime rates than smaller towns.

General Information & Warnings **Australian Department of Foreign Affairs & Trade** (⊕www.smartraveller.gov.au). **Consular Affairs Bureau of Canada** (⊕www.voyage.gc.ca). **U.K. Foreign & Commonwealth Office** (⊕www.fco.gov.uk/travel). **U.S. Department of State** (⊕www.travel.state.gov).

GEAR

Even though this is a warm Caribbean country, you should always bring some kind of clothing (a light shawl or hooded sweatshirt) appropriate for frigid, air-conditioned cars and buses. From September through November, be sure to have a good folding umbrella.

If you'll be spending time in Santo Domingo, you'll find that residents dress up more. Women in particular dress up every day; high heels are the norm, and women never wear sneakers, flip-flops, or shorts, always a dress, skirt, or slacks and stylish shoes (more often with heels). In fact, some museums and churches will not allow tourists to enter if they're wearing skimpy tops or shorts. Similarly, men will find that a *guyaberra* short will take them anywhere, but Dominican men never wear shorts or flip-flops, reserving those for the beach. Younger Dominican men may wear designer jeans and polo shorts. But the more casually you dress, the more you'll be sniffed at as a rich *turista*.

The North Coast is typically cooler and windier, particularly from December to March. At night, you'll want long sleeves and perhaps even a jacket. Along the Southeast Coast and in Punta Cana, the weather is warm year-round, but you may still want something to protect yourself from the chill of nighttime air-conditioning.

If you're going to the mountain areas such as Jarabacoa, Constanza, or Valle Nuevo, you must be prepared for chilly weather at night because of the elevation. In the hilly parts of the Southwest, temperatures are not as cold but certainly drop at night, when winds pick up. But during the day, it can be unbearably hot.

Generally, public restrooms in the D.R. are unsanitary and do not have toilet paper. Always pack small tissue packets, travel-size wipes, and hand sanitizer.

If you'll be shopping for groceries, bring a tote bag; plastic bags at supermarkets are very low in quality, when available.

Cosmetics and toiletries, sunscreen, and mosquito repellent are difficult to find if you want the usual American brands, and they are much more expensive than in the United States (expect to pay two to three times what you would normally pay). Over-the-counter medications, baby formula, disposable diapers, tampons, and contact lens supplies are similarly expensive and sometimes difficult to find.

PASSPORTS & VISAS

For a stay of 30 days or less, U.S. citizens entering the Dominican Republic must have a valid passport with six months of validity remaining. The new passport card is *not* sufficient for travel by air to the Dominican Republic. Upon arrival, you must purchase a Tourist Card for US$10, which is valid for a maximum of 30 days (after that you must appear in person at the airport to extend your visa, a process that requires another $10 fee and much paperwork). Some tour operators include the tourist card in packages, so ask about that when you make your booking. Business travelers must always get a business visa at a diplomatic mission or consulate in their home country.

A nonparent or single parent traveling with a child must have a notarized statement of permission from the absent parent(s).

■TIP→ Before your trip, make two copies of your passport's data page (one for someone at home and another for you to carry separately). Or scan the page and e-mail it to someone at home and/or yourself.

U.S. Passport Information U.S. **Department of State** (☎877/487–2778 ⊕http://travel. state.gov/passport).

HEALTH ISSUES

For more information, see ⇨*Health under On the Ground in the Dominican Republic, below.*

At this writing, there are no required immunizations for adults or children traveling to the Dominican Republic.

Especially after heavy tropical storms or hurricanes, dengue fever has been reported. Unlike others, the black Aedes mosquitoes that carry dengue bite during the day. To ward them off, wear long sleeves, socks, and shoes, and apply a strong repellent containing DEET to exposed areas. Malaria has also been reported in the D.R. after hurricanes, but at this writing there was no current malaria alert from the CDC regarding the Dominican Republic. In late 2007 and early 2008 avian or bird flu was reported in certain areas of the D.R. (associated with fighting cocks), but there are no further reports at this writing.

■TIP➜ **If you travel a lot internationally— particularly to developing nations—refer to the CDC's** Health Information for International Travel **(aka Traveler's Health Yellow Book). Info from it is posted on the CDC Web site (www.cdc.gov/travel/yb), or you can buy a copy from your local bookstore for $24.95.**

Health Warnings **National Centers for Disease Control & Prevention** (CDC ⊕www. cdc.gov/travel). **World Health Organization (WHO** ⊕www.who.int).

TRIP INSURANCE

What kind of coverage do you honestly need? Do you even need trip insurance at all? Take a deep breath and read on.

Comprehensive travel policies typically cover trip-cancellation and interruption, letting you cancel or cut your trip short because of a personal emergency, illness, or, in some cases, acts of terrorism in your destination. Such policies also cover evacuation and medical care. Some also cover you for trip delays because of bad weather or mechanical problems as well as for lost or delayed baggage. Another type of coverage to look for is financial default—that is, when your trip is disrupted because a tour operator, airline, or cruise line goes out of business. Generally you must buy this when you book your trip or shortly thereafter, and it's only available to you if your operator isn't on a list of excluded companies.

If you're going abroad, consider buying medical-only coverage at the very least. Neither Medicare nor some private insurers cover medical expenses anywhere outside of the United States (including time aboard a cruise ship, even if it leaves from a U.S. port). Medical-only policies typically reimburse you for medical care (excluding that related to preexisting conditions) and hospitalization abroad, and provide for evacuation. You still have to pay the bills and await reimbursement from the insurer, though.

Expect comprehensive travel insurance policies to cost about 4% to 7% or 8% of the total price of your trip (it's more like 8%–12% if you're over age 70). A medical-only policy may or may not be cheaper than a comprehensive policy. Always read the fine print of your policy to make sure that you are covered for the risks that are of most concern to you. Compare several policies to make sure you're getting the best price and range of coverage available.

■TIP➜ **OK. You know you can save a bundle on trips to warm-weather destinations by traveling in the hurricane season. But there's also a chance that a severe storm will disrupt your plans. The solution? Look for hotels and resorts that offer storm/hurricane guarantees. Although they rarely allow refunds, most guarantees do let you rebook later if a storm strikes.**

Trip Insurance Resources

Insurance Comparison Sites		
Insure My Trip.com	800/487–4722	www.insuremytrip.com.
Square Mouth.com	800/240–0369 or 727/490–5803	www.squaremouth.com.
Comprehensive Travel Insurers		
Access America	800/729–6021	www.accessamerica.com.
CSA Travel Protection	800/873–9855	www.csatravelprotection.com.
HTH Worldwide	610/254—8700	www.hthworldwide.com.
Travelex Insurance	800/228–9792	www.travelex-insurance.com.
AIG Travel Guard	800/826–4919	www.travelguard.com.
Travel Insured International	800/243–3174	www.travelinsured.com.
Medical-Only Insurers		
International Medical Group	800/628–4664	www.imglobal.com.
International SOS		www.internationalsos.com.
Wallach & Company	800/237–6615 or 540/687–3166	www.wallach.com.

BOOKING YOUR TRIP

There are a few things to keep in mind when booking a trip to the Dominican Republic, the most notable of which is that you can sometimes still get the best deals through a traditional or online travel agency. For more information, read on.

■ ACCOMMODATIONS

The government rates the hotels with a star system, doling out one to six stars. Star ratings take into consideration the facilities that the property has to offer, including restaurants, spas, tennis courts, bathroom amenities, and service, but ratings do not make qualitative judgments. Therefore, a so-called five-star resort in the D.R. may not be up to the same standards as a similarly rated resort in Mexico or the United States. Generally Americans may not be satisfied with any resort having a rating lower than four stars.

WHAT IT COSTS IN U.S. DOLLARS		
¢	under $80	under $125
$	$80–$150	$125–$250
$$	$150–$250	$250–$350
$$$	$250–$350	$350–$450
$$$$	over $350*	over $450**

*EP, BP, CP **AI, FAP, MAP Hotel prices are per night for a double room in high season, excluding 16% tax, customary 10% service charge, and meal plans (except at all-inclusives).

Most hotels and other lodgings require you to give your credit-card details before they will confirm your reservation. If you don't feel comfortable e-mailing this information, ask if you can fax it (some places even prefer faxes). However you book, get confirmation in writing and have a copy of it handy when you check in.

Be sure you understand the hotel's cancellation policy. Some places allow you to cancel without any kind of penalty; others require you to cancel a week in advance or penalize you the cost of one night. Small inns and B&Bs are most likely to require you to cancel far in advance. Most hotels allow children under a certain age to stay in their parents' room at no extra charge, but others charge for them as extra adults; find out the cutoff age for discounts.

■TIP➔ Hotels may operate on the European Plan (**EP**, no meals), the Breakfast Plan (**BP**, with full breakfast), Continental Plan (**CP**, continental breakfast), Full American Plan (**FAP**, all meals), Modified American Plan (**MAP**, breakfast and dinner) or an all-inclusive plan (**AI**) including all meals, drinks, and most activities.

APARTMENT & HOUSE RENTALS

Rental villas in the D.R. are often the second homes of wealthy absentee owners. In some resorts like Casa de Campo, they are the norm, though more often they are freestanding homes.

In Juan Dolio, you can find a wide variety of villas in the Metro Country Club as well as ocean-front condos. In "old" Juan Dolio, there are more moderately priced apartments and homes for rent, many of which are suitable for singles or long-term renters.

On the North Coast, much of the new high-end construction is designed to be privately owned but entered into a rental pool that is managed by the developers. Apartments are more common in Cabarete. The well-established Sea Horse Ranch development, between Sosúa and Cabarete, is a prestigious residential enclave a beach club, restaurant, and world-class equestrian center. In the Cabrera/Abreu area, about an hour west of Cabarete, the properties are in luxurious gated communities, where most rentals are managed by North Coast Management, a Cabrera-based agency.

HOTELS

The Dominican Republic is best known for its all-inclusive resorts that offer all you can eat, drink, and do for one moderate rate. These hotels, especially in the Punta Cana area, continue to be the big draw for this Caribbean island. Even though the escalating cost of food has driven costs up, they are still a great value, keeping the D.R. at the forefront of cheap destinations in the Caribbean. But newer hotel developments are increasingly luxurious (and have high prices to match).

Perfectly nice small independent B&Bs still exist in the Southwest near Barahona and are well-priced, offering a more personal experience. In the mountain areas surrounding Jarabacoa, Constanza, and Valle Nuevo, rustic complexes—often with fireplaces—are the favored lodgings.

In Santo Domingo, most of the better hotels are on or near the Malecón, with a growing collection of small, desirable properties in the trendy Colonial Zone, allowing you to feel part of that magical Old World neighborhood. But these hotels are still among the cheapest in the Caribbean.

▌ AIRLINE TICKETS

Most domestic airline tickets are electronic; international tickets may be either electronic or paper. With an e-ticket the only thing you receive is an e-mailed receipt citing your itinerary and reservation and ticket numbers.

The greatest advantage of an e-ticket is that if you lose your receipt, you can simply print out another copy or ask the airline to do it for you at check-in. You usually pay a surcharge (up to $50) to get a paper ticket, if you can get one at all.

The sole advantage of a paper ticket is that it may be easier to endorse over to another airline if your flight is canceled and the airline with which you booked

can't accommodate you on another flight.

CHARTER FLIGHTS

Charter companies rent aircraft and offer regularly scheduled flights (usually nonstops). Charter flights are generally cheaper than flights on regular airlines, and they often leave from and travel to a wider variety of airports. For example, you could have a nonstop flight from Columbus, Ohio, to Punta Cana, Dominican Republic, or from Chicago to Dubrovnik, Croatia.

You don't, however, have the same protections as with regular airlines. If a charter can't take off for mechanical or other reasons, there usually isn't another plane to take its place. If not enough seats are sold, the flight may be canceled. And if a company goes out of business, you're out of luck (unless, of course, you have insurance with financial default coverage; ⇨ *Trip Insurance under Things to Consider in Getting Started, above*).

Charter Companies Apple Vacations (⊕ www.applevac.com), reputed to be the largest tour-operator in the United States, offers 32 charter flights a week into Punta Cana from the U.S. **Funjet** (⊕ www.funjet.com) operates flights from Philadelphia, Newark, Chicago (O'Hare), Pittsburgh, and Hartford/Bradley into Punta Cana. **USA 3000 Airlines** (⊕ www.USA3000airlines.com) operates from Philadelphia, Newark, Chicago (O'Hare), Pittsburgh, and Hartford/Bradley to Punta Cana and sells its flights directly to consumers as well as to larger tour operators.

▌ RENTAL CARS

When you reserve a car, ask about cancellation penalties, taxes, drop-off charges (if you're planning to pick up the car in one city and leave it in another), and surcharges (for being under or over a certain age, for additional drivers, or for driving across state or country borders or beyond a specific distance from your point of rental). All these things can add substantially to your costs. Request car seats and extras such as GPS when you book.

Rates are sometimes—but not always—better if you book in advance or reserve through a rental agency's Web site. There are other reasons to book ahead, though: for popular destinations, during busy times of the year, or to ensure that you get certain types of cars (vans, SUVs, exotic sports cars).

▐ TIP→ **Make sure that a confirmed reservation guarantees you a car. Agencies sometimes overbook, particularly for busy weekends and holiday periods.**

At the major agencies, you'll have a choice of compact, mid-size, and large vehicles (including mini-vans and quite a few SUVs). They're usually all automatics with air-conditioning. The condition of these vehicles can vary greatly, but they may not be of the same quality as cars you would rent in the United States. You'll need a four-wheel-drive SUV to reach some more remote areas, like the hills west of Barahona or the mountainous regions beyond Jarabacoa.

The week between Christmas and New Year's and Easter Week are typically the busiest times of the year for car-rental companies, so make your reservations far in advance.

A U.S. driver's license is sufficient to rent a car in the D.R. Renters must be between the ages of 25 and 80. Infant car seats are difficult to get and can be expensive (as much as a car during busy periods). You'll be better off if you bring your own. Laws are similar to those in the United States, though they are not well enforced. If you need a car seat, always reserve it with your car.

Allow plenty of time to drop off your rental car at any airport. It may be a breeze to drop off a car at a small airport such as La Romana, but at Las Americas you must allow 45 minutes to an hour, 30 minutes in Punta Cana. The agency will tell you how far in advance to arrive at the airport, and believe those estimates since things rarely move as quickly in the D.R. as in the United States.

Major Agencies Avis (☎800/331–1084 ⊕www.avis.com ✉Las Américas Airport ☎809/549–0468 ✉Gregorio Luperon International Airport, Puerto Plata ☎809/586–0214 ✉Castillo Marquez, corner Duarte, La Romana ☎809/550–0600). **Budget** (☎800/472–3325 ⊕www.budget.com ✉Las Américas Airport ☎809/549–0351 ✉Gregorio Luperon International Airport, Puerto Plata ☎809/586–0413). **Europcar** (✉Las Américas Airport ☎809/549–0942 ✉Gregorio Luperon International Airport, Puerto Plata ☎809/586–7979 ✉Punta Cana International Airport, Bavaro, Punta Cana ☎809/686–2861). **Hertz** (☎800/654–3001 ⊕www.hertz.com ✉Las Américas Airport ☎809/549–0454 ✉Puerto Plata ☎809/586–0200).

Local Agencies MC Auto Rental Car (✉Las Américas Airport ☎809/549–8911 ⊕www.mccarrental.com). **McBeal** (✉Santo Domingo ☎809/688–6518). **Nelly Rent-a-Car** (✉Las Américas Airport ☎809/530–0036, 800/526–6684 in U.S.)

CAR-RENTAL INSURANCE

Some credit cards offer collision-damage waiver (CDW) coverage, but it's usually supplemental to your own insurance and rarely covers SUVs, minivans, luxury models, and the like. If your coverage is secondary, you may still be liable for loss-of-use costs from the car-rental company. But no credit-card insurance is valid unless you use that card for *all* transactions, from reserving to paying the final bill. All companies exclude car rental in some countries, so be sure to find out about the destination to which you are traveling.

■TIP→ Diners Club offers primary CDW coverage on all rentals reserved and paid for with the card. This means that Diners Club's company—not your own car insurance—pays in case of an accident. It *doesn't* mean your car-insurance company won't raise your rates once it discovers you had an accident.

Some rental agencies require you to purchase CDW coverage; many will even include it in quoted rates. All will strongly encourage you to buy CDW—possibly implying that it's required—so be sure to ask about such things before renting. In most cases it's cheaper to add a supplemental CDW plan to your comprehensive travel-insurance policy (⇨ *Trip Insurance under Things to Consider in Getting Started, above*) than to purchase it from a rental company. That said, you don't want to pay for a supplement if you're required to buy insurance from the rental company.

Unless you have a separate car-rental insurance policy, you should buy CDW from your agency in the D.R. Generally, the cost of CDW is not included in the quoted price, and it will add substantially to your costs. For example, Budget rents an intermediate-size car for $41.58 per day during shoulder season, but CDW will cost an additional $21.95 per day, but this is not significantly different from the cost of insurance in the U.S. and also covers you for theft. You can often get insurance through your credit card—or even through a separate car-rental insurance policy—for significantly less. Most U.S. car-insurance policies that cover you for rentals do not cover you in the Dominican Republic; if you are unsure

what your own policy covers, be sure to call and ask before your trip.

■TIP→ You can decline the insurance from the rental company and purchase it through a third-party provider such as Travel Guard (www.travelguard.com)—$9 per day for $35,000 of coverage. That's sometimes just under half the price of the CDW offered by some car-rental companies.

▌ VACATION PACKAGES

A package that combines the cost of your airfare (sometimes on a charter flight), your all-inclusive resort, and your airport transfers can still be a good value for travel to the D.R., even though prices have risen significantly over the past year. Low season—from September through mid-November—can offer good values, though this period also coincides with the peak hurricane season, so some rain is bound to fall. Another good value period begins after Easter week and continues through early June, when most U.S. schools are out for the summer. Summers are popular, particularly for Europeans, so there are not many deals after mid-June, when European schools are out; and August is particularly busy.

You can save enough money with one of these packages that you could still finance a couple of days of independent travel in a less expensive area such as the Southwest, where hotels are inexpensive and the scenery beautiful.

Organizations American Society of Travel Agents (ASTA ☏703/739–2782 or 800/965–2782 ⊕www.astanet.com). **United States Tour Operators Association** (USTOA ☏212/599–6599 ⊕www.ustoa.com). ■TIP→ Local tourism boards can provide information about lesser-known and small-niche operators that sell packages to only a few destinations.

TRANSPORTATION

It was once said that all roads lead to Rome. In the Dominican Republic, the same could be said for the capital, Santo Domingo. All of the island's major highways radiate from the capital, so this is the place from which bus and air service are the best. Puerto Plata and Santiago are key cities in the north, while Punta Cana and La Romana key destinations in the southeast. Several charter services and helicopter service connect places not covered by regular flights, but these are typically expensive connections.

The D.R. has an excellent highway system connecting major destinations, and there are decent secondary roads that are improving every year, though some still have more potholes than a lunar moonscape. Driving can be hazardous, which is why many tourists avail themselves of the reliable and inexpensive first-class bus system. If you're going to smaller cities and towns, then you may have to rely on the local *gua-guas,* which will get you to your destination, but certainly not with much comfort or speed.

TRAVEL TIMES FROM SANTO DOMINGO		
To	By Air	By Bus
La Romana	30 mins	1½ to 2 hours
Punta Cana/ Bávaro	45 mins	4½ hours
Santiago	30 mins	1½ to 2 hours
Puerto Plata	1 hour	4 to 4½ hours
Santa Barbara de Samaná	1 hour	5–6 hours
Barahona	1 hour	3 ½ to 4 hours

▌ BY AIR

The Dominican Republic has more international airports than any other island in the Caribbean, but it's important that you fly into the airport that is closest to your resort. You don't want to fly into Santo Domingo if you're staying in Punta Cana since this is an expensive, three- to four-hour drive. Here are some sample flight times to the D.R.: New York to Santo Domingo or Puerto Plata: 4 hours; Miami to Santo Domingo: 2 hours 10 min.; Miami to Puerto Plata 2 hours; San Juan to Punta Cana: 1 hour.

Domestic flights can be less numerous, and at present there are no domestic flights between Santo Domingo and Puerto Plata. To make this trip, you must charter a plane, take a bus, rent a car for the four-hour drive, or pay over $150 for a taxi.

Security checks and check-in at Dominican airports can be slow, so you definitely must arrive 2 or 3 hours before an international fight.

Airline Security Issues Transportation Security Administration (⊕ www.tsa.gov) has answers for almost every question that might come up.

AIRPORTS

The Dominican Republic has seven major international airports and one major domestic airport, including Cibao International Airport in Santiago (STI), which is convenient to the North Coast and central mountain regions of the island; Gregorio Luperon International Airport (POP) in Puerto Plata, about 7 mi (11 km) east of Playa Dorada; the new La Isabela International Dr. Joaquin Balaguer Airport (DHG), about 10 mi (16 km) north of Santo Domingo (you'll hear it called Higuero Airport and even Isabela, and it's used exclusively for domestic flights); La Romana–Casa de Campo International

Airport (LHR) in La Romana, which is being used increasingly for international flights; Las Américas International Airport (SDQ), about 15 mi (24 km) east of Santo Domingo, which has been beautified and improved over the past few years; El Catey International Airport (AZS), the new, impressive international airport about 25 mi (40 km) west of Samaná; and Punta Cana International Airport (PUJ, the island's busiest, handling some 1.5 million passengers a year).

Anticipate long lines and be sure to give yourself a full two hours for international check-in.

AIRPORTS

Cibao International Airport (STI ⊠ Santiago ☎ 809/582–4894). **El Catey International Airport** (AZS ⊠ Catey). **Gregorio Luperon International Airport** (POP ⊠ Puerto Plata ☎ 809/586–0107 or 809/586–0219). **La Isabella International Dr. Joaquin Balaguer** (DHG ⊠ Higuero ☎ 809/826–4003). **La Romana/Casa de Campo International Airport** (LRM ⊠ La Romana ☎ 809/556–5565). **Las Américas International Airport** (SDQ ⊠ Santo Domingo ☎ 809/412–5888). **President Juan Bosch International Airport** (AZS ⊠ El Catey ☎ 809/338–0150). **Punta Cana International Airport** (PUJ ⊠ Punta Cana ☎ 809/686–8790).

FLIGHTS TO & FROM THE DOMINICAN REPUBLIC

Most major airlines now have service to the Dominican Republic, including American Airlines/American Eagle, Continental, Delta, JetBlue (to Santiago, Puerto Plata, and Santo Domingo only), Spirit (to Santo Domingo only), and US Airways.

Many visitors fly nonstop on charter flights directly from the East Coast and Midwest, particularly into Punta Cana. These charters are generally part of a package and can only be booked through a travel agent.

Air Caraïbes and Air Antilles Express connect to the French West Indies (summer only); LIAT connects the D.R. mainly to the English-speaking Caribbean islands.

Incidents of theft, especially at Las Americas airport in Santo Domingo, is much less of a problem than it was in the past. At this writing, flights into Puerto Plata (particularly those connecting in Miami) have the worst reputation for pilfered baggage.

U.S. Airlines American Airlines/American Eagle (☎ 809/200–5151, 809/959–2420, 800/433–7300, or 809/542–5151 in Puerto Plata). **Continental** (☎ 809/262–1060 in D.R., 800/231–0856 in U.S.). **Delta** (☎ 809/200–9191, 809/233–8485, or 809/955–1500 in D.R., 800/221–1212 in U.S.). **JetBlue** (☎ 809/200–9898, 809/549–1793 in D.R., 800/538–2583 in U.S.). **Pan Am** (☎ 809/227–0330). **Spirit** (☎ 809/381–4111 in D.R., 800/772–7117 in U.S.). **US Airways** (☎ 809/540–0505, 809/549–0165 in D.R., 800/428–4322, or 800/622–1015 in U.S.).

Caribbean & Regional Airlines Air Antilles Express (☎ 809/621–8888). **Air Caraïbes** (☎ 809/621–8888, 0590/82–47–00 in Guadeloupe). **LIAT** (☎ 809/621–8888).

FLIGHTS WITHIN THE DOMINICAN REPUBLIC

Aerodomca and Air Century, flying out of Higuero Airport in Santo Domingo, offer charters and transfers. Helidosa Helicopters offers both charter flights and aerial sightseeing excursions. Caribair flies between Puerto Plata and La Romana. In addition to charter flights, Takeoff Destination Service has some scheduled flights.

Domestic Airlines Aerodomca (⊠ La Isabella International Dr. Joaquin Balaguer, Higuero ☎ 809/567–1195). **Air Century** (⊠ La Isabella International Dr. Joaquin Balaguer, Higuero ☎ 809/566–0888 ⊕ www.aircentury.com). **Caribair** (⊠ Gregorio Luperon International Airport, Puerto Plata ☎ 809/586–0131 ⊕ www.caribeair.com). **Helidosa Helicopters** (⊠ Punta Cana ☎ 809/688–0744 ⊠ Puerto Plata ☎ 809/320–2009). **Takeoff Destination Service** (⊠ Punta Cana ☎ 809/552–1333 ⊕ www.takeoffweb.com).

▋ BY BUS

Privately owned air-conditioned buses are the cheapest way to get around the country. They make regular runs to Santiago, Puerto Plata, Punta Cana, and other destinations from Santo Domingo. One-way bus fare from Santo Domingo to Puerto Plata is about $7.50, and it takes 3½ hours. Metro's deluxe buses have more of an upscale clientele; however, there are no movies. Caribe Tours sometimes shows bilingual movies, keeps the a/c on frigid, and is favored by locals and families. Buses are often filled to capacity, especially on weekends and holidays.

If you're going north, both Metro and Caribe Tours offer hourly service from Santo Domingo to Santiago, Puerto Plata, and Sosúa. Be forewarned that the bus music will be Dominican-loud. Caribe Tours also runs buses to Las Américas International Airport and the mountain town of Jarabacoa from Santo Domingo. Linia Gladys is a small bus line that will get you from the capital to Constanza; if you are in the town of Constanza, call them, and they might even pick you up at your hotel.

Espreso Baváro buses depart from Plaza Los Girasoles at Avenida Máximo Gómez at Juan Sánchez Ruiz; the buses are not the best, but the price is right, and the American movies current. If you're going to one of the Punta Cana resorts, you get off at the stop before the last and take a cab waiting at the taxi stand.

Frequent service from Santo Domingo to the town of La Romana is provided by Express Bus. Buses depart from Ravelo Street, in front of Enriquillo Park, every hour on the hour from 5 AM to 9 PM; the schedule is exactly the same from La Romana, where they leave from Camino Avenue. In Santo Domingo, there's no office and no phone, but a ticket taker will take your $4 just before departure. Travel time is about 1¾ hours. Once in town you can take a taxi from the bus stop to Casa de Campo ($18), Sunscape Casa del Mar ($25), or Iberostar Dominicus ($30).

Bus Information **Caribe Tours** (☎809/221–4422). **Espreso Bavaro** (☎809/682–9670). **Linea Gladys** (☎809/565–1223 in Santo Domingo, or 809/539–2134). **Metro Buses** (☎809/566–7126 in Santo Domingo, 809/586–6062 in Puerto Plata, 809/587–4711 in Santiago).

▋ BY CAR

Driving in the D.R. can be a harrowing and expensive experience, and the typical vacationer will not want to rent a car. We especially caution tourists against driving outside the major cities at night. Watch out for pedestrians, stray cows, goats, or horses, bicycles, and motorcycles. Some will not have headlights, and others will be riding on the shoulders, often against oncoming traffic.

If you limit your driving to a day-long excursion, you can probably manage in the Southeast and in Punta Cana. Similarly, on the North Coast, villa renters (especially those in the Cabrera area), may need to rent a car if their villa manager does not offer a good shuttle service. If you're traveling to the Southwest, you will probably need a car if you plan to do extensive independent exploring, and you may also need a four-wheel-drive vehicle (which must be rented in Santo Domingo or at Las Américas Airport).

Prices and service may both be lower if you rent from a local company. Local car-rental companies do not always maintain their vehicles, although some are reputable. For a day's car rental you can almost certainly go with a local. However, if you need a car for a full week, it's best to go with a major company, especially one that offers 24-hour roadside assistance.

Most major companies have outlets at Las Américas Airport outside Santo Domingo and at Gregorio Luperon International Airport in Puerto Plata, the airports of choice for most independent travelers who are likely to rent cars. At this time, there are no car-rental companies in the Barahona area, so if you are going there, rent at Las Américas or in Santo Domingo.

To rent a car in the D.R., you will need a valid driver's license, passport, and credit card; you must be between the ages of 25 and 80. In season you can expect to pay between $45 and $83 (Kia Picanto) for an automatic with insurance from a major company like Budget, which is one of the more reasonably priced companies. SUVs can cost as much as $160 daily (about $130 in low season) including insurance.

Take advantage of corporate rates, advance booking discounts, or hotel discount. Also, inquire if you can rent a car that takes diesel, which is generally cheaper than gasoline. If you want to rent a car for a day, you can often do so at a car-rental desk at your resort and have it delivered.

GASOLINE
Fill up—and watch—the gas tank; stations are few and far between in rural areas. Prices are usually a couple of dollars more expensive than those in the United States. Make certain that attendants don't reach for the super pump, which is even costlier. Also, watch as the attendant starts the pump to see that it reads 000; when he is finished make certain matches the amount you have paid.

ROAD CONDITIONS
Although some roads are still full of potholes, the route between Santo Domingo and Santiago is a modern, four-lane, divided highway, and the road between Santiago and Puerto Plata is a smooth blacktop. The highway from Santo Domingo to Casa de Campo, and from there to Punta Cana, is also a fairly smooth ride. A new highway between Santo Domingo and the Samaná Peninsula has just been completed, cutting the

driving time there in half. Surprisingly, many of the scenic, secondary roads, such as the "high road" between Playa Dorada and Santiago, are in good shape. Conversely, some in more remote areas are not only unlighted but have no lines.

ROADSIDE EMERGENCIES
It's particularly important to rent from an agency that offers emergency roadside assistance. For car theft, you can call 911 for the national police. For a simple flat tire, which is a common occurrence, you can have the tire repaired almost every *bomba* (gas station) until around 7 PM, but it's best to look for a *gomero* (tire shop), which will give you the best service.

RULES OF THE ROAD
Driving is on the right, the 80-kph (50-mph) speed limit is strictly enforced, seatbelts are mandatory. Otherwise, driving rules are similar to those in most of the United States. Right turns are allowed on red after you stop.

There are certain issues with driving in the D.R. Drunk driving is a problem, and the laws are not well enforced. The allowable blood alcohol level of 0.10 is higher than in most other countries, but it's particularly unwise to drink and drive in an unfamiliar place. You'll need to have all your wits when those around you don't.

Dominicans can be reckless drivers. They do not always stop at red lights, they often pass in a no-passing zone, and they don't always use their headlights at night.

Police corruption can also be a problem. You may see police officers standing on the side of the road, waving you down. You should always stop. One officer may smile and tell you that you were speeding or have made some other small violation, even if you have not. Always be polite, and speak as much Spanish as you can muster. He will do the same in his limited English. You can say something like: *"Que puedo hacer?"* (What can I do?).

He may tell you that you can pay the fine directly to him; if he agrees, discreetly pull out RD$150 (less than five bucks). Hopefully, he isn't too greedy. Otherwise, offer more in small increments, about RD$50 at a time, and work it out. Unfortunately, that's the way these things are done here.

Under no circumstances should you drive across the Dominican border into Haiti.

▌ BY MOTOCONCHO

Motoconchos are a popular and inexpensive mode of transportation in such areas as Puerto Plata, Sosúa, Cabarete, and Jarabacoa. You can flag down one of these motorcycle taxis along rural roads and in town; rates vary from RD$20 per person for a short run, to as much as RD$100 to RD$150 between Cabarete and Sosúa (double after 6 PM).

▌ BY TAXI

Taxis, which are government-regulated, line up outside hotels and restaurants. They're unmetered, so ask about the rates before entering. Though they are more expensive, hotel taxis are the nicest and the safest option. Freelance taxis aren't allowed to pick up from hotels, so they hang out on the street in front of them. Carry some small bills because drivers rarely seem to have change.

Recommendable radio-taxi companies in Santo Domingo are Tecni-Taxi (which also operates in Puerto Plata) and Apolo. Tecni is the cheapest, quoting RD$80 as a minimum per trip, Apolo RD$90. Hiring a taxi by the hour—with unlimited stops and a minimum of two hours—is often a better option if you're doing a substantial sightseeing trip. Tecni charges RD$240 per hour but will offer hourly rates only before 6 PM; Apolo charges RD$280 per hour, day or night. When booking an hourly rate, be sure to establish clearly the time that you start.

You can use taxis to travel to out-of-town destinations at quoted rates. Check with your hotel or the dispatcher at the airport. For example, from the Colonial Zone in Santo Domingo to Playa Dorado with Tecni-Taxi is $150. If you book through your hotel concierge, it can be more.

Taxi-Queen is the company that works through the Santiago hotels. Drivers have passed security checks and wear their ID tags around their necks. Their cars are not wonderful, and they're unlikely to speak English, but their prices are especially reasonable. Also, they'll take you the distance to Sosúa for $45 and Cabarete for $10 more. The going rate for a taxi between Sosúa and Cabarete is $12. However, the rate is the same for one or five persons, night or day. Taxi-Tourismo, the company that services the Cibao Airport in Santiago, charges $80 to Sosúa, $90 to Cabarete, but has safer, more commodious vehicles, mostly SUVs and minivans.

Information **Apolo Taxi** (☎809/537–0000, 809/537–1245 for a limo, which must be booked far in advance). **Taxi-Cabarete** (☎809/571–0767 in Cabarete). **Taxi-Queen** (☎809/570–0000, 809/233–3333 in Santiago). **Taxi-Sosúa** (☎809/571–3097 in Sosúa). **Taxi-Tourismo** (☎809/829–3007 in Santiago). **Tecni-Taxi** (☎809/567–2010, 809/566–7272 in Santo Domingo, 809/320–7621 in Puerto Plata).

ON THE GROUND

▌ COMMUNICATIONS

INTERNET

Paid Internet access of some kind is available in almost every hotel, though you may sometimes have access to only one slow and old terminal in the lobby, maybe with a Spanish keyboard. Many all-inclusives have concessionaires who operate a bank of computers in either a separate room or in the back of one of the shops, but you will likely pay as much as $5 for only 30 minutes.

Wi-Fi is becoming more prevalent in the better hotels, particularly in Santo Domingo; it's usually free but generally exists only in the lobby and some public areas rather than in your room. Chapter service can be found in Internet cafés, which are common in almost all the major resort areas.

Contacts **Cybercafes** (⊕ www.cybercafes. com) lists over 4,000 Internet cafés worldwide.

PHONES

Calling from a hotel is almost always the most expensive option; hotels usually add huge surcharges to all calls, particularly international ones. In some countries you can phone from call centers or even the post office. Calling cards usually keep costs to a minimum, but only if you purchase them locally. And then there are mobile phones *(⇨below)*, which are sometimes more prevalent—particularly in the developing world—than land lines; as expensive as mobile phone calls can be, they are still usually a much cheaper option than calling from your hotel.

To call the D.R. from the United States, dial 1, then the area code 809 and the local number.

CALLING WITHIN THE DOMINICAN REPUBLIC

To make a local call, you must dial 809 plus the seven-digit number (dial 1-809 if you're calling a cell phone). Directory assistance is 1411. Rates for calling within the D.R. vary by the hotel, but local calls are sometimes only a few pesos per minute.

CALLING OUTSIDE THE DOMINICAN REPUBLIC

From the D.R., just dial 1 plus the area code and number to call the U.S. or Canada. Some, but not all, U.S. toll-free numbers can be dialed from the D.R. by dialing 1-880.

Many savvy travelers these days now use Skype, the international calling program that you can download directly to your laptop. It's a fraction of the cost of traditional options. If you don't want to lug your notebook, many of the better Internet centers and cafés have Skype on their computers and have headphones, too.

Access Codes **MCI** (☎ 800/888–8000). **Sprint** (☎ 800/266–2255).

CALLING CARDS

Phone cards, which are sold at gift shops and supermarkets, can usually give you considerable savings if you're calling the United States or Canada, for which a hotel might charge $1 to $2 a minute. Codetel Comminicards can be used in most hotels (but check to see if you will incur a connection or other fee). Codetel calling centers have equally good rates to the States, about 35¢ a minute, but you'll have to pay cash.

You don't hear of that many visitors using calling cards from U.S. companies in the D.R. Why? Many hotels block these numbers to force you to go through the international telephone operator. Some hotels charge a connection fee that might range from $1.75 to ludicrous $10 (be sure to verify with your resort if there is a connection fee before attempting to use a calling card). Calling cards can be used successfully from pay phones when you can find one (such as in the airport) that works.

MOBILE PHONES

If you have a multiband phone (some countries use different frequencies than what's used in the United States) and your service provider uses the world-standard GSM network (as do T-Mobile, Cingular, and Verizon), you can probably use your phone abroad. Roaming fees can be steep, however: 99¢ a minute is considered reasonable. Be sure to ask your telecommunications' provider before leaving home. Remember that when you are out of the country you almost always pay the international toll charges for incoming calls. It's almost always cheaper to send a text message than to make a call, since text messages have a very low set fee (often as little as 5¢).

If you just want to make local calls, consider buying a new SIM card (note that your provider may have to unlock your phone for you to use a different SIM card) and a prepaid service plan in the destination. You'll then have a local number and can make local calls at local rates. If your trip is extensive, you could also simply buy a new cell phone in your destination, as the initial cost will be offset over time.

■ TIP → **If you travel internationally frequently, save one of your old mobile phones or buy a cheap one on the Internet; ask your cell phone company to unlock it for you, and take it with you as a travel phone, buying a new SIM card with pay-as-you-go service in each destination.**

Orange and CLARO (the mobile communication division of Codetel) are the two major cell phone companies. If you have a tri-band GSM phone, it will probably work on the island. Mobile phones in the D.R. operate at 1900 MHZ frequency, the North American standard.

If you're spending more than a week or two in the D.R., you can also get a local phone. You cannot rent from Orange, but you can from CLARO; however, it's more economical to buy a phone for less than $50 and prepaid phone cards of various denominations for air time. These are sold

at pharmacies, supermarkets, and *colmados* (small local grocery stores.) You can then call locally or long distance.

Contacts **Cellular Abroad** (☎800/287–5072 ⊕www.cellularabroad.com) rents and sells GMS phones and sells SIM cards that work in many countries. **Mobal** (☎888/888–9162 ⊕www.mobalrental.com) rents mobiles and sells GSM phones (starting at $49) that will operate in 140 countries. Per-call rates vary throughout the world. **Planet Fone** (☎888/988–4777 ⊕www.planetfone.com) rents cell phones, but the per-minute rates are expensive.

▌ CUSTOMS & DUTIES

Customs inspections on arrival to the D.R. are usually over quickly and painlessly. All travelers to the Dominican Republic are allowed to bring in one liter of alcohol, 200 cigarettes, and gifts not to exceed $100 in value. If you're carrying prescription medication—particularly controlled substances—be sure that you have a copy of the prescription and are carrying only enough for your personal use. Duties are particularly high for new electronic goods, and you'll be charged an import duty if the customs inspector believes you're bringing, say, a new laptop to someone in the D.R.

If you buy antiques on your trip, by all means carry the sales receipt with you. You can legally buy antique coins, including Spanish pieces of eight that are centuries old, at La Atarazana Museum in the Colonial Zone. Just produce your receipt and declare them as you exit the country.

Pets accompanying travelers from the United States must have a health certificate from a U.S. veterinarian signed within 15 days of your arrival. Dogs must have current rabies and parvo vaccinations. Airlines have other specific requirements, which you should inquire about before traveling to the D.R.

You're always allowed to bring goods of a certain value back home without having to pay any duty or import tax. But there's a limit on the amount of tobacco and liquor you can bring back duty-free, and some countries have separate limits for perfumes; for exact figures, check with your customs department. Cuban cigars are never allowed into the U.S. (and customs inspectors will check). The values of so-called "duty-free" goods are included in these amounts. When you shop abroad, save all your receipts, as customs inspectors may ask to see them as well as the items you purchased. If the total value of your goods is more than the duty-free limit, you'll have to pay a tax (most often a flat percentage) on the value of everything beyond that limit.

U.S. Information **U.S. Customs and Border Protection** (⊕ www.cbp.gov).

▌EATING OUT

The country's culinary repertoire includes Spanish, Italian, Middle Eastern, Indian, Japanese, American, certainly Dominican and *nueva cocina Dominicana* (contemporary Dominican cuisine). Depending on where you go, you can usually find restaurants at all levels, low, moderate, and high. Santo Domingo, the country's capital, has the best dining scene, as cosmopolitan as any in the Caribbean, with many ethnic restaurants, Italian prevailing. Fresh seafood is universal in the country, the exception being in the mountain areas, where meat is more the norm.

Restaurants that cater solely to tourists, as do many in the Colonial Zone, often dole out mediocre fare with poor service, yet their prices are escalating. Some of the best choices are in the business districts of the modern cities and in the upscale residential neighborhoods, where the menu prices offer a far better value.

Beach shacks serving simple but fresh seafood can be a fine way to make a great beach day even better. The quality of the food is usually fine, but you should always avoid ice and water unless it's bottled. Stands that serve cheap eats are an integral part of the culture and landscape, but eat street food at your own risk.

Dominican food does not have a stellar reputation, and it's doubtful that, despite some fusion movements, it will ever be world-class. Rice dishes prevail, and they're usually only "seasoned" with chicken or meat as well as tomato paste. Root vegetables, such as plantains and yucca, are staples, again with just a small amount of meat, and usually the less expensive cuts. *Mofango,* which consists of mashed green, roasted plantains mixed with shredded pork (or chicken) is very popular. *Moro,* a combination of seasoned rice and beans (usually brown pigeon peas) is ubiquitous. Soups can be the most flavorful, and the best thick stew is *sancocho,* usually made with five meats and poultry and served with white rice and avocado slices.

True vegetarian cuisine is rare in the D.R., but vegetarians can usually make do with the vegetable offerings, though you must always ask if vegetable dishes have any meat in them. If you eat dairy, one of the best Dominican specialties is *queso frito* (fried cheese). Children's menus are about as lackluster as they are in the States, usually listing chicken or fish fingers and *hamburgeresas.*

For information on food-related health issues, see Health below.

MEALS & MEALTIMES
As in most Spanish-speaking countries, breakfast is called *desayuno,* lunch *almuerzo,* and dinner *cena.* Breakfast can begin as early as 6 AM in a hotel, but usually it's 7 and will run until 10, 10:30. Most all hotel rates include some kind of breakfast, and in major properties a buffet is the norm. Some are elaborate, such as the breakfast buffet at the Sofitel Nicolas Ovando in Santo Domingo. Breakfast at the Iberostar resorts is among the best at the all-inclusives.

A Dominican breakfast is usually fresh fruit and/or juice, eggs scrambled with deli ham, mashed green plantains, and strong Dominican coffee. The European-owned B&Bs are more likely to serve a continental breakfast with a selection of cheeses and cold meats, German bread or French croissants, and yogurt. Out on the street, breakfast is harder to come by, but you can always find a cup of strong coffee.

Almuerzo can begin as early as 11 AM in the less-expensive eateries, where a daily *plato* is a mound of *moro* with chicken for $3 to $4; you'll pay the same price for a bland ham and cheese sandwich. Restaurants that cater more to tourists and business people usually serve from noon to 2:30 or 3. These will offer a more upscale Dominican special (but most people still want their *moro* at lunch) as well as lighter fare for the younger crowd, which is adopting a healthier eating pattern.

For dinner your hotel dining rooms and better establishments will open as early as 6, but Americans may be the only patrons until 8:30 or 9, when the Dominicans start roll in. Restaurants in the capital and its Colonial Zone, as well as those in Cabarete and Sosúa, may serve as late as 11 or midnight during the week, even later on Friday and Saturday. Many independent restaurants are closed on Sunday night since the main meal on Sunday is usually in the afternoon. When all else fails, you can hit a *colmado* or gas station that has a minimart.

Unless otherwise noted, the restaurants listed in this guide are open daily for lunch and dinner.

PAYING
Credit cards are widely accepted in upscale restaurants, particularly in the capital. Most of restaurants in Cabarete or Sosúa, whether expensive or cheap, don't take them. Elsewhere, small local restaurants rarely accept credit cards. American Express is usually only taken in the better restaurants and in hotel dining rooms.

For guidelines on tipping see Tipping below.

WHAT IT COSTS IN U.S. DOLLARS	
¢	under $8
$	$8–$12
$$	$12–$20
$$$	$20–$30
$$$$	over $30

Restaurant prices are for a main course at dinner and do not include 16% tax or 10% service charge.

RESERVATIONS & DRESS
Regardless of where you are, it's a good idea to make a reservation if you can. We only mention them specifically when reservations are essential (there's no other way you'll ever get a table) or when they are not accepted. (Large parties should always call ahead to check the reservations policy.) We mention dress only when men are required to wear a jacket or a jacket and tie.

WINES, BEER & SPIRITS
The Dominican market is dominated by the three Bs—Brugal, Barcelo, and Bermudez—all very popular brands of locally made rum. Presidente is the most widely known and distributed local beer. It comes in green bottles and is sometimes called *agua verde* (green water). Brahma and Bohemia beers are the other two *cervezas* brewed here. Local Dominican restaurants may only serve rum and beer, or they may have a full bar, but if it's an inexpensive place, you may be able to get only cheaper, domestic brands. Small, local *colmados* also sell wine and liquor. Upscale restaurants usually have only international brands, with the exception of the national rums and beers.

The official drinking age is 18, but usually no one is counting, except at the hip clubs, which attempt to adhere to the law for fear of losing their club license. In Santo Domingo a curfew allows bars and restaurants to serve only until midnight during the week, until 2 AM on Friday and Saturday; exceptions are bars, clubs, and casinos in tourist hotels. That is why a lot of young people have adopted clubs like LED in the Hotel Hispanola. All-inclusive resorts can serve alcohol 24 hours a day. In Cabarete some beachfront clubs must now close as early as 1 AM if they're next to a hotel; all bars must close by 3 AM.

▮ ELECTRICITY

The current is 110–120 volts/60 cycles just as in North America. Electrical blackouts occur less frequently than in the past and tend to last only one to two minutes (when they're over, everyone claps), but most hotels and restaurants have generators.

▮ EMERGENCIES

In Santo Domingo and major destinations, 911 is the general emergency number; you'll normally find an operator who can speak some English.

If you need to speak to the police, contact Politur, which is the police force that has been created and specially trained to aid tourists. Most officers speak some English, are polite, and are not as accustomed to thinking about money on the side. The telephone numbers for local Politur offices are given in each regional chapter.

A private ambulance service now exists in Santo Domingo, Puerto Plata, La Romana, and Santiago, and they will sometimes go to outlying areas. Movi Med will inform you when you call that they will want to be paid in cash on the spot. When the victim is delivered to a hospital, if there is not an ATM within it or nearby, tell them to drive you to one.

Santo Domingo and Santiago have the best medical facilities in the country. These cities have 24-hour pharmacies. It's rare to find them outside of these cities. You'll be able to recognize *farma-*

---

cias by their large red or green crosses. In most places, 9 PM is closing time for pharmacies.

Emergencies Movi Med (☎809/532–000 in Santo Domingo, 1-200-0911 elsewhere in D.R.).

U.S. Embassies & Consulates U.S. Consulate (✉Calle Cesar Nicolas Penson, corner of Maximo Gomez, La Esperilla, Santo Domingo ☎809/221–2171). **United States Embassy** (✉Leopoldo Navarro, at Calle Cesar Nicolas Penson Gascue, Santo Domingo ☎809/221–2171).

▮ ETIQUETTE & BEHAVIOR

Wearing shorts, short skirts, and halter tops in churches is considered inappropriate. Men in Santo Domingo never wear shorts. If you have to go to a government office and are wearing shorts, a clerk may refuse entry to you.

Security at hotels and resorts is tight, particularly regarding having guests in your room, especially if they're Dominican and of the opposite sex. Indeed, if you do have one overnight, you may find that you're charged double.

▮ HEALTH

For information on travel insurance, shots and medications, and medical-assistance companies see Shots & Medications under Things to Consider in Before You Go, above.

SPECIFIC ISSUES IN THE DOMINICAN REPUBLIC

Water sanitation is a constant problem across the island, and you should never drink water from the tap in the D.R. Many travelers choose to brush their teeth with bottled water, which is a reasonable precaution. Reports of food-borne illnesses in the D.R. are actually down, primarily as a direct result of the Cristal program of food safety; look for resorts and restaurants with a Cristal certificate to indicate that the current food-safety procedures are followed. At most upscale resorts and restaurants, ice is made from purified water, and drinking water served to you is either bottled or purified (insist on bottled water if you're concerned). If you have a stomach ailment, see a physician immediately.

Stray dogs and cats can be a problem; do not feed these animals, and if you are bitten or scratched, attend to the wound immediately. Do not hesitate to see a doctor if infection is evident.

Sexually transmitted diseases such as Hepatitis B and AIDS (known as SIDA in the D.R.) are prevalent among the local prostitutes, yet another reason why it is unwise to choose the D.R. for a sex-tourism vacation. Certainly, men should always use a latex condom, and women should insist that their local sex partners use a condom. Because the quality of condoms in the D.R. can be questionable, you should always bring some from home.

Most often, however, the worst malady that tourists are affected by is bad sunburn. Be smart, and protect your skin. Wear a hat, visor, or cap, and apply sunscreen (SPF 30 and up) on your body and face (especially your nose and ears). Reapply lotion after swimming. As for lying on the chaise getting that tan, like mad Englishmen, avoid that noonday sun. Most markets and pharmacies sell sunscreen, but expect to pay twice what you would pay at home, often for a local brand.

Large resorts will have a medical clinic on-site. You'll have to pay a fee (about $65) to use the services of the physician, but if you have travel medical insurance, you can often have this amount reimbursed. Medications can be expensive. If you have a more serious issue, you'll find private clinics and hospitals in the capital and most major tourist areas. You'll have to pay for services up front, but your medical insurance (or travel medical insurance) may reimburse you for out-of-pocket expenses. Some private clinics accept payment by credit card.

Mosquito coils are available in supermarkets, but you'll only need those if you're renting a house. Do buy your mosquito repellent (with DEET) before you leave home; the same major U.S. brands are sold in the D.R., but you'll pay double the price. It's important to protect yourself from mosquitoes and the illnesses they can carry. If you do get a mosquito bite, do what the locals do and rub a wedge of fresh lime on it to take the itch out.

OVER-THE-COUNTER REMEDIES

You can find the usual over-the-counter medications in *farmacias* (pharmacies), in some *supermercados* (supermarkets), and even some essentials in the local *colmados* (small grocery stores). Look for the discount store California, which is the Dominican equivalent to Wal-Mart.

▌ HOURS OF OPERATION

Banks are open weekdays from 8:30 to 4:30. Post offices are open weekdays from 7:30 to 2:30. Offices and shops are open weekdays from 8 to noon and 2 to 6, Saturday from 8 to noon. About half the stores stay open all day, no longer closing for a midday siesta.

HOLIDAYS

Major public holidays are New Year's Day, Ephiphany—known also as Three Kings Day (Jan. 6), Our Lady of La Altagracia Day (Jan. 21), Duarte's Birthday (Jan. 26), Independence Day (Feb. 27),

Good Friday, Labor Day (1st Mon. in May), Corpus Christi (May 14), Restoration Day (Aug. 16), Our Lady of Las Mercedes Day (Sept. 24), Constitution Day (Nov. 6), and Christmas.

LANGUAGE

Spanish is spoken in the D.R. Staff at major tourist attractions and front-desk personnel in most major hotels speak some English, but you may have difficulty making yourself understood. Outside the popular tourist establishments, restaurant menus are in Spanish, as are traffic signs everywhere. Using smiles and gestures will help, and though you can manage with just English, people are even more courteous, kind, and hospitable if you try to speak their language. It's a matter of respect. Buy one of those skinny phrase books or get Spanish audio discs from the library, and just try, *si*?

MAIL

Airmail postage to North America for a letter or postcard is RD$40; letters may take more than two weeks to reach their destination or never make it. Or you can pay big money, RD$695, for a "fast mail" stamp (which will take three days) through a new service called EMS INPOSDOM, which is also named EPS, the equivalent of our UPS. You can send packages and get a tracking number, but the success rate is not so high.

The main branch of the post office in Santo Domingo is on Calle Heroes del Luperon at Rafael Damiron La Ferla. If you need to send a package home, it's more reliable to use FedEx or DHL, though they cost a small fortune. Do save your receipt and tracking number; one Fodorite sent a present to Martinique from Santiago's main post office using DHL, via Miami, for a cost of US$37 and it was never seen again.

MONEY

The cost of a week's vacation in the Dominican Republic will vary widely depending on where you stay. A package that includes airfare and an all-inclusive resort will usually be the best value, but this can vary from $4,000 per person for a week at a luxurious resort in Uvero Alto to less than $2,000 per person for a week at a less luxurious resort in Playa Dorada. It's also possible to do the trip for a much cheaper price if you go during the off-season (September to October) or lower your standards. But these days, the teaser offers of $1,000 usually have a lot of fine print (and are usually limited to three-night stays). You will not need any local currency if you're staying at an all-inclusive resort. But if you're traveling independently, then cash is definitely king in the D.R.; however, don't carry more than $100 on your person unless you're on your way to an upscale restaurant that does not take credit cards. Large hotels, upscale restaurants in major cities, and expensive stores take credit cards (though Amex is not accepted as often), but some local establishments will take credit cards only if you pay a 3% to 4% supplement.

ITEM	AVERAGE COST
Cup of Coffee	$1
Glass of Wine	$4
Glass of Beer	$2.50
Sandwich	$4.50
One-Mile Taxi Ride in Capital City	$4.50
Museum Admission	$1.50

Try to carry smaller-denomination bills for cab drivers, who never seen to have change. And even in all-inclusive resorts, staff are quite happy to get their tips as US$1 bills.

Prices throughout this guide are given for adults. Substantially reduced fees are almost always available for children, students, and senior citizens.

■TIP➡ Banks never have every foreign currency on hand, and it may take as long as a week to order. If you're planning to exchange funds before leaving home, don't wait until the last minute.

ATMS & BANKS

Your own bank will probably charge a fee for using ATMs abroad; the foreign bank you use may also charge a fee. Nevertheless, you'll usually get a better rate of exchange at an ATM than you will at a currency-exchange office or even when changing money in a bank. And extracting funds as you need them is a safer option than carrying around a large amount of cash.

■TIP➡ PIN numbers with more than four digits are not recognized at ATMs in many countries. If yours has five or more, remember to change it before you leave.

ATMs are widely available in the capital and tourist towns, like Cabarete. As you get out into the country, they become scarce. In the Southwest for example, there are several in the main city of Barahona but none in the countryside, and barely any in the hill towns. Banco Popular has many locations throughout the country, as do BHT and Scotiabank. Most ATMS—called ATHs or *cajeros automaticos* in the D.R.—are members of Cirrus, Plus, or other international networks but will give you pesos.

In nearly all ATMs you'll have a choice of language, so just choose English. Generally, 10,000 pesos is the maximum you can take out at one time. The commands are self-explanatory on the machine itself, with the exception of "Valid" or Validate," which is the equivalent of hitting "Enter."

Some ATMs may seem to have their own agenda. For example, if your debit card normally draws from your checking account and does not process, you may be able to take funds from your savings account. Hit the button to get your card back; if you don't take your debit card immediately, the machine may take it back.

Always think safety. It's best to go to ATMs that are inside or just outside banks, during daylight hours only. The safety reasons are obvious, but if the machine swallows your card, you immediately have some recourse other than to call the number for the bank the next day. Most banks do have security guards next to the outdoor ATMs at night, but always shield your PIN number as you enter it.

CREDIT CARDS

Throughout this guide, the following abbreviations are used: **AE**, American Express; **D**, Discover; **DC**, Diners Club; **MC**, MasterCard; and **V**, Visa.

It's a good idea to inform your credit-card company before you travel, especially if you're going abroad and don't travel internationally very often. Otherwise, the credit-card company might put a hold on your card owing to unusual activity—not a good thing halfway through your trip. Record all your credit-card numbers—as well as the phone numbers to call if your cards are lost or stolen—in a safe place, so you're prepared should something go wrong. Both MasterCard and Visa have general numbers you can call (collect if you're abroad) if your card is lost, but you're better off calling the number of your issuing bank, since MasterCard and Visa usually just transfer you to your bank; your bank's number is usually printed on your card.

If you plan to use your credit card for cash advances, you'll need to apply for a PIN at least two weeks before your trip. Although it's usually cheaper (and safer) to use a credit card abroad for large purchases (so you can cancel payments or be reimbursed if there's a problem), note that some credit-card companies *and* the banks that issue them add substantial percentages to all foreign transactions, whether they're in a foreign currency or not. Check on these fees before leaving home, so there won't be any surprises when you get the bill.

Major credit cards (American Express not as often) are accepted at most hotels, large stores, and restaurants.

Reporting Lost Cards American Express (☎809/227–3190 in Santo Domingo, 866/751–2797 in other provinces [24 hours], 336/393–1111 collect from abroad ⊕www.americanexpress.com). **Diners Club** (☎800/234–6377 in U.S., 303/799–1504 collect from abroad ⊕www.dinersclub.com). **Discover** (☎800/347–2683 in U.S., 801/902–3100 collect from abroad ⊕www.discovercard.com). **MasterCard** (☎800/627–8372 in U.S., 636/722–7111 collect from abroad ⊕www.mastercard.com). **Visa** (☎800/847–2911 in U.S., 410/581–9994 collect from abroad ⊕www.visa.com).

CURRENCY & EXCHANGE

You may need to change some money, particularly if you're not staying in an all-inclusive resort, where dollars are usually accepted. Prices quoted in this chapter are in U.S. dollars unless noted otherwise. The coin of the realm is the Dominican peso (written RD$). At this writing, the exchange rate was approximately RD$34 to US$1.

Independent merchants willingly accept U.S. dollars, but because the peso can fluctuate, change will be in pesos. Considering the recent decline of the dollar relative to most world currencies, the Dominican peso has remained fairly stable, hovering between RD$32 and RD$34 to the dollar since 2006. Always make certain you know in which currency any transaction is taking place and carry a pocket calculator.

You can find *cambios* (currency exchange offices) at the airports, as well as on the street, and in major shopping areas throughout the island. A passport is usu-ally required to cash traveler's checks, if they're taken. Save some of the official receipts with the exchange transaction, so if you end up with too many pesos when you are ready to leave the country, you can turn them in for dollars. Some hotels provide exchange services, but, as a rule, hotels and restaurants will not give you favorable rates—casino cages are better.

■TIP➔ Even if a currency-exchange booth has a sign promising no commission, rest assured that there's some kind of huge, hidden fee. (Oh . . . that's right. The sign didn't say no *fee*.) And as for rates, you're almost always better off getting foreign currency at an ATM or exchanging money at a bank.

TRAVELER'S CHECKS

Some consider this the currency of the cave man, and it's true that fewer establishments in the Dominican Republic will accept traveler's checks these days. Banks still cash them without a hitch, although money changers at the *cambios* may balk, even with a passport. Nevertheless, they're a cheap and secure way to carry extra money, particularly on trips to urban areas. Both Citibank (under the Visa brand) and American Express issue traveler's checks in the United States, but Amex is better known and more widely accepted; you can also avoid hefty surcharges by cashing Amex checks at Amex offices. Whatever you do, keep track of all the serial numbers in case the checks are lost or stolen.

Contacts American Express (☎888/412–6945 in U.S., 801/945–9450 collect outside of U.S. ⊕www.americanexpress.com).

▋ PROSTITUTION

Although the D.R. has had a reputation for prostitution and sex tourism, officials are making efforts to curb the problem. In the late 1990s Sosúa was like one big red-light district, with European male tourists coming specifically for sex tourism. Town fathers have made vigorous efforts to clean things up—and they have—but prostitution still exists in the now designated *Zona Rojas*. It's traditionally been a different story in Cabarete, where young, local surfer boys target northern European girls, who end up paying the freight. The real action goes down in Punta Cana, with the infamous "sanky hanky" boys—staffers, often waiters, bartenders, and animation staff—who prey on single female guests, especially older ones, lavishing attention on them, saying, "Meet me in the disco." Such a rendezvous often ends up in a seedy, drive-up, by-the-hour motel. What some unsuspecting ladies don't realize is that not only will they have to pay for the room but for the boy's services as well.

In Santo Domingo, prostitutes are alive and not always well (diseases are a real threat). They ply their trade, roaming casinos and hotels, though top properties vigilantly thwart their efforts. Throughout the D.R., sex bars are usually called "gentlemen's clubs." There's substantial gay prostitution as well. Child prostitution has almost been stamped out, but not entirely, and the government will prosecute tourists who have sex with minors (under age 18), who may also be prosecuted in their own country.

SAFETY

Violent crime against tourists in the D.R. is rare, and the island has a history of being safe. It definitely is safer now that President Lionel Fernandez is back in power. Nevertheless, you should exhibit the same caution you would in any unfamiliar destination. Poverty is everywhere in the D.R., and petty theft (particularly of cell phones), pickpocketing, and purse snatching (thieves usually work in pairs) are most frequent in Santo Domingo. Pay attention, especially when leaving a bank, a *cambio,* or a casino, despite the very visible police. Crime has even come to Santiago, so be cautious at night, and lock the doors of your car or taxi. Armed

private security guards are a common sight at clubs and restaurants.

Security at the all-inclusive resorts is really good, but petty theft still occurs. Punta Cana remains one of the safest regions, Ulvero Alto even more so. In this region, a pot salesman is more often a boy hawking shiny, stainless-steel pots. However, should anyone approach you to buy drugs, know that the penalties in this country are extremely tough—jail (not pretty), fines, and no parole—and don't even think of bringing drugs from home. Take hotel-recommended taxis at night. When driving, always lock your car and never leave valuables in it, even when doors are locked. If you have a safe in your hotel room, use it; many now are of a size to accommodate a laptop. If it doesn't, camouflage it. If a computer costs $600 in the states, it would be twice as much in the D.R.

▇TIP➔ **Distribute your cash, credit cards, IDs, and other valuables between a deep front pocket, an inside jacket or vest pocket, and a hidden money pouch. Don't reach for the money pouch once you're in public.**

TAXES

Departure tax—separate from the $10 tourist card you must purchase on entering the country—is $20 and almost always included in the price of your ticket. The government tax (IBIS) is a whopping 16% and is added to almost everything—bills at restaurants, hotels, sports activities, rental cars, and even items at the *supermercados* that are not considered basic, including anything imported.

TIME

Atlantic Standard Time is observed year-round. From November to March, when it's 9 AM in New York Boston and Miami, it's 10 AM in the Dominican Republic. During Daylight Savings Time in the

States, it's the same time on the island as it is on the East Coast.

▌ TIPPING

Generally a 10% service charge is included in all hotel and restaurant bills; it's the Dominican law. In restaurants, the bill will say *propino incluido* or simply *servis*. When in doubt, ask. Even then it's still expected that you will tip an extra 5% to 10% if the service was to your liking. In resorts, it's customary to leave at least a dollar per day for the hotel maid. Taxi drivers expect a 10% tip, especially if they've had to lift luggage or to wait for you. Skycaps and hotel porters expect at least $1 per bag.

Some guests have started to tip other service staff at all-inclusive resorts, even though tipping is supposed to be included in the cost of your trip. Bellboys, waiters, concierges, and bartenders (who may have a tip cup) are starting to expect a dollar, and they tend to give far better service to those who ante up. Remember, you're under no obligation to do this, but many travelers bring a stack of U.S. singles for this purpose. If you leave a present for your maid, write a note with it so they can show security that it was a *regalo*.

The staff at a private villa also expect some kind of a gratuity. The management company from which you rent should be able to give you an idea of the tip expected, but it's usually about 10% of the total cost of the villa.

▌ WEDDINGS

The relative ease of getting married in the D.R. has made it a major destination for Caribbean weddings. There are no residency requirements, nor are blood tests mandatory. Original birth certificates and passports are required. Divorce certificates must be stamped by the Dominican Consulate. If a woman has been divorced, it must have been at least 10 months ago.

Single certificates that indicate the bride and groom are indeed single, must be stamped by that same consulate. If either party is widowed, a death certificate must be produced along with the previous marriage certificate. These documents must be translated into Spanish and legalized. You must usually submit documents at least two weeks in advance of your wedding, and the cost for processing is at least $75 per person.

As elsewhere in the Caribbean, civil ceremonies, performed by a judge, are easier and require less documentation than those performed in churches. They'll be in Spanish unless you arrange for an English translator. Similarly, the legalized wedding certificate will be in Spanish and may not be delivered for a week or more. Most couples arrange their wedding ceremonies through the wedding coordinator at their resort.

A number of resorts cater to the wedding market and provide a gorgeous backdrop for the occasion. The famed Casa de Campo has handpicked staffers who are near magicians at coordinating celebrity weddings, often in secrecy. Conversely, many a young couple have married here surrounded by family and friends hosted in a handful of villas.

At Natura Cabanas, in Cabarete, you can be married in the palatial yoga pavilion or on the beach. This eco-lodge lends itself to creative, offbeat, wedding celebrations. In nearby Sosúa, Piergiorgio's (Palace Hotel) is a romantic Victorian-esque inn with an amazing view of Sosúa Bay from the white rotunda that serves as its picturesque wedding gazebo.

The all-inclusive resorts are seasoned at handling wedding celebrations, with some like Sunscape and Dreams resorts having wedding coordinators who earn kudos from the brides and their mothers.

For those wanting a more intimate a high-end venue, ultraluxurious vacation villas on the beach give a lifetime of memories.

In Cabrera's Orchid Bay Estates, Villa Castellamonte is designed like an Italian palazzo. Its dedicated wedding coordinator performs magical transformations at this 15,000 square-foot mansion with eight bedrooms, a resort-size pool complex and golden beach. A neighbor in this gated community, Flor de Cabrera, is a multilevel (18,500 square foot) 10-bedroom, exquisitely furnished with a separate master casita for the bride and groom.

INDEX

NOTES

NOTES

NOTES